The Surrealist Menagerie

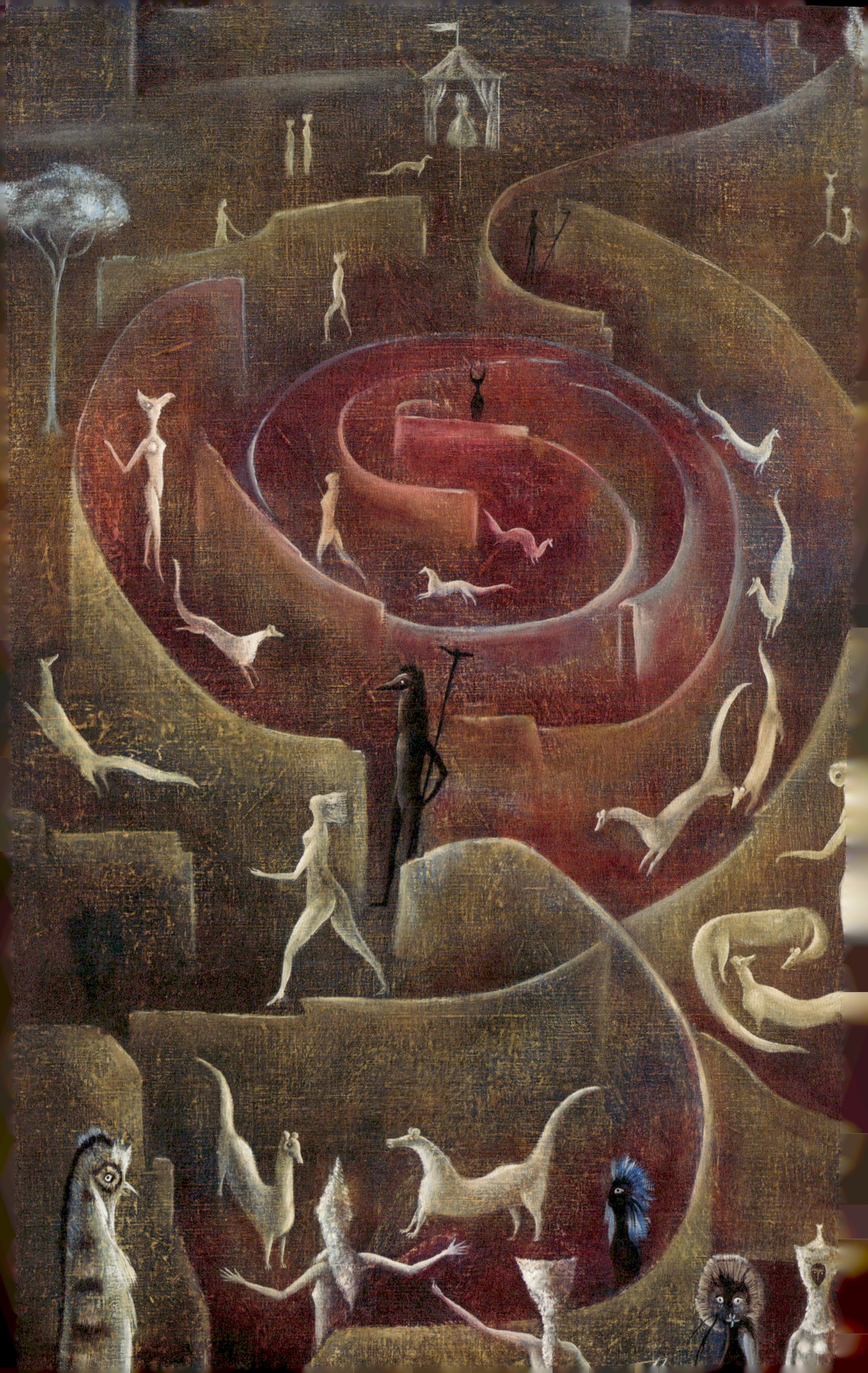

DESMOND MORRIS

The Surrealist Menagerie

Strange Beasts & Fantastic Visions

T&H

Contents

Introduction

Animals have played a significant role in the art of the surrealists. Their purpose has been threefold – factual, visual and symbolic. By 'factual', I mean the actions that animals perform during their lives – flying, swimming, crawling, fighting, mating, feeding, hiding, playing, fleeing. 'Visual' relates to their iconic shapes, patterns and colours. And by 'symbolic', I refer to the way in which animals can be used to represent something else, such as freedom, power, love, anger or sexuality.

Some surrealist animals embody all three of these qualities. Others have only a single role to play. Some are painted in a naturalistic style but are placed in an irrationally inappropriate environment. Others are wildly distorted. There is also the popular concept of a chimera – a creature made up of mismatched parts – an elephant with the legs of a spider, or a bird with the arms of a human.

There have been two main sources of invention: familiar animals that have been given the surrealist treatment, and mythical creatures that bear no relation to any living species but are the creations of perversely imaginative surrealist brains. This volume has been confined to the former. It would be possible to fill a second book with the invented beasts alone.

Apart from a few bestiaries, there have been no previous publications devoted purely to this subject, which is surprising, considering what a rich field it is. Even more surprising is the fact that I myself have ignored it. For 80 years, I have lived a double life as a professional zoologist and an active surrealist. In 1944 my first zoological study appeared in print, and it was in that same year that I made my first surrealist drawings. Since then, I have remained active in both fields. My response to the suggestion of a book on the subject was immediate, and I plunged into my library in pursuit of unusual surrealist animal images. As there are more than 700 volumes in the surrealist section of my library, this preoccupied me for quite a while. After weeks of searching, I emerged with a collection of over 750 surrealist animals. It was tempting to include the wonderful creatures that appeared in the works of proto-surrealists such as Hieronymus Bosch, but the field is so rich that I decided to concentrate instead on the works by the official members of the surrealist movement that began in Paris in the 1920s. I use the word 'official' because, uniquely, this was an art movement from which you could be expelled if you broke its golden rules – rules laid down by its charismatic leader, the French poet André Breton, whose first *Surrealist Manifesto* of 1924 served as its foundational text.

From my collection of animal images, the best examples have been selected to illustrate this volume. I had to make a decision as to whether they should be presented 'artist by artist' or 'animal by animal'. I decided on the latter arrangement because I found it more revealing.

I should perhaps explain my inclusion of two artists who are not usually identified as being surrealists – the painter Francis Bacon and the sculptor Henry Moore. Bacon originally wanted to be a member of the surrealist group and hoped that his work would be included in the International Surrealist Exhibition in

London in 1936, the event that introduced the movement to Britain. But he was foolishly rejected by the organizers of that exhibition. Henry Moore was an active member of the organizing committee of the 1936 exhibition, but his involvement with the surrealists was short-lived as he was expelled from the movement in 1947 because, to earn some money, he had made a religious statue for a church. These two unfortunate rejections resulted in the surrealists losing two of the greatest artists of the 20th century and it seemed fitting to reinstate them here.

Another major artist whom I felt had to be included is the Swiss-born German painter Paul Klee. He was a surrealist who anticipated the surrealist movement. He was a few years ahead of the surrealists, but he had already discovered the joys of irrational visual invention. He likened his method to 'taking a line for a walk' – a perfect description of surrealism's approach to creativity. Finally, a word about the titles of the surrealist paintings. There are four kinds:

1. *A short descriptive title.* Some artists did not concern themselves with titles and gave their works simple labels. In a few cases, an untitled work was given a descriptive title at a later date by a private gallery, an art museum or the author of an artist's monograph.

2. *A literary title.* Artists often applied erudite literary references to their works. This is a reminder of the fact that surrealism began as a literary movement before it moved on to become a predominantly visual art form.

3. *An imaginative description that embodies the essence of the subject matter of a painting.* It may convey the mood of the scene depicted or a psychological aspect of it.

4. *A deliberately meaningless, irrational title, sometimes in direct contrast to the subject matter of a painting.* Some surrealists felt that it was too 'traditional' to give helpful titles to their work, so they plucked words from the air that perversely bore no relationship to the subject matter. Magritte was the most extreme example of this approach. When he had completed a new painting, he would sometimes invite his friends round to look at it and challenge them to come up with the most unrelated titles they could devise. He would then select the best of these to give to his new work. This surrealist game has not stopped some art historians from doing their best to find a meaning in these titles.

The Invent

ebrates

Mollusc

The shells of snails appear in so many wonderful forms that it is not surprising to find that many of the surrealists have included them in their paintings. The most inventive use of them is to be found in the work of the French painter Félix Labisse. His dramatic composition *The Field of the Cloth of Gold* (1943) celebrates a famous historical encounter that took place near Calais on 7 June 1520, between the English king Henry VIII and Francis I of France. In the hope of securing continued peace, the meeting was staged as a lavish entertainment, in which each side tried to outdo the other with extremes of regal luxury. There were nearly three weeks of banquets, feasts and tournaments, and this symbolic competition became so fierce that later conflict was inevitable.

Labisse presents the two kings not on magnificent steeds, but instead emerging from huge mollusc shells, as if they were slow-moving snails that had been roused into ornate competition by the occasion. He adds a further insult by portraying them as the kings seen in playing cards and even makes one of them, specifically, the King of Spades.

The French surrealist Pierre Roy enjoyed decorating his coastal landscapes with large shells. In *Andromeda Prisoner* (c. 1930),

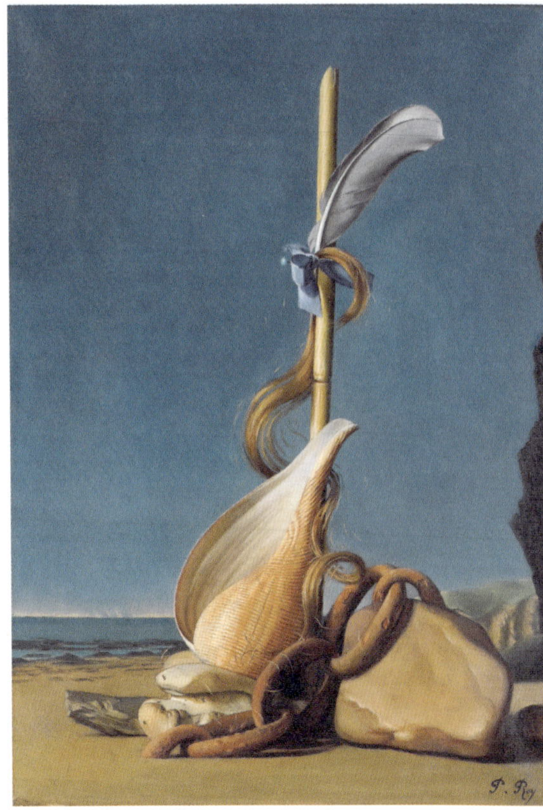

Pierre Roy, *Andromeda Prisoner*, c.1930

Félix Labisse, *The Field of the Cloth of Gold*, 1943

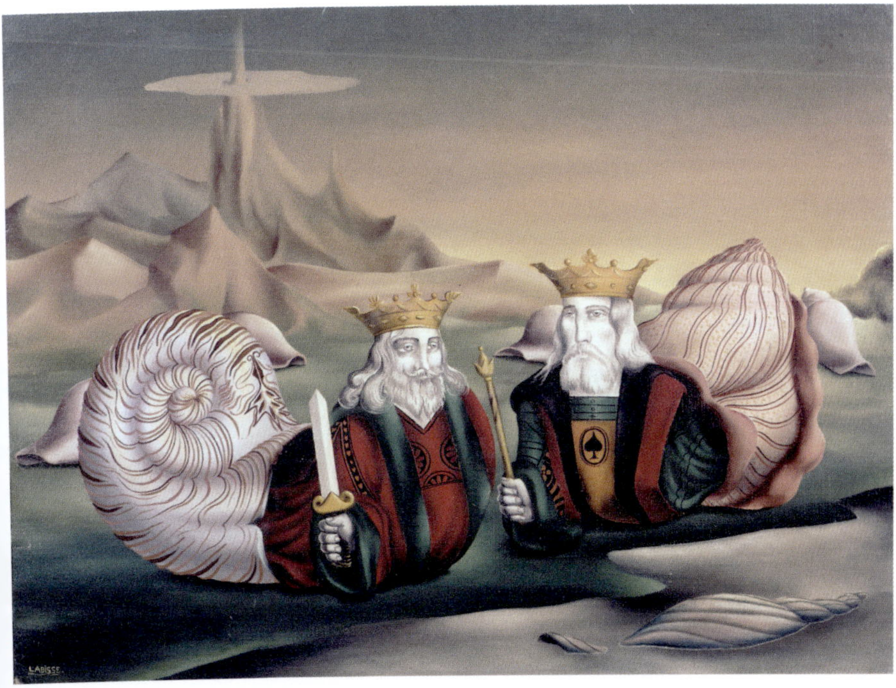

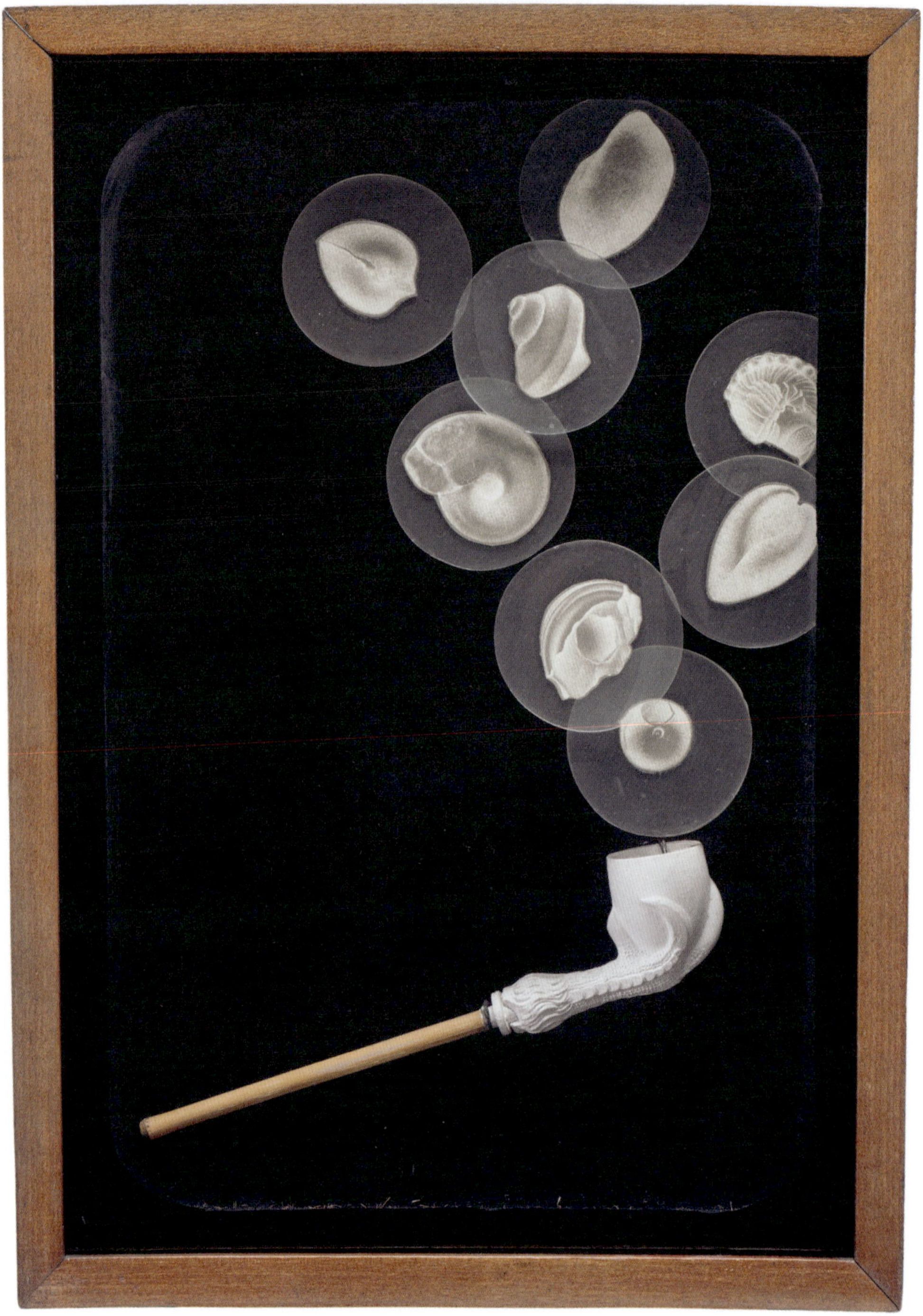

Joseph Cornell, *Object (Soap Bubble Set)*, 1941

a beach forms the backdrop for an unnaturally large shell, lying at a graceful angle that gives it an almost erotic quality. The shell is propped against a post to which a tendril of hair and a feather are tied with a blue ribbon. At the foot of the post are a rusty chain and a rock – references to the Andromeda of Greek myth, who is chained naked to a rock as a human sacrifice to the sea monster Cetus but is rescued by Perseus.

In Joseph Cornell's *Object (Soap Bubble Set)* of 1941, an antique clay pipe is blowing bubbles and, mysteriously, inside each of the eight bubbles there floats a small shell. This glass-fronted, framed box belongs to the American artist's acclaimed series of shadow boxes, in which he used everyday found objects to create miniature universes, many of which reflect his fascination with geology and the cosmos.

Starfish

The familiar shape of the starfish, with its five radiating arms, does not easily lend itself to surrealist appropriation. Its meaning in modern slang – referring to someone who is passive during sex – might have helped its cause, but this appears to be too recent a term to have influenced the surrealists.

In *The Star Dancer* (1991), the Belgian surrealist Marcel Mariën plays with the notion of a starfish having five 'arms' by attaching a small plastic high-heeled shoe to one of its limbs. Originally given the French title *La Danseuse étoile* – a term used at the Paris Opera Ballet to describe female dancers who have achieved the highest rank – this mixed-media piece features a real starfish against a sea-blue background.

Eileen Agar and Joseph Cornell also incorporated real starfish into their works. In Agar's *Fish Circus* (1939), which the British artist is believed to have made after a holiday on the Mediterranean coast, the shape of the starfish pinned to the centre of the collage visually draws together the organic and geometrical elements of the composition as a whole. Cornell's *Untitled (Sand Tray with Map and Starfish)* (1952), on the other hand, needs to be handled to be fully appreciated, as a lengthy catalogue caption explains:

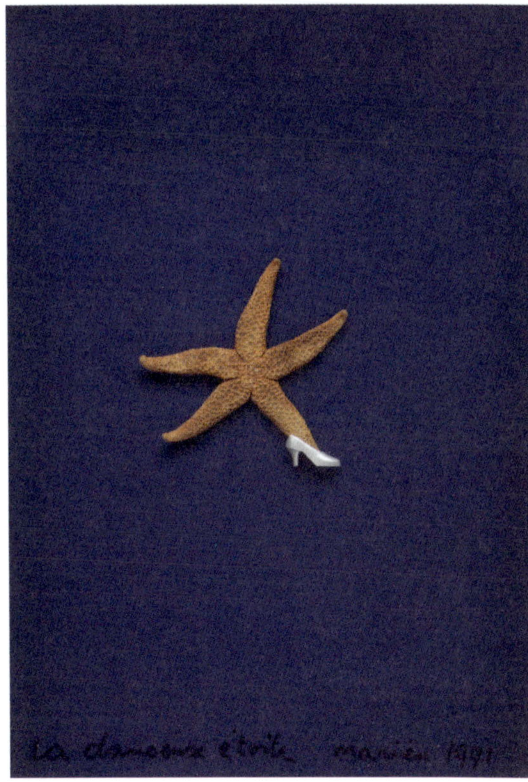

Marcel Mariën, *The Star Dancer*, 1991

Eileen Agar, *Fish Circus*, 1939

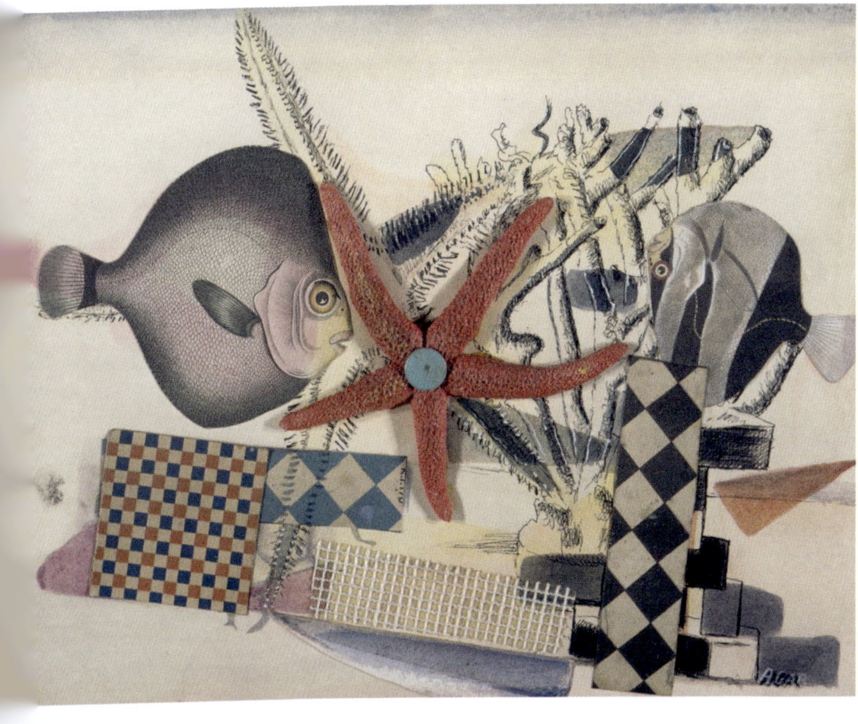

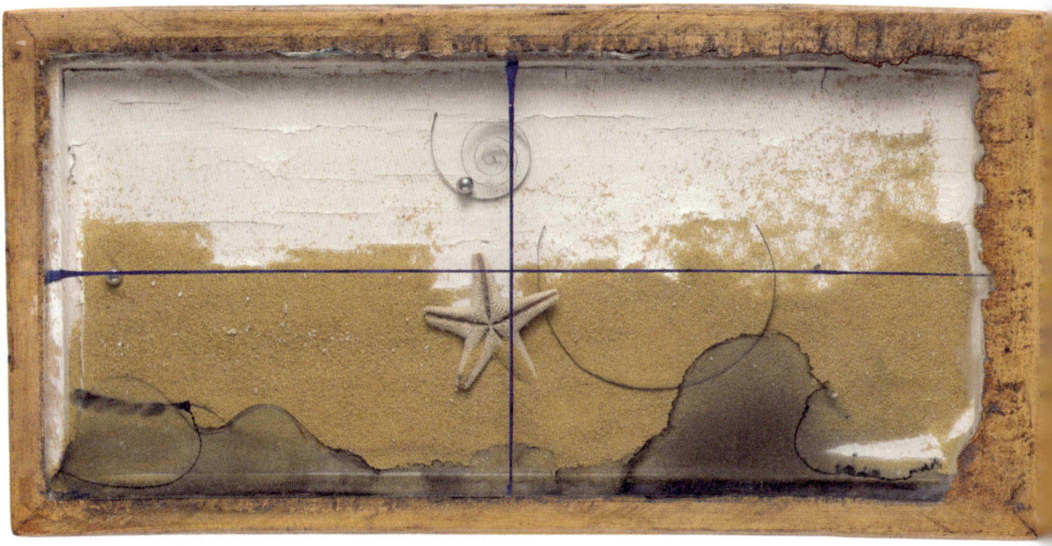

Joseph Cornell, *Untitled (Sand Tray with Map and Starfish)*, 1952

Edward Wadsworth, *The Beached Margin*, 1937

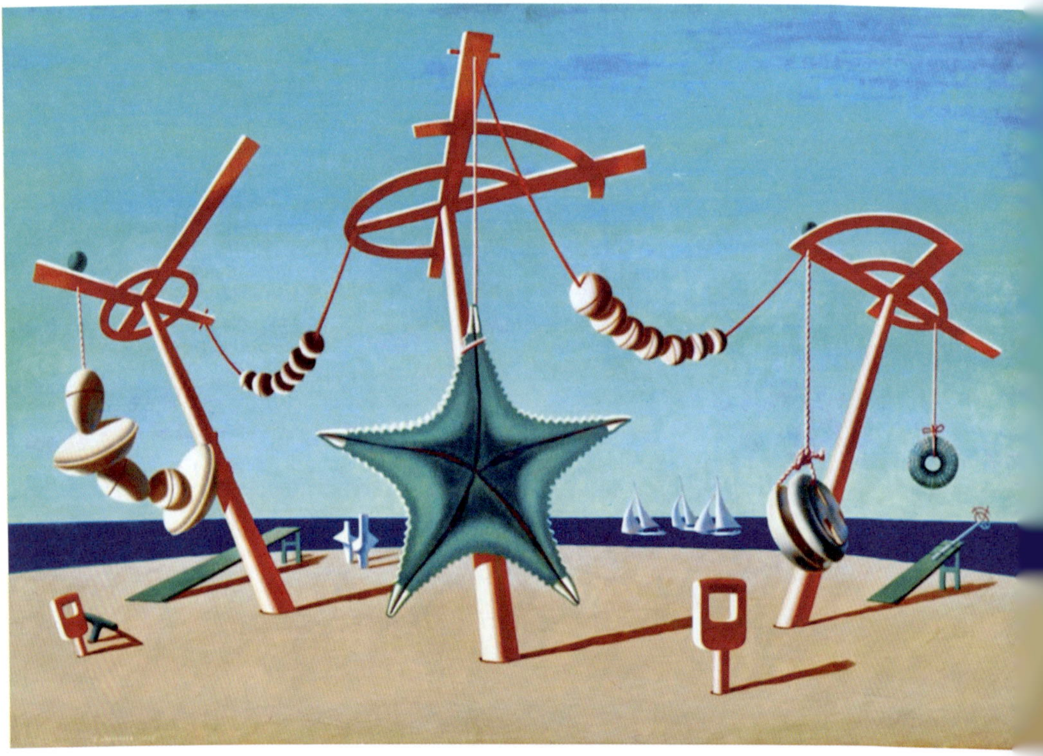

'The tidal rhythms of the sea, governed by the moon, are enacted as the box is handled. Two layers of sand, strewn with flotsam and jetsam, zoom in on what could be a patch of beach, an underwater perspective of the ocean floor, night sky or even a subatomic field.... A shiny blue marble is at once a toy, a distant planet and an emblem of the geometric notion of the sphere; in the same spirit, a dried starfish might be understood as a particular realisation of the eternal concept ... a volume the size of a shoebox, Cornell celebrates his love of stargazing and beachcombing.'

The seaside enthusiast Edward Wadsworth, who transformed objects found in harbours, docksides or on beaches into highly stylized still-life compositions, enjoyed adding an occasional starfish. In *The Beached Margin* (1937), a huge starfish takes centre stage: suspended from a stake in the sand (one of three such posts from which various objects hang in unexpected juxtapositions), it recalls photographs of a deep-sea fisherman's star catch on show for all to see. By displaying the starfish in this manner, the artist transforms it from a small reef creature into a marine monster.

Lobster

One surrealist, Salvador Dalí, was obsessed with the image of the lobster and made it his own to such an extent that nobody else could use it without seeming to imitate him. His most famous lobster appears in *Lobster Telephone* (1938), perched on an old-fashioned desk phone. The plaster lobster has been hollowed out to fit over the receiver, and a hole has been cut in the tail for the cord. Dalí created several versions of *Lobster Telephone*, including both a red lobster sitting on a black phone and a white lobster sitting on a white phone. As his alternative title *Aphrodisiac Lobster* suggests, the telephone lobster is a sexual statement, hugging the receiver as if trying to mate with it. It has also been pointed out that the tail of the lobster, where its sex organs are situated, is placed directly over the telephone's mouthpiece.

Dalí was skittish when discussing lobsters. In his autobiography, *The Secret Life of Salvador Dalí*, originally published in 1942, a drawing of a lobster telephone is accompanied by the caption: 'I do not understand why, when I ask for a grilled lobster in a restaurant, I am never served a cooked telephone; I do not understand why champagne is always chilled and why on the other hand telephones, which are habitually so frightfully warm and

Salvador Dalí, *Lobster Telephone*, 1938

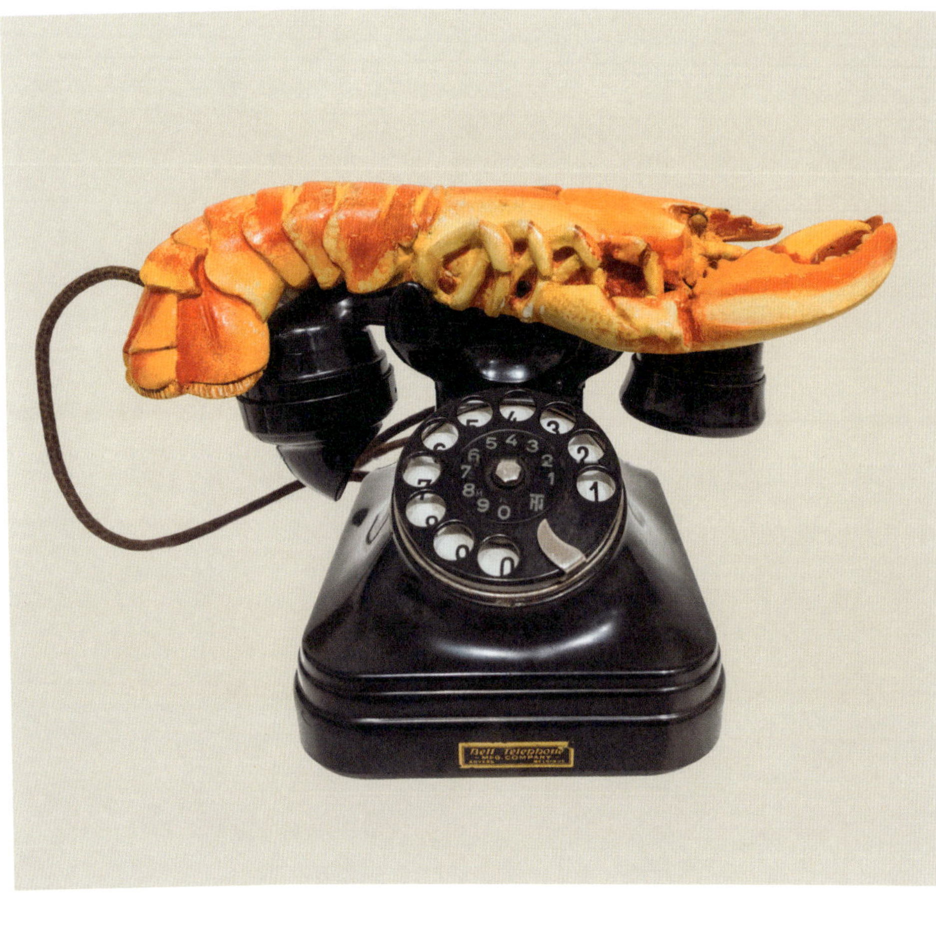

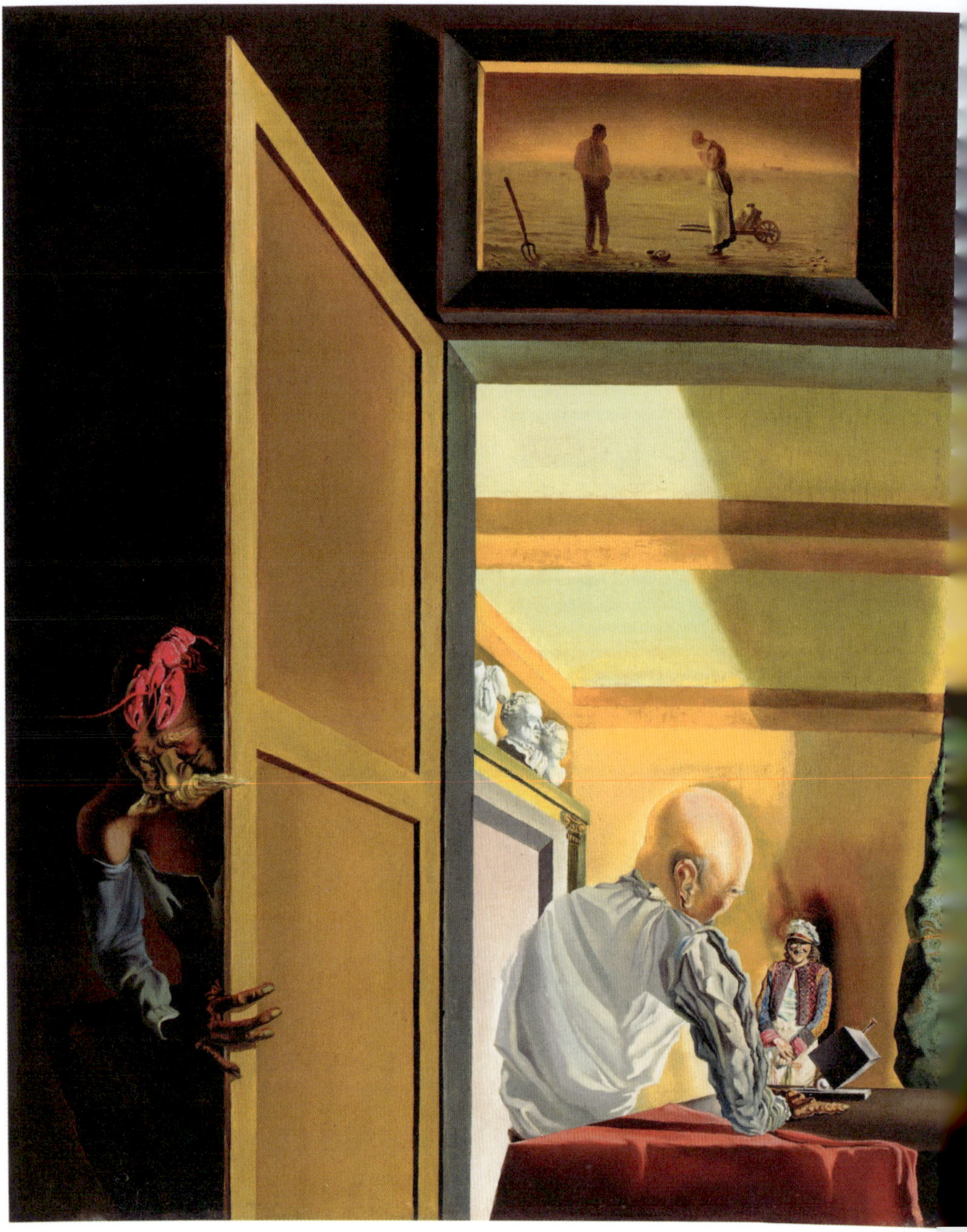

Salvador Dalí, *Gala and the Angelus of Millet Immediately Preceding the Arrival of the Conic Anamorphoses*, 1933

disagreeably sticky to the touch, are not also put in silver buckets with crushed ice around them.'

The telephones were not Dalí's first involvement with the lobster. Back in 1933, he had included one in his painting *Gala and the Angelus of Millet Immediately Preceding the Arrival of the Conic Anamorphoses*. Here, a red lobster is placed on the head of a strange-looking figure behind a door on the left. A copy of Jean-François Millet's *The Angelus* (1857–59), a painting that Dalí was obsessed with at the time, hangs above the door to a room where Dalí's muse and soon-to-be wife, Gala, is sitting. Anamorphosis refers to an image or drawing that is distorted and requires the viewer to look at it from a specific angle – or through a special device – in order to make out what it is, although it is not altogether clear how this works in this particular painting.

In 1937, Elsa Schiaparelli offered Dalí a new way of displaying his favourite sea creature: as a decorative element on one of her dresses, a now-iconic off-white, high-waisted organza gown. Dalí wanted his print to show a swooping red lobster with parsley scattered around it and blobs of mayonnaise. Schiaparelli permitted the parsley but rejected the idea of adding mayonnaise – presumably because it would look as though the gown had been stained by real food.

In 1939, lobsters made a notorious appearance in Dalí's specially designed pavilion at the New York World's Fair, which he called 'Dream of Venus'. The pavilion was described as 'a multimedia experience' and involved dressing nude female models in fresh seafood, including lobsters, which were used to cover their genital region.

Scorpion

The scorpion is rarely seen in the works of the surrealists, but one does put in a dramatic appearance, floating in the sky of a tarot-inspired piece of 1969 by the British-Mexican painter Leonora Carrington. Forming part of a larger composition that is dominated by a mysterious hybrid figure with wings, stingerlike legs, a human hand and multiple eyes, this scorpion is clearly a reference to the astrological star sign Scorpio – the eighth sign of the zodiac, derived from the constellation Scorpius. Scorpius has around 18 main stars that have long been associated with the distinctive shape of a scorpion, with its curved tail. Carrington's scorpion, although not a strictly faithful map of the stars that shape the constellation, contains its beating heart, the super-giant star Antares – a Greek name roughly translated as 'rival of Ares', likely given to the star because of its reddish hue. Standing directly above the hybrid figure's largest eye, the red circle of Antares, set against a black background, lights up the night sky.

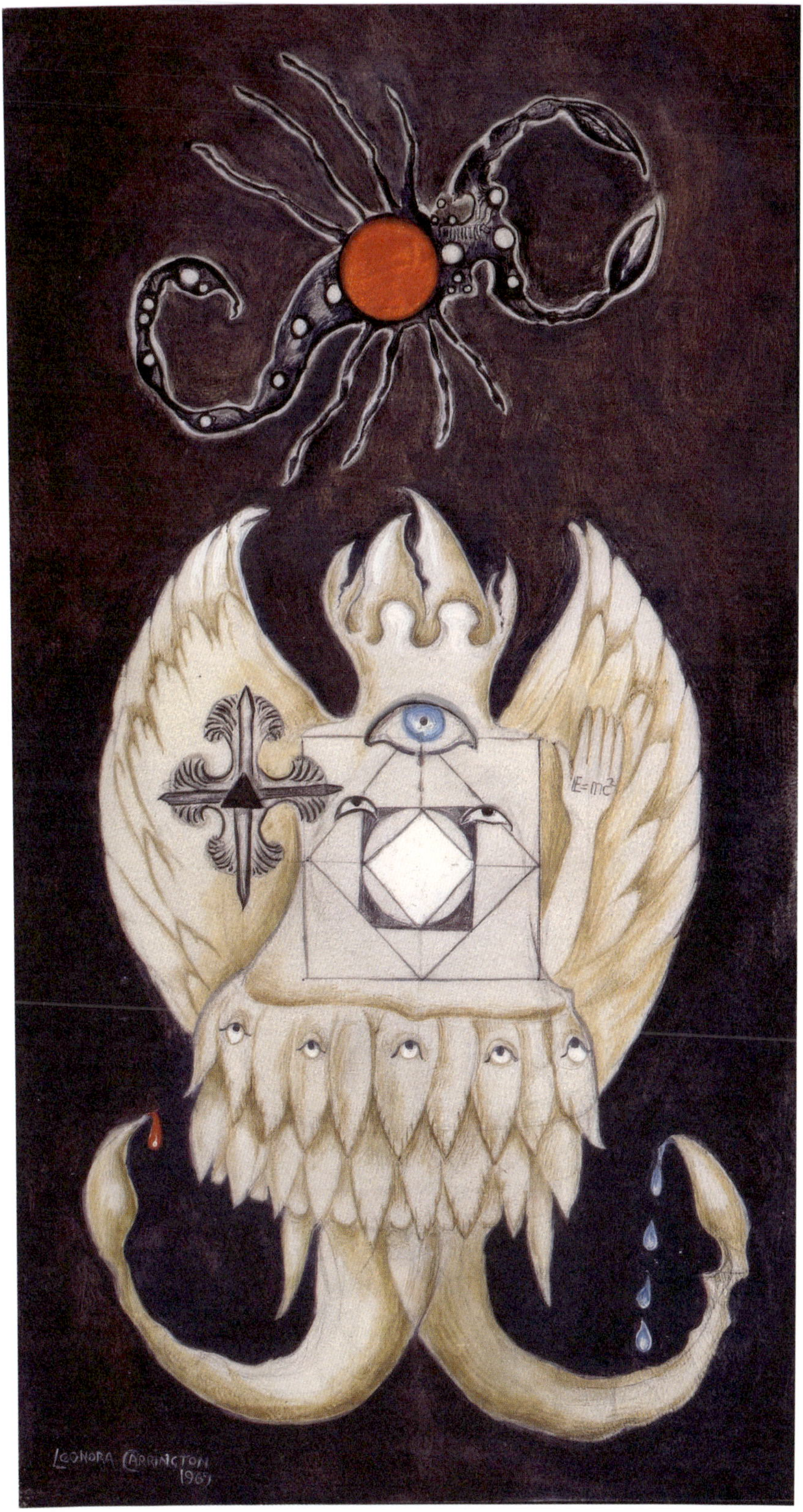

Leonora Carrington, *Untitled*, 1969

Insect

Symbolically, insects are nearly always viewed as pests, sent to plague humanity in innumerable ways. The list is a long one: locusts, fleas, lice, bed bugs, mosquitoes, gnats, ants, wasps, cockroaches, house flies, bluebottles and clothes moths are just some of the insects that have caused problems for humans, from mere irritation to deadly infection. So how have the surrealists treated these unwanted companions?

The French surrealist André Masson painted a number of works on the subject, such as *Summer Divertissement* (1934), in which a swarm of angry, multicoloured insects fills every corner of the composition – an overwhelming infestation that has driven all other forms of life out of the picture. Painted when the artist was living in Spain, on the eve of the Spanish Civil War, this is an animal rebellion, and it is we who have been ousted.

Belgian artist Roger Van de Wouwer's strange portrait of 1961, *Tartuffe's Hairshirt*, shows a uniformed soldier whose head has completely vanished under a dense insect swarm. The poor man stands dutifully to attention, watched by a smiling human swarm of commandos, all wearing red berets. The title of this work suggests that the soldier is suffering a mode of penance worthy of

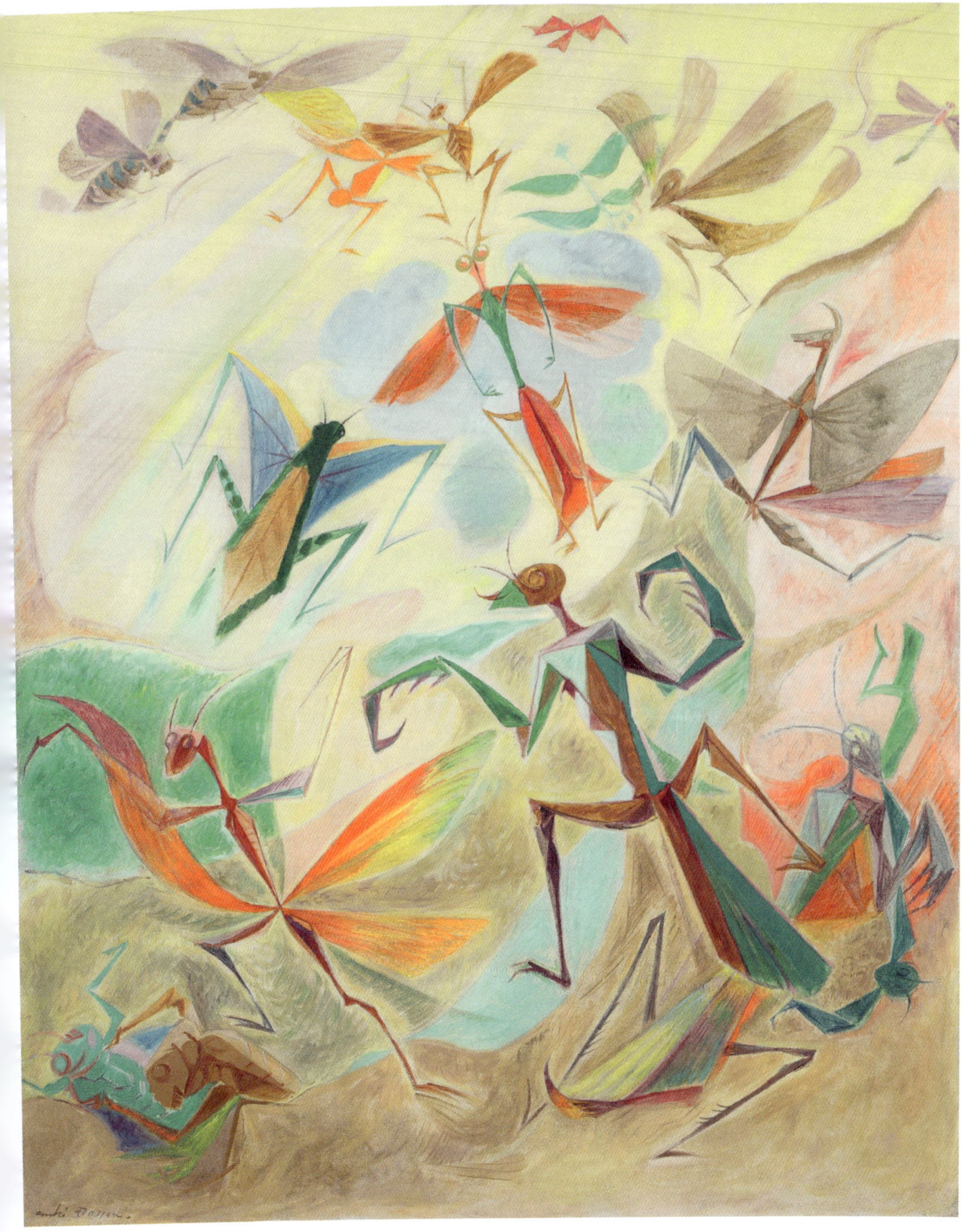

André Masson, *Summer Divertissement*, 1934

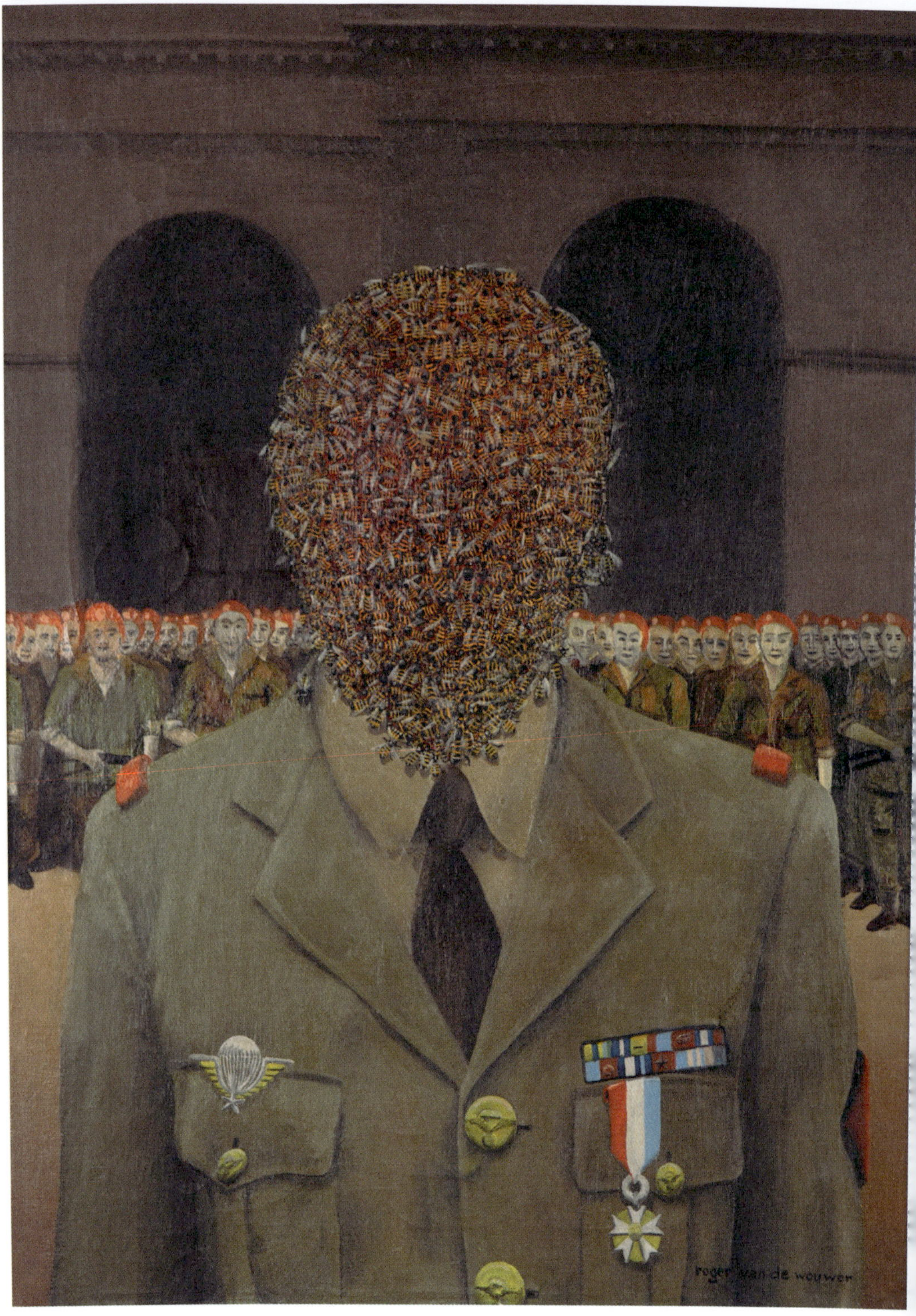

 Roger Van de Wouwer, *Tartuffe's Hairshirt*, 1961

the character Tartuffe, but in this case the hairshirt – an item made of rough cloth that penitents sometimes wore to punish themselves – has become a smothering mask of stinging wasps. Tartuffe, of course, is the hypocritical scoundrel in Molière's theatrical comedy of the same name who can adopt any role and become the master of it, duping the central character Orgon into believing he is extremely pious when in fact he is betraying him.

A giant wasp also makes a sinister appearance in Remedios Varo's *The Double Agent* (1936). Clinging to the back of a standing male figure, it presses him face-first against the wall of a room and appears to have sliced through his neck, while multiple staring eyeballs watch the scene unfold. At the bottom of the work, a partial head is seen emerging from a crack in the floor, the first of many self-portraits by the Spanish-Mexican artist.

In John Tunnard's *Self-Portrait* of 1959, the depiction of the artist is given less prominence than the sawfly in the foreground, with its distinctive apical clubs. Tunnard's head, thrust into a corner of the composition, appears almost to fade into the sombre background as he carefully observes his oversized subject. The English painter was a keen entomologist in later life, and in this work it is as though his whole world has become consumed by the insect.

In Dalí's classic painting *Face of the Great Masturbator* (1929), a large grasshopper sits, inverted, on the mouth of the human face that dominates the composition. A swarm of ants, representing sexual anxiety in Dalí's paintings, gathers on the grasshopper's abdomen.

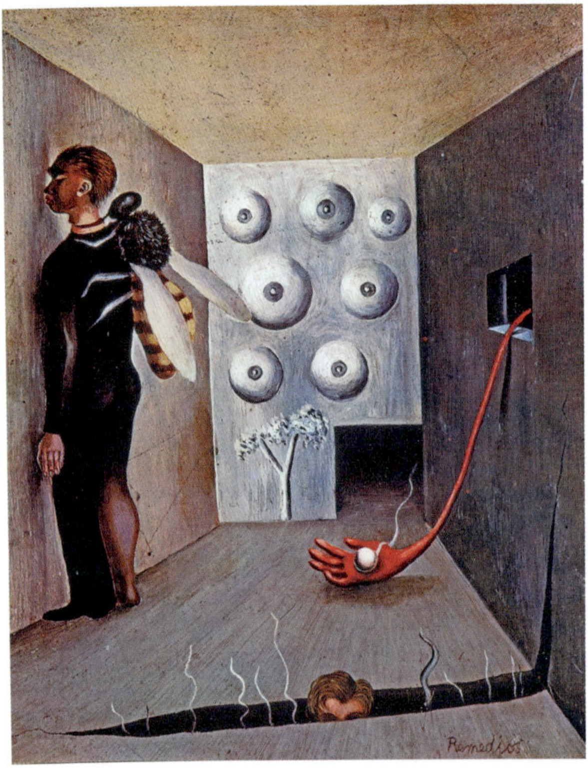

Remedios Varo, *The Double Agent*, 1936

Salvador Dalí, *Face of the Great Masturbator*, 1929

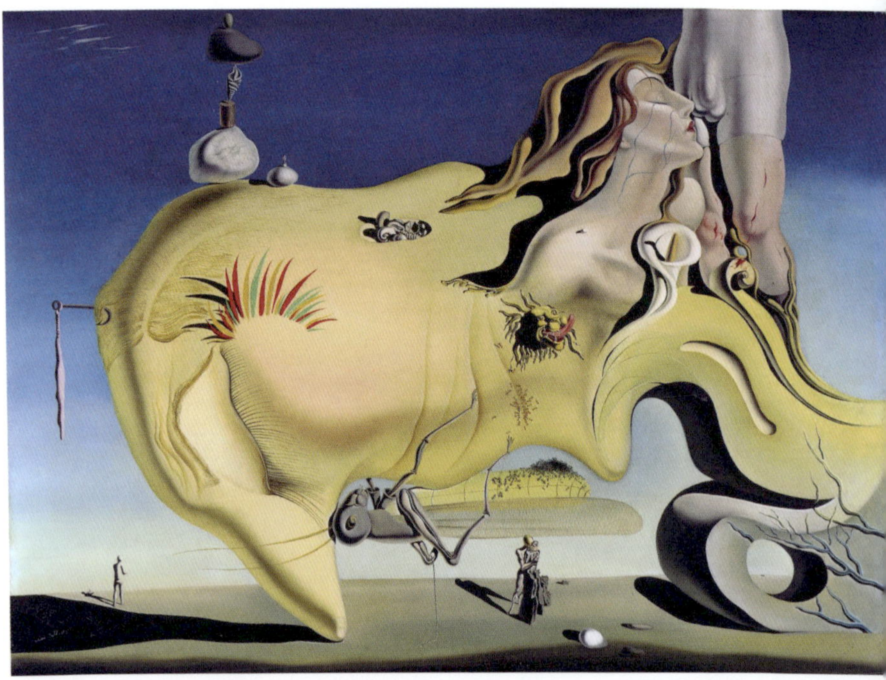

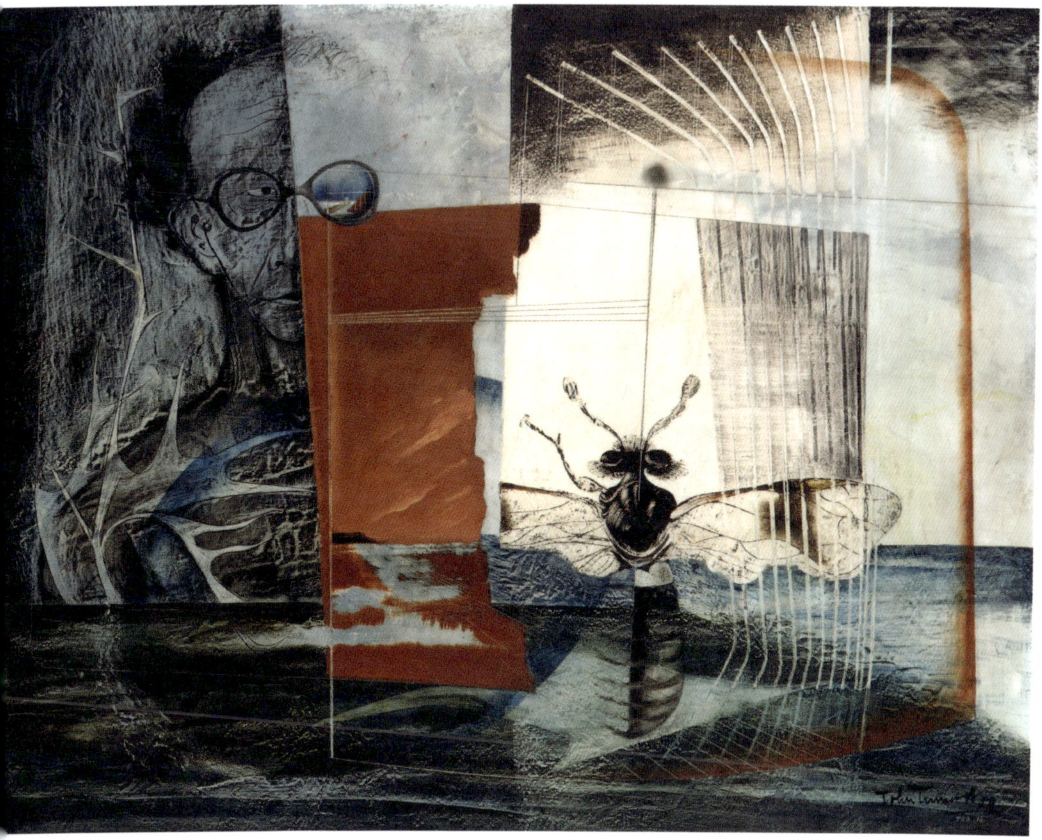

John Tunnard, *Self-Portrait*, 1959

Mantis

The sinister praying mantis was bound to have surrealist appeal for three reasons. The first concerns its name – and the fact that it appears to be praying when it is preying. As it sits quietly camouflaged, waiting for its prey to pass by, its powerful front legs are bent up in what appears to be a posture of prayer. These are called raptorial legs because they are designed to seize and hold prey: folded back like the blades of a pocket knife, until the mantis strikes out and grasps its victim, they are equipped with sharp spines that stop it from escaping. The idea of a lethal posture of prayer would have appealed to the anti-religious surrealists. The second reason is that, after it has mated, the female mantis sometimes eats her male partner. This bizarre link between sex and feeding also had surrealist appeal. Finally, the head of the mantis has a dramatic shape in which the huge compound eyes give it the appearance of an interplanetary alien.

These three qualities made the insect especially attractive to Félix Labisse, who featured mantises in a number of paintings. In the example shown here, *Amorous Mantises* (1946), the female is caught in the act of eating the male's head as he mates with her.

The German surrealist Max Ernst also painted this insect. In his ironically titled *The Joy of Life* (1936), rampant foliage creates a dense forest scene in which various creatures are hiding. The painting is a twist on a work of the same name by Henri Matisse, dating from 1905–6, but Ernst has replaced Matisse's colourful, sensual vision of Arcadia with a suffocating mass of twisted, entangled undergrowth – an expression of the deteriorating situation in Europe in the 1930s. His mantis is cleverly hidden in the leaves at the bottom of the composition but, once spotted, is unmistakable.

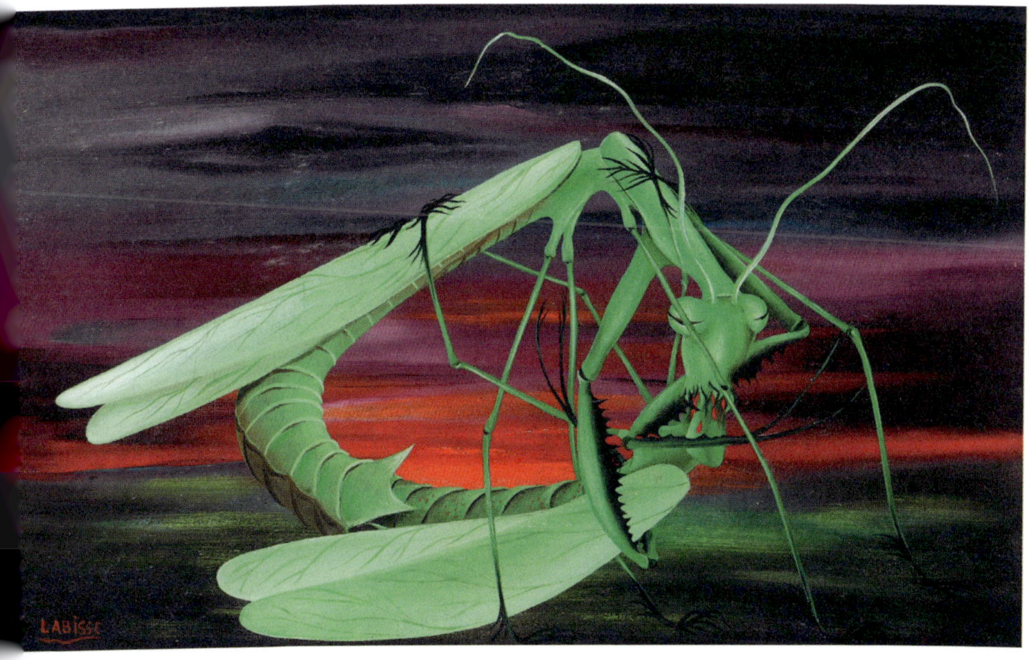

Félix Labisse, *Amorous Mantises*, 1946

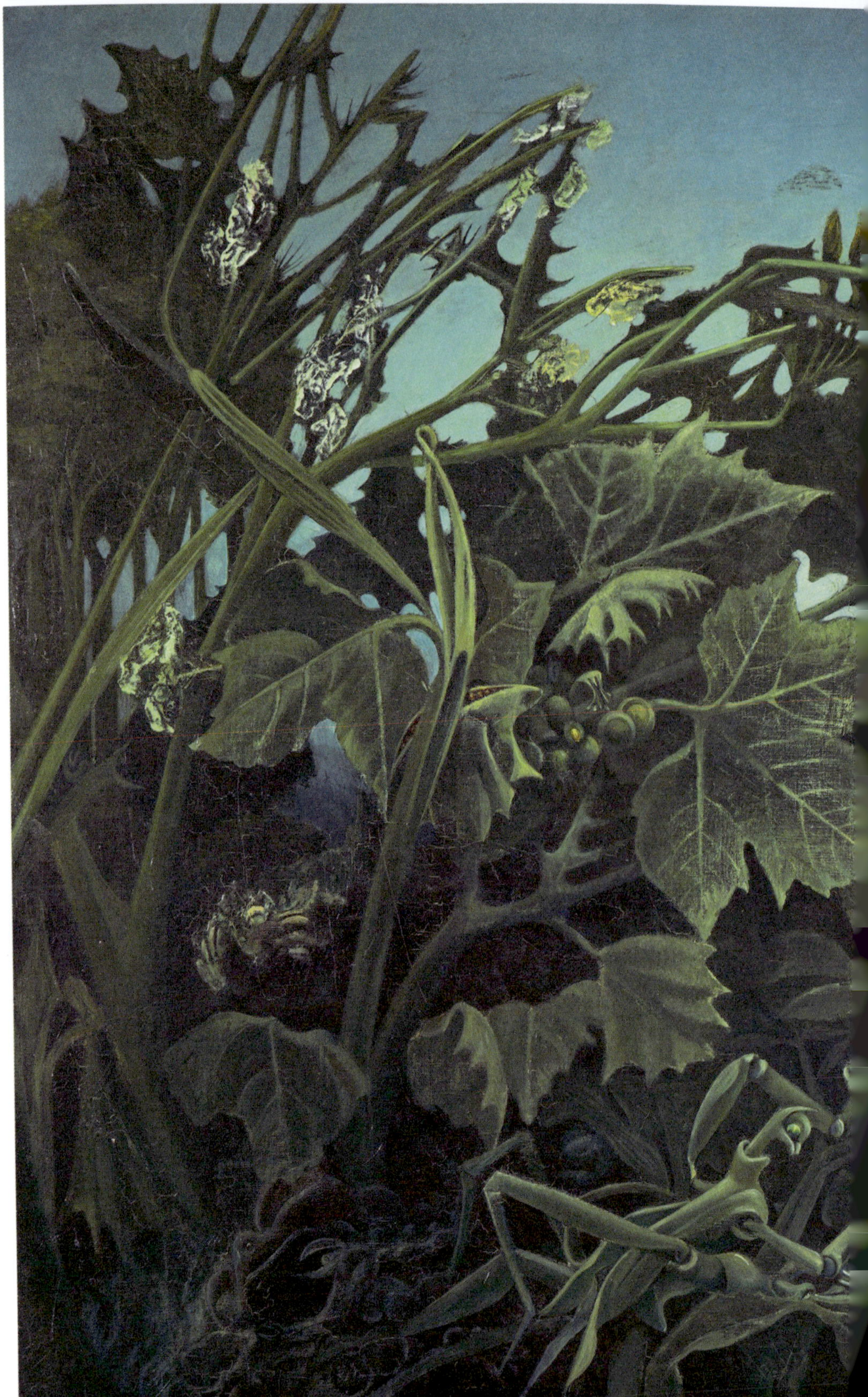

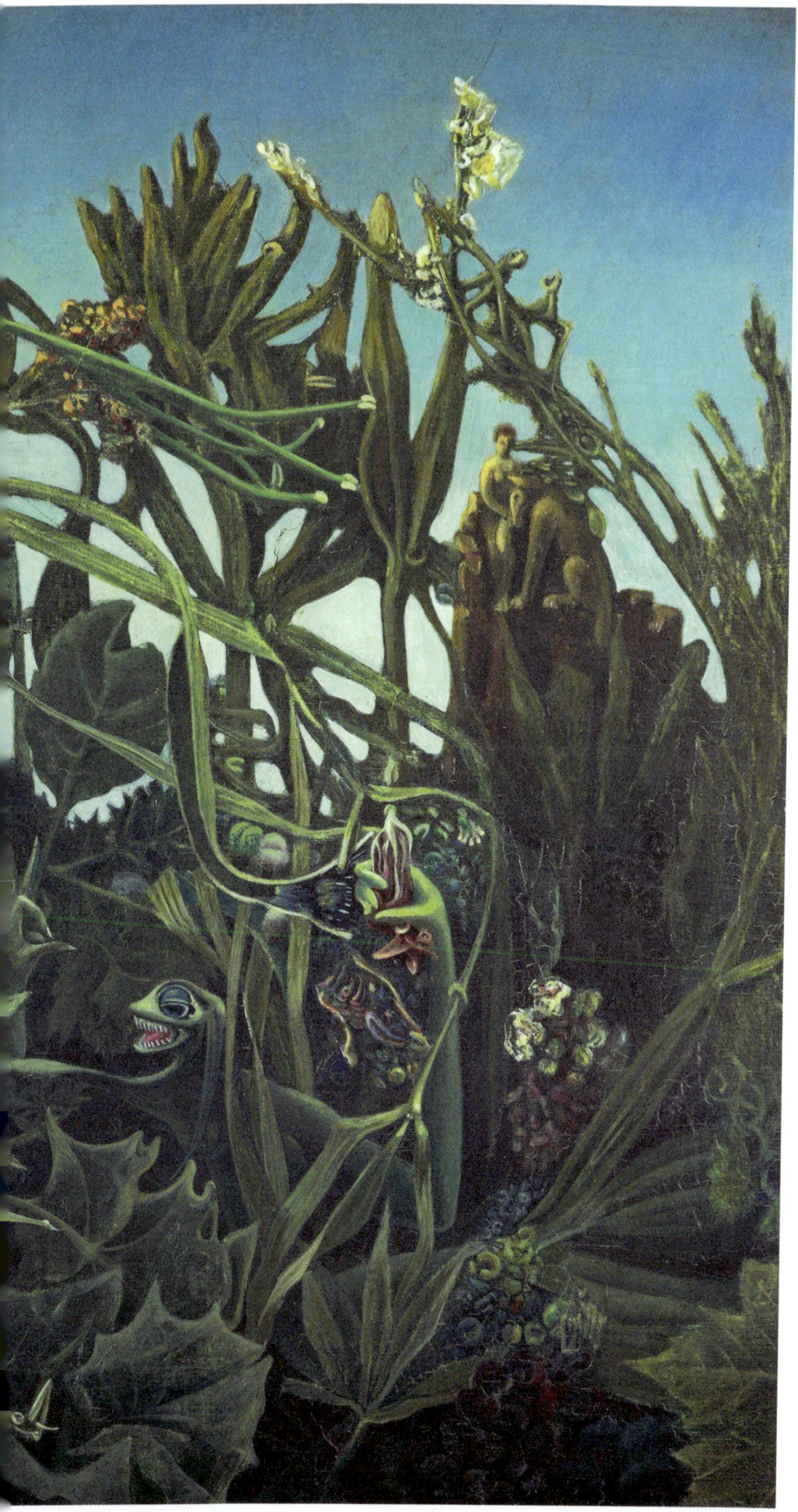

Max Ernst, *The Joy of Life*, 1936

Butterfly

Symbolically, the butterfly represents transformation, fragility and endurance. Its metamorphosis from a caterpillar to a chrysalis to an adult is perhaps the ultimate symbol of renewal and reshaping. With its delicate body and soft, fluttering wings, the butterfly must adapt to diverse and often hostile environments to survive. For the surrealists, however, the butterfly's colourful, fragile beauty posed a problem. How can something so pretty exist in the darkly humorous world of surrealism?

In an early work by Victor Brauner, *The Crime of the Butterfly King* (1930), the Romanian artist presents a terrifying hybrid being in a sinister, dark landscape. While the title points to a butterfly king, this central figure would appear to be his victim: it has the head and legs of a woman; the body is a dull-brown winged creature that looks more like a fly than a butterfly. The creature's eyes have become the woman's breasts, its legs are her pencil-thin arms, and its wings have spread to become her clothes. Blood runs down the woman's face and neck, and the bodies of two blood-soaked women and another flying insect – which also appears to be dead – can be seen in the background.

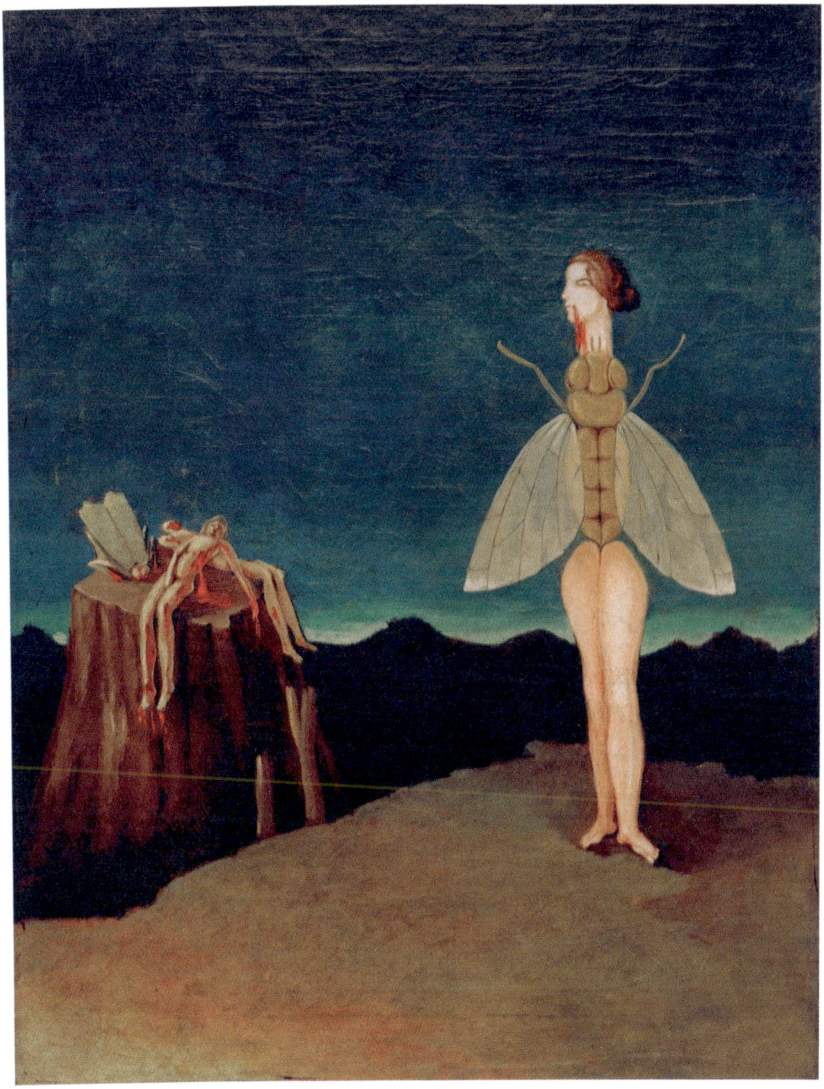

Victor Brauner, *The Crime of the Butterfly King*, 1930

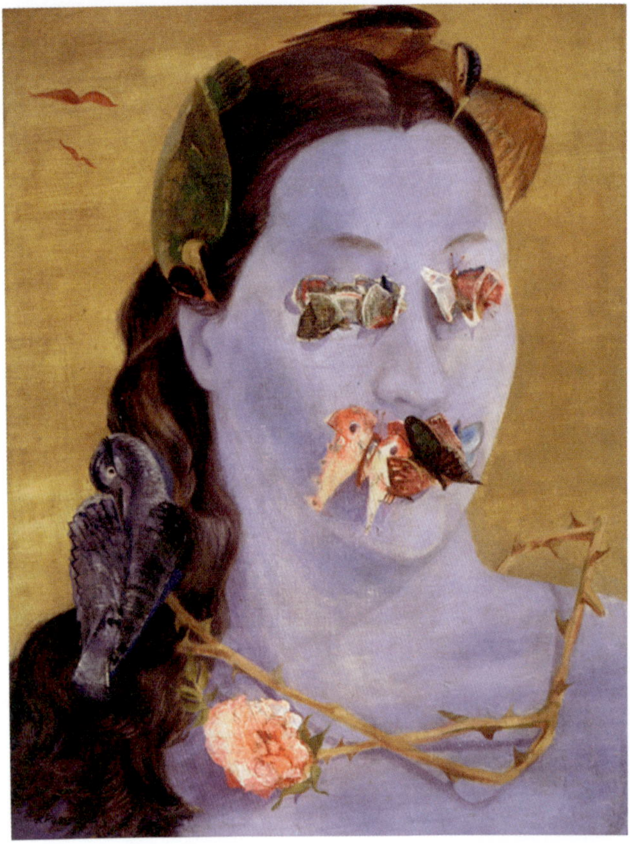

Roland Penrose, *Winged Domino: Portrait of Valentine*, 1937

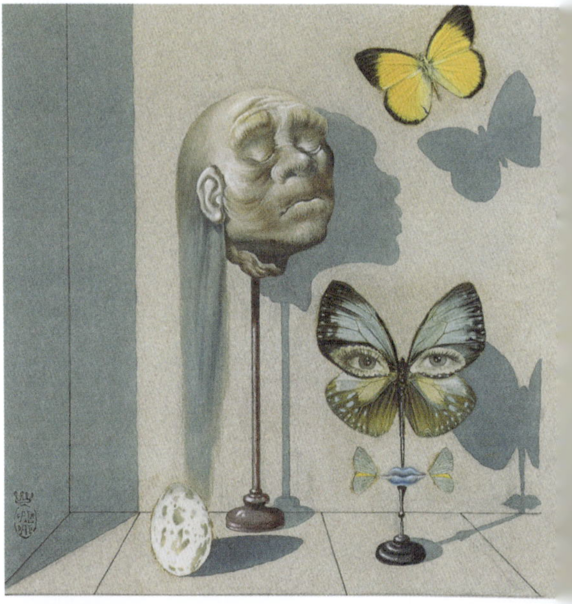

Salvador Dalí, frontispiece for *La Limite*, 1951

Roland Penrose's *Winged Domino: Portrait of Valentine* (1937) is a deeply personal portrait. The Valentine of the title is the English artist's first wife, Valentine Boué, painted shortly after the breakdown of their marriage. Her eyes and mouth are covered with clusters of butterflies, rendering her both blind and mute, and she wears a necklace of thorns. The result is a deeply disturbing image, with the butterflies seeming to suck the sustenance from the woman's face.

Butterflies appear in a number of works by Salvador Dalí, often as a symbol of freedom or hope. In the frontispiece of Maurice Sandoz's book, *La Limite* (1951), which Dalí illustrated, a beautifully marked butterfly – displayed on a stand – has been transformed into a female face by the addition of a pair of attractive eyes with long lashes. The cheeks of the woman are defined by two more butterflies, seen resting on either side of her blue lips. However, a shrunken head in the background, also on a stand, provides an ominous contrast.

In the late 1920s and 1930s, the French artist Francis Picabia experimented with layering images to achieve a 'transparent' effect, producing a series of superimposed heads, figures and objects. His *Woman with Butterfly* (1927), while not strictly superimposed, continues the theme by placing a near-naked woman inside the head of a man with deliberately exaggerated features. Kneeling, she wears only black stockings and black gloves, and reaches up to touch a huge butterfly, whose abdomen has taken on a phallic quality.

In Óscar Domínguez's *Le Plus clair du temps II* (1943), the focus is on objects rather than the human form: eight butterflies have been pinned inside a glass display case. A sundial and an hourglass dominate the foreground, while the background is a web of straight lines and strangely contorted, angular forms. In 1943, the Spanish artist was living in occupied Paris, having been

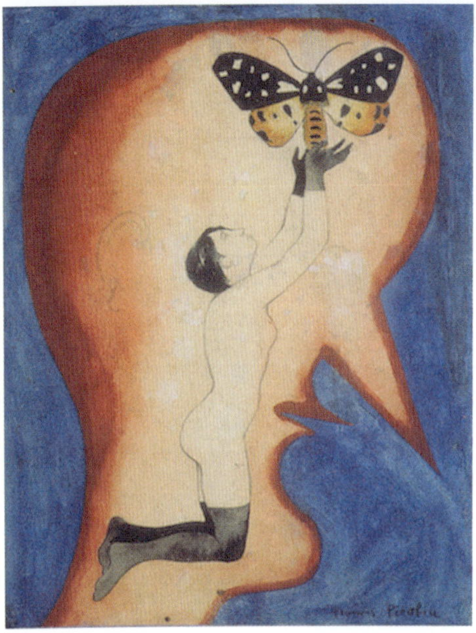

Francis Picabia, *Woman with Butterfly*, 1927

Jindřich Štyrský, *Untitled*, 1940

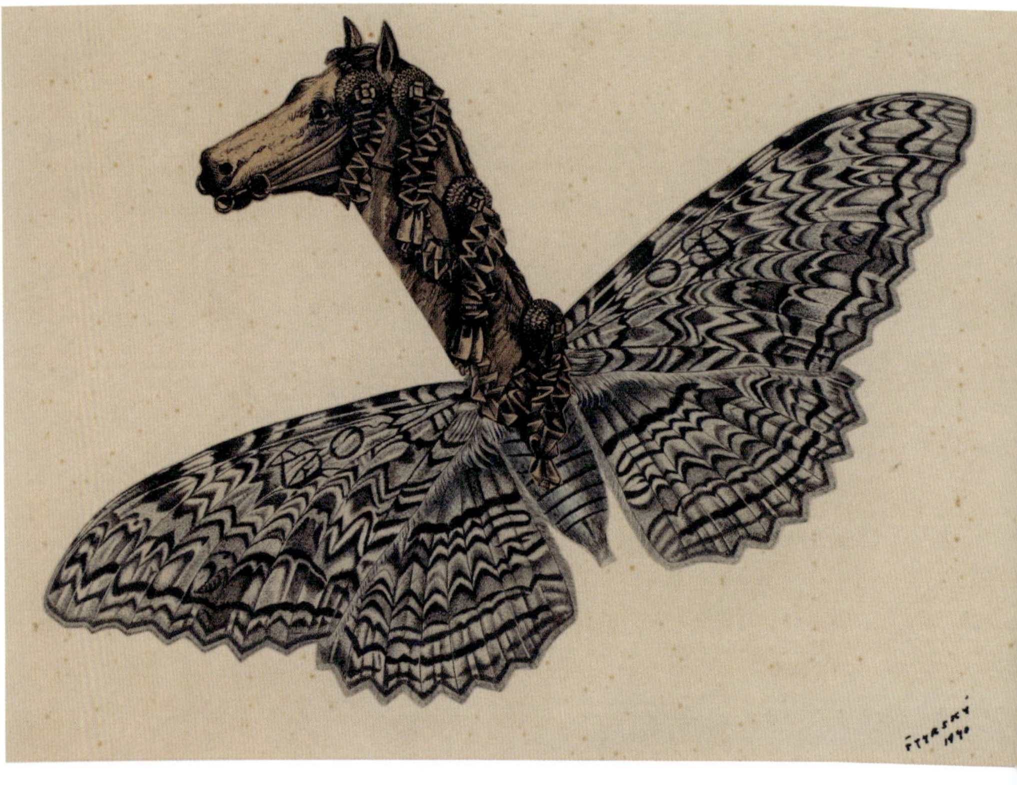

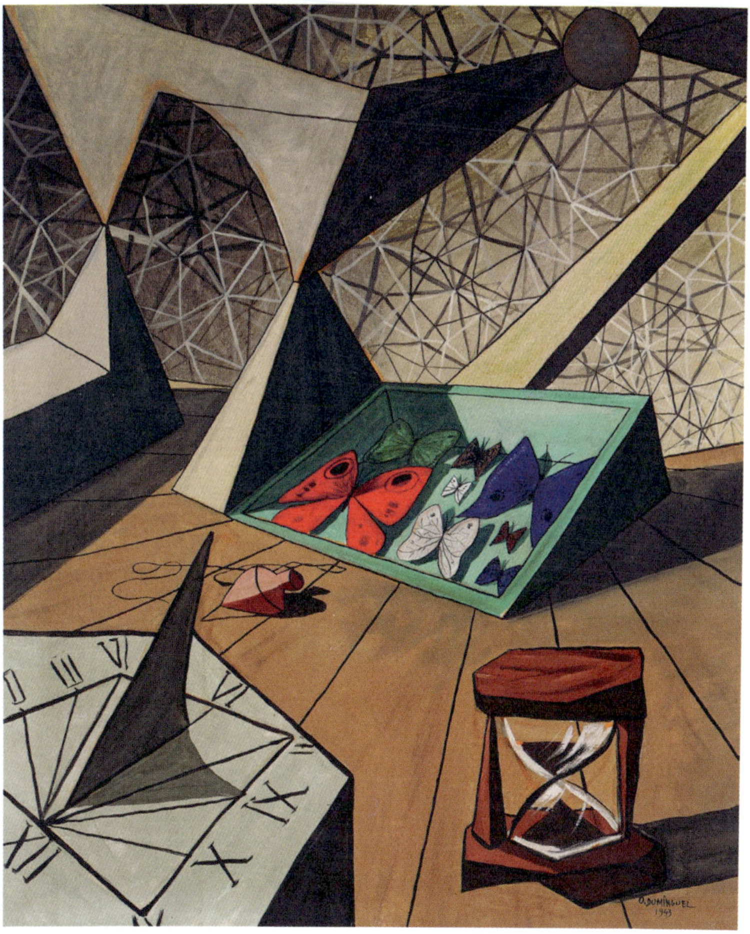

Óscar Domínguez,
Le Plus clair du temps II, 1943

Henry Moore, *Large Divided Oval: Butterfly*, 1982 (cast 1985–86)

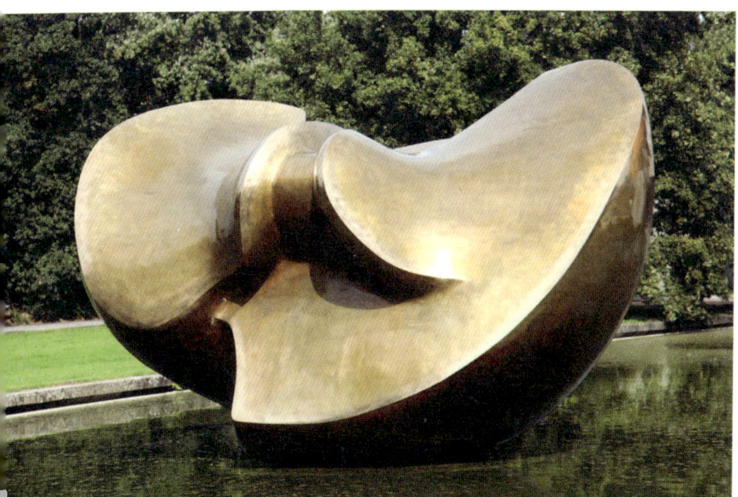

unable to secure an exit visa. The case of butterflies belonged to his father and is a recurring motif in Domínguez's works, a symbol of nostalgia.

In 1967, the British master sculptor Henry Moore did the unthinkable: he portrayed the most delicate of insects as a solid block of white marble. In *Divided Oval*, a piece Moore went on to cast in various media, only the smooth contours of the wings help us identify the source of his inspiration.

In his *Untitled* collage (1940), the Czech surrealist Jindřich Štyrský also does the unthinkable, giving his butterfly the neck and head of a horse. Jane Graverol, meanwhile, uses a lighter touch, transforming her four-eyed butterfly into the bow that ties the hair of her *Lolita* (1960). This detail is a reference to the author of the classic book, Vladimir Nabokov, who was passionate about butterflies. Nabokov is known to have spent his summers travelling through the western US on the hunt for rare species.

Finally, the English artist Edith Rimmington, in *The Decoy* (1948), one of her remarkable 'false collages', depicts a female hand inside which a chrysalis snugly sleeps, while three more dangle from the subject's fingertips and four adult butterflies flit about, against a plain background.

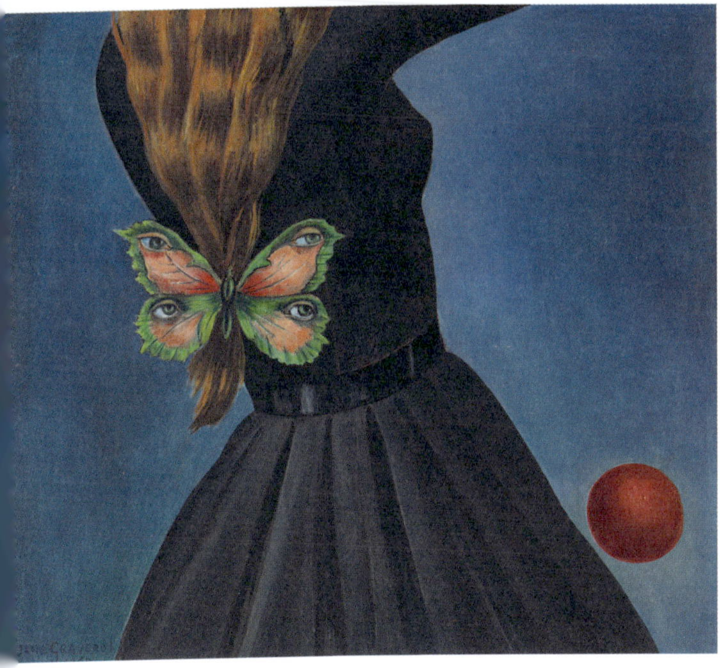

Jane Graverol, *Lolita*, 1960

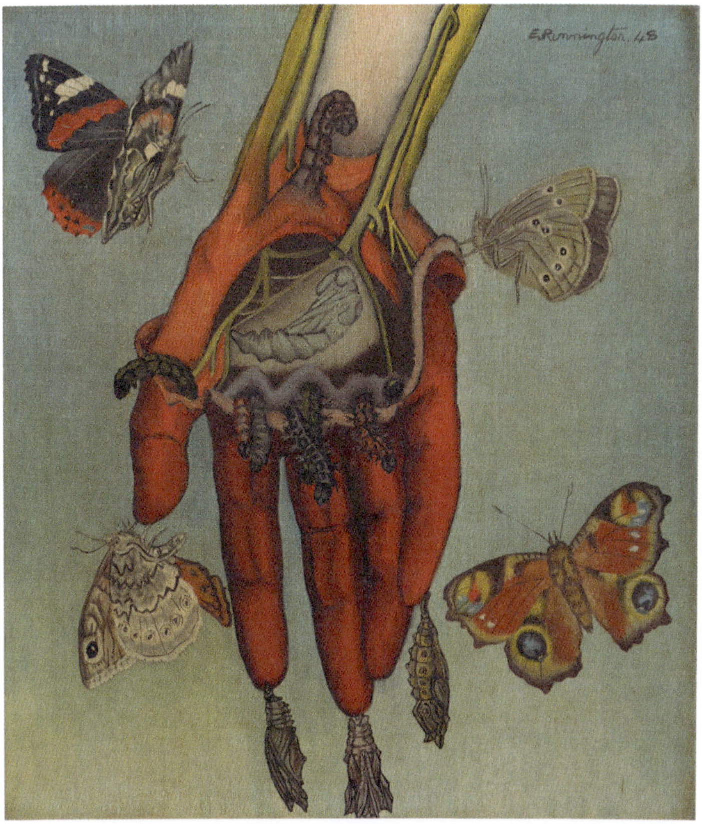

Edith Rimmington, *The Decoy*, 1948

The Cold

Bloods

Fish

The fish is a surrealist favourite. Its iconic shape has lent itself to countless visual interpretations. What can the surrealist imagination turn a simple fish-shape into? A small sample of works will show the amazing range of adaptations that have been offered to us over the years.

In *Sirens* (1926), by the French artist Georges Malkine, the focus is on eyes. Malkine turns a tankful of small aquarium fish into alluring female eyes, which seem drawn to the miniature naked human forms in the top left of the painting. A woman watches on, her own eyes obscured by a bar at the top of the tank.

Ithell Colquhoun takes a completely different approach in her still life *Sardine and Eggs* (*c.* 1941). The painting shows a fish and two hen's eggs tightly pulled together in a string bag – on the surface, an innocent, domestic purchase. However, the double meaning is unmistakable, with the objects symbolizing the male genitalia: the fish becoming the penis, and the two eggs the testicles. By using eggs, typically associated with female reproduction, to represent the testicles, the British artist cleverly fuses the male and the female.

In René Magritte's *Collective Invention* (1935), the Belgian artist turns his fish into the head and torso of a mermaid. A typical mermaid, of course, has the top half of a woman combined with the tail of a fish, but Magritte has reversed this arrangement to create an unforgettable surrealist image.

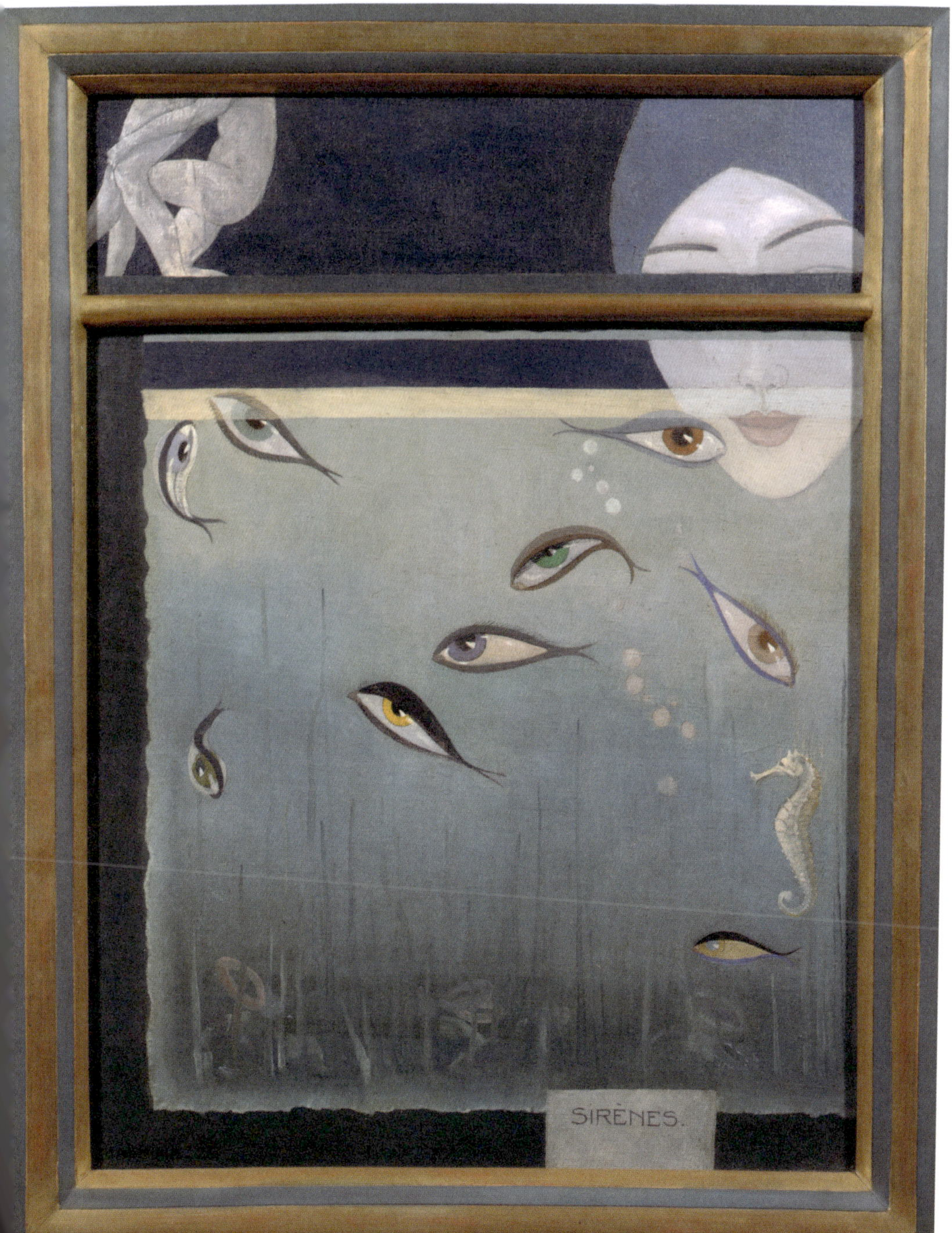

Georges Malkine, *Sirens*, 1926

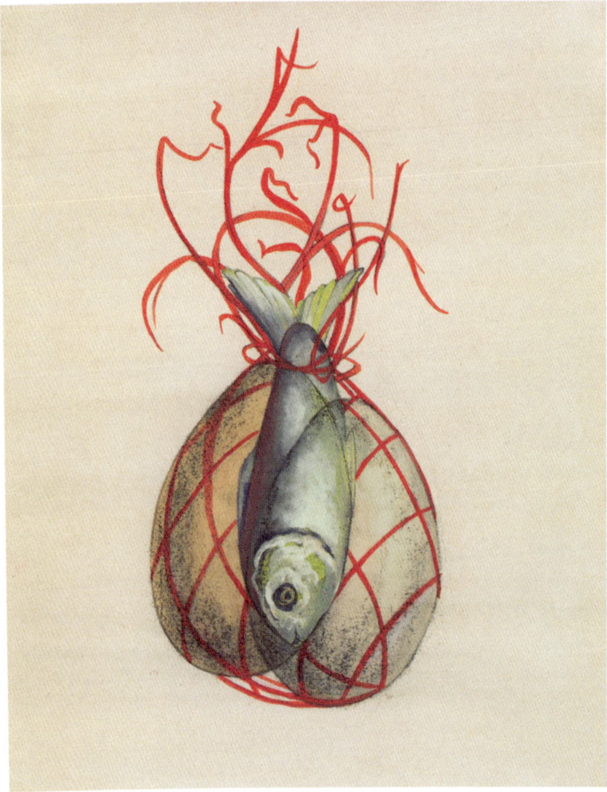

Ithell Colquhoun, *Sardine and Eggs*, c. 1941

René Magritte, *Collective Invention*, 1935

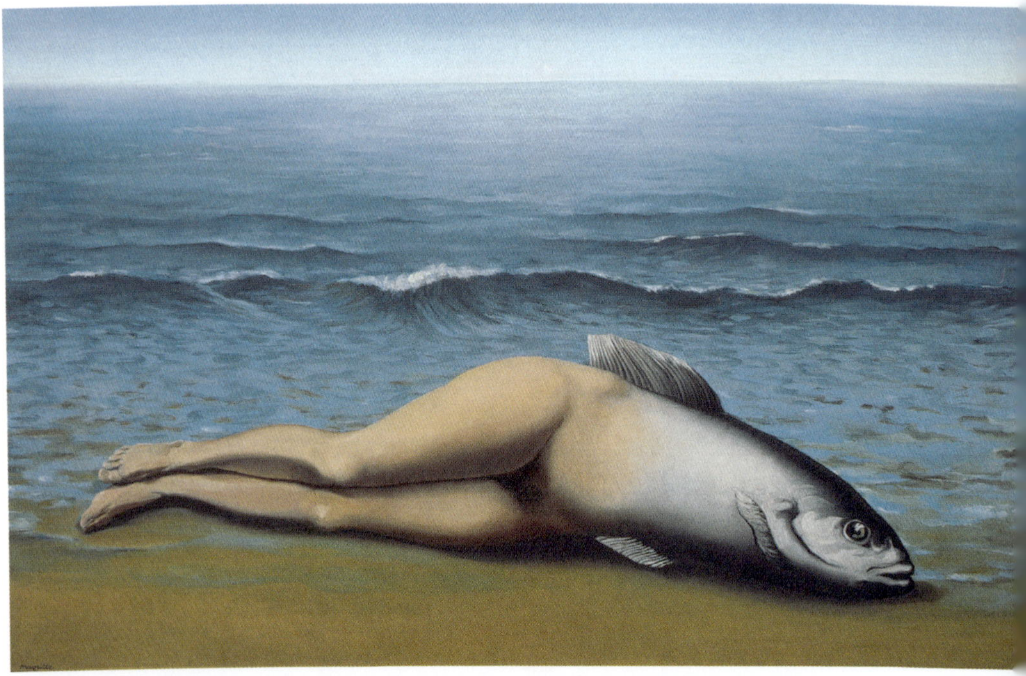

But it is Marc Chagall, in *Time Is a River without Banks* (1930–39), who gives us perhaps the most outrageous of all these imaginative fish images. Instead of dorsal fins, his fish has wings that glow red, as if they have burst into flames. As it soars over the river below, possibly recalling Chagall's hometown of Vitebsk (then part of the Russian Empire, now in Belarus), it 'carries' a grandfather clock while playing a violin with a human hand that emerges from its body. The painting was completed as war was breaking out and, as well as looking into his past, evokes the dangers facing the Jewish artist: a couple in the bottom right corner

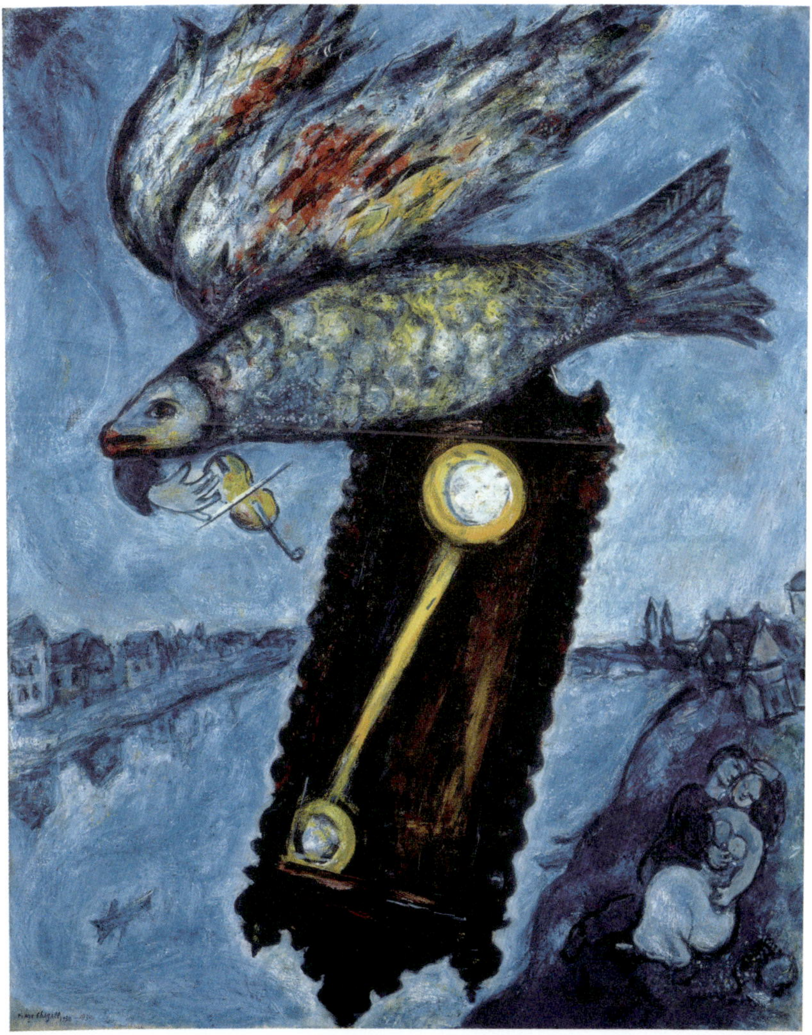

Marc Chagall, *Time Is a River without Banks*, 1930–39

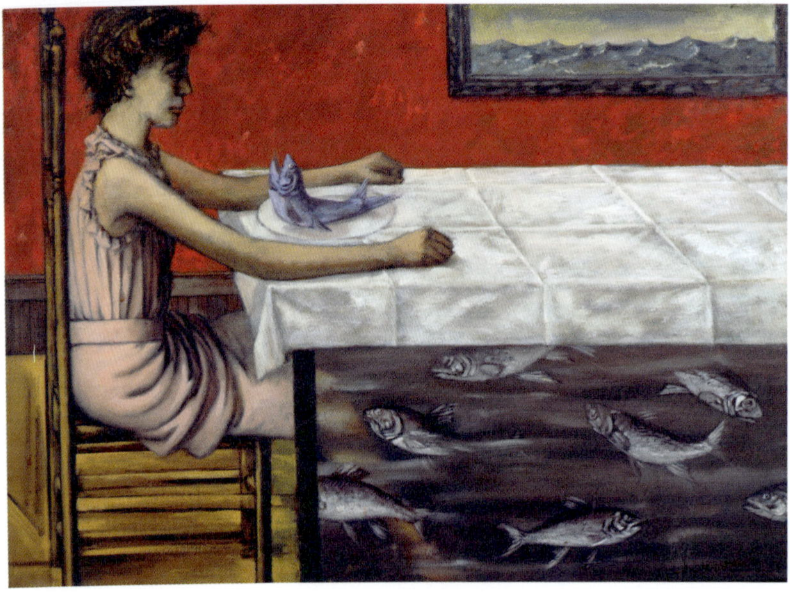

Dorothea Tanning, *Poached Trout*, 1952

Félix Labisse, *Charlotte Corday*, 1946

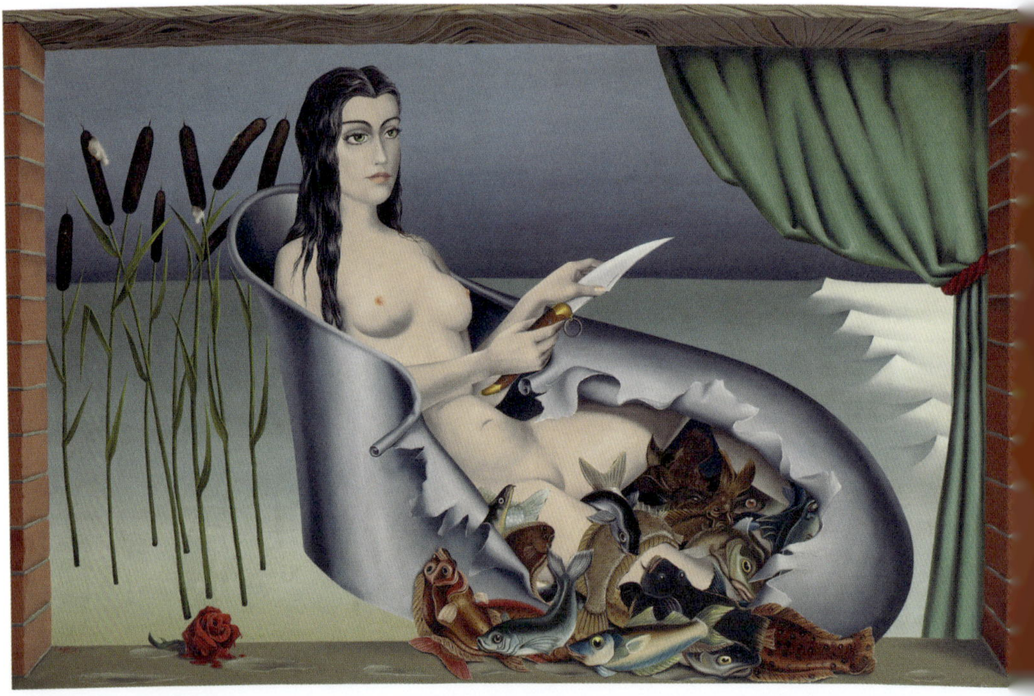

have been interpreted as Chagall and his wife, locked in a melancholy embrace.

Charlotte Corday (1946), by Félix Labisse, depicts a naked woman reclining in her bath. In one hand she holds a savage-looking knife, and with the other she runs her fingers along the blade. The bath has been sliced apart, releasing a shoal of fish that has spilled out onto the floor. A figure of the French Revolution, Charlotte Corday became known as the 'Angel of Assassination' after murdering her political opponent, Jean-Paul Marat, in 1793. She stabbed him to death when he was taking a medicinal bath. Four days later, she was executed by guillotine.

Poached Trout (1952), by the American artist Dorothea Tanning, shows a young woman sitting at a dining table, staring at a fish that rears up on the plate in front of her. But on closer inspection, we see that this table has bizarrely become an aquarium. The woman's legs disappear into the water of a tank, in which several large fish thrash about.

Victor Brauner gives us a curious transformation in *Fish on Wheels* (1965), in which his fish has become a road vehicle of some kind, inside which a drama is unfolding. It is hard to make out what is happening in the belly of the fish, but it seems to involve a pregnant woman whose hair has become a vomiting snake.

In Toyen's *Between the Long Shadows* (1943), a sombre figure, shrouded in white, is shown from the side. She sits on a white chair, behind which there clusters a frightened shoal of huge fish, which appear to be floating in the sky. On the right, the remains of a skeletal shoal can be seen. Painted during the Second World War, when Toyen was forced underground by the Nazi occupation of Czechoslovakia, this haunting image reflects the themes of threat and devastation that permeate the artist's work at this time. Toyen (née Marie Cermínová) was a gender-neutral pseudonym adopted by the artist, who resisted the rigid attitudes towards

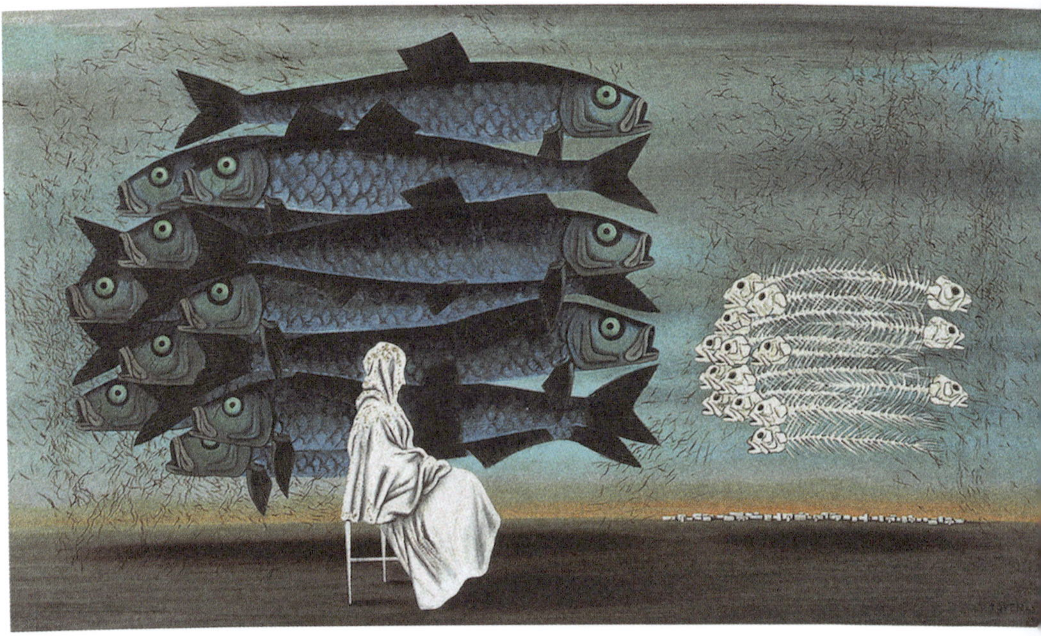

Toyen, *Between the Long Shadows*, 1943

Paul Klee, *Around the Fish*, 1926

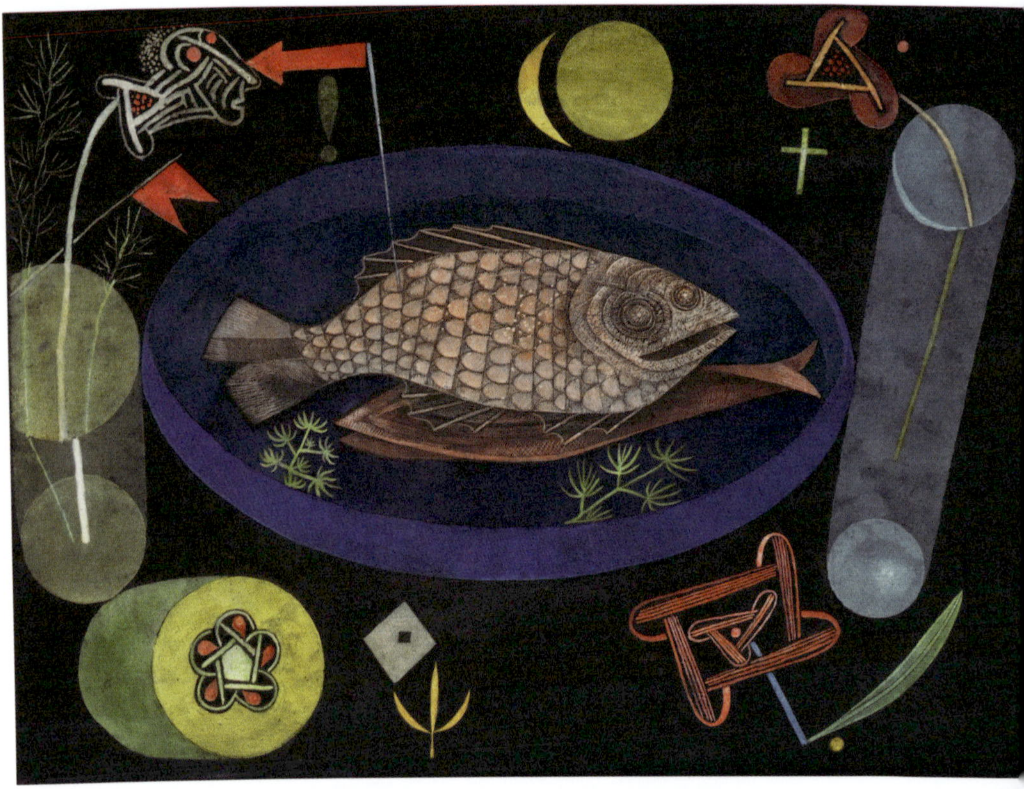

gender and sexuality at the time. Toyen rejected being labelled as female, used the masculine singular form in Czech, and adopted both women's and men's attire.

The final example comes from the Swiss proto-surrealist Paul Klee, whose *Around the Fish* (1926) celebrates the fish in a special way by making it the dominant centrepiece of this carefully constructed composition. Depicted on a blue plate, the fish (or are there more than one, as suggested by reflections below the fish?) is surrounded by all manner of shapes and objects, including moons, a transparent cylinder, an arrow, a cross and a red-eyed, mask-like head.

Few occupants of the surrealist menagerie can have enjoyed such a varied symbolic outing as the fish.

Victor Brauner, *Fish on Wheels*, 1965

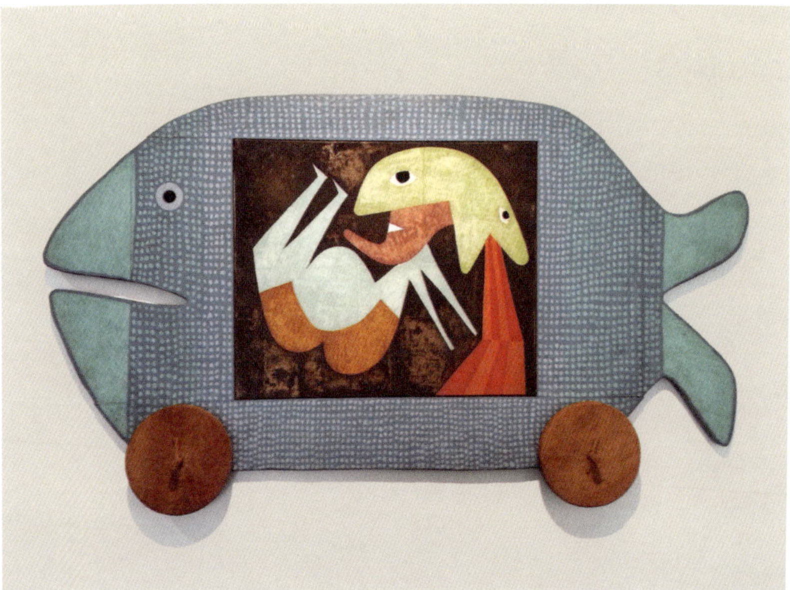

Frog

Frogs seem to have had little appeal for the surrealist artists. The ones that do occasionally manage to hop into the corner of a composition are usually minor figures.

One exception is the large frog that appears in the centre of Victor Brauner's *The Object that Dreams II* (1938). A simple interpretation of this work is that it shows a sleeping, red-haired woman who is dreaming of kissing a frog and thereby turning it into a handsome prince. This is the well-known fairy tale, but it is surely too sickly sweet for a surrealist imagination as darkly perverse as that of Victor Brauner. Or is he deliberately mocking us by abandoning his usually arcane compositions to present us with his version of a hackneyed fairy tale?

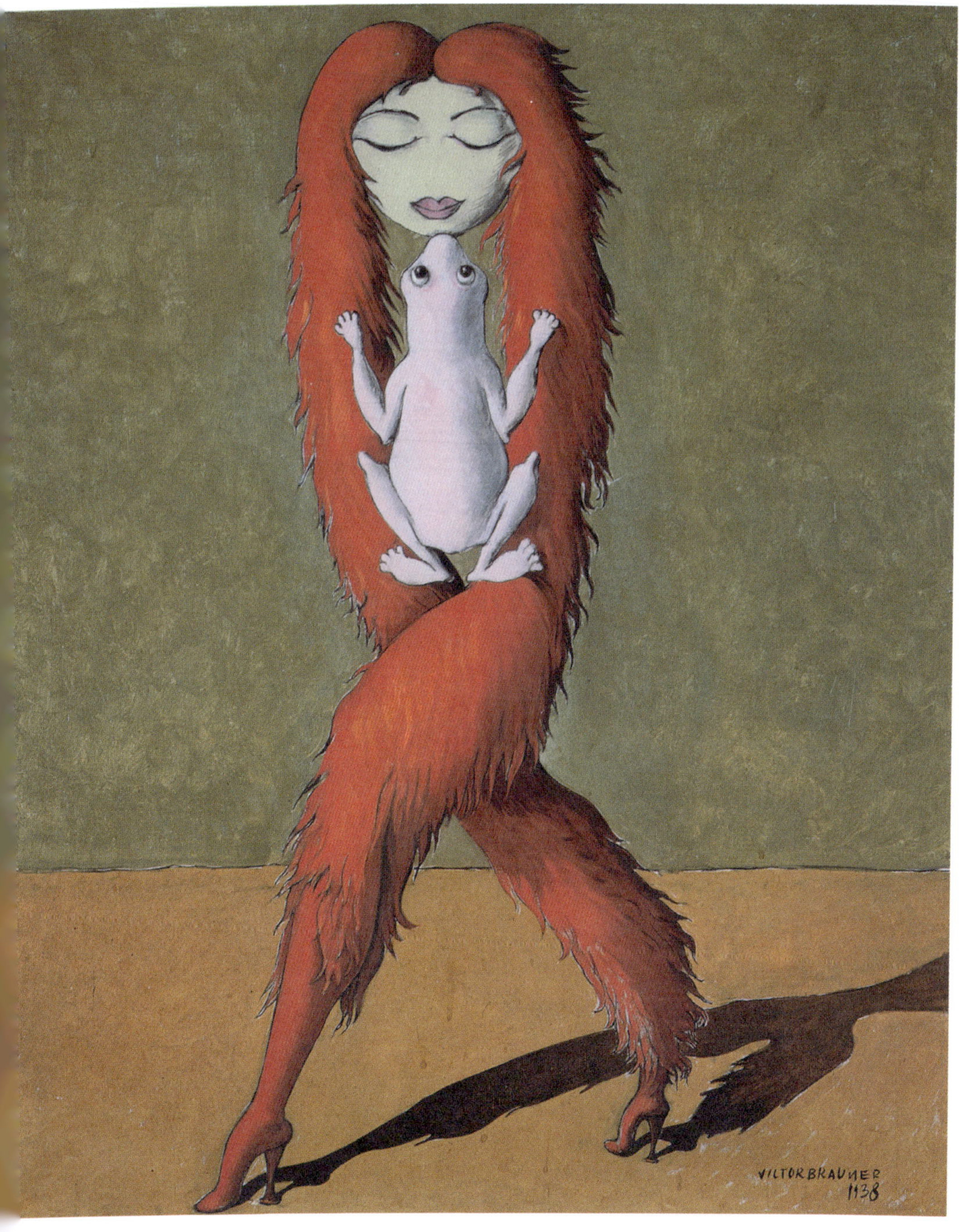

Victor Brauner, *The Object that Dreams II*, 1938

Chameleon

As a creature of startling appearance, with its independently rotating eyes, spirally coiled tail, and immensely long tongue with a bulbous, sticky tip, and an ability to change colour to blend into the surroundings, one would expect the chameleon to be a familiar presence in the surrealist menagerie. This is not, however, the case. Perhaps the chameleon is such a surreal creature in its own right that artists felt they could do little to add to its oddities. As far as this particular creature is concerned, they were unable to compete with nature.

In *The Lure of Death* (1930), Victor Brauner proves the exception, finding a novel way to exploit this bizarre animal. In nature, the chameleon often sits quietly on a branch waiting for food to pass its way. Camouflaged against the foliage, and lying very still, it can remain undetected. Then, when the prey animal – usually a large insect – gets close enough, the chameleon opens its mouth and shoots out its amazingly long tongue. If the tongue strikes the prey, its adhesive tip renders the victim helpless, and it is very easy for the chameleon to quickly withdraw its tongue and swallow its meal.

In this painting, the Romanian artist seems to ask himself what would happen if, instead of an insect, an absurd contraption flew by. Would a chameleon be so rigidly programmed to strike, that it would attack almost anything? A propeller-driven air balloon has come dangerously close, and the chameleon, having struck it, now faces the impossible task of swallowing the balloon whole.

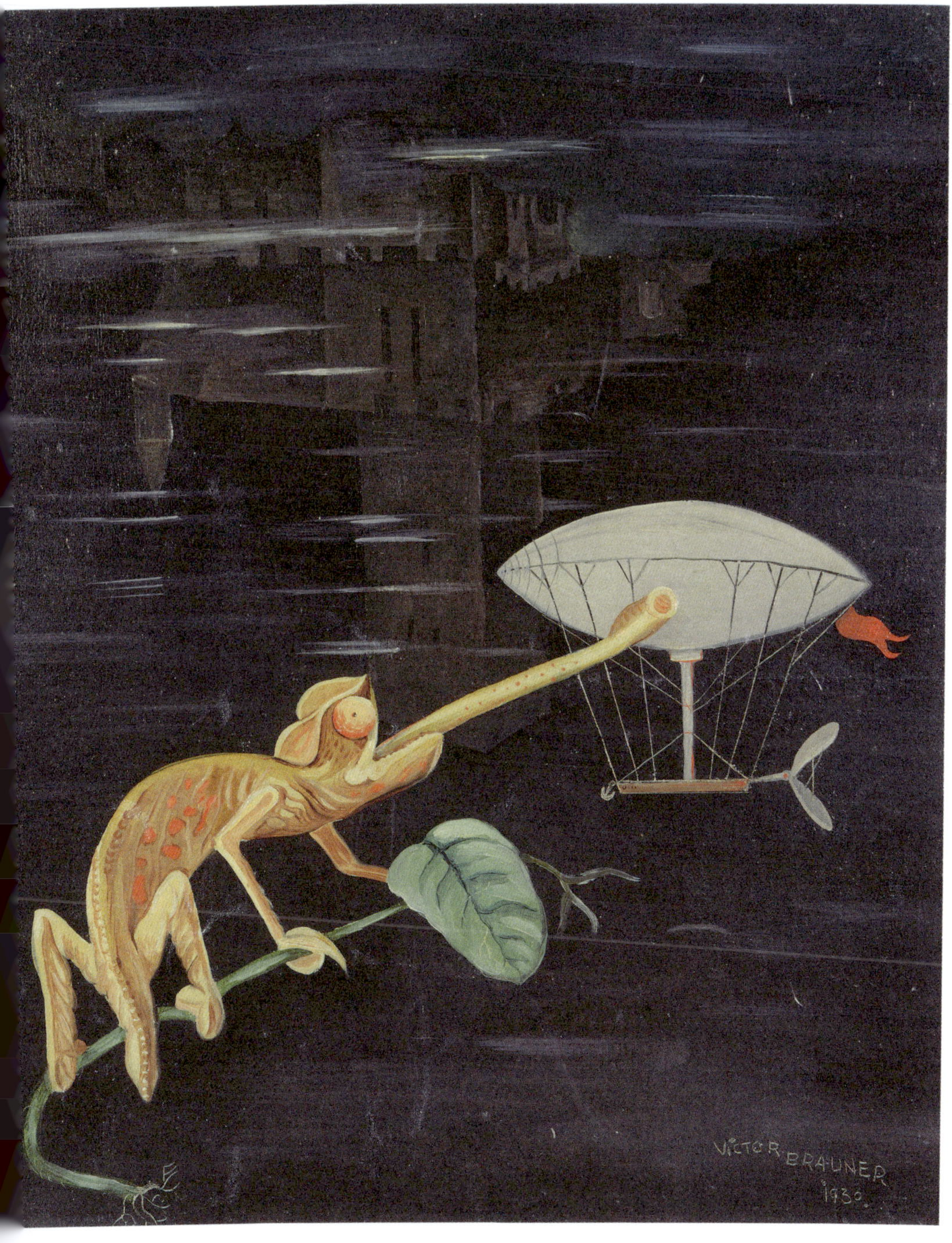

Victor Brauner, *The Lure of Death*, 1930

Snake

The snake is particularly rich in symbolic meanings. Because it sheds its skin several times a year, and on each occasion emerges shiny and new, the ancient Egyptians saw it as a symbol of renewal, reincarnation and immortality. They were deeply concerned with the afterlife and gave serious attention to anything that might ensure passage into this later form of existence. The practice of circumcision is thought to have originated in this symbolism, with ancient Egyptians equating the surgical removal of the foreskin in men with the snake's shedding of the skin and continual process of renewal. The snake is also a well-known phallic symbol, of course.

In terms of behaviour, the snake is known for its stealth and cunning in hunting prey and evading predators. Many snakes use their environments to conceal themselves, hiding under objects or in vegetation until an unsuspecting victim comes within striking distance. Because they cannot close their eyes, snakes can also symbolize the threat of an unblinking, fixed stare. And finally, they are associated with venom and the ability to poison their prey, although most snakes are not venomous.

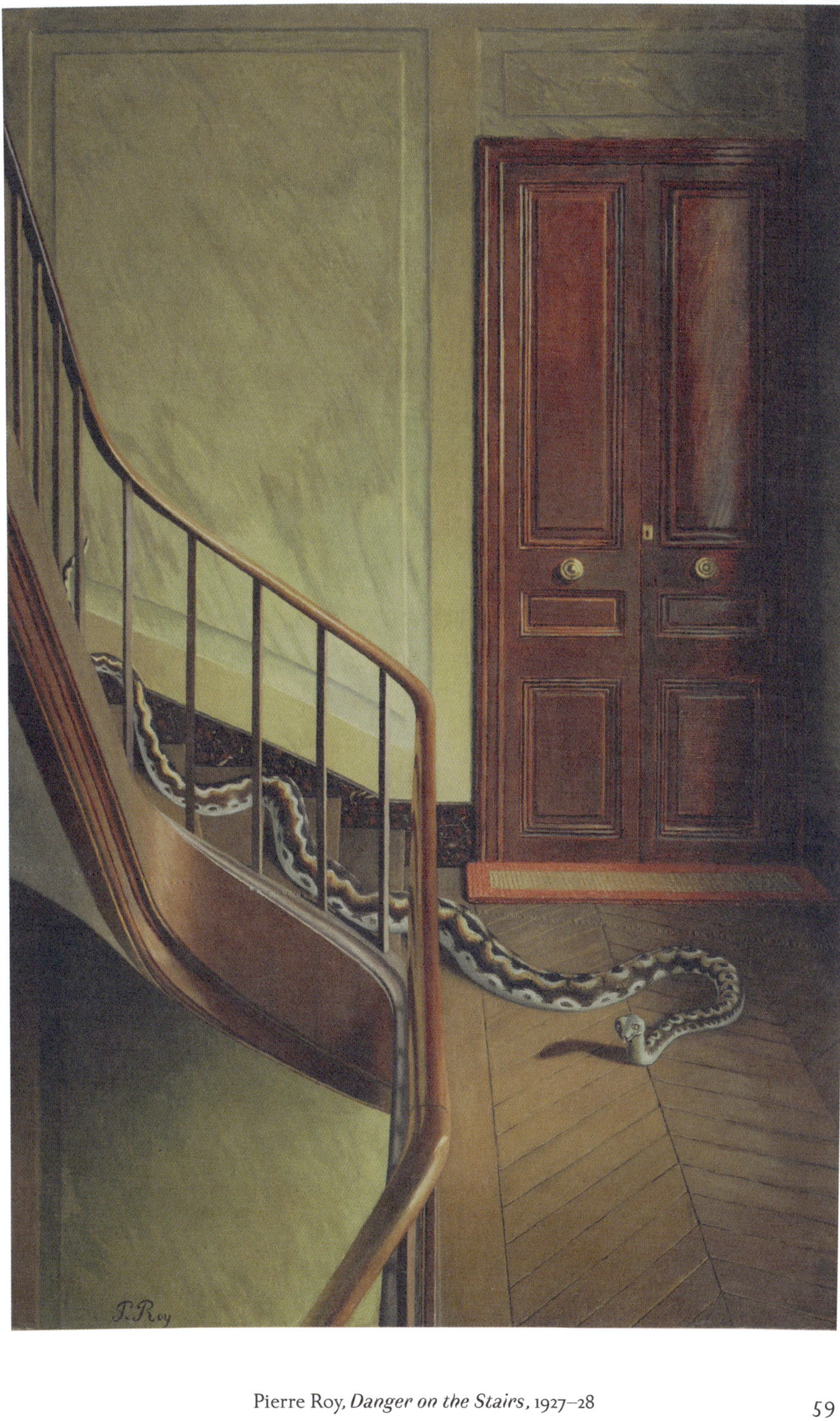

Pierre Roy, *Danger on the Stairs*, 1927–28

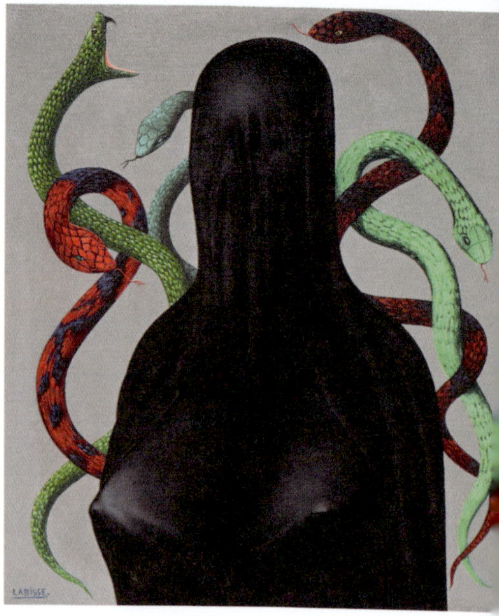

Félix Labisse, *The Daughter of Tiresias*, 1973

Leonora Carrington, *Forbidden Fruit*, 1969

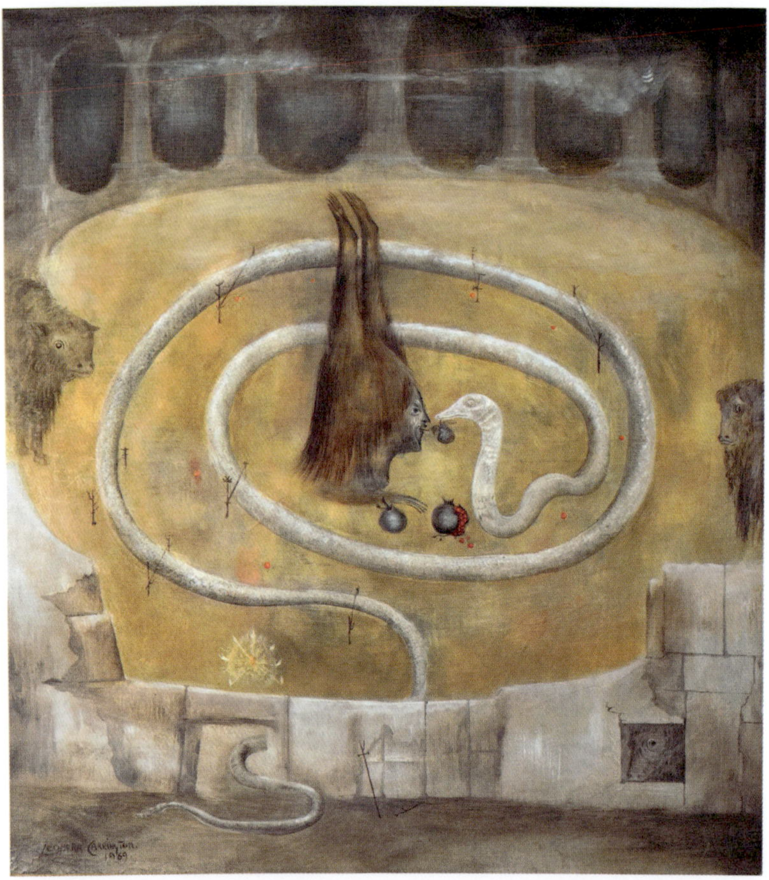

With all these attributes, it is not surprising that snakes appear repeatedly in surrealist art. In *Danger on the Stairs* (1927–28), Pierre Roy shows us the landing of an ordinary Paris apartment block. The eye is drawn to the tall double doors on the right, before moving to a giant snake that crawls towards us, its long body disappearing up the twisting staircase. Here, Roy taps a familiar childhood fear that there may be dangerous beasts lurking in the place we should feel most safe: the monster under the bed, waiting to pounce.

In Félix Labisse's *The Daughter of Tiresias* (1973), a mass of red and green snakes writhes around a sinister female figure covered in a thin black shroud. In Greek mythology, Tiresias was a blind prophet who came across a pair of mating snakes and hit them with a stick. The goddess Hera was so angry with him that she turned him into a woman, and he stayed as such for seven years, before turning back into a man. The title indicates that the shrouded figure is his daughter Manto, who also possessed the gift of prophecy.

In her *Forbidden Fruit* (1969), Leonora Carrington shows us a very long snake that has completely encircled a horned female head covered in fur. The snake appears to be offering her some kind of fruit – perhaps the forbidden fruit from the Garden of Eden, as the title would suggest, but seen in the context of other works by the artist, who drew on imagery and ideas from a vast range of cultures and belief systems, this is more likely a positive interaction – a gesture of exchange. Two more of these fruits lie on the ground nearby, while the snake's tail creates a spiral, a symbol of spiritual evolution in Theosophy.

The Wing

ed Animals

Bird

Symbolically, birds represent freedom. Many of us envy their ability to fly, to escape the confines of the earth, and wish we could do the same. In his analysis of dreams, Freud identified birds with sexual desire, arguing that a bird taking flight is a symbol of human male erection. Like many of Freud's equations, this may seem far-fetched, but there is no doubt that, in some surrealist depictions of birds, there is an erotic undertone. Equally, anatomical features of birds are often brought into play as design elements. In such cases, there need be no symbolism, but merely the joy of including a sharp beak, a spread wing or a grasping talon.

The surrealist who was most obsessed with birds was the German Max Ernst. His fixation began early, when he was only fourteen. It is said that, at the very moment his mother gave birth to a sixth child, Ernst's beloved parrot, Hornebom, died. For Ernst, it was as if the new baby had robbed his bird of its soul. From that point on, a bird became his totem, his lifelong preoccupation. He subsequently came to view himself as a bird, creating an ambiguous avian alter ego called Loplop, 'the Bird Superior', which appears in a series of works from the late 1920s onwards. People have puzzled over this name, but it seems to be the nickname of another pet parrot – Pol Pol – spelled backwards.

Although Loplop may have begun as the ghost of a parrot, in Ernst's depictions he quickly loses any parrot-like qualities to

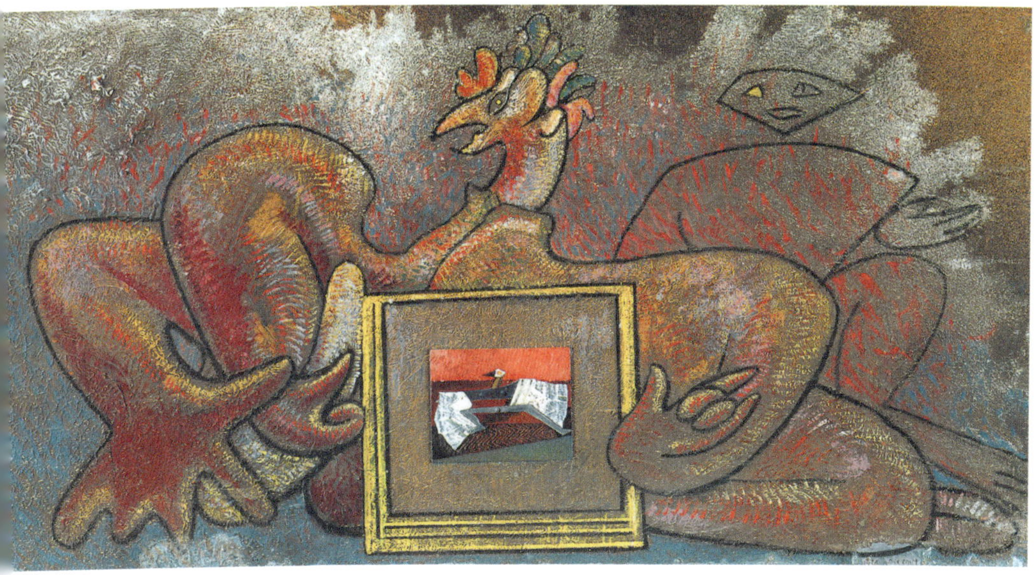

Max Ernst, *Loplop Introduces Loplop*, 1930

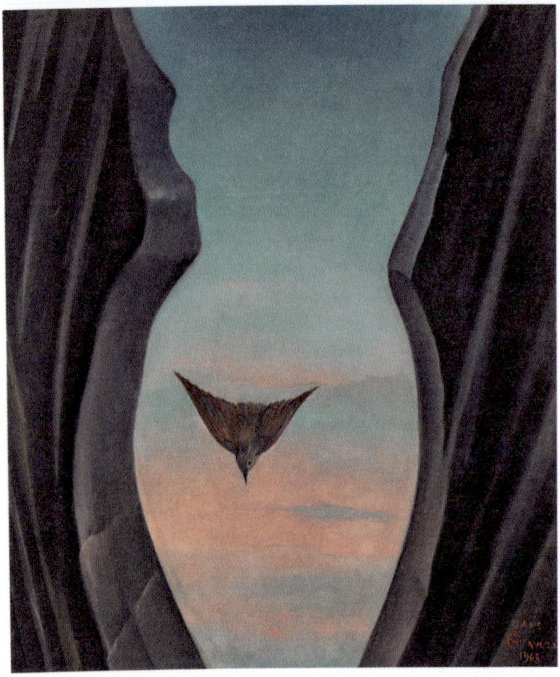

Jane Graverol, *The Holy Spirit*, 1965

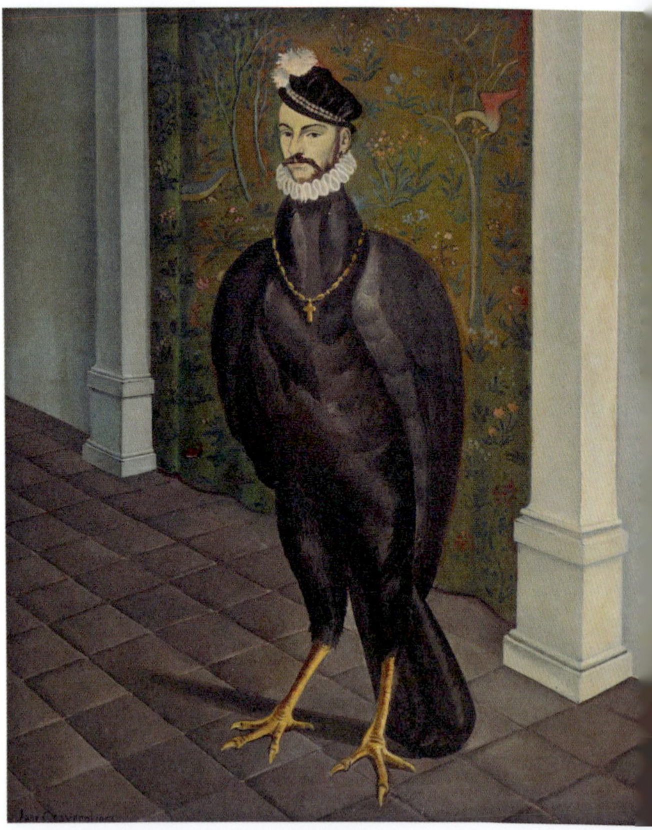

Jane Graverol, *Cruelty of Memory*, 1956

reveal a darker edge. In one of the earliest paintings to feature Loplop (*Loplop, Superior of the Birds*, 1928), the head of the bird still retains its downward-curving, parrot-like beak, but two years later, in *Loplop Introduces Loplop* (1930), where Loplop is shown holding a framed portrait of himself, the mysterious creature is unlike any bird – a strange species all of its own. This continues in other works in the Loplop series.

Commenting on his sinister bird companion, Ernst wrote: 'In 1930 ... I had an almost daily visit from the *Head of the Birds*, called Loplop, a very special phantom of exceptional faithfulness, who is attracted to my person. He presented me with a *heart in a cage, the sea in a cage, two petals, three leaves, a flower and a girl, and also the man with black ink eggs* and *the man with the red cloak*.... one evening he told me some jokes that were not funny.'

An ominous feathered creature also appears in Ernst's masterpiece, *Attirement of the Bride* (1940, see p. 115). It has a slender neck and head with an elongated, savage beak. From inside its long, curved plumage, a human arm emerges holding a broken spear, the tip of which is pointed straight at the bride's genital region. Here, the bird-man has become the symbolic male who will deflower the bride, but – in light of Ernst's avian alter ego – it may also be interpreted as a depiction of the artist himself.

Birds are a favourite subject of the Belgian artist Jane Graverol, appearing in various guises. In *The Holy Spirit* (1965), she plays with the principles of gestalt: a bird with outstretched wings soaring across a pastel sky becomes the pubic triangle of a female silhouette, depending on how you look at the picture. In the earlier *Cruelty of Memory* (1956), a bird is transformed into a historical male figure. In his courtly pose, with neck ruff and pendant crucifix, he stands stiffly erect, as if engaged in some important social event, made ridiculous by his dark plumage and his bird's clawed feet.

In *The Lovers (Messengers of the Number)* (1947), Victor Brauner draws on esoteric imagery to create a composition full of surrealist meaning. The two figures are derived from the tarot: the male, on the left, represents the Magician, symbolizing will-power and creativity, while the female – presented as an eagle-headed human in elegant royal regalia – is the High Priestess, associated with intuition and hidden knowledge. However, subtle clues within the work reveal additional layers of meaning. The numbers below the High Priestess, '17' and '13', are a reference to André Breton, co-founder of the surrealist movement, who 'claimed' them as his own due to their graphic resemblance to his initials, the letters A and B, and even had '1713' on a plaque at the entrance to his studio. The papal triple tiara on the eagle's head also points to Breton, who was known as 'the pope' due to his power and disciplinarian approach within the surrealist group.

Birds are a recurring theme in Leonora Carrington's extraordinary, often unsettling compositions. *Bird Bath II* (1978) shows a bemused-looking bird being given a bath by two female figures – an elderly woman dressed in black, in the foreground, who is spraying the bird with white paint, and a companion in a bird mask holding out a white cloth, in a baptism-like ritual that perhaps suggests transformation. Behind them, a structure that resembles Carrington's childhood home, Crookhey Hall in northwest England, features a prominent bird motif and forms a bleak, ominous backdrop. The themes of entrapment, trauma and escape, which Crookhey Hall represents in Carrington's works, are central to another bird-themed painting, *Crow Catcher* (1990). Here, a terrifying woman, reminiscent of the 'old crone' of fairy tales, is chasing a black bird across a muted landscape and has it by the leg, while two crows swoop in a frenzy at the edge of the scene.

René Magritte takes a more lyrical approach to birds. In a handful of works, the earliest of which – entitled *The Return*

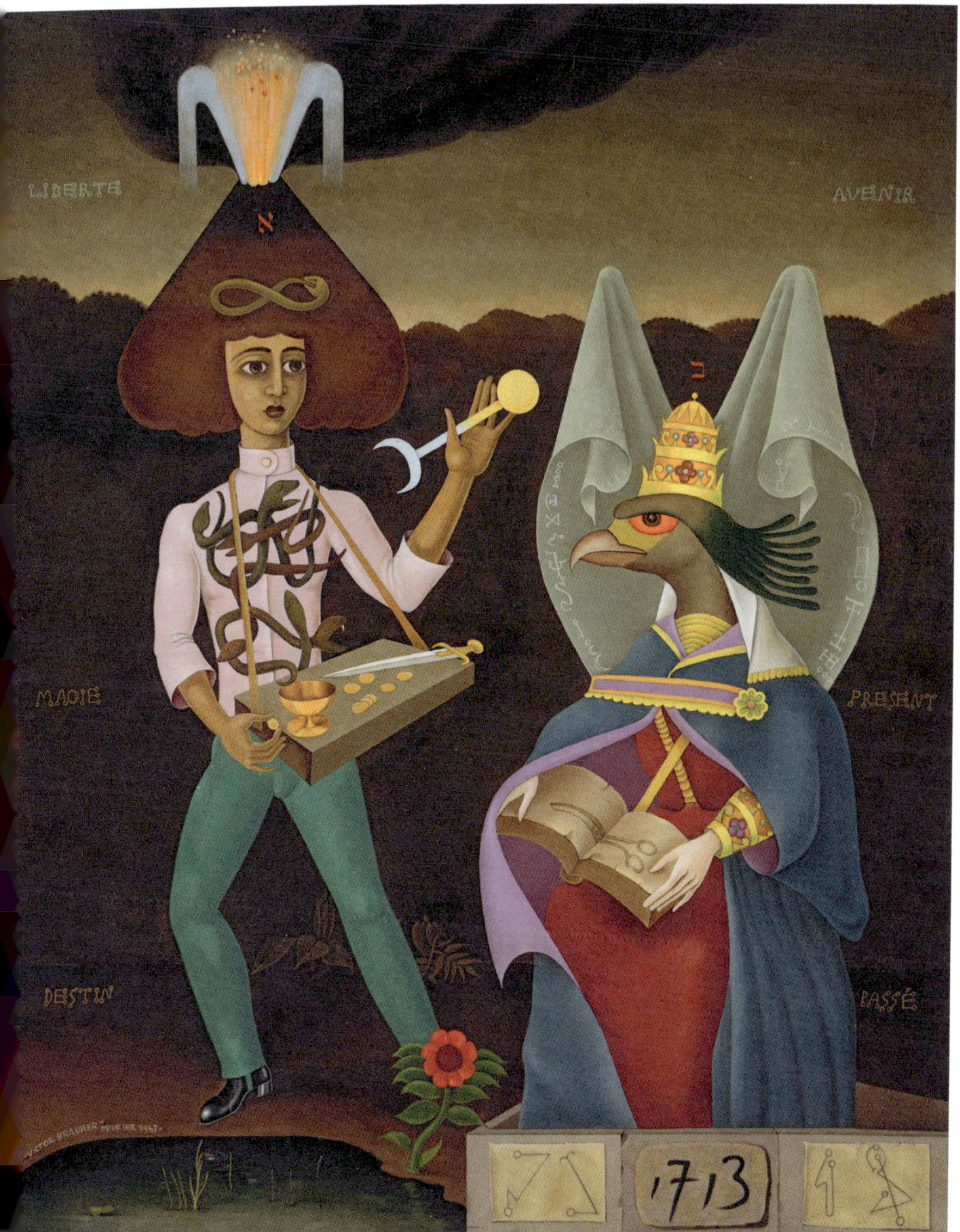

Victor Brauner, *The Lovers*
(Messengers of the Number), 1947

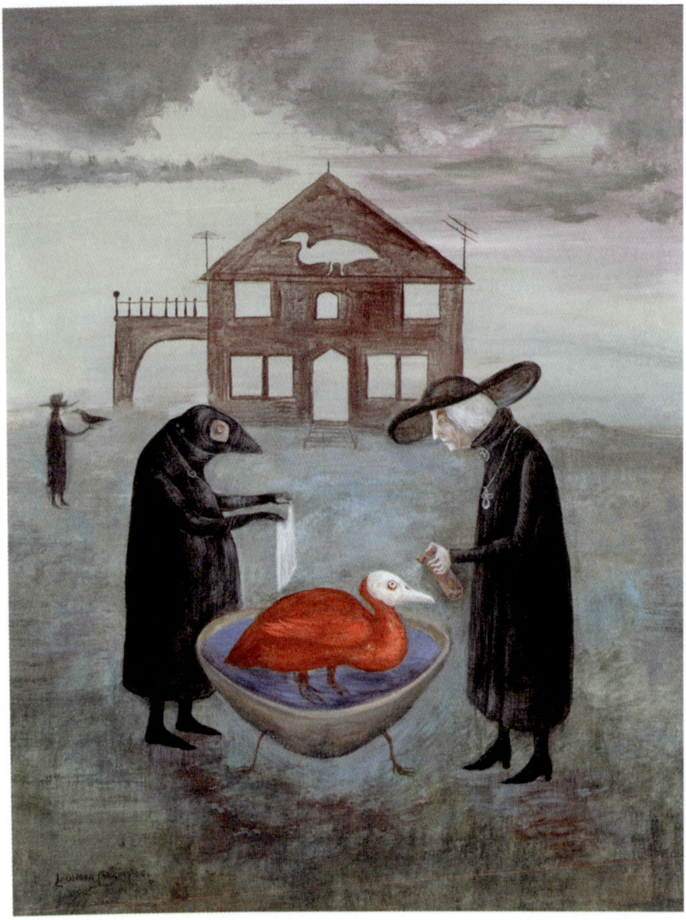

Leonora Carrington, *Bird Bath II*, 1978

Leonora Carrington, *Crow Catcher*, 1990

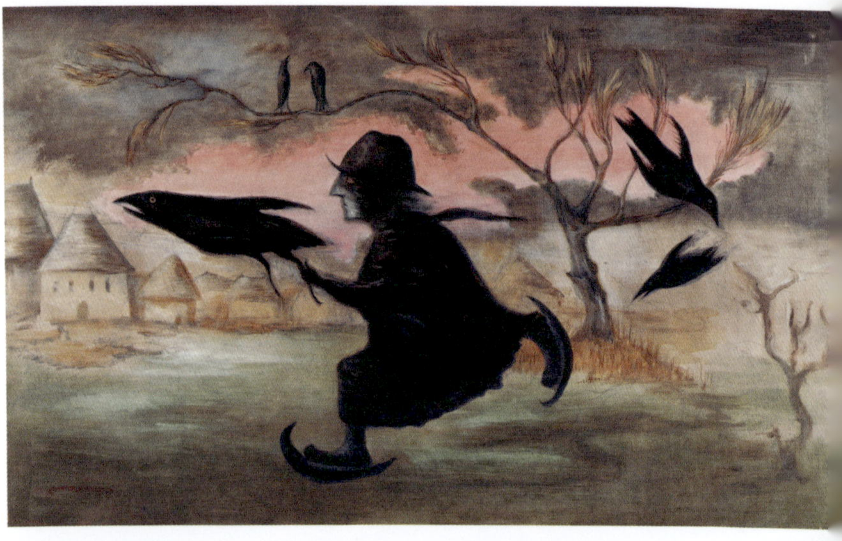

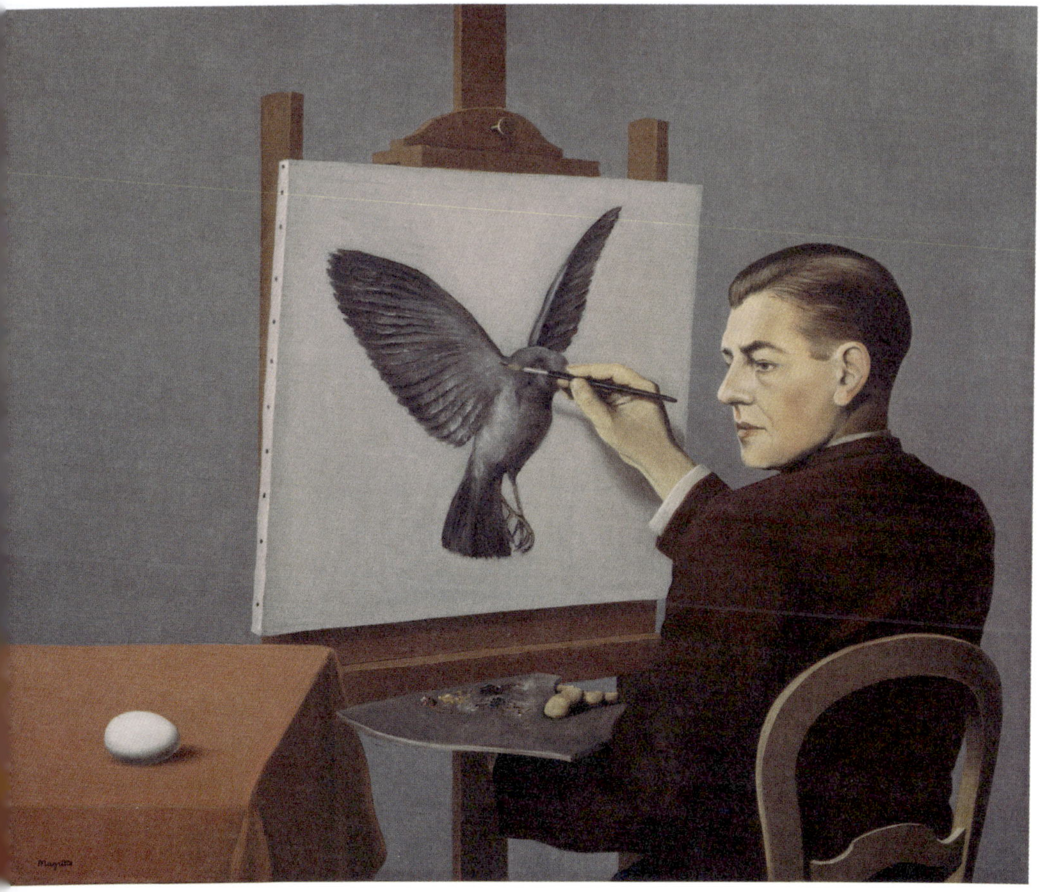

René Magritte, *Clairvoyance*, 1936

– dates from 1940, he revisits a motif that has become synonymous with the artist: the silhouette of a bird soaring through the sky. Bizarrely, the bird appears to have been cut from the sky – its body and wings have become a bright-blue expanse dotted with white, fluffy clouds. In another of his surrealist visual jokes, Magritte paints a portrait of himself at his easel. He can be seen studying his subject, an egg on a nearby table, but on the canvas he has painted a completely different subject: a bird in flight. Titled *Clairvoyance* (1936), the painting appears to suggest that the artist has the ability to capture things that do not yet exist.

Another joke is played on the viewer in Edith Rimmington's *The Oneiroscopist* (1947), which centres on a nightmarish cloaked figure sitting patiently on a deck above a sea of clouds. This curious chimera has the feet of a gigantic bird and human hands, and its head is made up of the skull of a long-beaked guillemot (*Uria aalge*) and an insect's eye. It is wearing a deep-sea diver's heavy collar, and a diver's helmet lies on the ground next to it. Here, the joke is, of course, that the guillemot is a diving bird, and the bird's beak will never fit into the spherical helmet. The title suggests that this hybrid creature, an explorer of dreams, is poised to dive into the unconscious.

The subject of Salvador Dalí's *Bird* (1928) appears to be a raptor, or bird of prey. The work depicts a cross-section of a bird and reveals the contents of its stomach – an entire mammal of some kind. This final meal appears not to have agreed with the bird because both creatures lie in the ground in a state of decomposition – an impression made all the more striking by the incorporation of sand, pebbles and shingles into the painting.

Birds often seem to fare poorly at the hands of the surrealists. The English artist Oscar Mellor's three birds in *The Gathering* (1962) look seedy and barely capable of keeping their eyes open, as if they are hanging onto life by a thread. Although the title would

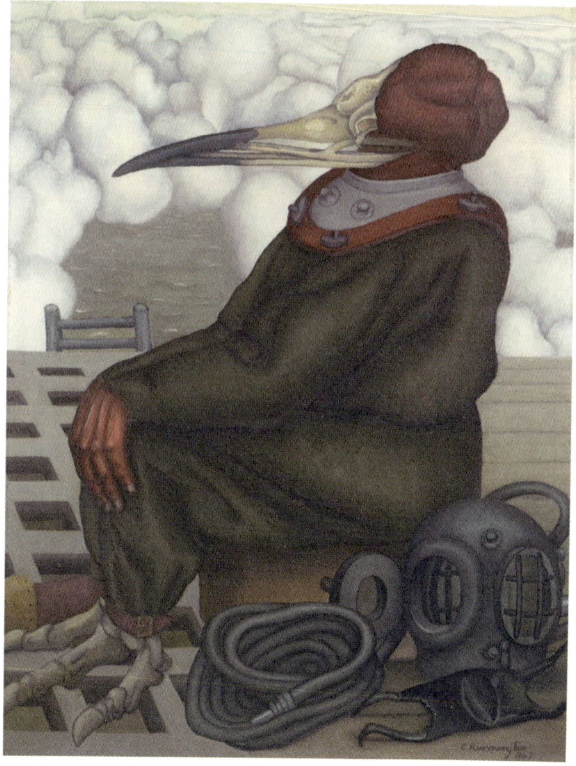

Edith Rimmington, *The Oneiroscopist*, 1947

Salvador Dalí, *Bird*, 1928

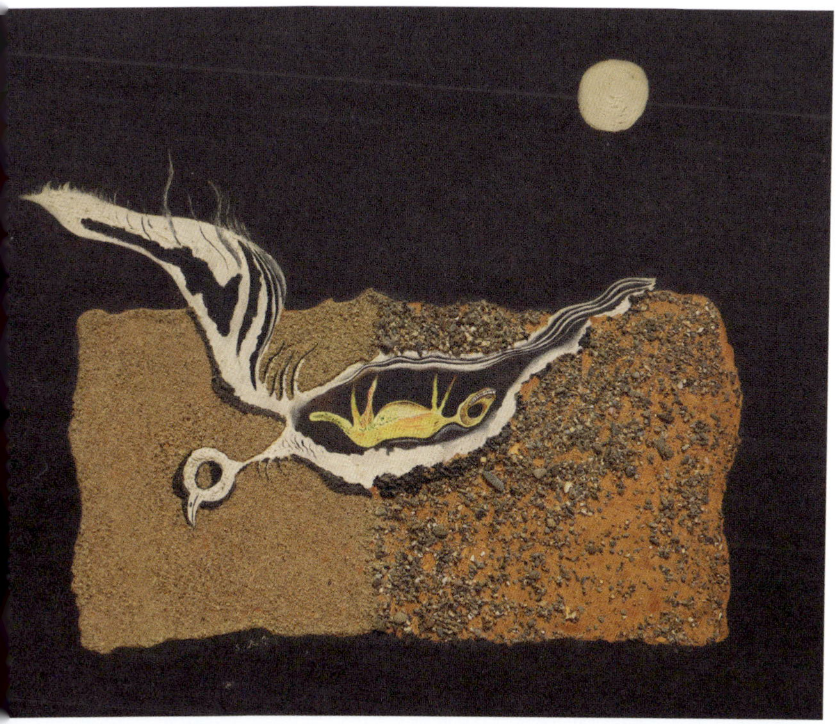

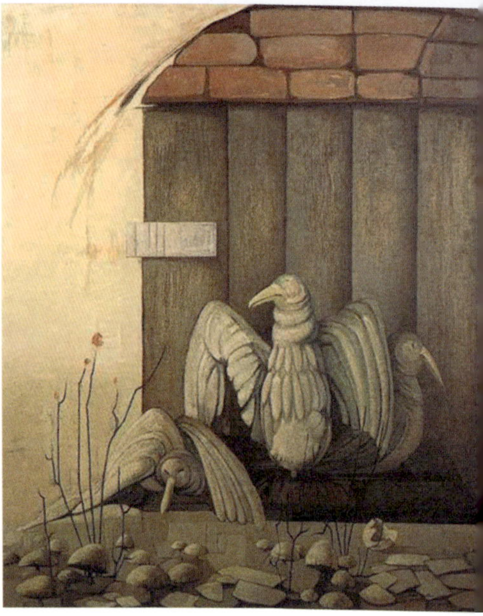

Oscar Mellor, *The Gathering*, 1962

Leonor Fini, *The Guardian of the Phoenix*, 1952

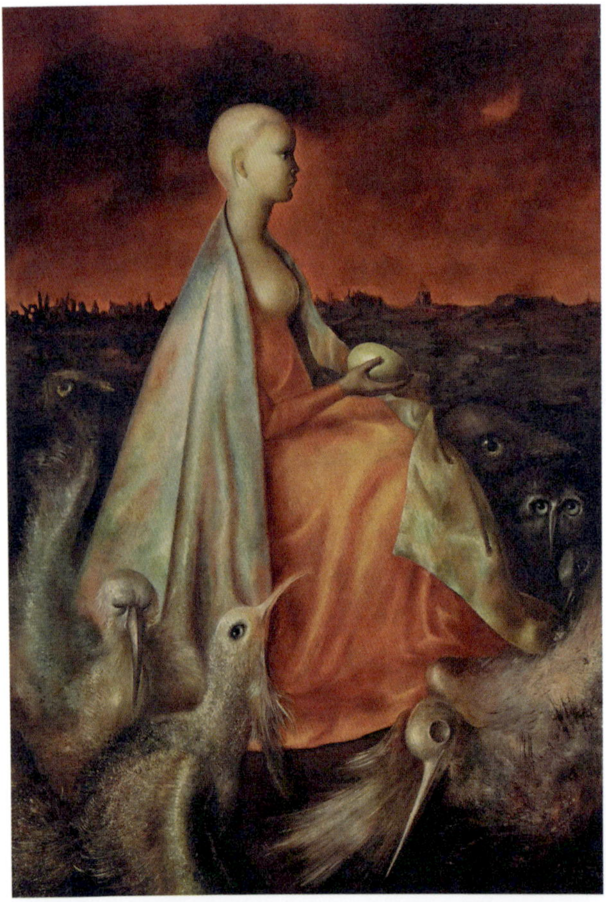

suggest otherwise, the birds at the feet of Argentine painter Leonor Fini's central female protector in *The Guardian of the Phoenix* (1952) also appear in a sorry state, with just a sparse covering of down. If we are to find happier birds, we must turn to the delightful bird-trees of the Outsider–surrealist Scottie Wilson, such as *Untitled (Tree of Birds)* (*c.* 1960), or the spritely, cheerful yellow birds of Paul Klee's *Landscape with Yellow Birds* (1923). In the strangely titled *The Misunderstood* (1938), meanwhile, by the American artist Man Ray, his characterful bird-of-paradise flower (*Strelitzia reginae*) has an eye, giving it an unmistakable birdlike appearance.

In Joan Miró's *The Bird's Song on the Dew of the Moon* (1955), a man watches a brightly coloured bird in flight, its beak wide open in song. The bird has two raised wings, a fanned-out tail and large, avian feet, each with three claws, but when it comes to the open beak, the Catalan artist has added a pair of sharply pointed teeth to the lower mandible. The ancestor of birds, *archaeopteryx*, did have teeth, but they are absent in modern birds.

The horse-headed, winged creature in Wifredo Lam's *Black Wings* (1972), which incorporates recurring themes in the Cuban artist's later works, also shows little respect for avian anatomy. As with Miró, his 'bird' is adapted to his highly personal style of imagery.

In terms of anatomy, one of the strangest of all surrealist birds appears in Félix Labisse's *The Foreign Leda* (1950). The blindfolded nude's right hand has grown into a bird's head, and its sharp beak is seen to be biting the nipple of her left breast. The title is odd, because the bird's head is black, with a white crest and a red cere – nothing like the swan in Greek mythology, the god Zeus in disguise, that raped Leda.

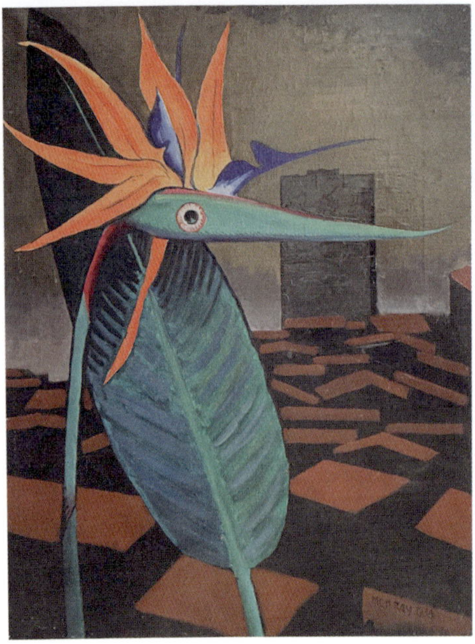

Man Ray, *The Misunderstood*, 1938

Paul Klee, *Landscape with Yellow Birds*, 1923

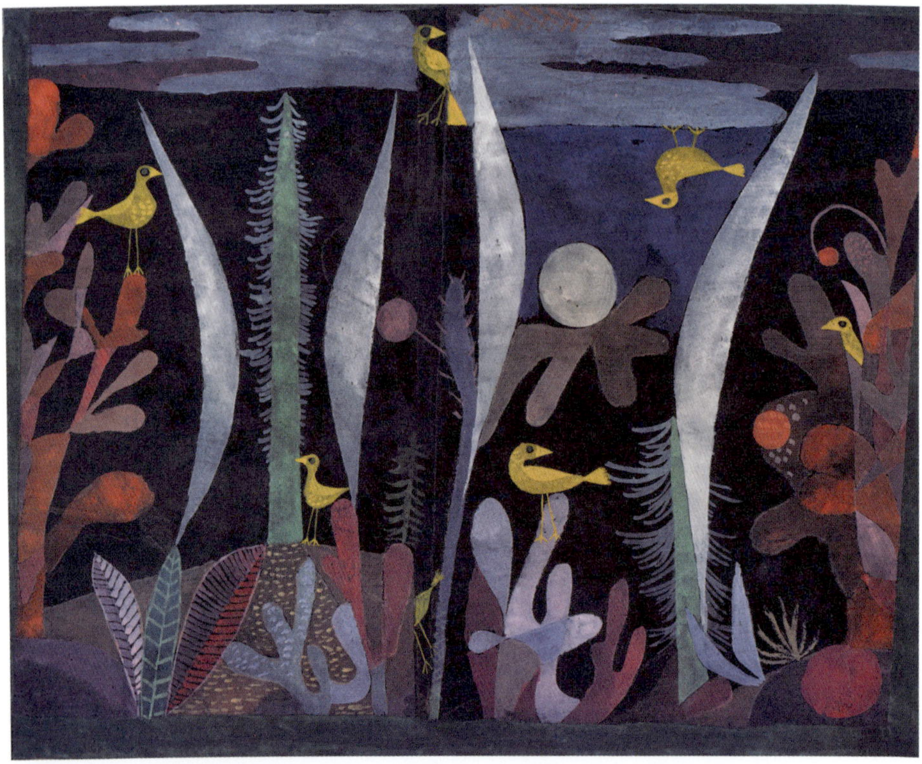

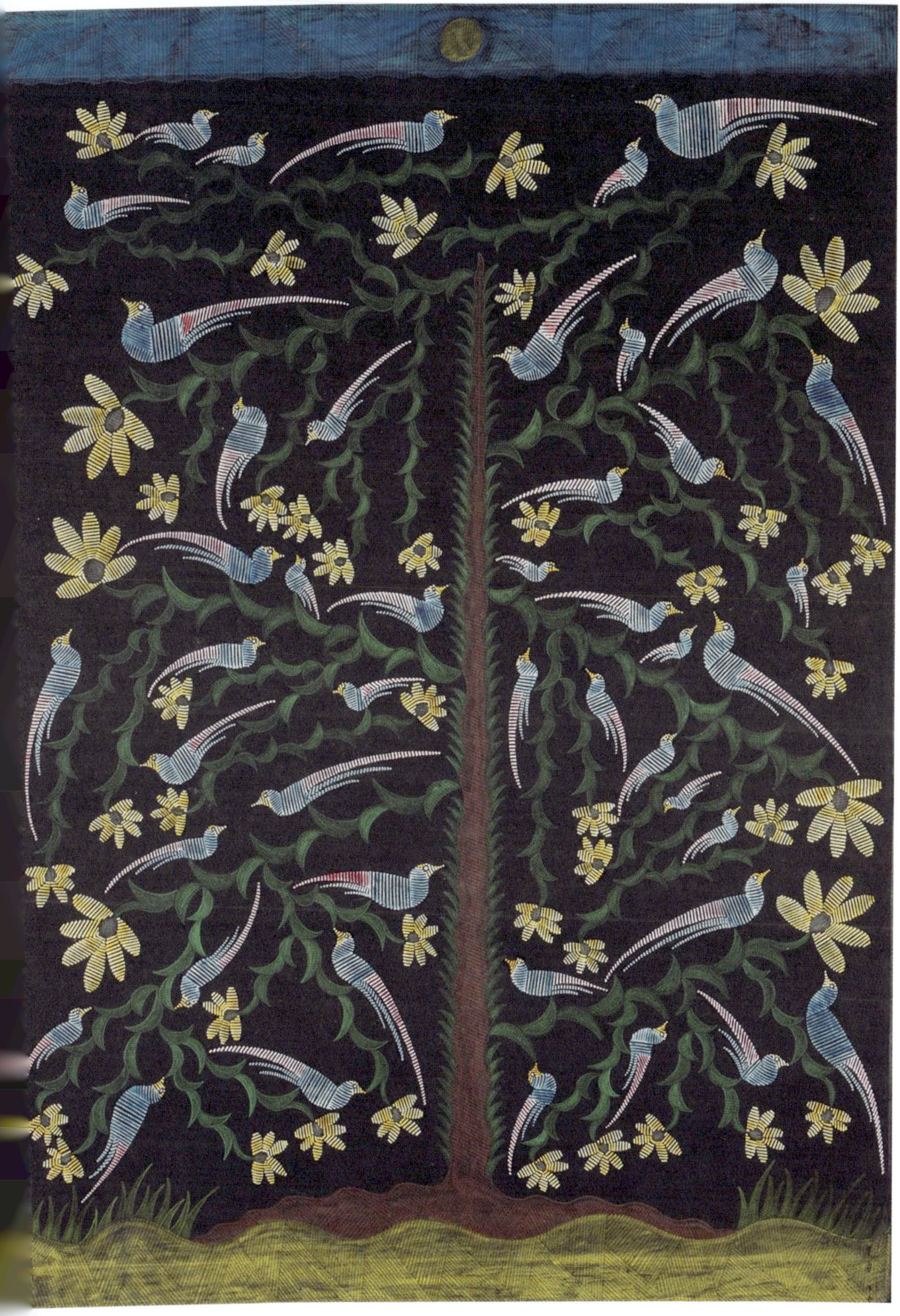

Scottie Wilson, *Untitled (Tree of Birds)*, c. 1960

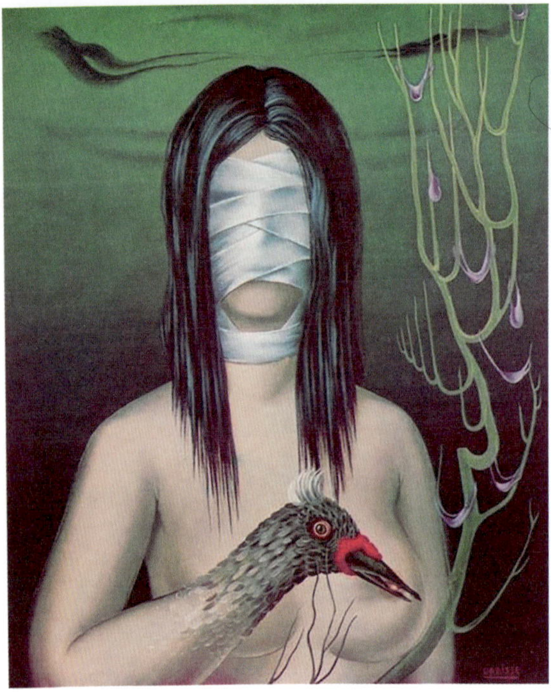

Félix Labisse, *The Foreign Leda*, 1950

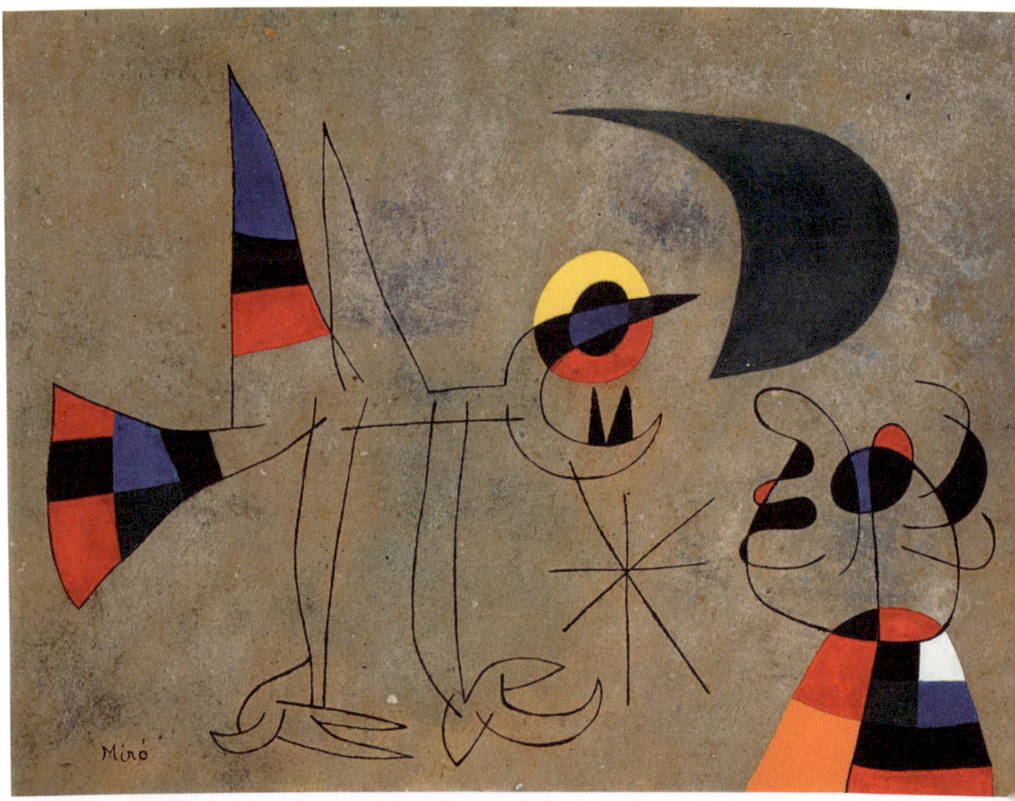

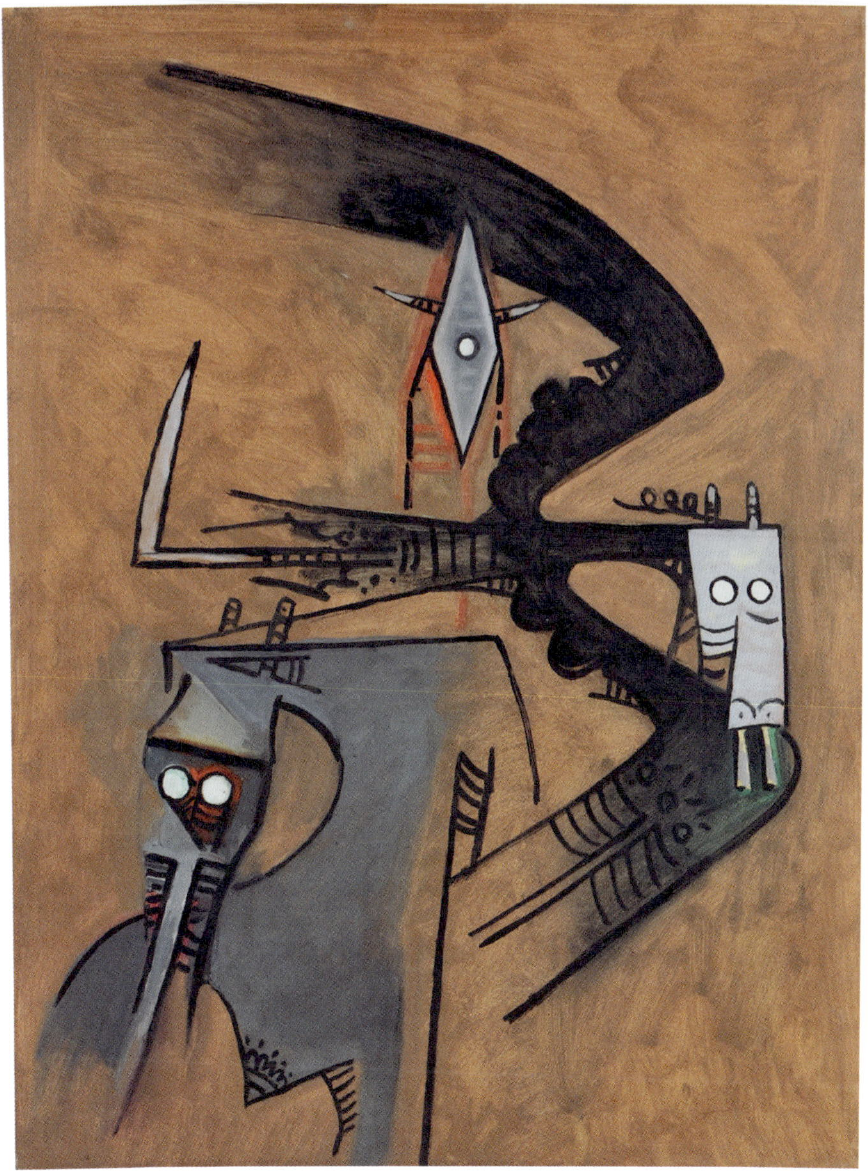

Wifredo Lam, *Black Wings*, 1972

an Miró, *The Bird's Song*
the Dew of the Moon, 1955

Swan

The swan fascinated the surrealists for several reasons. First, they were drawn to its iconic shape, with its heavy body, its huge, powerful wings, and its long, elegantly curving neck. Then, there is its dramatic plumage, pure white or jet black. And, for a bird, it is unusual in its behaviour – hissing like a snake and liable to attack if approached too closely. Above all, according to Greek myth, it was a swan – the god Zeus in disguise – that coupled with Leda, a story that inevitably appealed to the surrealist preoccupation with desire, sex and metamorphosis. Although Leda was raped by Zeus, artists through the ages – from Michelangelo to Cézanne – have often cast the god in the role of 'seducer'.

In *Leda Atómica* (1949), Dalí shows the swan being given a tender caress by Leda – modelled by the artist's wife, Gala – who sits naked on a pedestal. His is an ethereal vision of the story, with Leda appearing weightless as she reaches out her left hand to touch the swan's head. Here, Dalí uses a concept he called 'nuclear mysticism', fusing elements of traditional Catholic iconography, mathematics and atomic physics. The various objects we see in the painting – a book, a set square, an egg – appear to be held in a state of suspension, charged with an invisible energy but never touching.

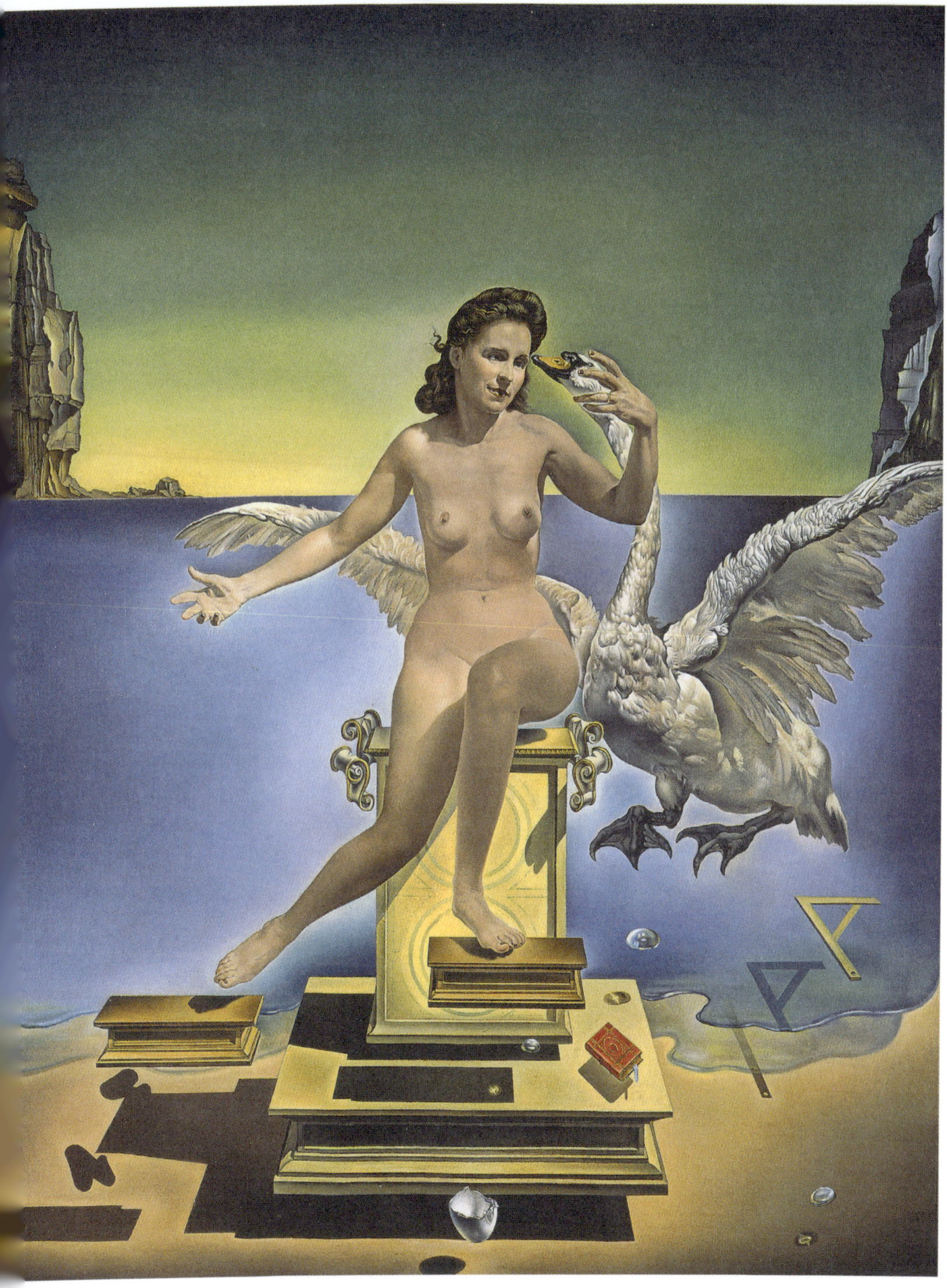

Salvador Dalí, *Leda Atómica*, 1949

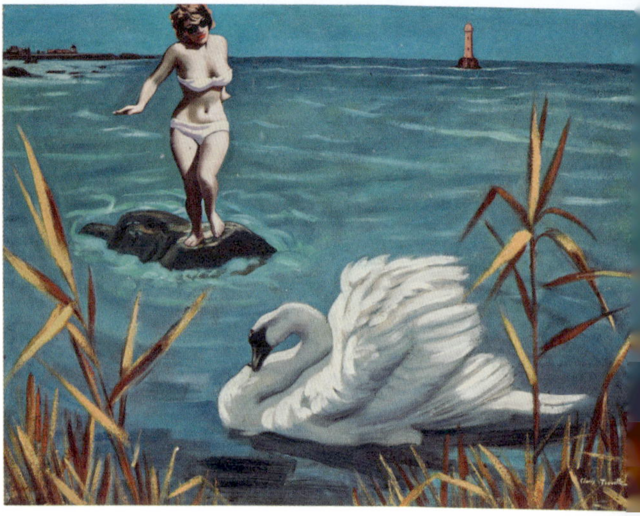

Clovis Trouille, *Make Me into a Swan*, 1959

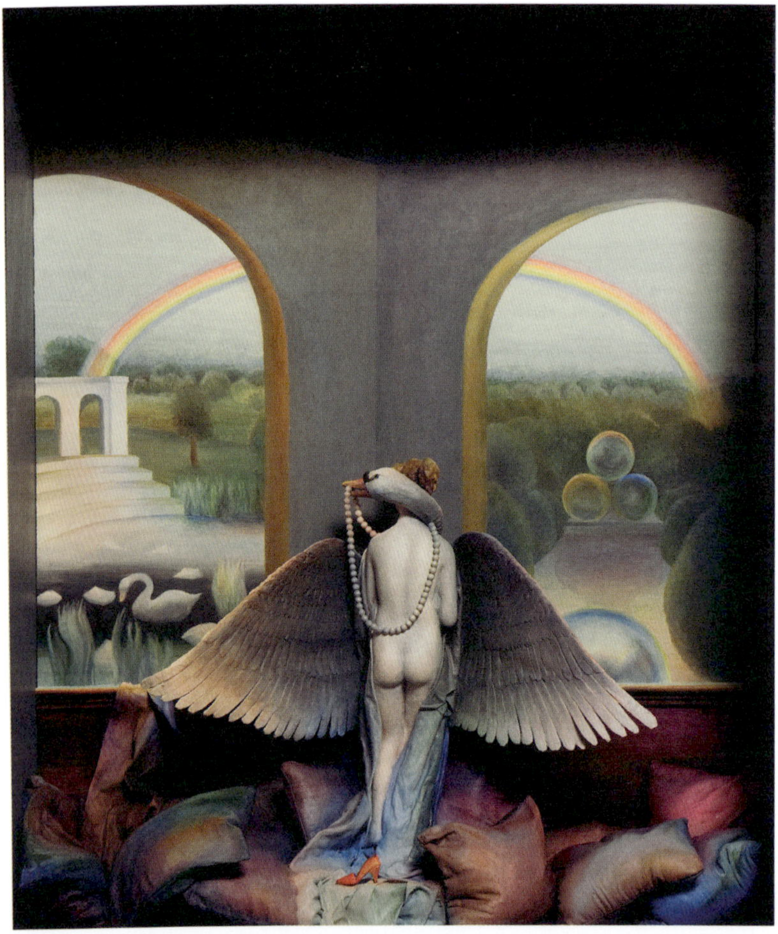

Mimi Parent, *Leda and the Swan*, 1997

In Clovis Trouille's *Make Me into a Swan* (1959), Leda is a modern woman wearing a bikini and sunglasses. She stands on a rock, but her body language suggests she is trying to get closer to a magnificent swan that has abandoned its usual river for the sea. The title and the phallic lighthouse in the background make her motive clear: she wants to be transformed into the swan's feathered mate.

In an unusual *Leda and the Swan* composition of 1997, the Canadian surrealist Mimi Parent has her standing with her back to the viewer. The swan pulls her to him by twisting his neck around hers, while in his beak he grasps a long necklace that cascades down her back, giving the impression that he holds her in a head lock. Amid the crumpled bed sheets and scattered cushions, the eye is drawn to a single red shoe, the only identifiable item of clothing – suggestive, perhaps, of a frenzied engagement.

Depictions of the encounter between Zeus and Leda appeared as early as 300 BC, and the incident has been reimagined countless times in classical and traditional art. The surrealists brought their own dark visions to the subject, but like earlier artists, they probably did not realize that there are two characteristics that make the swan – out of all the creatures that the Greeks could have picked as the aggressor – an oddly fitting choice. First, the male swan – unusually for a bird – possesses a penis. Most birds make only light cloacal contact when mating, but because swans mate in water, where sperm can be easily washed away, the male swan evolved a penis as a way of ensuring fertilization. Second, it is now known that many birds, including swans, become 'imprinted' with the first individual they see when they hatch from the egg. In nature, this is always their parent (unless they happen to be a cuckoo), but if a human being is present when an egg hatches, the chick responds to them as its parent and follows them wherever they go.

Apart from the Leda connection, the swan also had a special appeal to the surrealists because of its remarkably long neck and its wide wings. In Salvador Dalí's *Swans Reflecting Elephants* (1937), one of the artist's famous 'optical illusions', we see three swans sitting side by side in the water at the edge of a pond. Their shapes are reflected in the water, where they are magically transformed into the heads of elephants. The long necks become the trunks, and the large wings become the elephants' ears.

Dalí also created a majestic, blind swan with spread wings as the centrepiece of his set for the ballet *Bacchanale*, which premiered at the Metropolitan Opera House in New York in 1939. The story centres on the extravagant 19th-century King Ludwig II of Bavaria, the 'Swan King', who was known for his love of medieval legends, fantasy and fairy-tale castles. The front of the swan is a dark aperture – a doorway through which the dancers emerged – and there are cracks on the bird's plumage, indicating that it was meant to be a building in the shape of the bird.

In 1972, this same artist also offered us a mysterious chimera: a swan emerges from the rump of a strange-looking stallion with human teeth and the long tresses of a woman. The clue to such a curious combination comes from Dalí's title for the work: *Horace's Chimera*. In Greek mythology, the Chimera was a monster killed by Bellerophon, who was riding on the winged horse Pegasus. Dalí's horse/swan combination is a kind of chimera, but it does not have wings, and it is not the monster of ancient mythology. Horace is the key to unlocking this delightful surrealist muddle, specifically the famous opening lines of *Ars Poetica* (*c.* 19 BC), in which the Roman poet uses a chimera as a metaphor to criticize art that combines mismatched elements and lacks unity: 'If a painter had chosen to set a human head on a horse's neck, covered a melding of limbs, everywhere, with multicoloured plumage, so that what was a lovely woman, at the top,

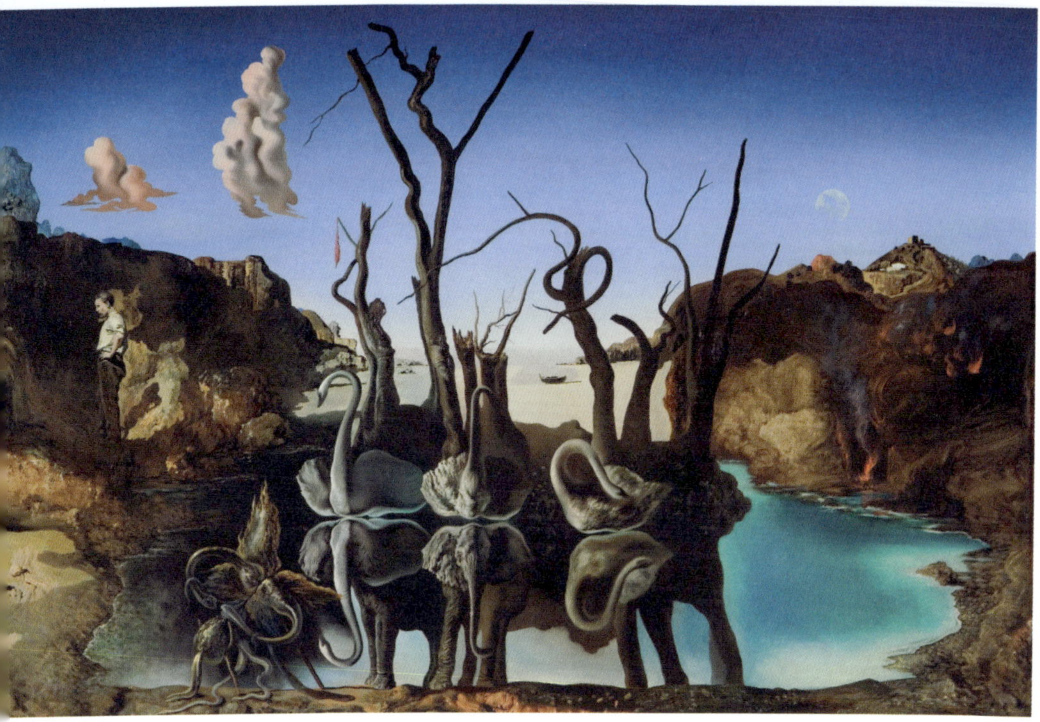

Salvador Dalí, *Swans Reflecting Elephants*, 1937

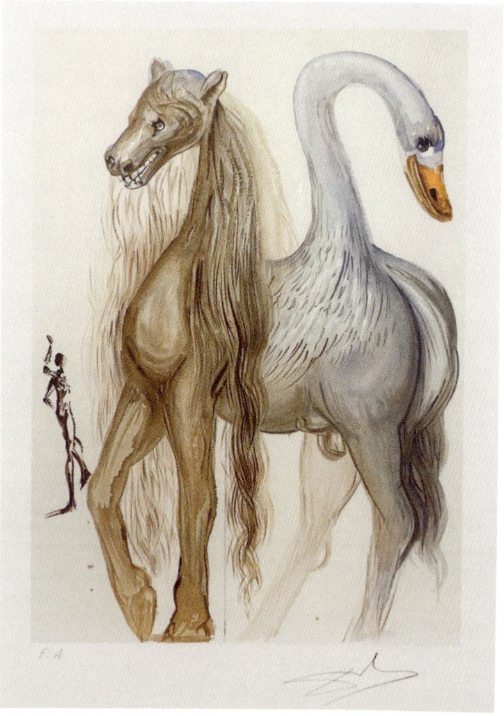

Salvador Dalí, *Horace's Chimera*, 1972

ended repulsively in the tail of a black fish: asked to a viewing, could you stifle laughter, my friends?'

Joseph Cornell takes a different approach in *Untitled (Object with Swan)* (1967). Here, a toy swan reflected in the glass of a hand mirror creates the impression of swimming across smooth water – yet another surrealist optical illusion.

Finally, there is a group of four black swans that appear at the bottom of *Lepidopteros* (1969) by Leonora Carrington. One of the birds is grooming its feathers and another is eating small red fruits from a grey bowl. Together with the masked figures around the table, they create a haunting, unsettling atmosphere.

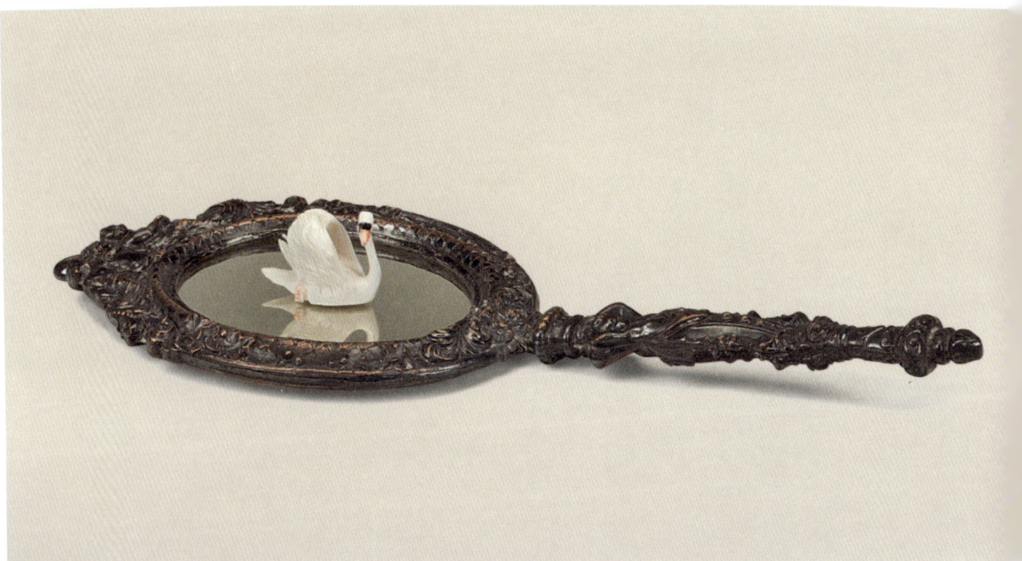

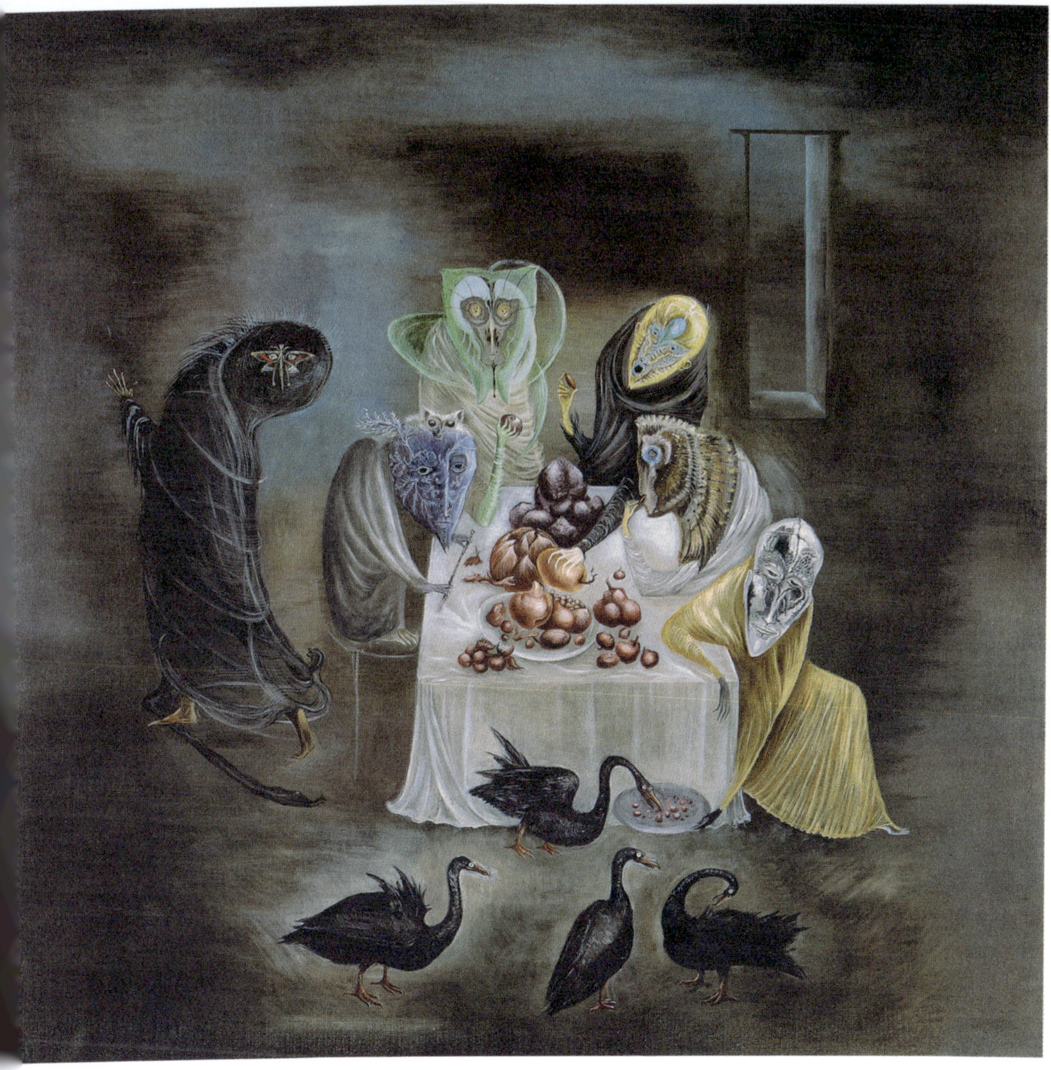

Leonora Carrington, *Lepidopteros*, 1969

Joseph Cornell,
Untitled (Object with Swan), 1967

Goose

The goose as a subject has appealed to two surrealists, Leonora Carrington and Salvador Dalí. In Carrington's *Grandmother Moorhead's Aromatic Kitchen* (1975), three sinister, hooded figures stand around a kitchen table (or is it an altar?) within a magic circle, surrounded by scattered items of food such as garlic cloves and sweetcorn cobs. Two masked figures work busily on the left of the canvas, and a horned creature with a broom stands on the right. But the eerie scene is dominated by a huge white goose that dwarfs everything else. The dedication in the title to Carrington's Irish grandmother, together with the Gaelic invocations inscribed at the outer edge of the magic circle, may provide a clue to its significance: the white goose is a magical creature in Celtic mythology.

This wonderfully mysterious painting has been subjected to the kind of scholarly analysis that Carrington hated. It has been suggested, for example, that she transforms the kitchen from a place of female oppression into one of female power. Unfortunately, such interpretations overlook the ambiguity of the composition: the figures at work in the kitchen are masked, their gender by no means certain. In any case, the figures pale into

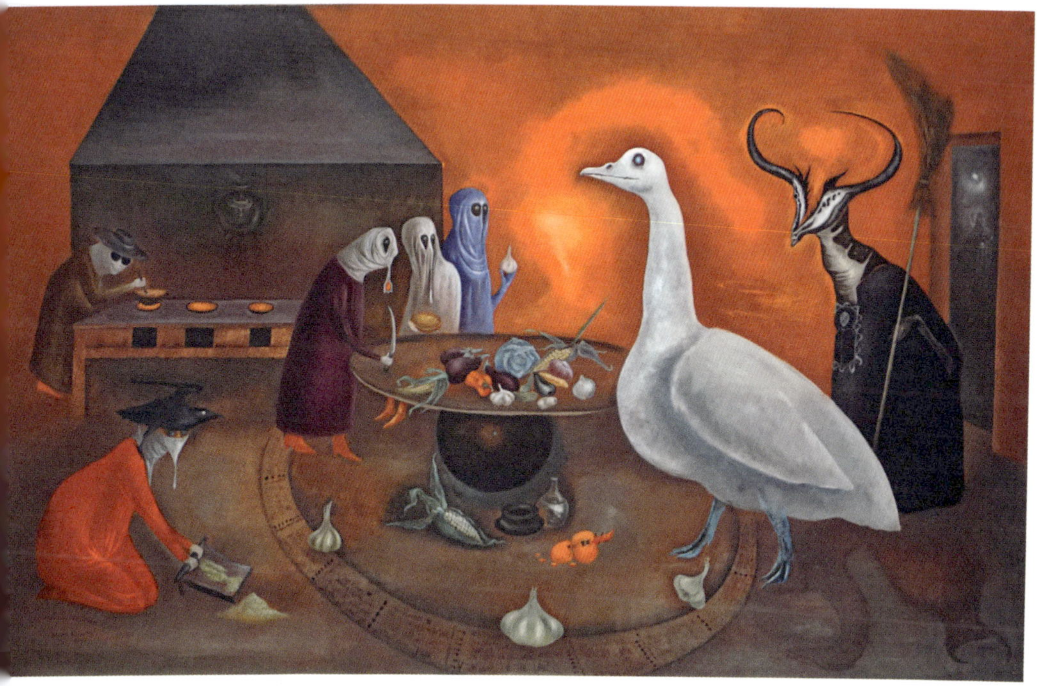

Leonora Carrington,
Grandmother Moorhead's Aromatic Kitchen, 1975

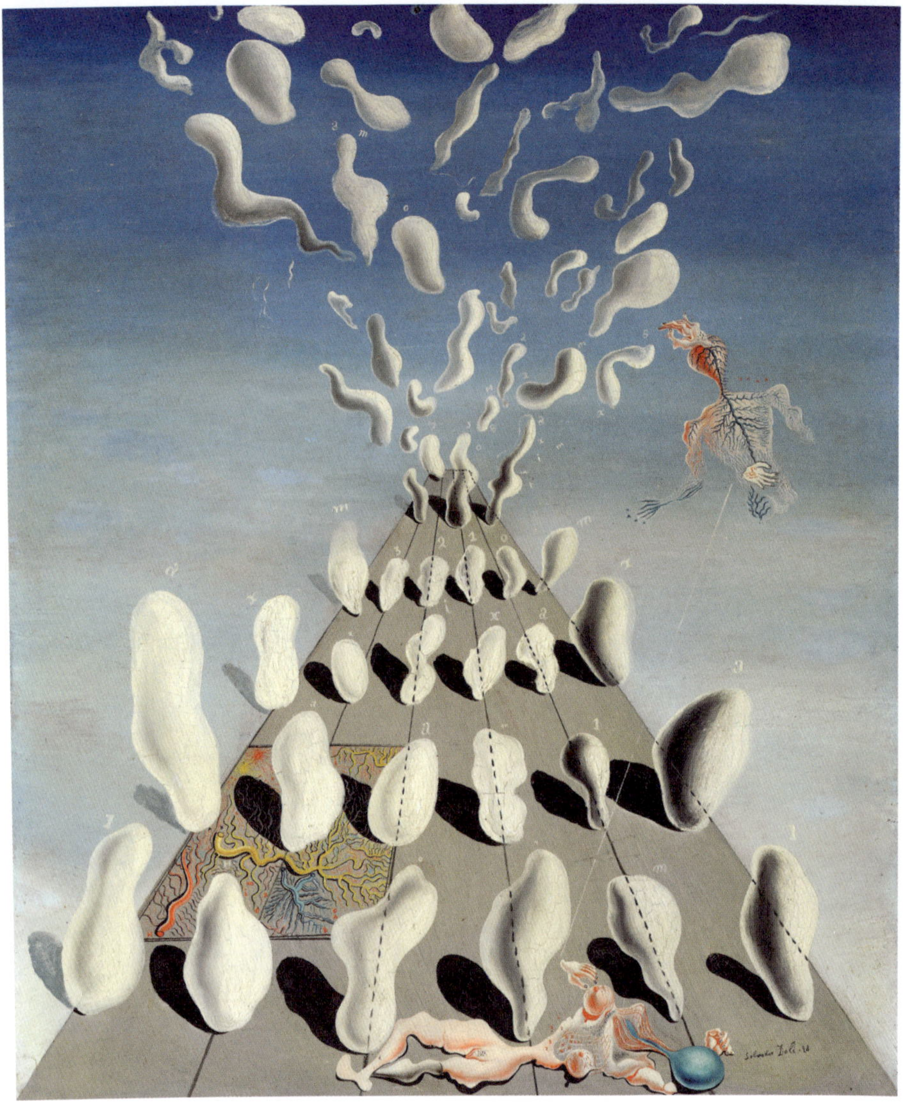

Salvador Dalí, *Inaugural Gooseflesh*, 1928

Salvador Dalí,
Allegory of Spring, c. 1979

insignificance beside the goose, which overwhelms the kitchen with its presence. If anything, it is the food – the goose – that has the power, towering over those who would, presumably, like to devour it. It is the tantalizing ambiguity of this kitchen scene that is the true quality of the painting, an ambiguity that Carrington fostered in so many of her complex surrealist works.

Dalí's *Inaugural Gooseflesh* (1928) takes a very different view of the goose. Here, its flesh has been packaged into about sixty smooth lumps of food. In the foreground they are lined up like soldiers on parade, but in the distance they have started to float up into the air like deformed balloons. As with Carrington's painting, this is a mesmerically ambiguous event that deliberately defies analysis.

A much later work by Dalí, *Allegory of Spring* (*c.* 1979), fuses surrealism with the neoclassical. In execution, it is surprisingly loose, compared with Dalí's usually meticulous, precise brushwork. The five human figures – four nude females and a reclining, bearded nude male – fill the panel with swirling lines and intense movement. The goose, realistically portrayed, is pushing between the legs of two of the women, as though it represents the reproductive force of nature, pressing to the fore as the spring season unfolds.

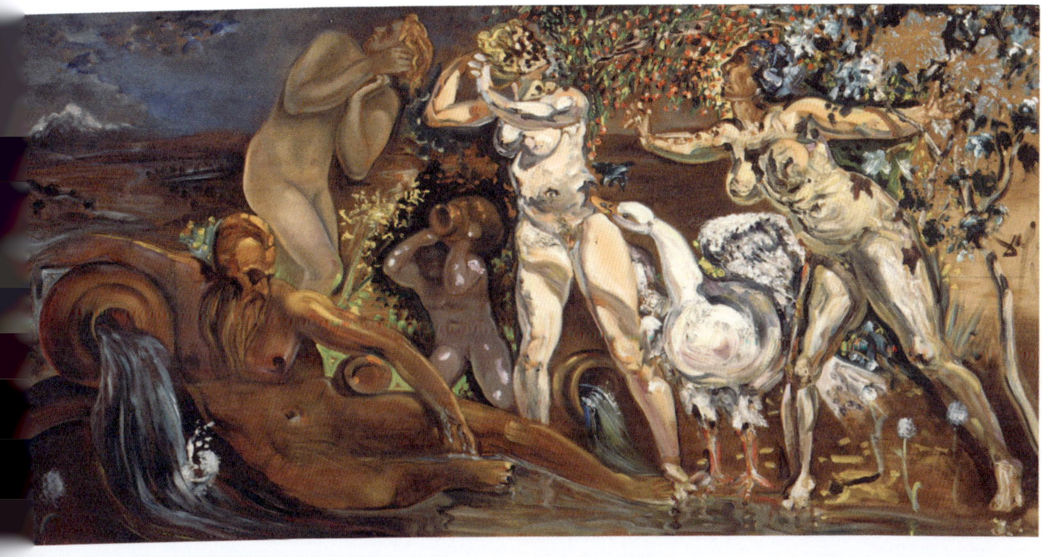

Vulture

In the West, the vulture is often seen as the herald of death. We picture it circling in the sky above a dying or dead animal, waiting for the moment to descend and start tearing it to pieces. It may come as a surprise, therefore, that this popular idea of vultures endlessly circling above carrion is false: once they spot a potential meal, they waste no time in investigating.

The vulture does not seem to have appealed to the surrealists, although it does feature in the work of Edith Rimmington, Meret Oppenheim and Salvador Dalí. In Rimmington's *Relative Strength* (1950), the vulture appears to be a collage, but this is deceptive. Working with pen, ink and watercolour on paper, Rimmington has faithfully copied 19th-century illustrations with remarkable technical skill. The vulture was taken from an engraving by Richard Polydore Nodder, who was active between 1793 and 1820. The species shown is the red-headed vulture (*Sarcogyps calvus*), otherwise known as the Pondicherry or Indian black vulture. The work also includes a butterfly and a moth. The butterfly, at the top of the composition, is Cassia's Owl-butterfly (*Opsiphanes cassiae*) and the moth, at the bottom, is the Light Crimson Underwing (*Catocala promissa*). These, too, were carefully copied

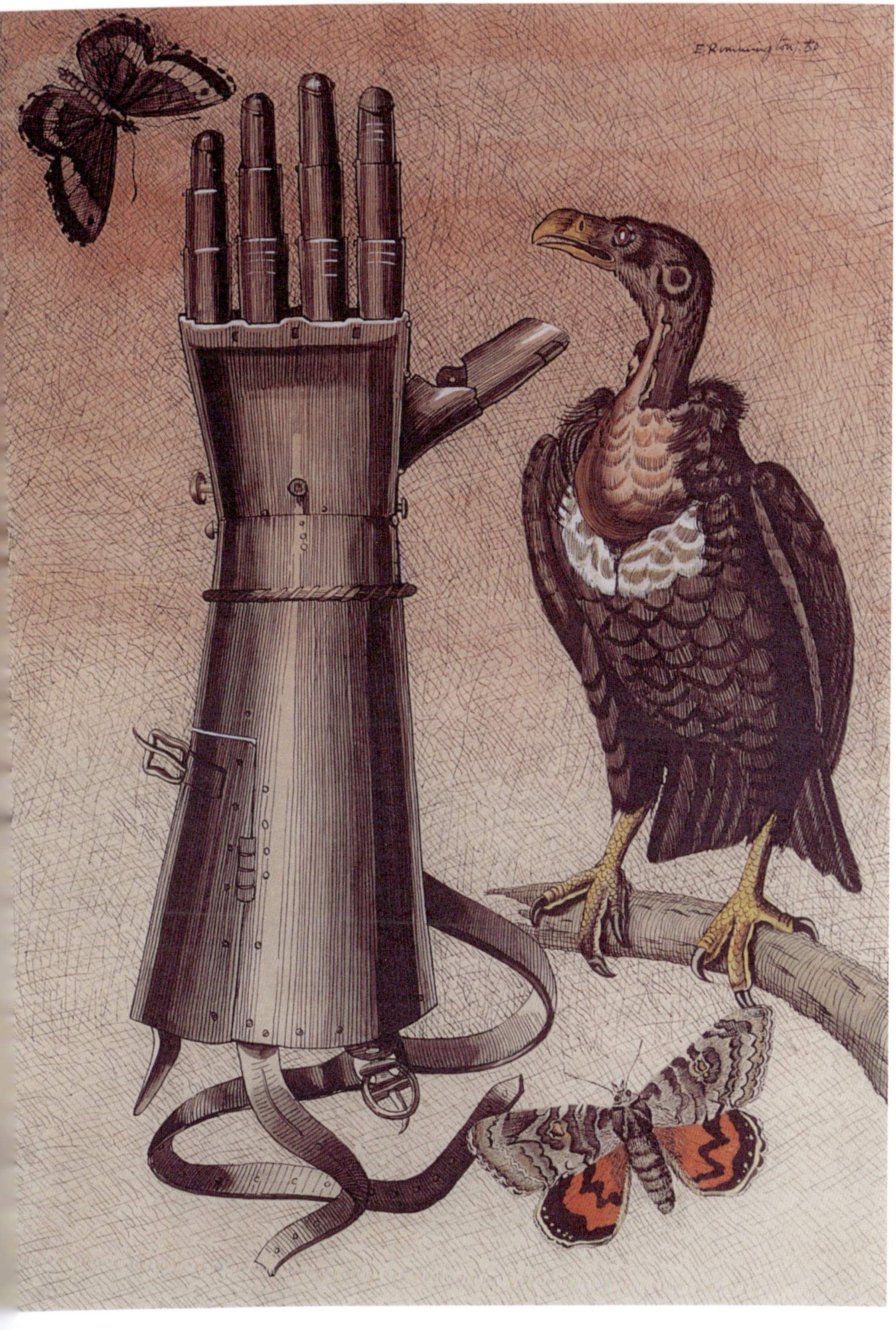

Edith Rimmington, *Relative Strength*, 1950

from illustrations by Nodder. The three zoological images surround a central image of an iron glove, presumably part of a suit of armour. It is the irrational juxtaposition of these elements that makes the work an attractively ambiguous surrealist statement.

A sketch by Meret Oppenheim, entitled *Vulture and Yellow-Red Object* (1975), centres on a sinister, black bird with open wings, above which there floats a strange object that resembles a flying saucer. The Swiss artist looked for inspiration in the world around her, with birds, snakes and butterflies often featuring in her expressions of dreams and the unconscious. Could she be making a surrealist joke about UFOs in this work, with the menacing bird – the opportunistic scavenger hovering overhead – itself being shadowed by an even more threatening object?

Dalí's *Chair with the Wings of a Vulture* (1960) offers an unconventional juxtaposition of objects. Twelve large wooden spoons have been attached to an upright kitchen chair. This odd construction has grown a large pair of vulturine wings, above which we can just see the upper half of a female face peeping out, as though it is the head of the bird. Thin wires radiate from a large wickerwork halo that encircles the young woman's head, giving the impression of beams of light. On the wall above the chair, there are votive candles and a Christian cross. In this mix of disparate objects and motifs, it is as if the Virgin Mary has become a messenger of death, rather than the giver of sacred life.

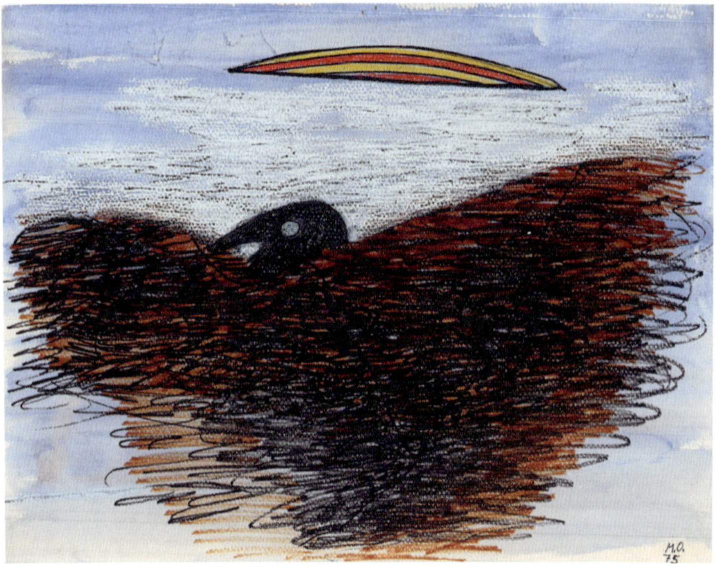

Meret Oppenheim, *Vulture and Yellow-Red Object*, 1975

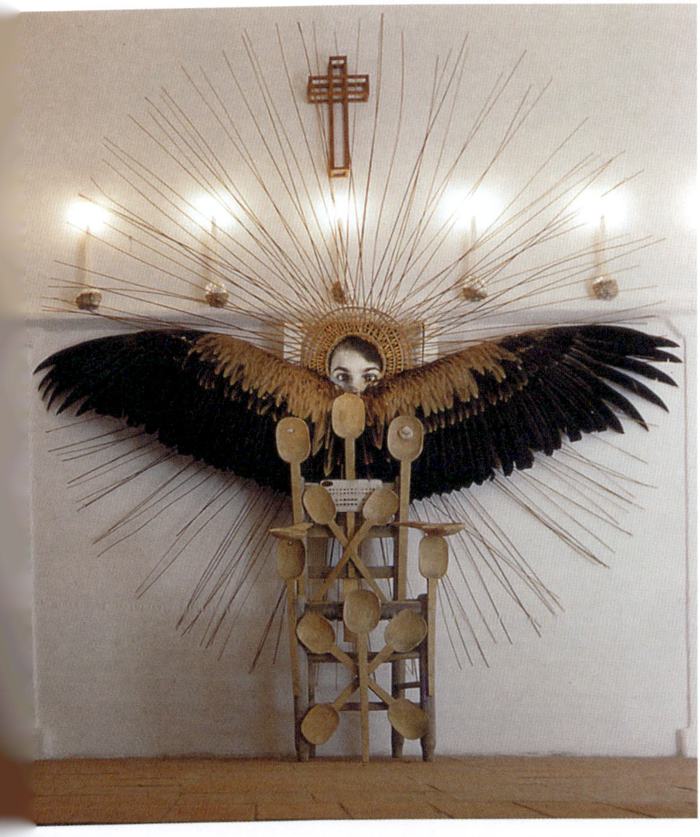

Salvador Dalí, *Chair with the Wings of a Vulture*, 1960

Eagle

In Western cultures, the eagle has long been a symbol of power and strength. Its thick neck and heavy, curved beak, along with its sharp talons, make it a visual metaphor for dominance and controlled aggression. As a result, it has repeatedly been used as a heraldic device and as an emblem of might. The American bald eagle, for example, has become a respected national icon, despite the fact that, in nature, this particular species happens to get much of its food from scavenging. Its proud shape overcomes this unfortunate fact.

When William Blake wrote 'To see a world in a grain of sand', he was expressing the idea that, with imagination, in the smallest detail of nature we can see the riches of the universe. In a series of works inspired by a colour photograph of a mountain later found among his papers, René Magritte finds the extraordinary in the ordinary. A drawing by the artist on the back of the photograph reveals that the shape of the mountain ridge reminded him of an eagle with outspread wings. It was a simple matter to add an eagle's head to this image and, in this way, to celebrate the mighty power of the great bird, now transformed into a massive wall of rock.

This recurring motif of the eagle-mountain is tentatively explored as early as 1926, in the painting *Wreckage of the Shadow*. Magritte returned to it in a series of works produced from 1938

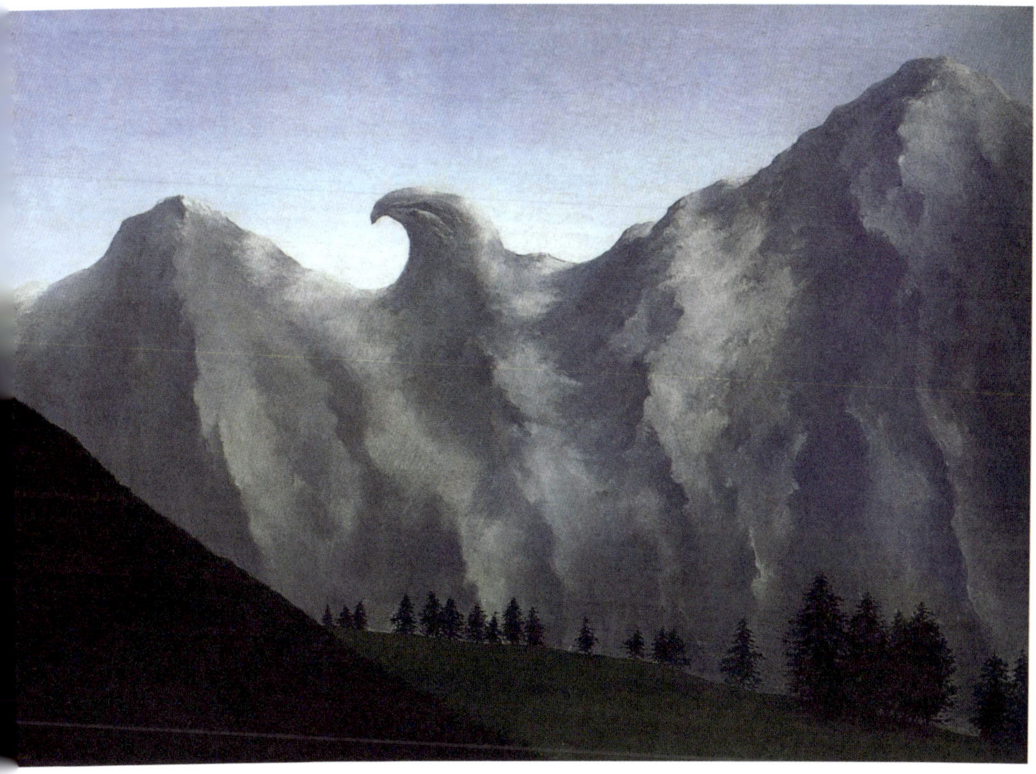

René Magritte, *The Domain of Arnheim*, 1938

onwards under the title *The Domain of Arnheim*, the earliest realization of which is shown here. But when the Nazis came to power, with the eagle as their emblem of terror, and war broke out in 1939, he decided it was time to curb the eagle's flight. In a work significantly called *The Present* (1939), he insults the great bird by dressing it in a buttoned-up jacket that will prevent it from spreading its wings over Europe.

A number of other surrealists have enjoyed depicting eagles in their work. One of the most impressive examples is by the Belgian Jane Graverol, who worked in Magritte's shadow but gave us some images that were just as powerful and mysterious as any of his. Her painting *The New Melancholy* (1956) shows a huge black eagle filling a whole room. This giant of a bird is staring menacingly at a tiny songbird that sits calmly on its perch inside its small, protective cage. The ambiguity of the relationship between the eagle and the songbird is fascinating.

Another intensely ambiguous eagle is created by Toyen in *The Dangerous Hour* (1942). In place of sharp talons, this bird has delicate human hands, which rest on a fence, one hand on top of the other. The top of the fence is protected by a line of sharply pointed, upright shards of broken glass, to deter anyone from climbing over it. The hands appear to cover unseen shards, which would likely cut into the flesh, but there is no sign of blood. The only touch of red in this painting is in the eye of the bird, which is human in shape but slitted, as if inserted into the bird's eye socket. This eagle was painted at the height of the Second World War, when Toyen was risking it all by hiding a Jewish surrealist, Jindřich Heisler, in the bathroom of the artist's small apartment in Prague, where he stayed for four long years. The symbolism of this work clearly has some connection with the eagle emblem of the Nazis, but its message is presented in a mysterious, irrational manner that transforms it into a surrealist masterpiece.

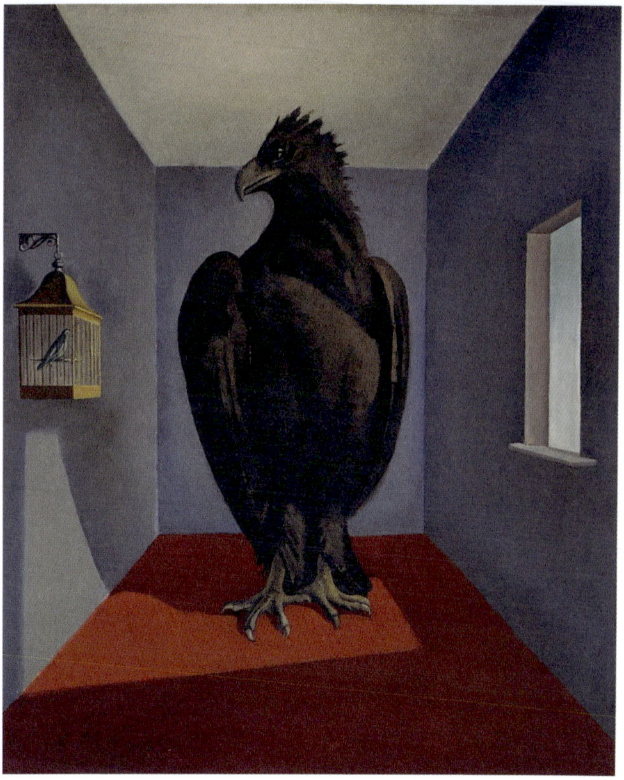

Jane Graverol, *The New Melancholy*, 1956

Toyen, *The Dangerous Hour*, 1942

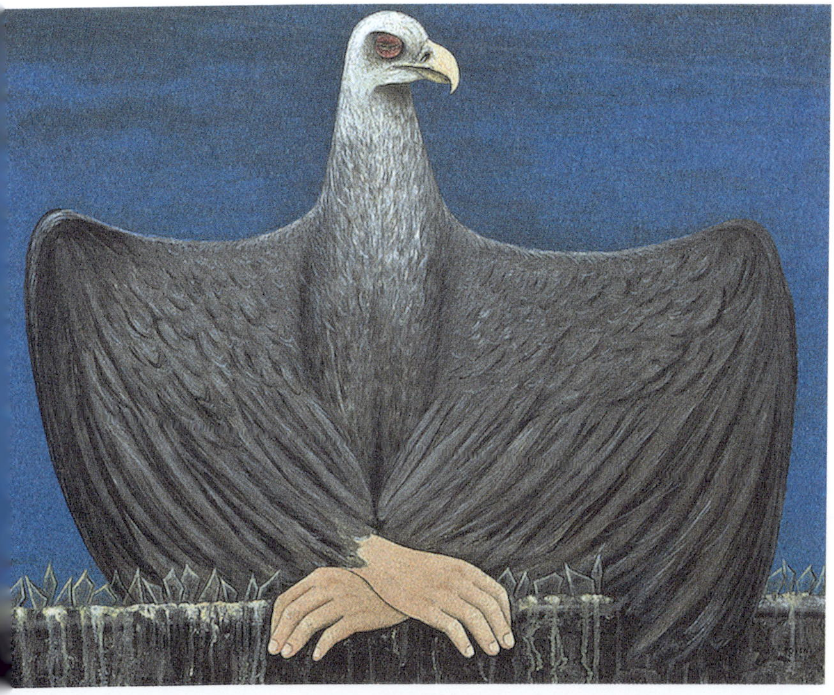

Poultry

Symbolically, poultry appear in two distinct, contrasting forms: as the aggressive cockerel or cock and the egg-producing hen. It will hardly come as a surprise to discover that almost all the surrealist portrayals of poultry are of young cockerels or adult cocks (roosters), usually in a belligerent mode.

André Masson's *Ibdes in Aragon* (1935) presents a view of this small Spanish village with two cockerels in the foreground. The whole scene is bright red, as though a savage fight has taken place and everything is soaked in blood. Masson had left Paris for Spain in 1934 and remained there until the Spanish Civil War broke out in July 1936, when he decided to return to France. During his stay he produced a series of landscapes, writing 'there is always an element of fantasy, either in the sky, or on the ground, or underground.' The fantasy is provided here not only by the cockerels, which bleed into the landscape, but a crocodile shaped by the rocks in the background. One can't help thinking that Masson is anticipating the conflict, with all its horrific bloodshed – his two cockerels becoming fiery symbols of the seething anger in Spanish society that was about to explode into out-and-out warfare.

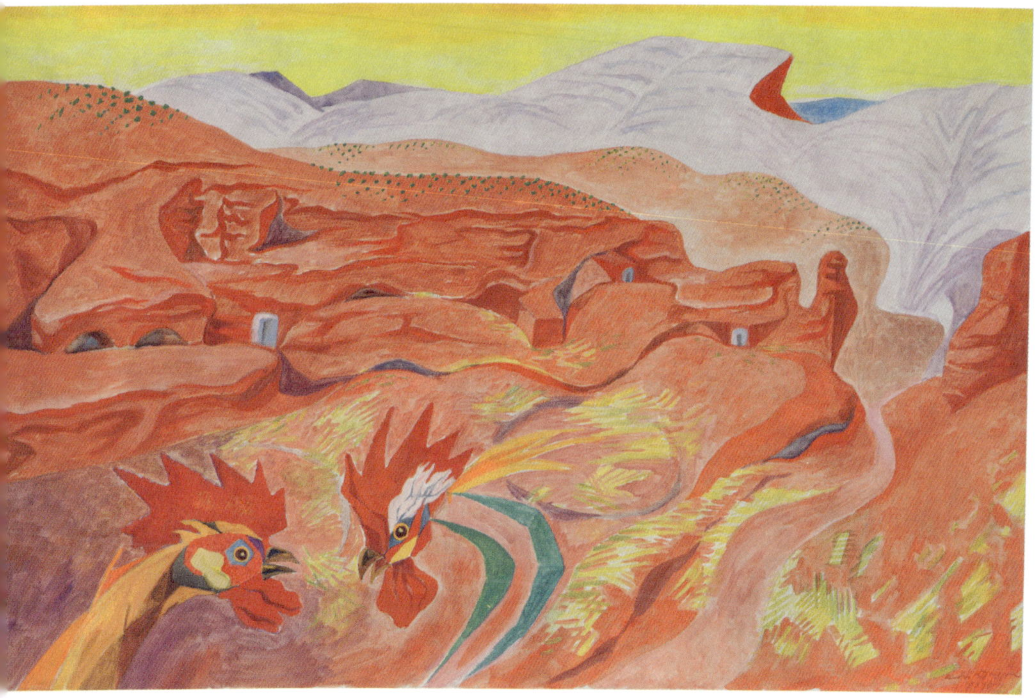

André Masson, *Ibdes in Aragon*, 1935

Toyen's strange painting *At the Green Table* (1945) also centres on fighting cocks. There are four pairs of them, with each pair facing up to one another. All the birds have red plumage and they are positioned in a dark green landscape near a derelict house. The scene is nocturnal and suggests imminent fighting. The title given to this painting seems out of place until one notices the presence on the green surface of three snooker or billiard balls. The dark green 'lawn' is also, it seems, a green tabletop, where a contest is taking place.

The splendid red bird in Marc Chagall's *Listening to the Cock* (1944) has no rivals, but appears ready to face any opponent that dares to cross its path. The title suggests it is crowing aggressively.

Two cocks sit quietly under the table in Remedios Varo's *Vegetarian Vampires* (1962), having been dramatically tamed. Each has silky white plumage and a bright red cockscomb, and both are on a lead, as though they have become family pets. Instead of two clawed feet, they have four legs like a domestic dog. These are domesticated, obedient cocks, their masculine fighting spirit no more than a fond memory. Like the cocks sitting patiently at their feet, the vampires of the title appear to have lost their thirst for blood and sit around the table sipping fruit juice through long straws.

In this selection of surrealist poultry, only Francis Picabia gives a friendly view of domestic hens. In *Chicken Coop* (1912), the hens are huddled together in a swirling mass of brightly marked feathers. They have become more an abstract pattern than a collection of individual birds.

Toyen, *At the Green Table*, 1945

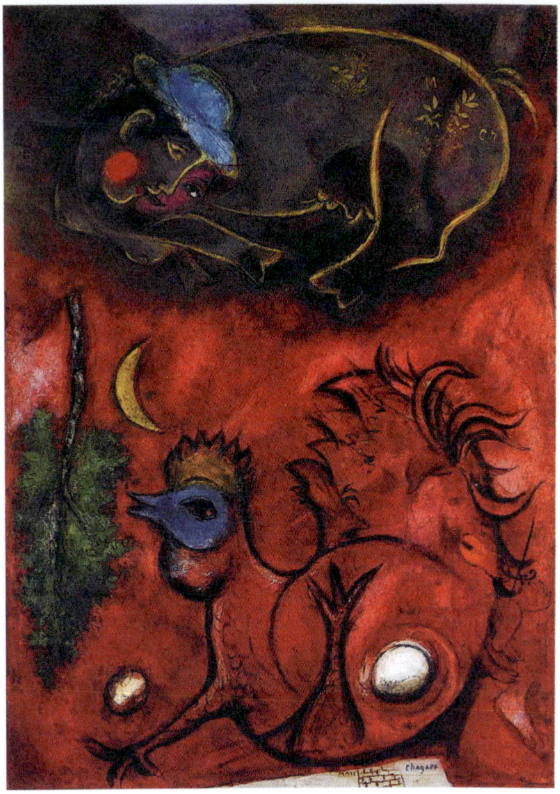

Marc Chagall, *Listening to the Cock*, 1944

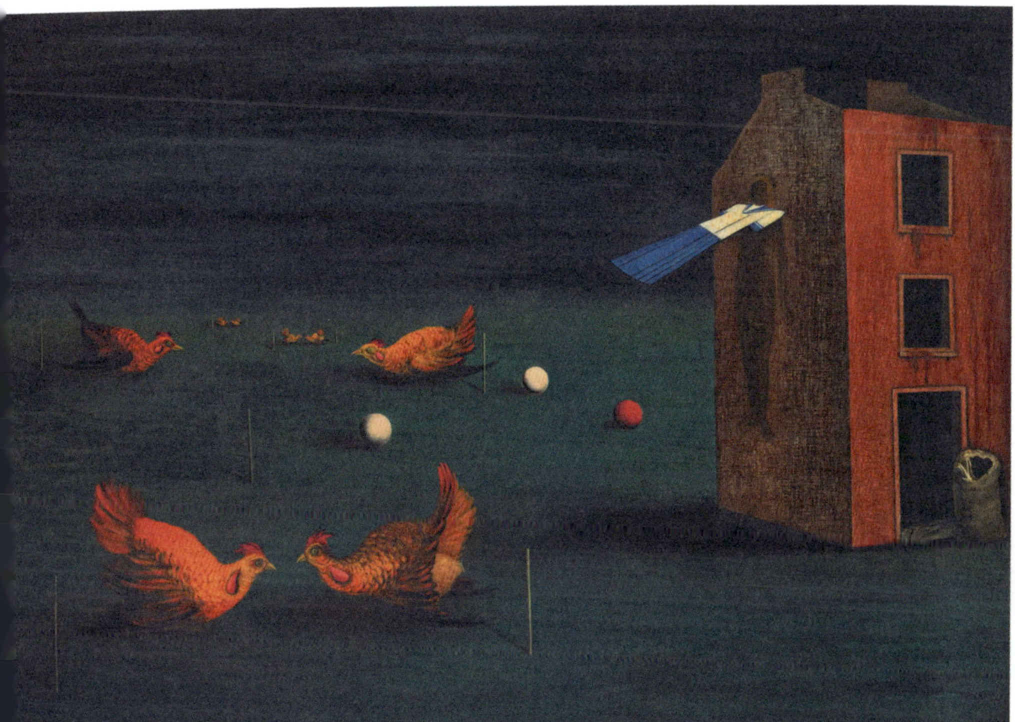

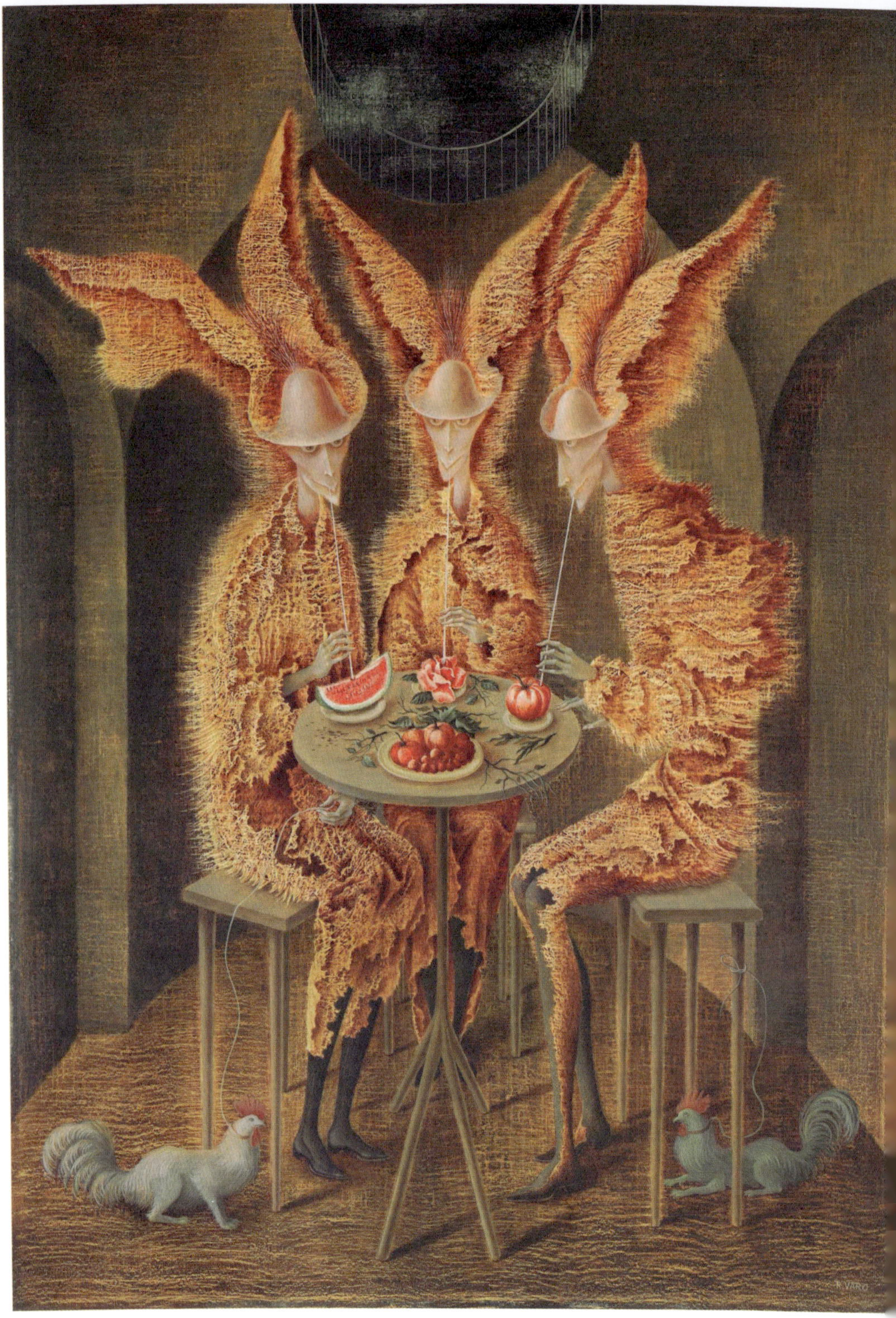

Remedios Varo, *Vegetarian Vampires*, 1962

Francis Picabia, *Chicken Coop*, 1912

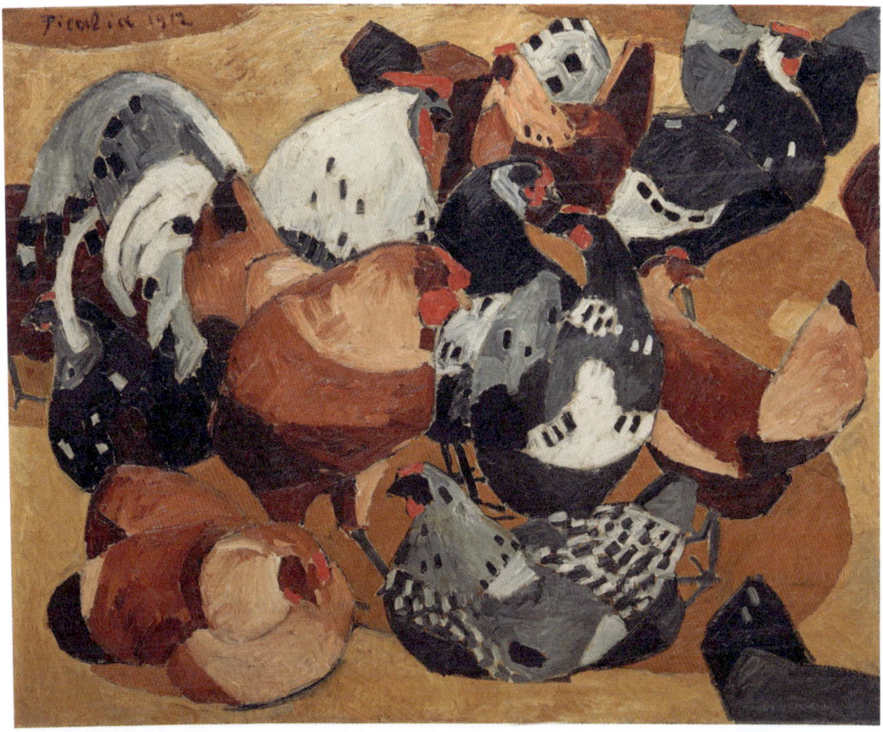

Pigeon/Dove

The dove has been an important symbol for thousands of years, but it is particularly associated with the biblical story of Noah's Ark. In Genesis, Noah sends a dove out from the Ark to find dry land: 'When the dove returned to him in the evening, there in its beak was a freshly plucked olive leaf! Then Noah knew that the water had receded from the earth. He waited seven more days and sent the dove out again, but this time it did not return to him.' The dove confirms for Noah that a time of calm and deliverance has come – a new start – becoming a lasting symbol of peace.

That is the accepted story, and it is natural to assume that the 'dove' was the dainty turtle dove (*Streptopelia turtur*), but the bird Noah sent was a rock pigeon (*Columba livia*), the ancestor of our domestic pigeon. Pigeons, not doves, had been trained since ancient times to act as homing birds. And it was pigeons that were used by early ships to bring back messages. The confusion arises because rock pigeons have sometimes been called rock doves.

Zoologically, there is little difference between pigeons and doves. They both belong to the family *Columbidae*, with the larger species being called pigeons and the smaller ones, doves. The general shape of birds in this family is so similar that, in surrealist paintings, it is sometimes hard to identify the species.

The collage *Physiomythological Diluvial Picture (Fatagaga)* (1920) – a collaboration between Max Ernst and Jean Arp – shows us two doves or pigeons, one sitting on a branch and the other acting as the head of a male human figure who is flexing the muscles of his right arm. His left leg is raised to display a bird's clawed foot, as

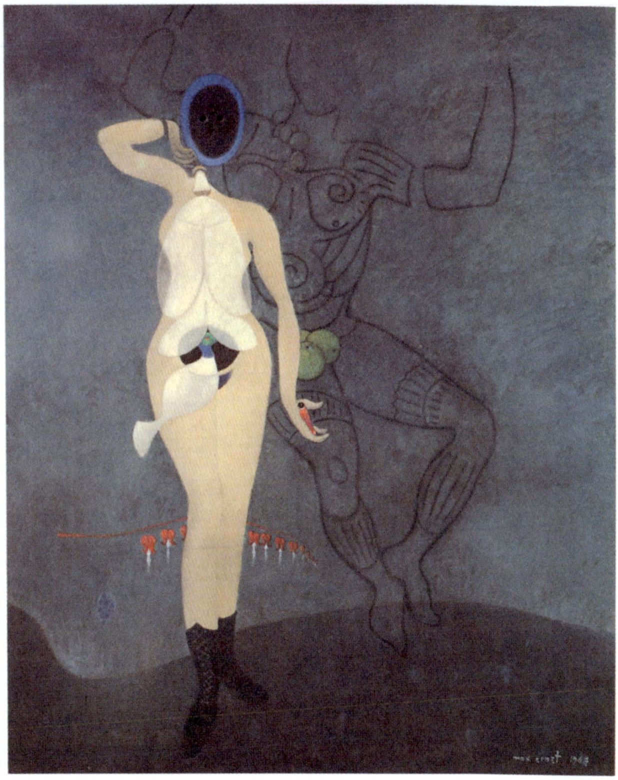

Max Ernst, *The Return of the Beautiful Gardener*, 1967

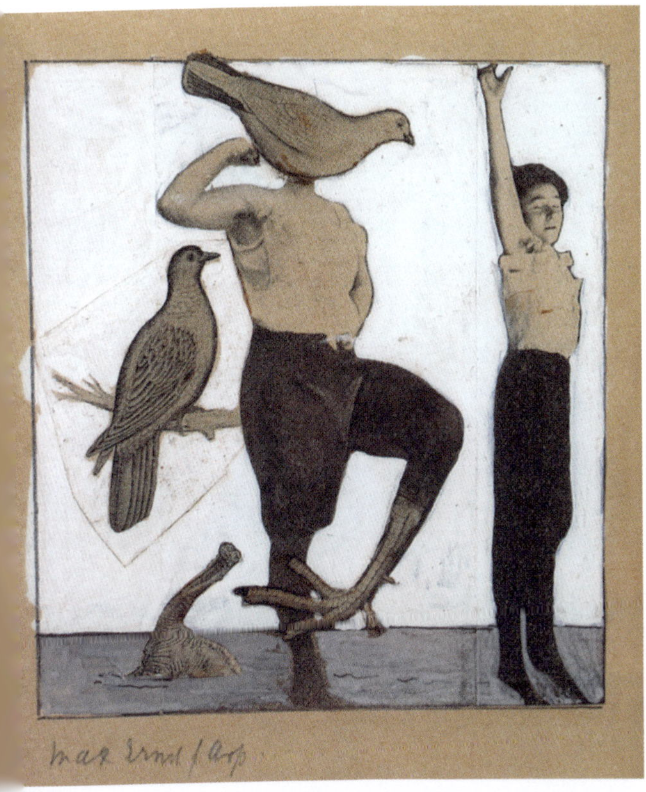

Max Ernst & Jean Arp, *Physiomythological Diluvial Picture (Fatagaga)*, 1920

if the man is slowly transforming into a bird. The scene, bizarrely, is being observed by a long-necked dinosaur in the background.

Ernst returns to the subject of the dove in a later work, *The Beautiful Gardener* (1923). Here, the bird sits high on the right thigh of a half-naked woman, so that its head is given a phallic positioning above her pelvis. This picture was removed from the Kunstmuseum in Düsseldorf in 1937 as part of the Nazi attack on modern art and included in the notorious 'Degenerate Art' exhibition in Munich the same year. Because the picture was lost, Ernst repainted it in 1967, calling his new work *The Return of the Beautiful Gardener*. This time, the head of the bird almost disappears into the woman's body. Ernst may have been aware of the associations made by Freud between a bird in flight and erect phallus (see p. 64).

René Magritte's *The Therapist* (1937) shows a seated, headless man whose upper body has been replaced, bizarrely, by a birdcage containing two white doves. A broad-brimmed hat sits where you would expect the head to be, and the cage is draped in a red cloak. It is a folly to attempt to analyse Magritte's compositions – they should always remain enigmatic riddles – but in this case, one cannot help but see the doves as representing inner peace and calm, which is, after all, the aim of a therapist's treatment. If this interpretation is correct, it means that this title is unusually relevant for a Magritte work – he nearly always made a point of choosing irrational and meaningless titles. His *Catalogue Raisonné* reveals the reason: this work was not, in fact, given its title by Magritte himself, but by one of his friends.

Magritte returned again and again to the subject of doves. In a series of works called *The Natural Graces*, begun in the 1940s, he explored what has become one of his most recognizable motifs, the 'leaf-dove', in which the leaves of a plant are transforming into a family of doves. Fascinated with the concept of metamorphosis,

Magritte experimented with this idea in different arrangements and media, sometimes depicting other birds (see pp. 118–19).

Other surrealists who included doves or pigeons in their compositions were Francis Picabia, Eileen Agar and Toyen.

René Magritte, *The Therapist*, 1937

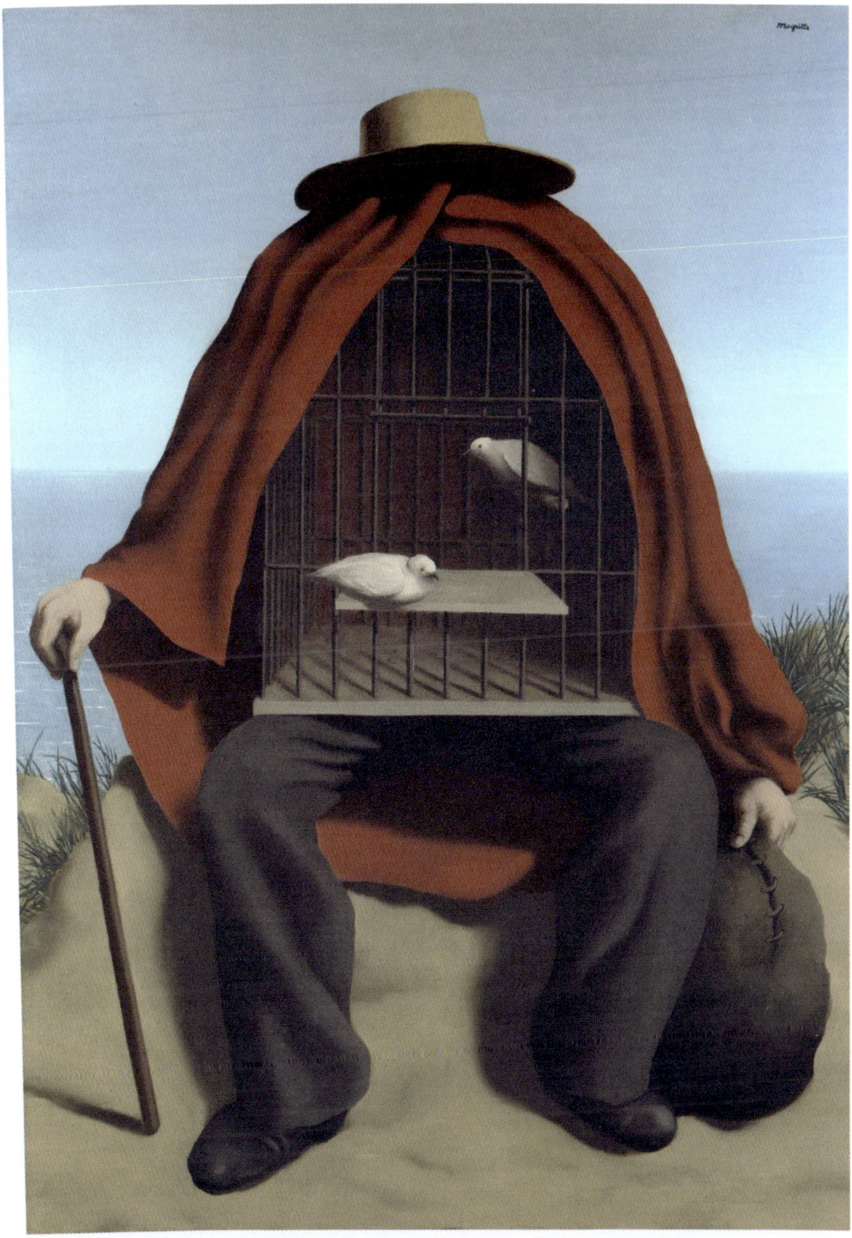

Parrot

The parrot was a favourite subject for the Mexican surrealist Frida Kahlo and the American Joseph Cornell. They appear in a handful of Kahlo's paintings and in many of Cornell's famous 'boxes'.

Saddened by her inability to bear children, Kahlo surrounded herself with animals. She had pet dogs, cats, monkeys, doves, turkeys, an osprey, a chipmunk, a deer, and two species of Amazon parrot – the Yellow-headed Amazon and the Lilac-crowned Amazon (*Amazona oratrix* and *Amazona finschi*). Her favourite, a Yellow-headed Amazon called Bonito, appears in several of her works. In her most famous parrot painting, *Me and My Parrots* (1941), she sits with a bird on each shoulder and with two more cradled in her arms. Bonito, the largest of them, is perched on her left shoulder and a second Yellow-headed Amazon is held on her right forearm. On her left forearm and on her right shoulder there are two Lilac-crowned birds. With Kahlo festooned in this way, it is as if she has given birth to a whole clutch of parrots.

Bonito was reportedly so tame that he would nestle under her blankets when she was resting on her bed. At mealtimes, he was allowed to fly around the table and would kiss the diners with his curved beak. Rather oddly for a parrot, he was especially fond of butter and would help himself at the butter dish. When he died in the winter of 1941, Kahlo gave him a special burial and, in a letter to a friend, wrote: 'I cried for him a lot since, you remember, that he was marvellous.'

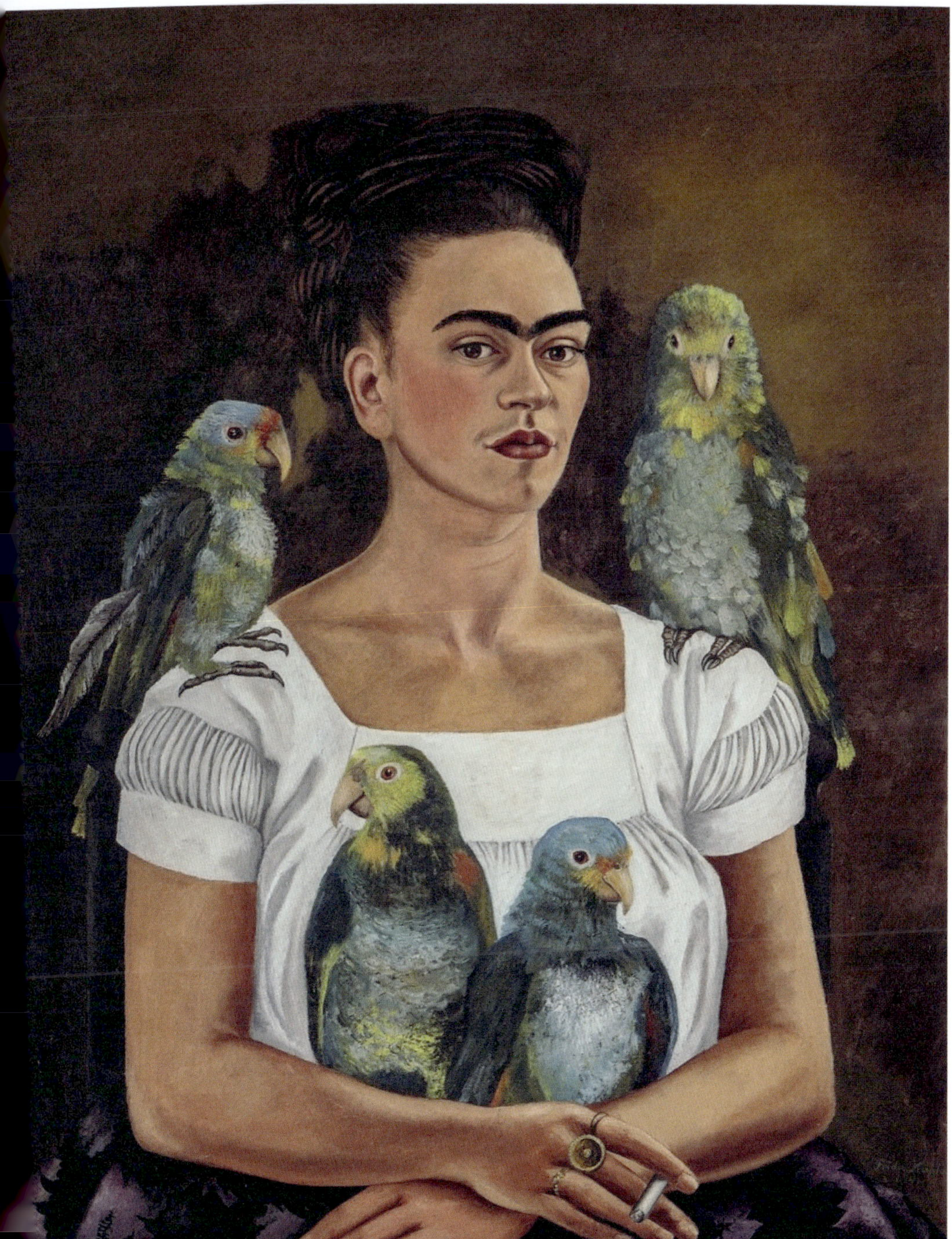

Frida Kahlo,
Me and My Parrots, 1941

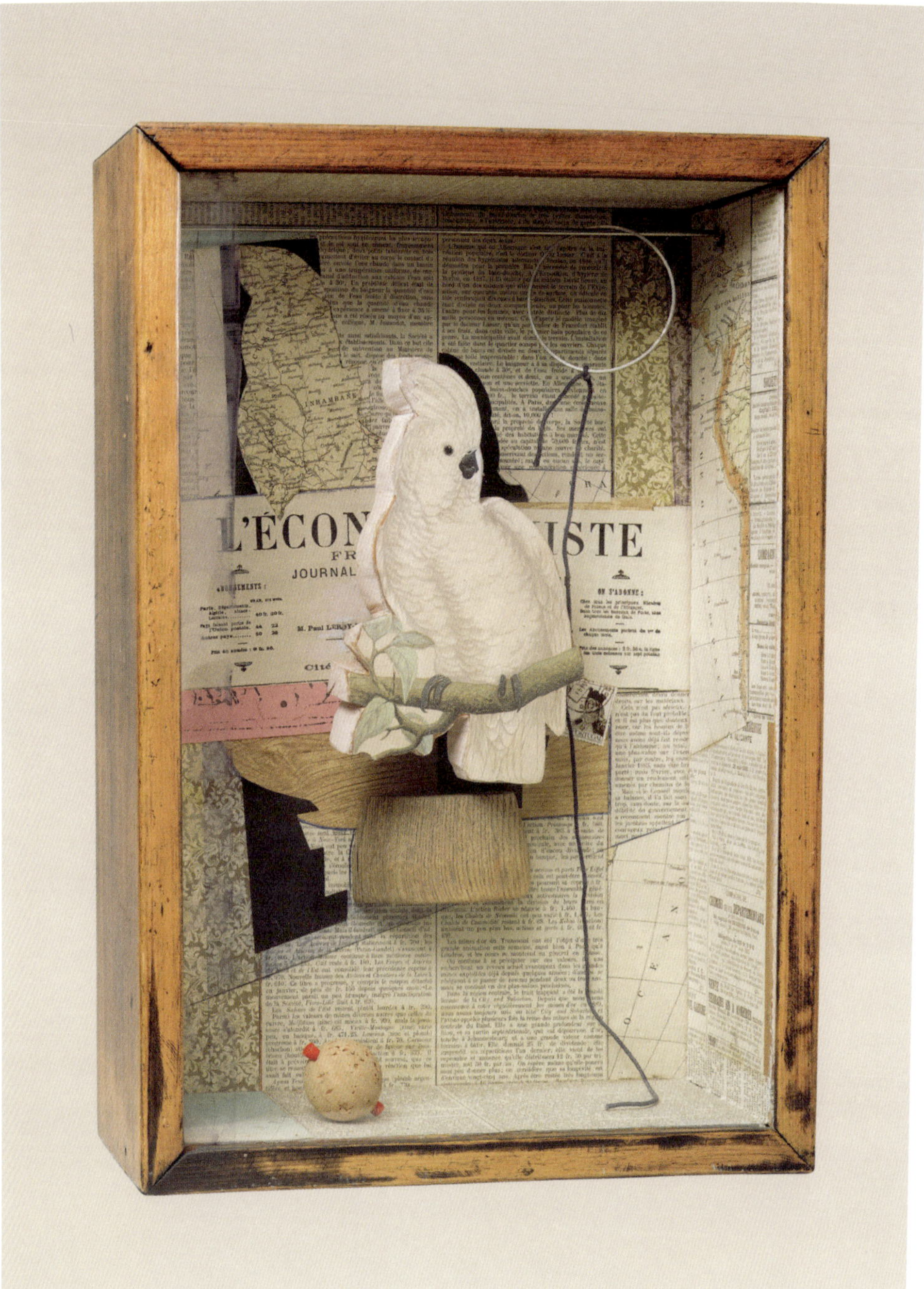

 Joseph Cornell, *A Parrot for Juan Gris*, 1953–54

For Joseph Cornell, parrots were happy reminders of his formative years. He said that they took him back to the 'magic windows of yesterday ... pet shop windows splashed with white tropical plumage ... and indelible childhood memories of a neighbour's pet parrot'. The white plumage seems to have lodged itself in his mind because many of the parrots in his artworks are white cockatoos. He shows them sitting in glass-fronted boxes, surrounded by strange objects.

It is said that he was impressed by the claim that cockatoos could imitate whole arias and he associated these birds, in particular, with the 19th-century Italian opera singer Giuditta Pasta. He described the atmosphere in which he created these white parrots as 'a warm and rich one ... [inspired by the] scintillating songs of Rossini and Bellini and the whole golden age of bel canto'.

In addition to white cockatoos, Cornell was also fond of eclectus parrots. The male eclectus is bright green with narrow patches of red under the wings, while the female is an intense red and purple-blue. In Cornell's works, the vivid green of the male becomes a washed-out yellow-green.

One of Cornell's earliest solo exhibitions, in 1949, was called simply 'Aviary' and consisted of 26 box constructions devoted to this theme. Displayed at the Charles Egan Gallery in New York, the boxes were hung at various heights as if the birds inside them were sitting in trees.

Owl

The ancients referred to the owl as the human-headed bird and it is this feature that has given it such wide appeal to artists. Its round head, its flat face and its large eyes give it a human quality that no other bird can match. Symbolically, it tends to have been cast in two contrasting roles: the wise old bird or the stealthy nocturnal killer. So there are 'good owls' and 'bad owls' in popular thinking, and the surrealists were fascinated by both.

Max Ernst's masterpiece *Attirement of the Bride* (1940) shows us one of the strangest owls ever depicted in a work of art. It has given rise to endless scholarly debate and a variety of interpretations. One thing is clear: Ernst set out to mystify the viewer of this work and in this he certainly succeeded. But as with much surrealist painting, it is the dark mystery that is at the very centre of the basic concept of the movement – the pleasure that is to be taken in the irrational world of dreams. As Ernst's great love, Leonora Carrington, once said irritably during an interview with her cousin, the journalist Joanna Moorhead, who was asking about the meaning of one of her paintings: 'It's a visual world. You want to turn things into a kind of intellectual game; it's not.'

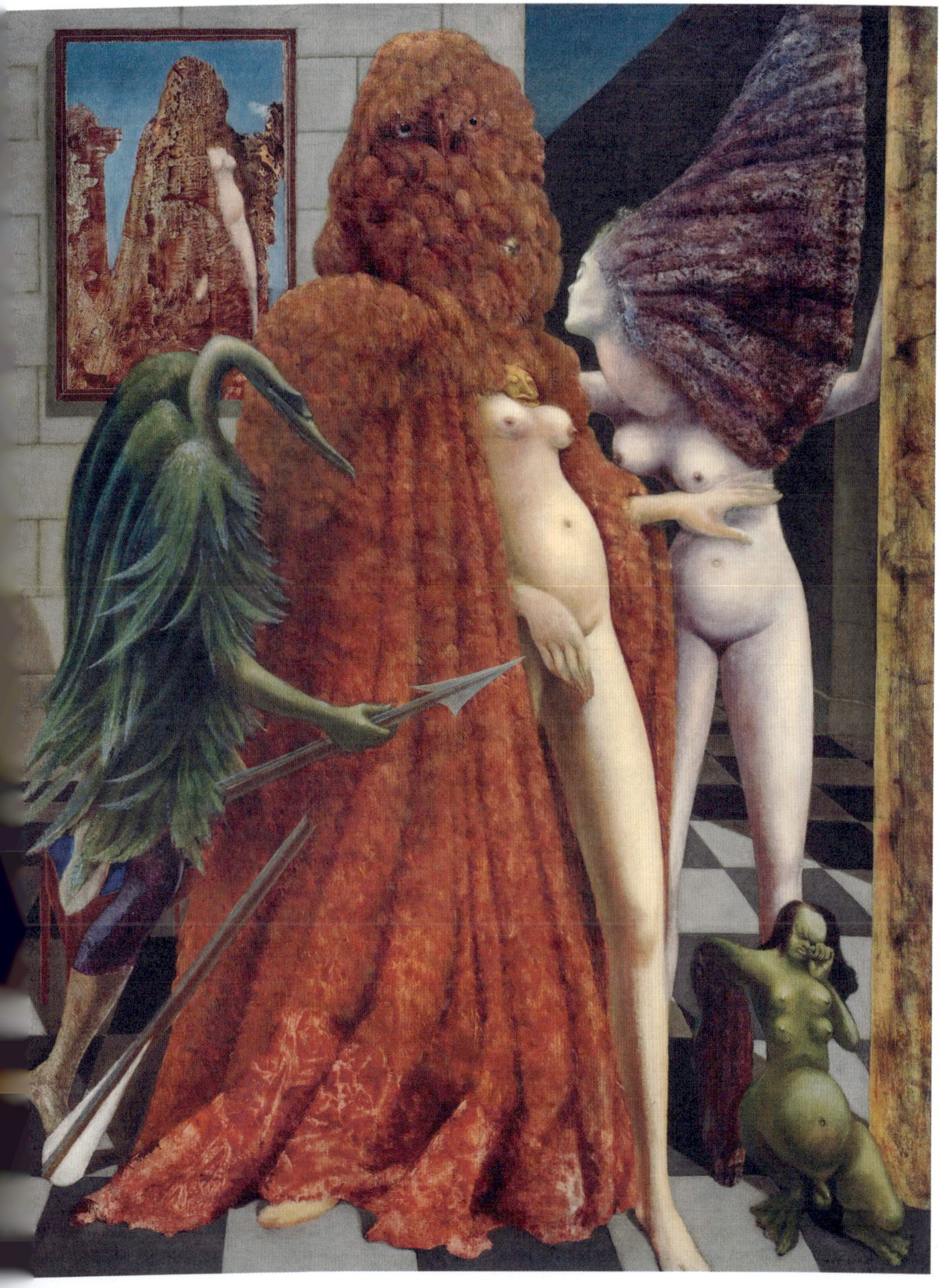

Max Ernst,
Attirement of the Bride, 1940

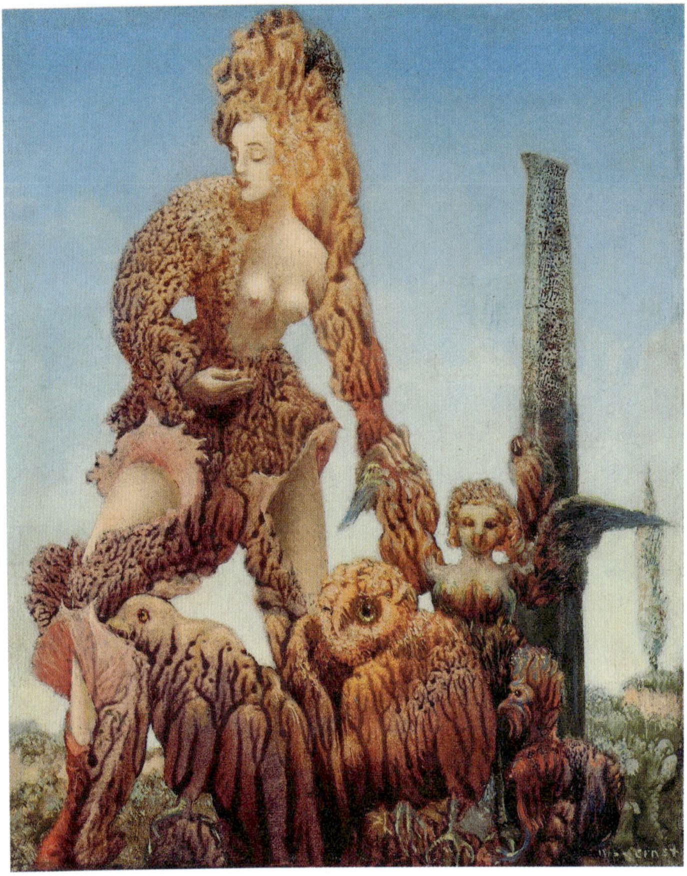

Max Ernst, *Marlene (Woman and Child)*, 1941

Morris Graves, *Little-Known Bird of the Inner Eye*, 1941

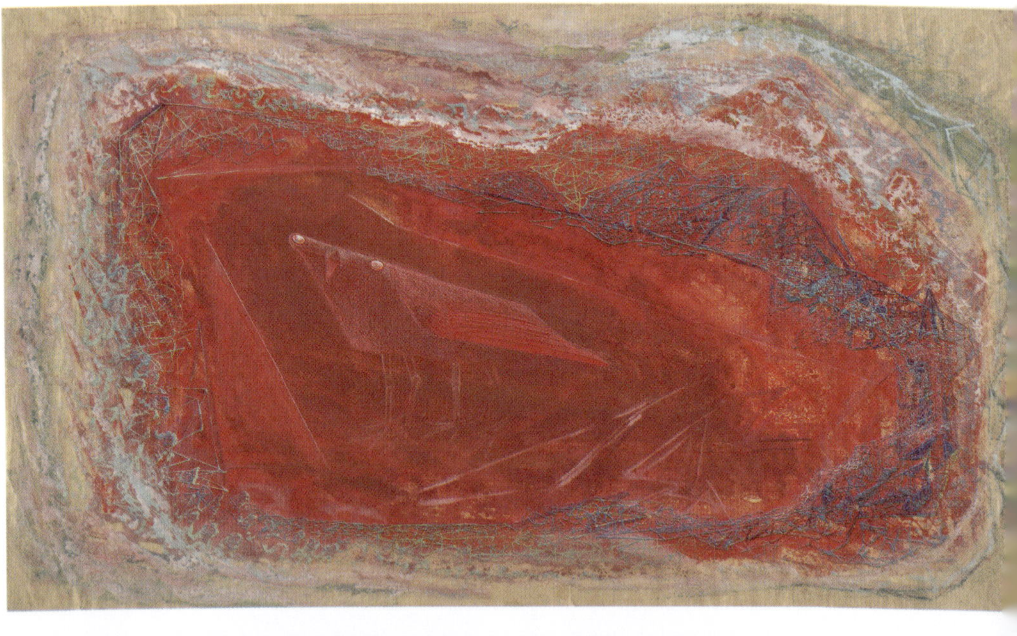

The visual world of Ernst's *Bride* is dominated by a naked young woman half-covered in a heavy feathered cloak. The upper part of this orange cloak has grown into the wings and head of a huge owl. One of the owl's eyes is orange and the other is blue. This bizarre woman/bird, or bird/woman, is being guarded by another human/bird hybrid that has the slender head and neck of a heron or crane, is covered in long, blue-green feathers, and has the arms and legs of a man. He carries a broken spear whose sharp point appears to be aimed directly at the bride's genitals.

Scholars have speculated that the bride is Carrington, and that her spear-carrying guardian is Ernst himself in the guise of a bird. But this tells us nothing about why the bride is being transformed into a gigantic owl. Ernst himself gives us no clue, of course, although he famously admitted to having an avian alter ego called Loplop (see p. 64).

His orange-feathered owl appears a year later in *Marlene (Woman and Child)* (1941). Here, it has become a complete bird, with clawed feet, crouching below the figure of Marlene, whose child is a winged bird/human hybrid. It has been suggested that this owl is Ernst himself, following another German, the actress Marlene Dietrich, who left Nazi-dominated Europe for America in the 1930s, where he too took refuge after the outbreak of the Second World War.

In the same year, 1941, the American artist Morris Graves created a memorable four-legged owl in a painting entitled *Little-Known Bird of the Inner Eye*. His bird stares at us from a dark cavity – some sort of burrow or cave – perhaps inspired by the real-life home of the small burrowing owl (*Athene cunicularia*) that lives in the western states of North America, where Graves himself had his studio. The 'inner eye' mentioned in the title prompted one critic to comment: 'This owl-inspired image expresses the artist's idea of a hidden part of the mind in which we know a higher reality than that of the daily world.' Graves himself said that he painted in order to rest from the external world, and that he made 'notations of its essences with which to verify the inner eye.' There are two other ways to interpret this wartime painting: on the one hand, this delicate creature may reflect the horrors of the Second World War by hiding itself away (just as humans were having to seek out air-raid shelters); on the other, it may symbolize wisdom in retreat from inhumanity.

René Magritte's owls are sombre beings. In his haunting work *The Companions of Fear* (1942), one of the earliest examples of his leaf-bird motif (see pp. 108–9) painted at the height of the Second World War, he depicts a bleak alpine landscape in which plants are growing into sinister owls, seen here in their role as night-time killers – like the bombers that filled the skies over Europe in those terrible years. Magritte, however, shows these solitary predators during the day, clustered together and rooted to the ground. When he painted this picture, he was living in a Belgium that was occupied by the Nazis and where fear of the Gestapo was a daily presence. It is as if he is saying that his whole world has become a deadly environment where even the vegetation has been infected by evil and can sprout death.

Magritte's title for this painting, suggested to him by his friend, the poet Louis Scutenaire, is significant. *Les Compagnons de la peur* is the French title of a book by the American thriller writer Rex Stout – a favourite of Magritte's. The original title of this book was *The League of Frightened Men* (1935), which fits the painting's wartime mood even more closely.

In 1944, with the war still raging, Magritte returned to this theme of owls growing out of plants, in a work called *Image in the Window*. But now the owls have turned white and become ghostlike. A new feature here is that the largest owl has a pair of long, pointed ears growing out of the top of its head. There are, of

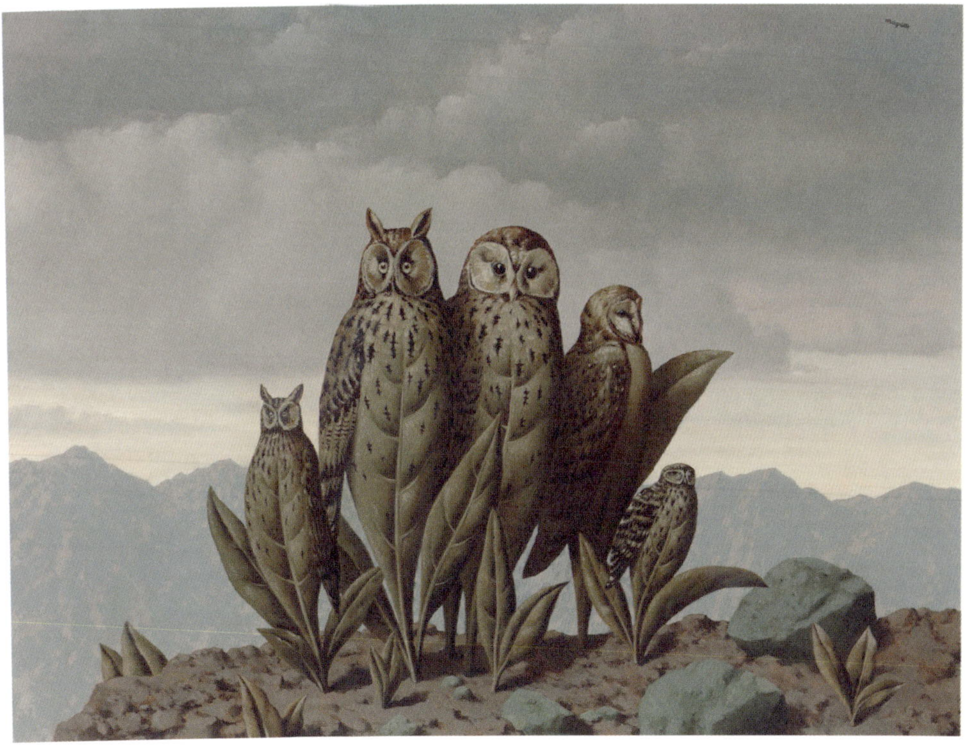

René Magritte, *The Companions of Fear*, 1942

course, species of eared owls known in nature, but these particular ears appear to bear little resemblance. Writing to a friend of his, the surrealist Marcel Mariën, Magritte commented: 'Notice that for some time now there has always been a pair of pointed ears in my pictures.... Could there be a relationship with Satanism?' Magritte seems puzzled by this urge to make his owls into demonic figures, and we are left to wonder whether his sinister birds – these deadly nocturnal killers – have become symbols of the Nazi evil that surrounded him.

Wifredo Lam's strangely spear-winged owl in *The Fear of a Bird* (1955) also has two projections on top of its head, but here the pointed ears have grown into a pair of curved horns, and its sharp claws have been transformed into humanoid feet. Despite

Remedios Varo, *Creation of the Birds*, 1957

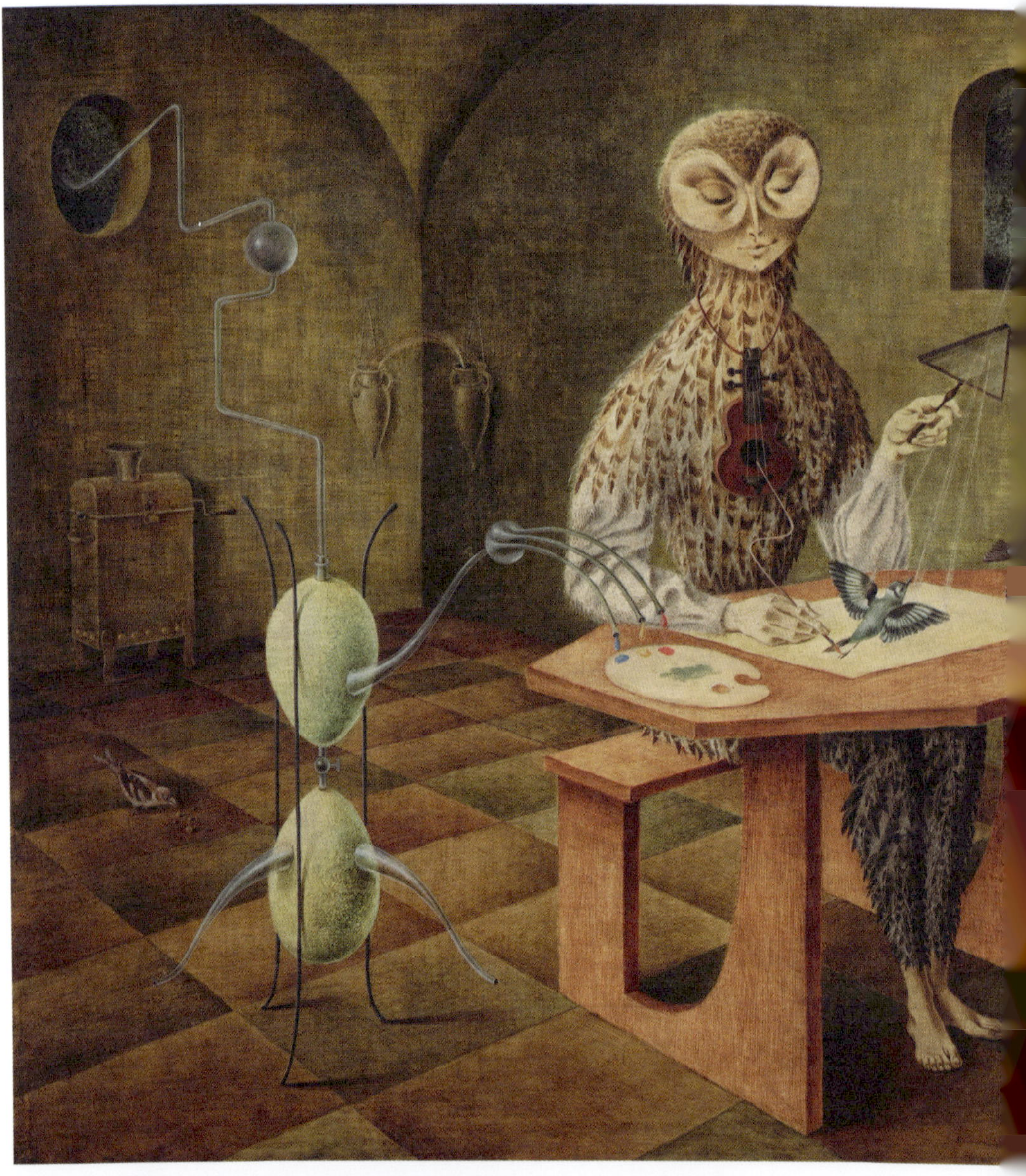

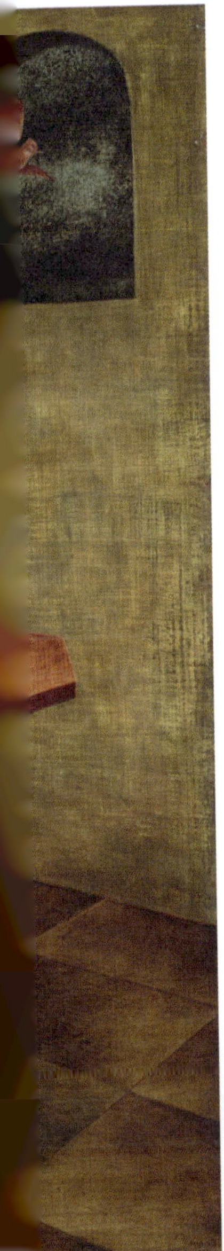

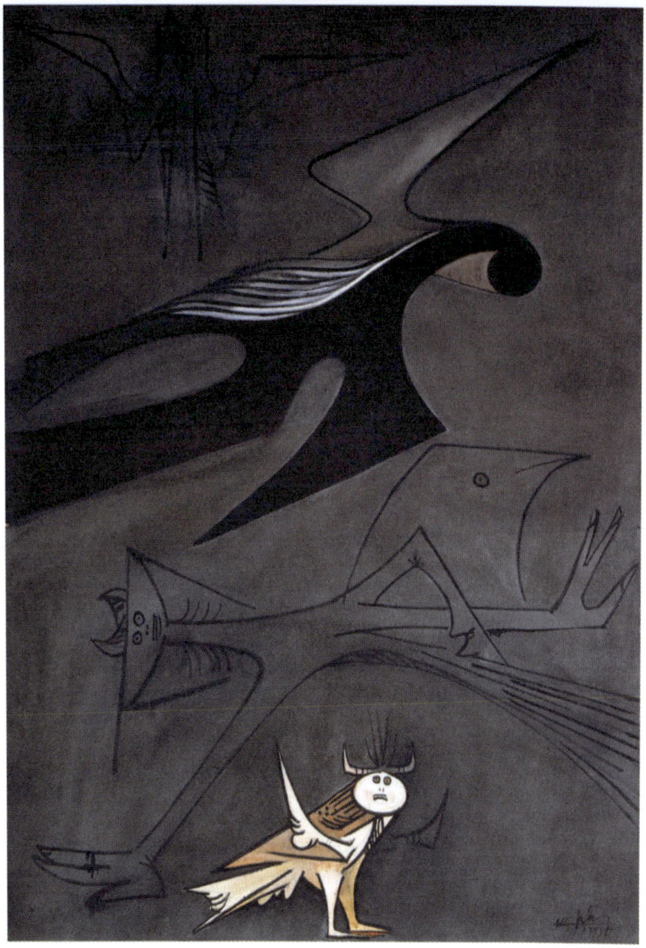

Wifredo Lam, *The Fear of a Bird*, 1955

these oddities, Lam's owl has a strong presence that makes you believe this is a portrayal of a creature that actually exists.

Finally, there is the extraordinary surrealist owl presented to us by Remedios Varo in *Creation of the Birds* (1957). The title of this painting gives a clear indication of what her bizarre owl-figure is doing. The central figure of the owl, with its feathered head, neck, shoulders and chest, has discernible, apparently female human features: a nose, lips, clothed forearms, hands and feet. Around the owl's neck hangs a small stringed instrument – halfway between a guitar and a violin – and from this there emerges a long, curved wire that ends in a paintbrush. Holding the brush in her right hand, she paints a bird that is so realistic it is flying off the page and up into the air. A second bird has already taken wing. This process is being aided by the triangular prism that she holds in her left hand, which is multiplying the ray of light that shines into the room from a bright star seen through the window. On the left-hand side of the composition, a bizarre apparatus that may be an alembic – used for distillation in alchemy – drips blue, yellow and red paint onto her palette. In this magical work, Varo shows us not the predatory owl, but the wise owl – one with the knowledge to create living birds merely by drawing them.

Swallow

The swallow plays an important role in Conroy Maddox's *The Conquest* (1977). The painting shows a large, desolate courtyard in which two white-clad children have been tragically isolated from the outside world. One stands immobile, and the other appears to be writhing on the ground, perhaps suffering from some kind of seizure. In the far distance we can see snow-covered mountain peaks. Flying high above this bleak scene are two graceful swallows, which immediately become symbols of freedom – the freedom that the two children have been so cruelly denied. As migratory birds, swallows cover vast distances, something that the two incarcerated children can only dream of – they are going nowhere. Maddox's meticulously created scene poetically contrasts confinement and liberty.

This painting was produced during an important phase in the English artist's oeuvre, when Maddox was obsessed with the psychiatric experiments conducted by Jean-Martin Charcot in the 19th century in the Parisian hospital of the Salpêtrière. Widely regarded as the father of modern neurology, Charcot described the hospital as the 'grand asylum of human misery', whose residents all female included the elderly, orphans, beggars,

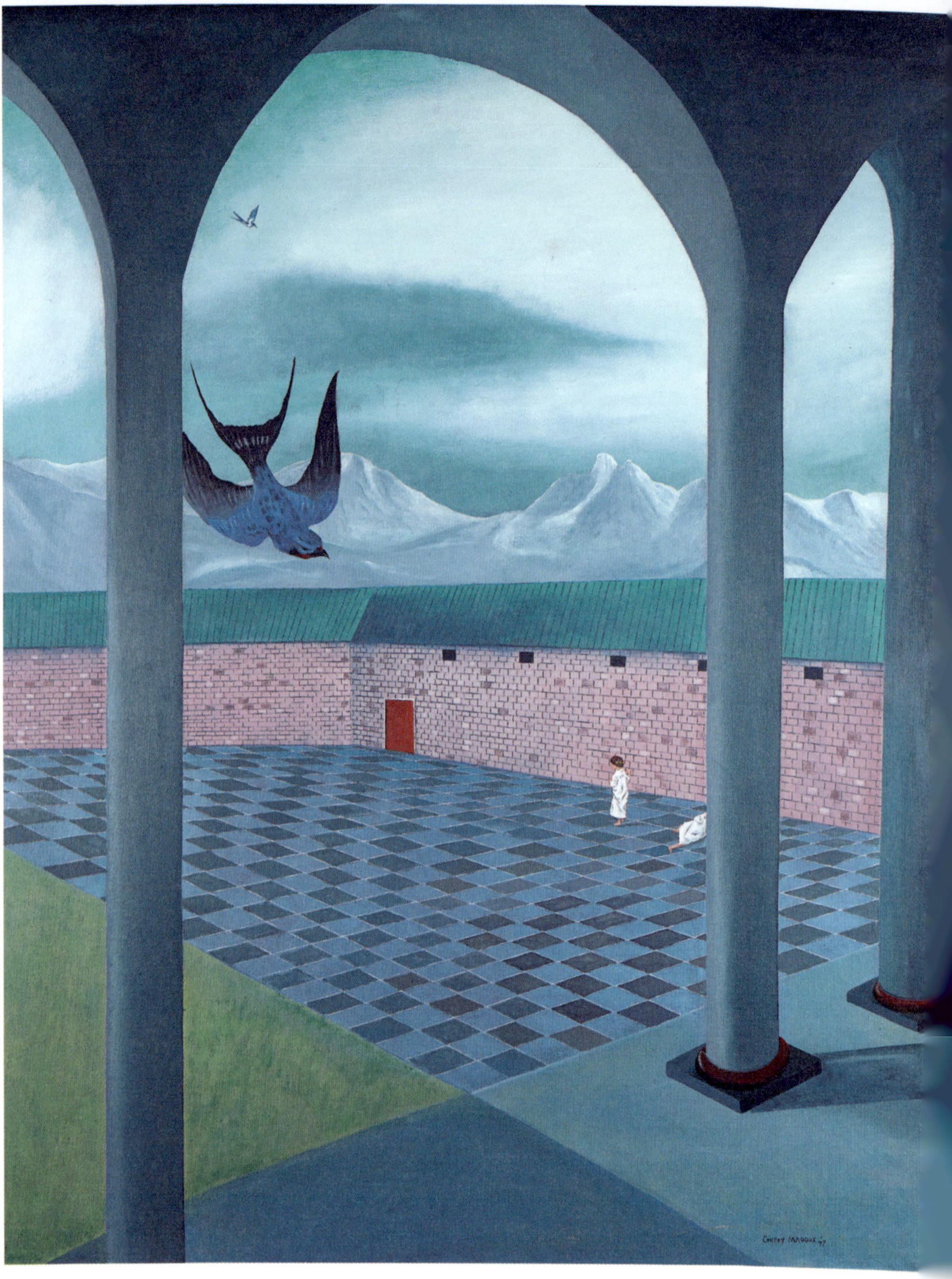

Conroy Maddox, *The Conquest*, 1977

epileptics, the blind, women with mental disorders, prostitutes and criminals. In 1940, Maddox wrote about 'the long-neglected playgrounds of Salpêtrière', adding, rather mysteriously: 'Your flight was thought to be the riddle of the birds' migration since it was you who fashioned freedom, who dreamed exclusively of yourself dreaming.' What he appears to be saying here is that, although the two wretched children have been physically imprisoned in the grounds of the hospital, they are able to gain their spiritual freedom in their daydreams, where they can go anywhere their unconscious imaginations take them.

There are, then, two contrasting explanations of Maddox's portrayal of the swallow. In the simple version, the physical freedom of the birds contrasts vividly with the physical confinement of the children. In the more subtle version, suggested by Maddox himself and seemingly reinforced by the title, the symbolic freedom of the birds echoes the mental freedom of the dreaming children. In other words, it may be possible to imprison, say, a tortoise, because tortoises are incapable of dreaming, but you can never truly imprison human beings, because they can always escape privately into a secret world of their imaginations. It was, of course, the enriched enjoyment of this other world that the surrealist movement set out to foster.

Nightingale

Symbolically, the nightingale is perhaps most strongly associated with love. It is a remarkable bird, able to produce over one thousand different sounds. The part of the brain responsible for creating sound is bigger in nightingales than in most other birds. If a nightingale appeared in a work of art, one might therefore expect it to play a positive role. Perversely, the one surrealist who portrayed the nightingale, Max Ernst, decided to make it a negative force, endowing it not with love, but with hate.

Produced during Ernst's Dadaist phase, *The Chinese Nightingale* (1920) is part of a series of collages created by the artist in 1919 and 1920 using photographs from military publications. It shows a bomb – the kind dropped by aircraft – lying on the grass. The shape of the weapon has been modified so that it looks like the giant head of a bird. It has also grown two arms and an eye, and it is topped by a decorative fan that becomes a crest. This image is Ernst's way of attacking a war that, a few years previously, he had fought as a reluctant member of the German artillery division.

In 1924, Ernst returned to the nightingale theme in one of his strangest compositions, *Two Children Are Threatened by*

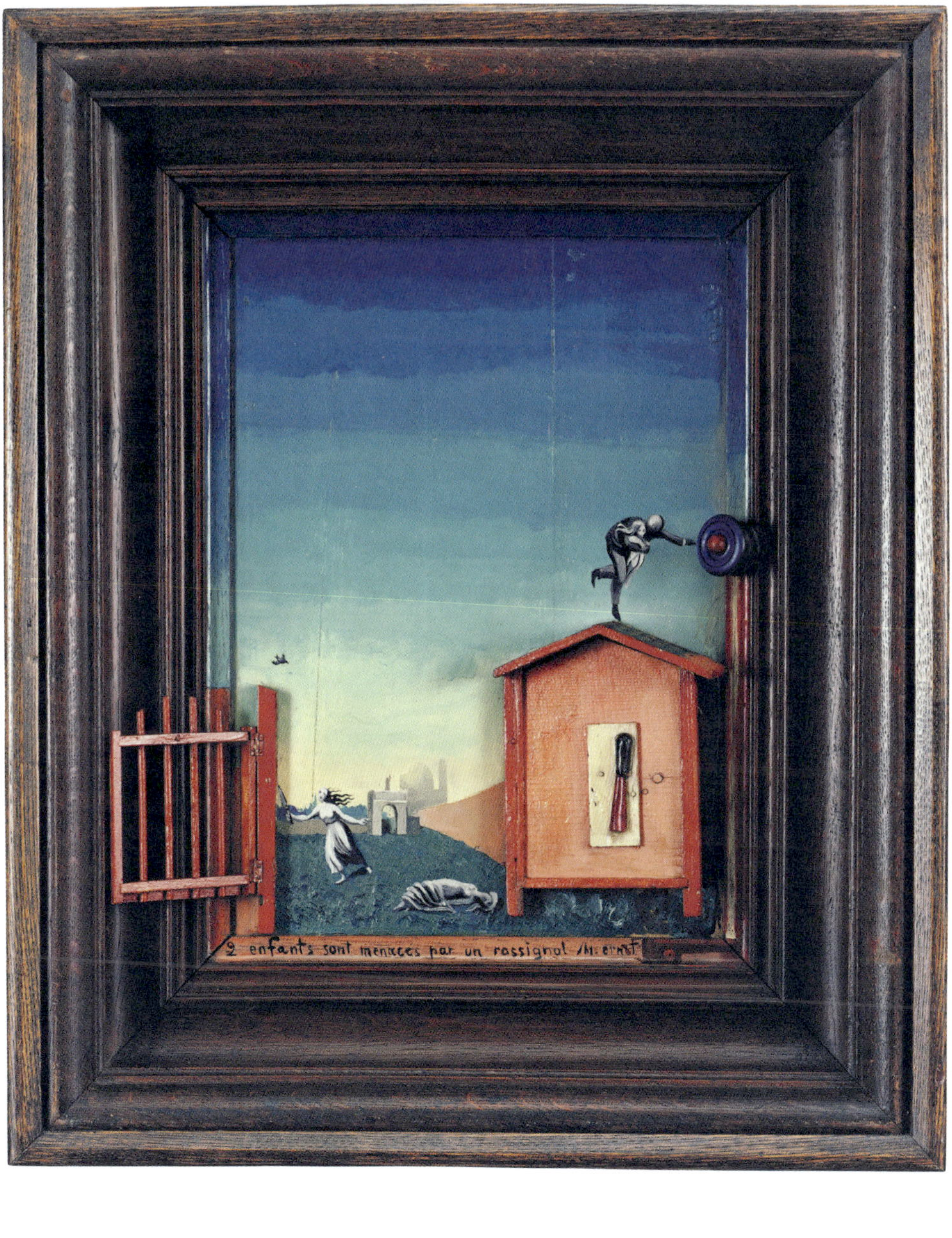

Max Ernst, *Two Children Are Threatened by a Nightingale*, 1924

a Nightingale. Merging collage and painting, he added elements of wood – including a gate and a knob – to the painted scene. The picture shows four human figures – the two children, a man and an infant. A tiny, inoffensive bird hovers in the air, so small that you would barely notice it. In the title of this work, we are told that this bird, the nightingale of love, is in fact threatening the children. One child appears to have fainted and lies on the ground, while the other child stands nearby, brandishing a knife at the bird. On the roof of a strange building, the man is seen fleeing with an infant clutched in his arms. The oddity of this scene lies in the way Ernst has chosen to portray the nightingale as a menacing threat that is creating panic, a bird that is normally seen as the least threatening being imaginable. It is this perverse symbolic inversion that gives the work its enduring appeal.

Bat

Symbolically, the bat represents night fears. The first of these fears comes from an old superstition that if a young woman went out at night, a bat would fly into her hair and become so entangled that she would have to have her hair cut off to release it. Of course, a bat's sensitive navigational system means that, flitting about at night, it would masterfully avoid coming too close to anyone's hair.

An eccentric British earl, who was particularly fond of bats, decided to prove this fear to be unfounded. He did this in a dramatic fashion, coming up behind female dinner guests and thrusting an adult bat into their hair. The bats quickly escaped and he easily proved his point, although it is doubtful his guests welcomed this piece of scientific fieldwork. When asked how his research was going, he replied: 'Not enough blondes.' He was worried because blonde hair is finer than dark hair, and he wanted to be sure that it, too, would survive the experience unharmed (it did).

But it is the second bat fear that appeals to the surrealist mind that of having your blood sucked by a vampire. In reality, you will only get bitten by a vampire bat (*Desmodus rotundus*)

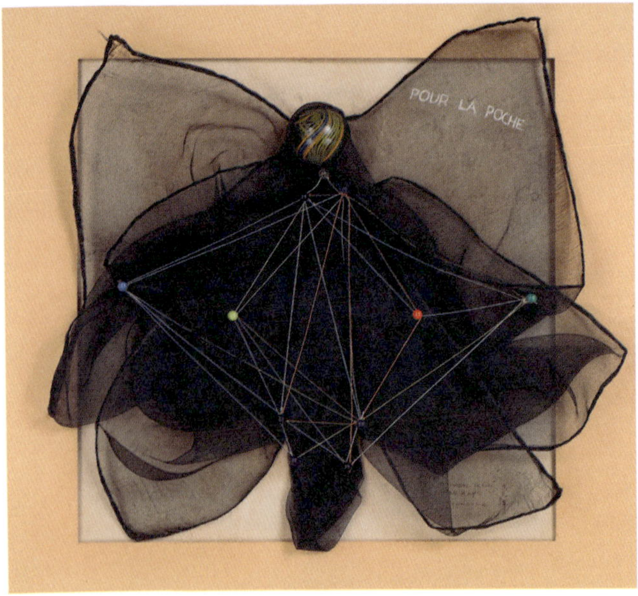

Jacqueline Lamba, *For the Pocket*, 1935

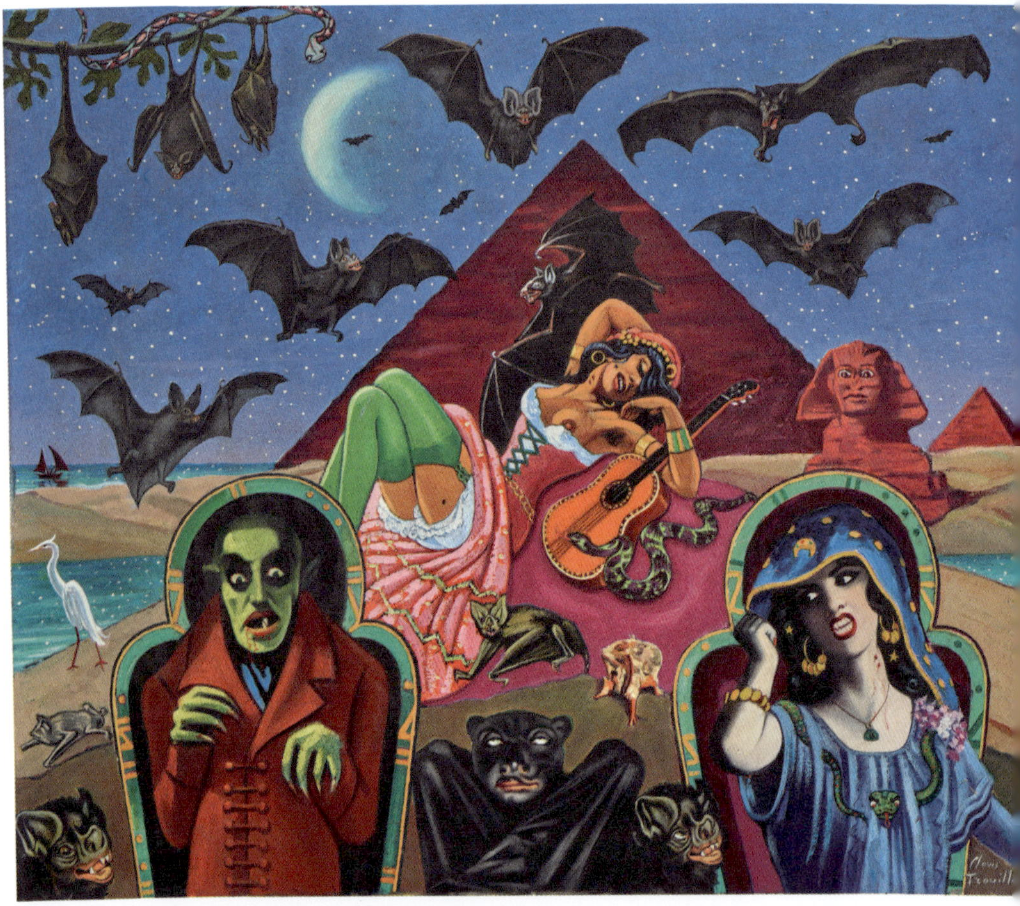

if you sleep out of doors in regions of the world where they exist (Mexico, Central and South America) and have part of your body exposed – and even then, it's rare. When this happened to a 20th-century British zoologist, Leonard Harrison Matthews, working in the field, he reported that the vampire bat has such sharp teeth that it was able to feed on him without waking him up. He only discovered the cuts on his legs the following morning. He later discovered that vampire bats, despite the legends, never suck blood. When it flows from their neat cuts, they lap it up like cats drinking milk. The vampire bat's saliva is now known to contain an anaesthetic agent that numbs the skin, making it a master of avoiding detection.

Several surrealist artists have portrayed vampire bats, including Toyen and Clovis Trouille. In Trouille's *Dream of the Vampire* (1960), bats fill the sky and hang from nearby branches as a young woman in a provocative pose sleeps peacefully below them.

In *For the Pocket* (1935), the artist Jacqueline Lamba, who was married to André Breton, offers a very different kind of bat. Hers is made of black silk – a fancy handkerchief that has been folded into the unmistakable shape of the winged mammal. It was dedicated in ink to 'My friend, Man Ray'.

ovis Trouille,
eam of the Vampire, 1960

The Carr

vores

Dog

There are over 1,000 breeds of dog, all descended from wolves over a long period of time. There are three basic types: the fierce dogs, the athletic dogs and the companion dogs. The fierce dogs are the guardians – those that protect livestock, property and people. The athletic dogs are those involved in a wide variety of sports or other human activities that require physical strength, stamina and dexterity – the racing dogs, the hunting dogs and the performing dogs. The companion dogs – 'man's best friend' – are the pet dogs and lapdogs. Sadly, there is one further kind of dog that is drawn from all these categories – the stray dog – and the surrealists have painted examples of each.

In *Frica Fear* (1950), Victor Brauner portrays one of the most savage dogs in the surrealist menagerie. A human couple are shown, sitting on the ground, confronting one another. The man's penis has become a vicious dog that is attacking the female body with its stiff tongue. The dog's wide-open jaws display rows of sharp teeth. The woman's arm, which bizarrely appears to protrude from her chin, reaches out towards the man, and her hair has become a strange purple animal that watches on.

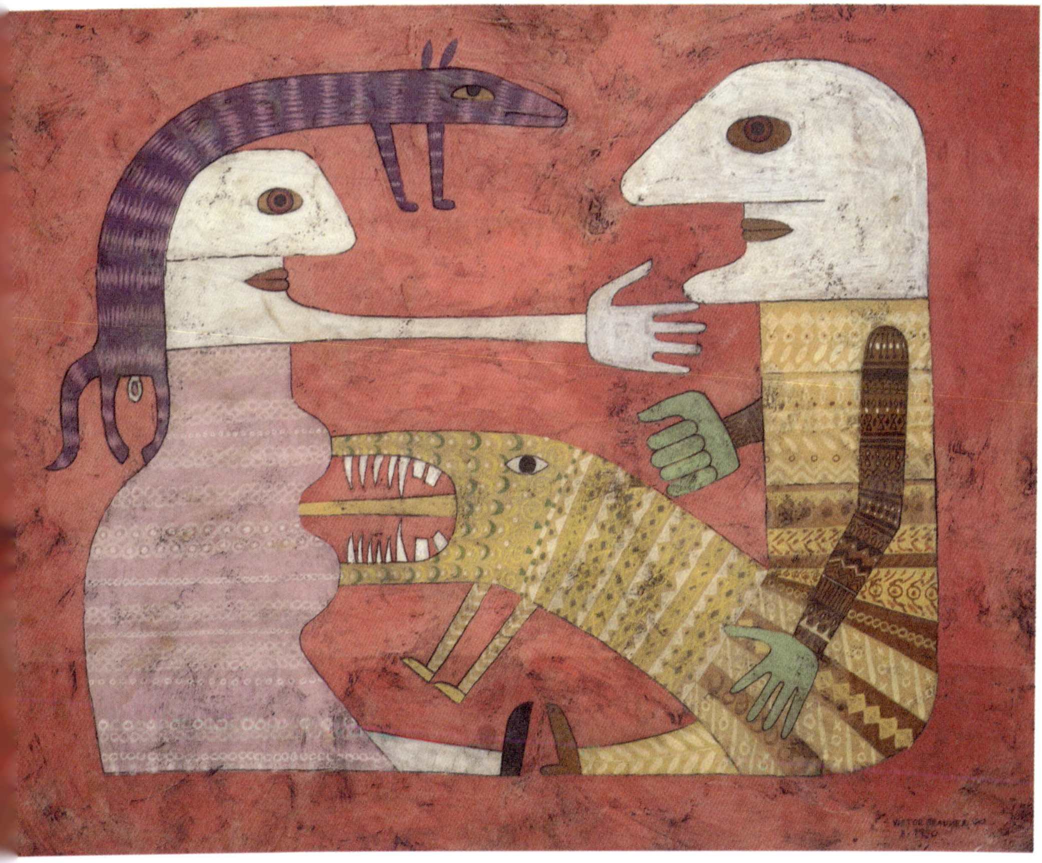

Victor Brauner, *Frica Fear*, 1950

Joan Miró's chirpy little animal in *Dog Barking at the Moon* (1926) is far less frightening. Perhaps this excitable guard dog has mistaken the bright moon for an intruder. Painted at the artist's family farm in Montroig, Spain, which inspired a number of early works, the scene has been reduced to the bare essentials, giving it an otherworldly feel. In a preparatory sketch for the painting, the dog's 'bow wow' is written out, unfurling towards the moon, which replies dismissively in a cartoon-style bubble – elements that were subsequently crossed out.

In the sports category, Toyen's *Fox Hunt* (1964) portrays two dogs that are certainly athletes. They are running so fast that their legs have become a blur and their tongues are hanging out. Unfortunately, Toyen does not seem to know about dog breeds, or perhaps does not care, because the animal portrayed is not a foxhound but a spotted dalmatian – a breed developed to run alongside coaches to protect them from highwaymen in the days before there were police and motor vehicles.

Francis Picabia's *Animal Trainer* (1923, falsely dated 1937) also takes us back to an earlier time, when circuses used all sorts of performing animals in their Big Top shows. Here, however, it is four dogs that take centre stage, accompanied by an owl on a stand that looks intently at the viewer. Picabia's trainer is cracking a whip, but only one dog appears to respond, leaping up towards him. One of the dogs remains lying on the ground, looking up at him, another scratches itself, and the fourth dog is walking way.

Frida Kahlo and Dorothea Tanning are among the artists to offer us companion dogs. In Kahlo's *Self-Portrait with Small Monkey* (1945), the artist sits with two of her favourite pets, a spider monkey and a Xoloitzcuintle, or Mexican hairless dog. Today this dog is a rare breed, in part because some people find its near-naked body ugly, but it has a charming temperament and makes a devoted companion. In ancient times, it was bred by

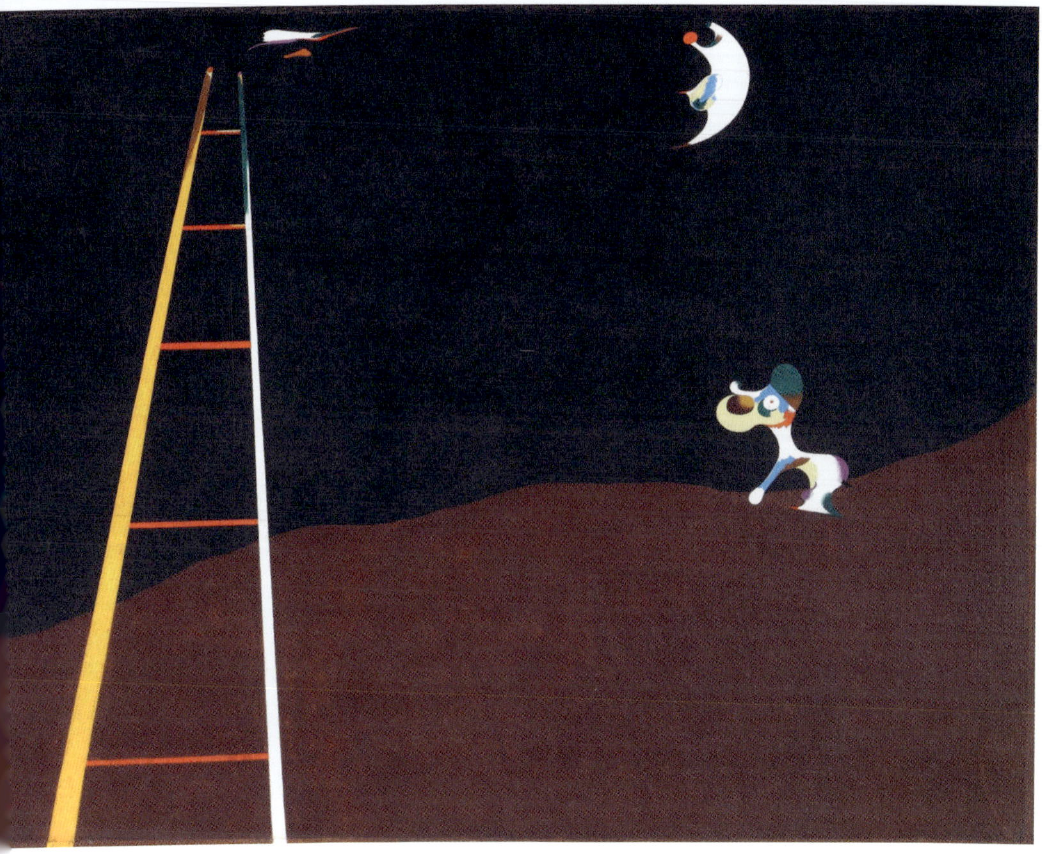

Joan Miró, *Dog Barking at the Moon*, 1926

Toyen, *Fox Hunt*, 1964

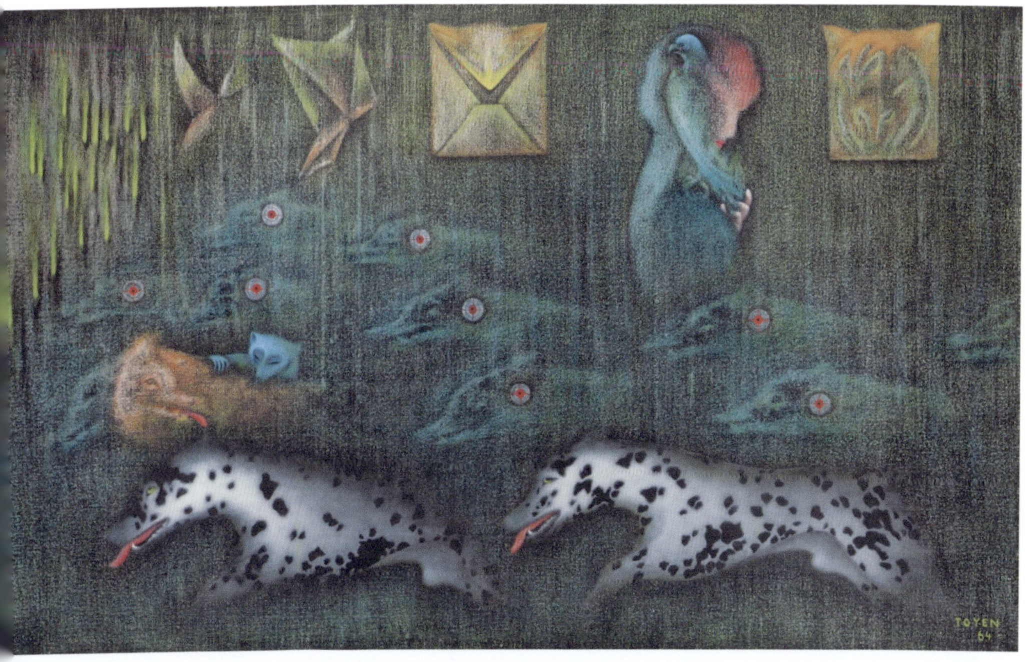

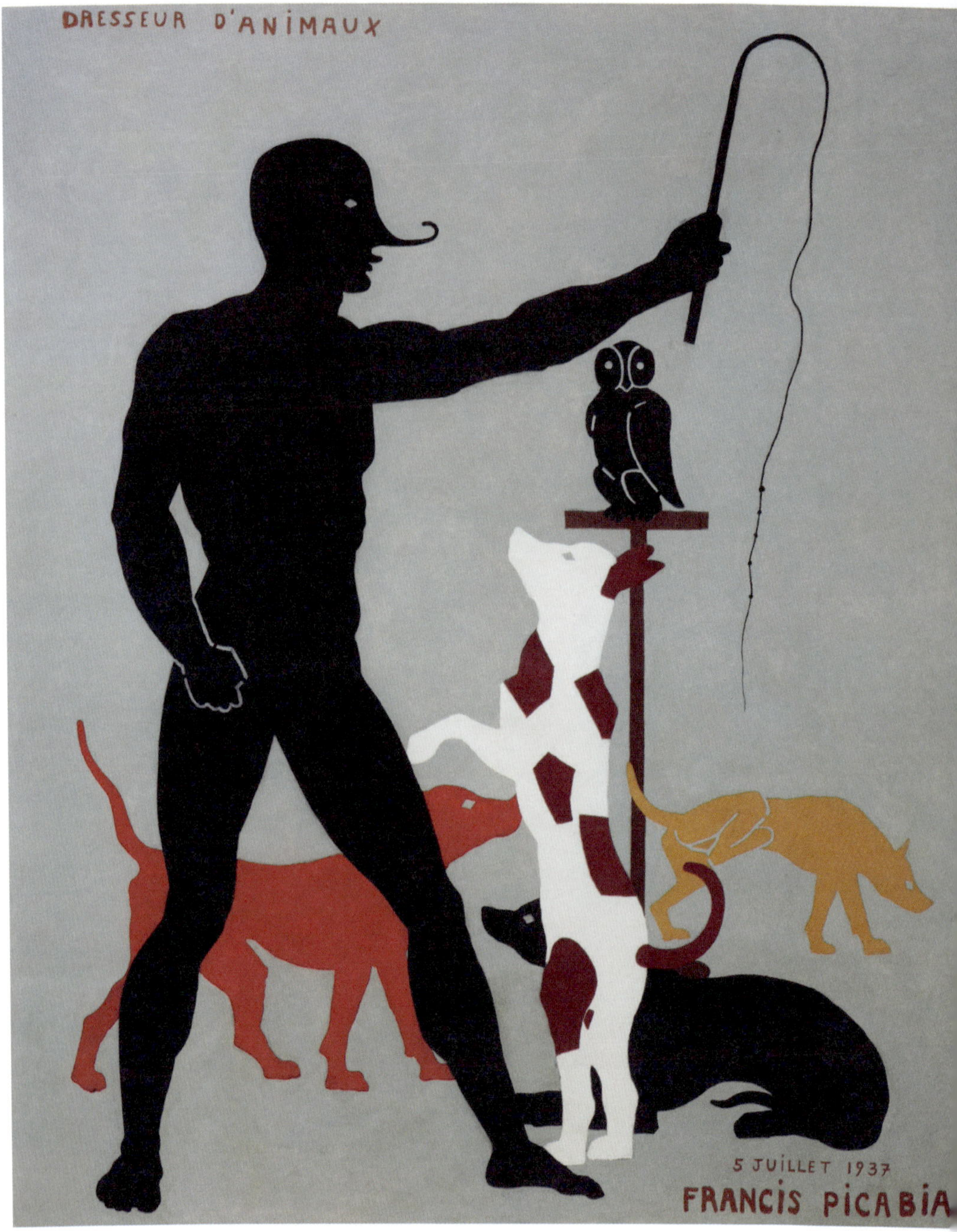

Francis Picabia, *Animal Trainer*, 1923

Mesoamerican peoples for two reasons: as a food source and to provide heat on cold nights. Its fur-free skin is remarkably warm to the touch, making it an effective substitute hot-water bottle. The name Xoloitzcuintle, pronounced *show-low-eats-queent-lee*, comes from the Aztecs, who revered them as guardians and believed they had healing properties.

The lapdog in Tanning's *Living Picture* (1954) has grown so huge that it will no longer fit on her lap. Instead, it rears up to embrace her, or perhaps to possess her – the meaning is unclear. The Lhasa Apso terrier in the picture originally belonged to Peggy Guggenheim, Max Ernst's third wife, but was shared by Ernst and Tanning after they married in 1946. It appears in a number of Tanning's works, where it sometimes becomes the American artist's alter ego.

Finally, in the 1950s, Francis Bacon painted several memorable portraits of feral dogs, one of which is shown overleaf. Based on the dog from Eadweard Muybridge's late 19th-century photographic studies of animal locomotion, *Dog* (1952) depicts an isolated, snarling creature, the smears of paint evoking a sense of vulnerability as well as aggression. This example and Bacon's other portraits in the same series brilliantly capture a very different side of modern canine existence, a mile away from the posh portraits of pampered pets we know so well.

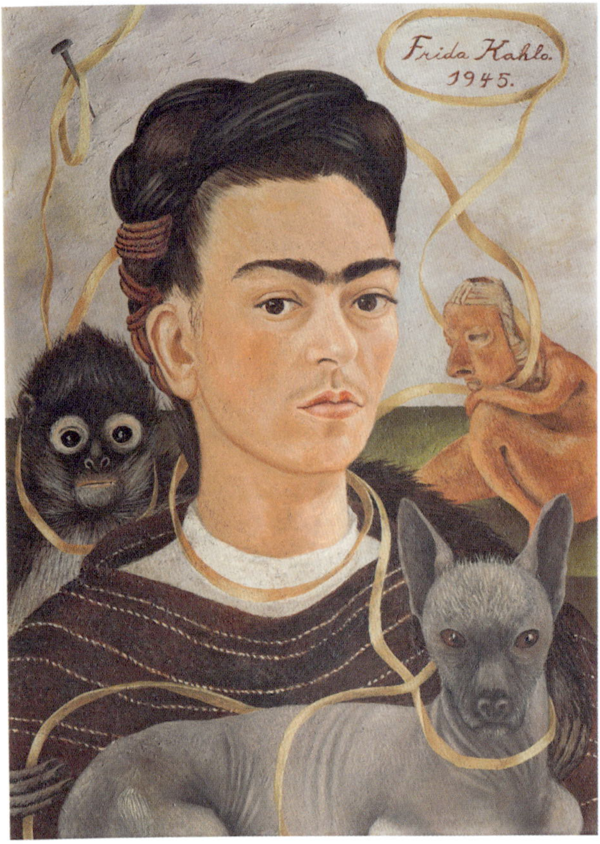

Frida Kahlo, *Self-Portrait with Small Monkey*, 1945

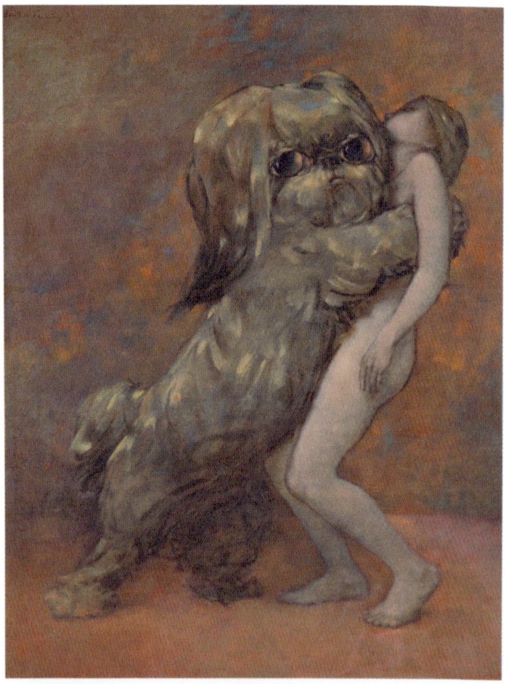

Dorothea Tanning, *Living Picture*, 1954

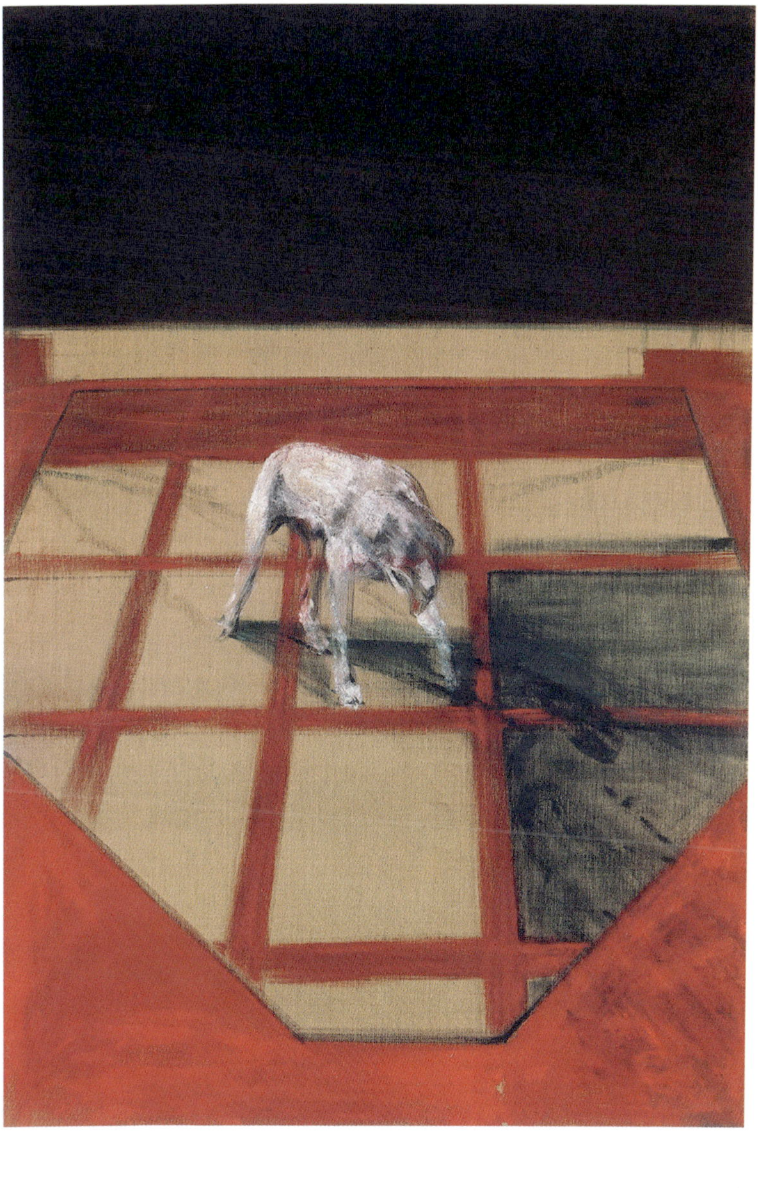

Francis Bacon, *Dog*, 1952

Fox

The fox has not been a popular image among surrealist artists, but there have been three striking examples, from Toyen, Victor Brauner and Leonora Carrington.

In a work entitled *At the Château Lacoste* (1943), Toyen's fox appears at first glance to be a wall graffito, then comes to life before our very eyes: the wily predator is caught in the act of killing a pigeon. The head of the fox is well-defined, although its tail is a sad stump rather than the long, traditional bush that it should be. The absence of the diagnostic red colour of the vulpine fur is perhaps another shortcoming. But, despite these omissions, Toyen's fox has an intense presence, with its teeth bared against an unseen rival who, presumably, is interested in stealing the dying bird. Toyen's title for this painting adds to its chilling presence, for the French castle of La Coste was the 18th-century home of the notorious Marquis de Sade. With this connection, the fox's predatory behaviour becomes a symbol of the Marquis's reputation for extreme cruelty. The painting was triggered by a set of photographs taken by Toyen's partner, the Czech surrealist Jindřich Štyrský, who was obsessed with de Sade. He had undertaken a pilgrimage to the ruined castle, where he had lovingly

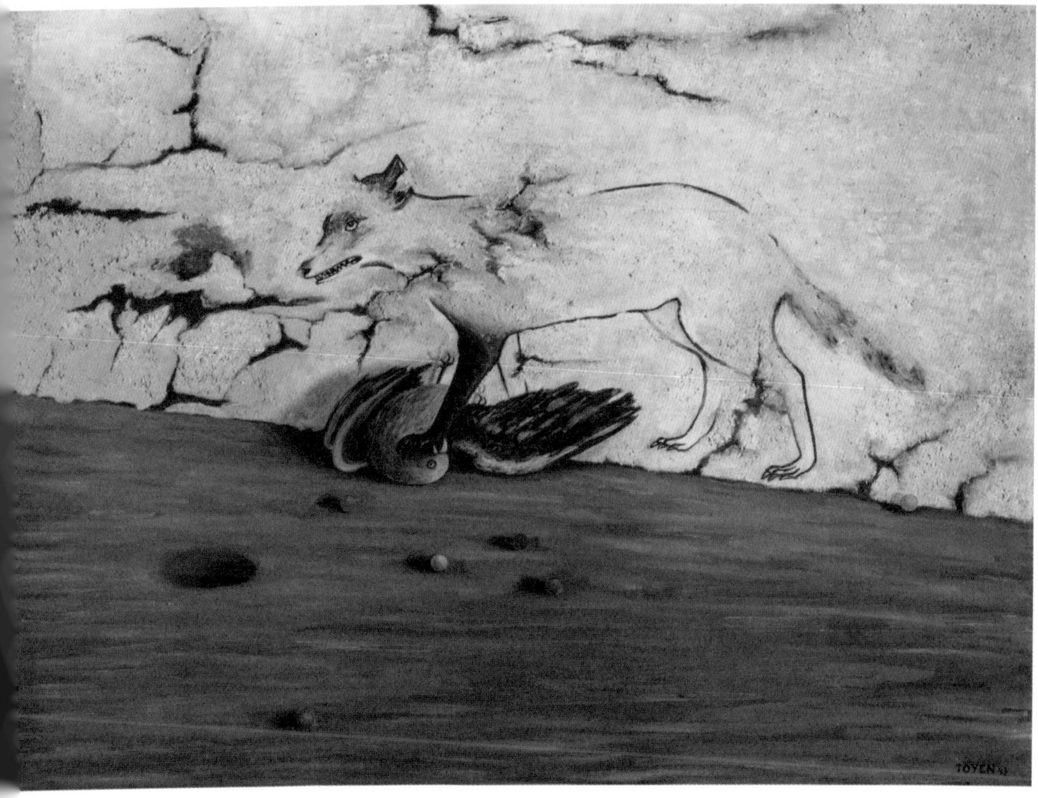

Toyen, *At the Château Lacoste*, 1943

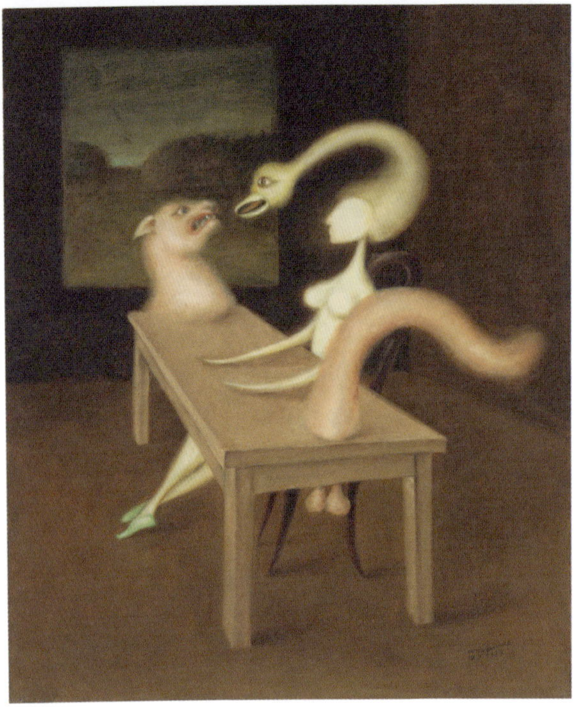

Victor Brauner, *Fascination*, 1939

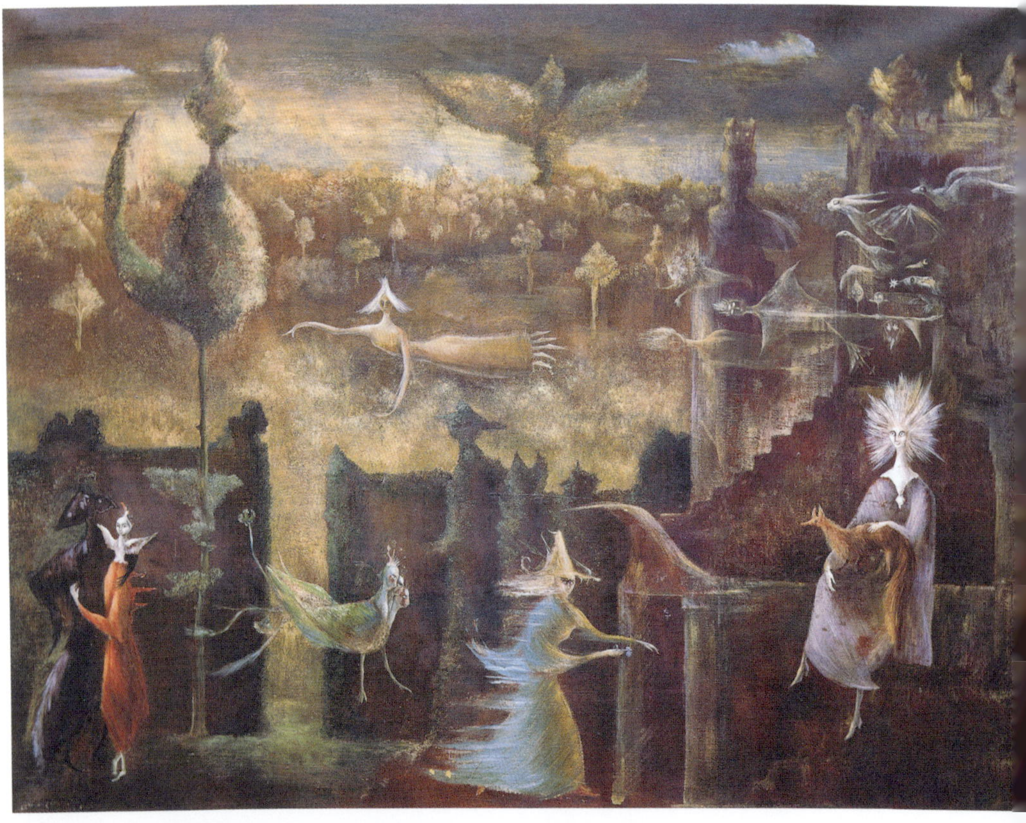

photographed the decaying walls and crumbling stonework. Toyen was fascinated by these images and began to incorporate them into paintings – as in the case of this menacing fox.

Victor Brauner's fox comes in two versions. The first is an object, a wooden table mounted with the stuffed head and tail of a taxidermied fox. The second is a painting of the same subject, but now with the addition of a strange nude female seated at the table, whose hair has grown into the head and neck of a bird that is threatening the fox. Brauner's misleading title for his surrealist object is *Loup-table* (*Wolf-Table*, 1939–47) – poetic licence, since the animal parts he used obviously came from a stuffed fox rather than a wolf. The title was presumably meant to give the work a more powerful predatory impact. The painting, on the other hand, is called *Fascination* (1939).

In *Nine, Nine, Nine* (1948), Leonora Carrington's fox lies like an exotic pet in the lap of a witch-like female whose hair shoots out from her head, as if electrified. Her fox has a disproportionately small head and a disproportionately large bushy tail. They sit in the corner of a complex, dreamlike landscape populated by strange female entities that, as in many of her works, appear to be drawn from folklore, myth and fantasy. Carrington lived for many years in Mexico, where there is a popular myth about a trickster fox that may have inspired the image in this painting. Indeed, the sword-wielding fictional character El Zorro, which means 'The Fox' in Spanish, was likely rooted in Mexican folklore.

onora Carrington,
ne, Nine, Nine, 1948

Ferret

The white, domesticated ferret (*Mustela furo*) is thought to have descended from the wild European polecat (*Mustela putorius*). For centuries, these small, inquisitive creatures have been used to control pests, including rodents on ships. They have also proved effective hunting companions, flushing out rabbits.

Symbolically, they represent playful curiosity. The English phrase 'ferreting something out' relates to this. There is only one major surrealist representation of ferrets, Leonora Carrington's *Ferret Race* (1952). This could have been a mundane event, but she transforms it into a magical scene in which thirteen white ferrets are seen scampering around a maze that has no end point. There is no way that they can actually win this race. They are enjoying the chase but, perhaps like the artist herself at this point in her life, they have no idea where they are headed. Significantly, they are accompanied in the maze by several naked young women and various other strange beings.

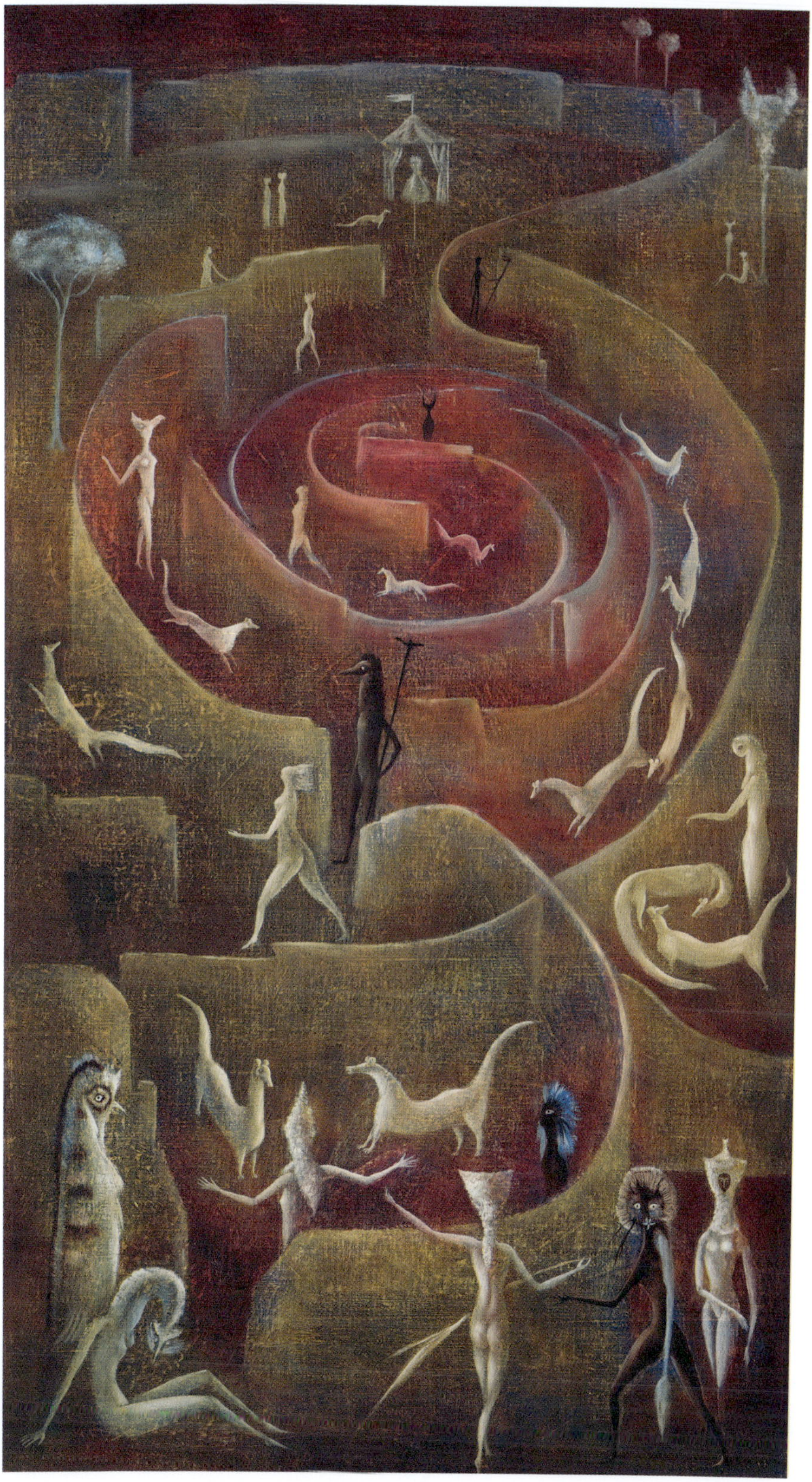

Leonora Carrington, *Ferret Race*, 1952

Hyena

The hyena has been described as the only major carnivore that lacks grace and dignity. The refined anatomy and elegant movements of the big cats are things of beauty. The perceived ugliness and ungainliness of the hyena offer a striking contrast. Yet, in nature, it is an efficient and successful killer and scavenger, with massive jaws and bulging neck muscles, capable of tearing its prey to pieces with ease.

The hyena makes a noteworthy appearance in the work of Leonora Carrington and Victor Brauner. In Carrington's *Self-Portrait* (*c.* 1937–38), it plays a major role. The artist herself sits alone in a strange, almost empty room, her only companion a female striped hyena (*Hyaena hyaena*) that is conspicuously lactating. A tailless rocking horse floats behind her, and through an elaborately dressed window a white horse can be seen galloping away. There is a sinister tale behind Carrington's relationship with the hyena, which we know from a short story she wrote around the same time, called 'The Debutante' (1938). She was herself a debutante in real life – the daughter of a rich industrialist who had her presented at court. But she found herself at odds with the vacuous pomp of high society and, when she encountered

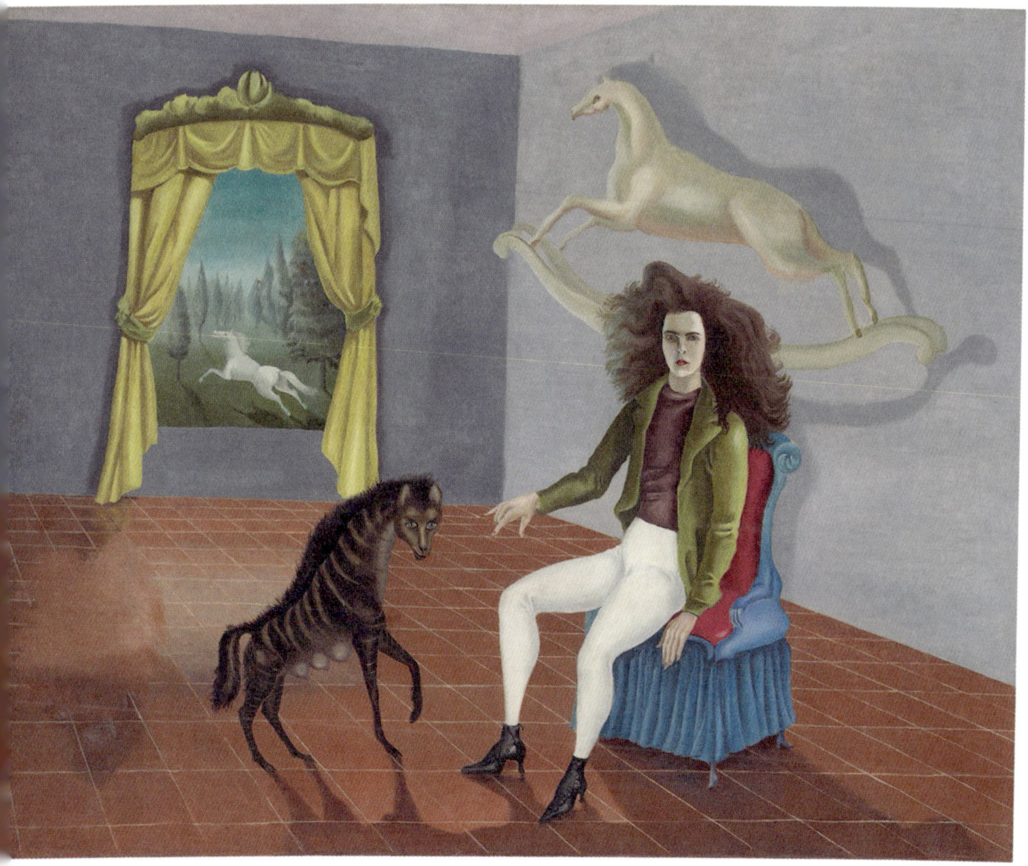

Leonora Carrington, *Self-Portrait*, c. 1937–38

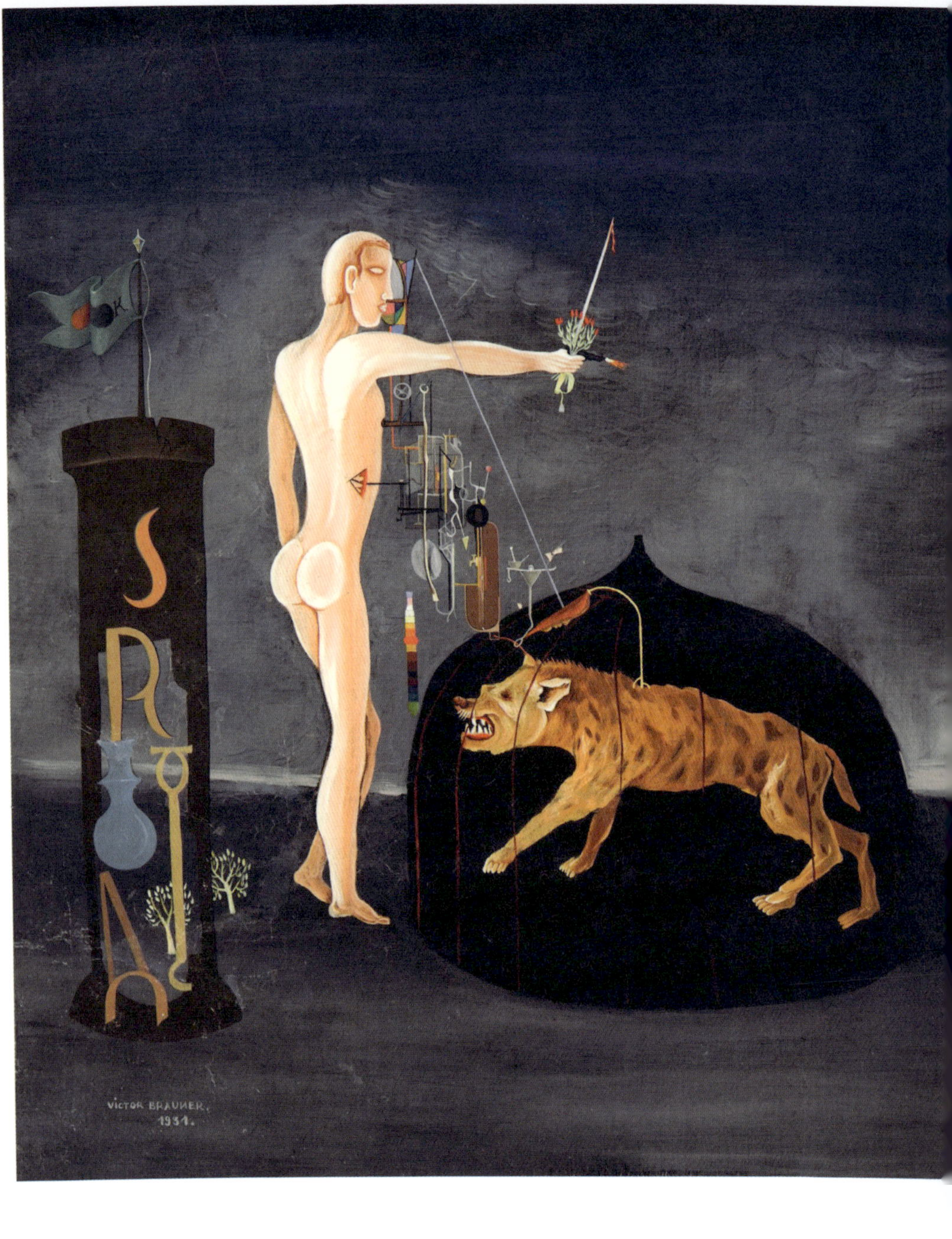

Victor Brauner, *Person with a Dragon*, 1931

the surrealists in London in 1936, she became a member of their rebellious group and was soon in a relationship with Max Ernst.

In 'The Debutante', the girl at the centre of the story hates her rigid upbringing and befriends a hyena she meets at the zoo. She tells the animal that she is dreading a glamorous ball that is being held in her honour, and the hyena offers to go in her place. The problem is disguising the hyena's face, but the animal solves this difficulty by tearing the human face off the girl's maid and wearing that. The hyena also has a pungent smell and is just about to sit at the table with the rest of the party, when one of the guests complains that she stinks. 'I smell a little strong, eh?' the hyena says, before eating her disguise – the face of the maid – and escaping out of a window.

Lurking behind this tale is Carrington's desire to remove herself from the restrictions of polite society and a natural affinity with the wild animal, free of formalities and able to do as she wishes. Much later in life, in an interview conducted in 1999, Carrington identifies with this creature, saying: 'I am like a hyena, I get into the garbage cans. I have an insatiable curiosity.'

In Victor Brauner's *Person with a Dragon* (1931), the 'dragon' is clearly an adult spotted hyena (*Crocuta crocuta*). A naked man stands with his back to us, firing a gun at something unseen. A complicated piece of laboratory apparatus connects the man and the hyena, which is caged. Showing its formidable teeth, the animal snarls aggressively as if preparing to launch a savage attack.

Cat

Cats have fascinated a host of modern artists, including Andy Warhol, who had 26 – all but one named Sam – and even created an illustrated book about them. And the Argentinian surrealist Leonor Fini surrounded herself with a whole colony of them. At one time she had no fewer than 23 living with her in her apartment.

Just to be different, Salvador Dalí had a pet ocelot (*Leopardus pardalis*), a wild feline that came from Colombia. He called it Babou and would take it to restaurants with him on a collar and lead. It often caused trouble and, when one diner demanded its removal because it was a wild animal, Dalí retorted that it was only a domestic cat that he had painted to look wild.

Symbolically, the cat stands for haughty independence, perversity, predatory cunning and stealthy savagery. Its soft, strokable fur also identifies it as a symbol of sexual contact and it is the slang word for female genitals in a number of languages, including French, German and English (*la chatte, Muschi* and 'pussy', respectively). But, for the surrealist artists, it is the cat's key anatomical features that have most appeal. It is possible to say 'cat' visually with only a few lines. In Miró's *Head (The White Cat)* (1927), the cat has been reduced to nothing more than a pair of eyes and long, curved whiskers.

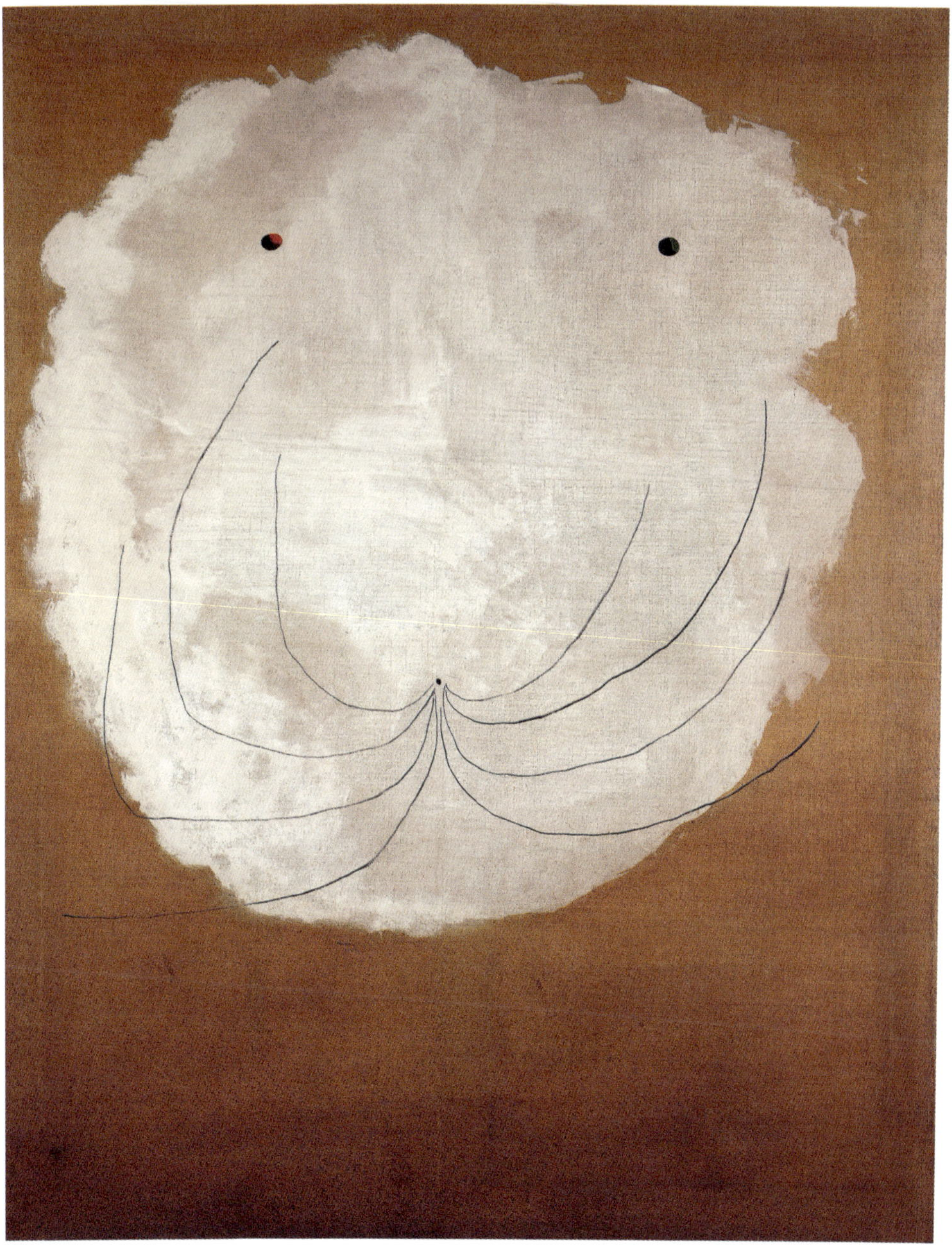

Joan Miró, *Head (The White Cat)*, 1927

In the paintings of Leonor Fini, the cat is a soft, erotic being, smoothly rounded and inviting you to caress its fur. There is a famous photograph of her with one of her long-haired pet cats held between her thighs, leaving little doubt as to its sexual symbolism. Cats dominated her life, sleeping in her bed and even roaming freely on her dining table, sampling the food, to the dismay of her guests. When she was painting, she was surrounded by cats. They even sat on her palette. It has been said that a work by Fini is only genuine if it has cats' hairs embedded in the paint. She summed up her adoration of cats with the words: 'The cat is for us the warm, furry, moustached and purring memory of a lost paradise.'

In the dreamlike *Sunday Afternoon* (1980), Fini portrays two of her great loves – the form of a young woman and her pet cats. She was openly bisexual and this painting erotically combines the softness of the woman's body with the soft feline fur.

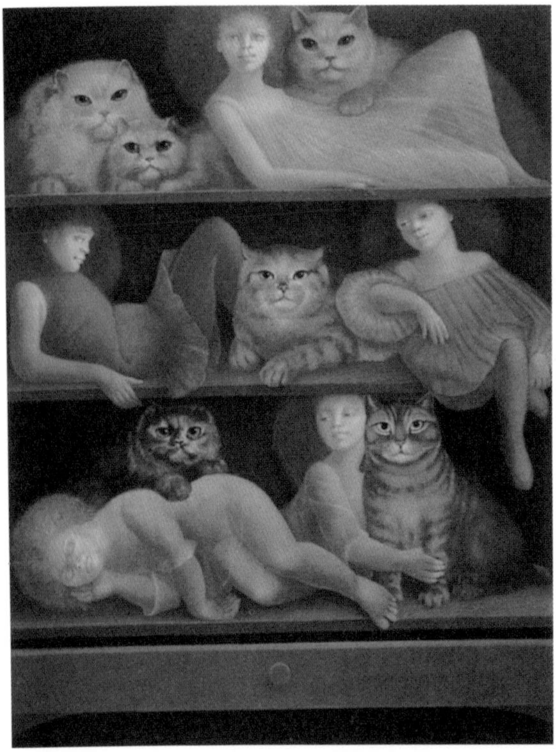

Leonor Fini, *Sunday Afternoon*, 1980

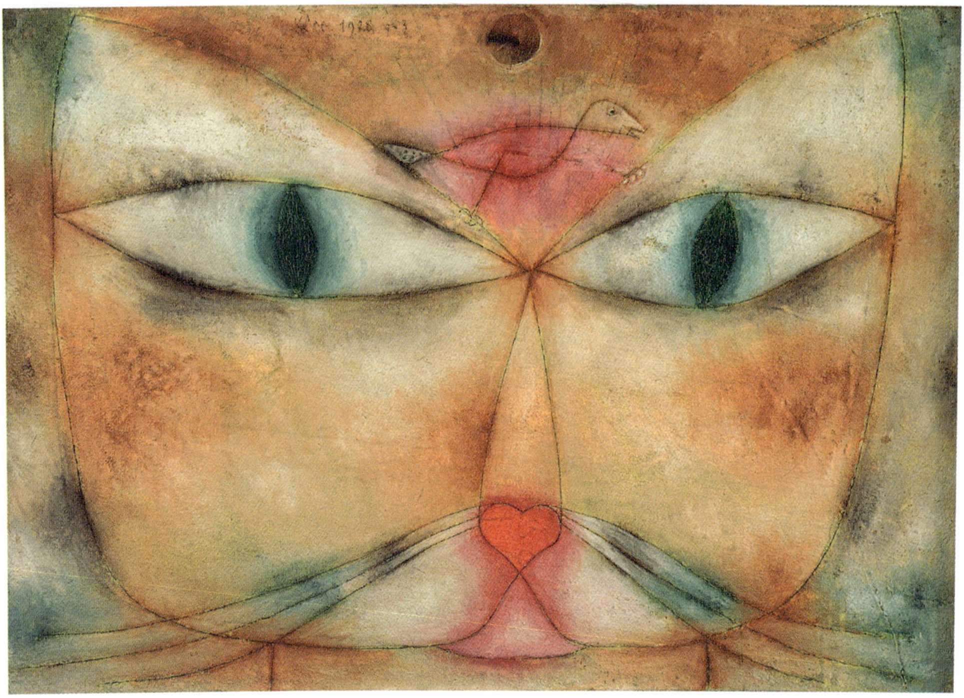

Paul Klee, *Cat and Bird*, 1928

Paul Klee nearly always had a pet cat as a companion in his studio. The first of these arrived in 1902 and was followed by a string of others until the artist's death in 1940. The most important was Bimbo, whom Klee and his wife adopted from their close friend, the dancer Karla Grosch, after her move to Tel Aviv in 1933. Bimbo was a long-haired white cat that followed the artist everywhere and was photographed climbing his shoulders. With his great love of cats, it is not surprising to find that they appear in some twenty paintings. The most famous of these is *Cat and Bird* (1928), which captures the intense facial expression of a hunting cat. The bird in this picture appears to be not just on the cat's mind but inside its brain – an impression that is emphasized by the focus on the cat's head, which takes up the entire canvas. In an earlier abstract work on paper, *The Mountain of the Sacred*

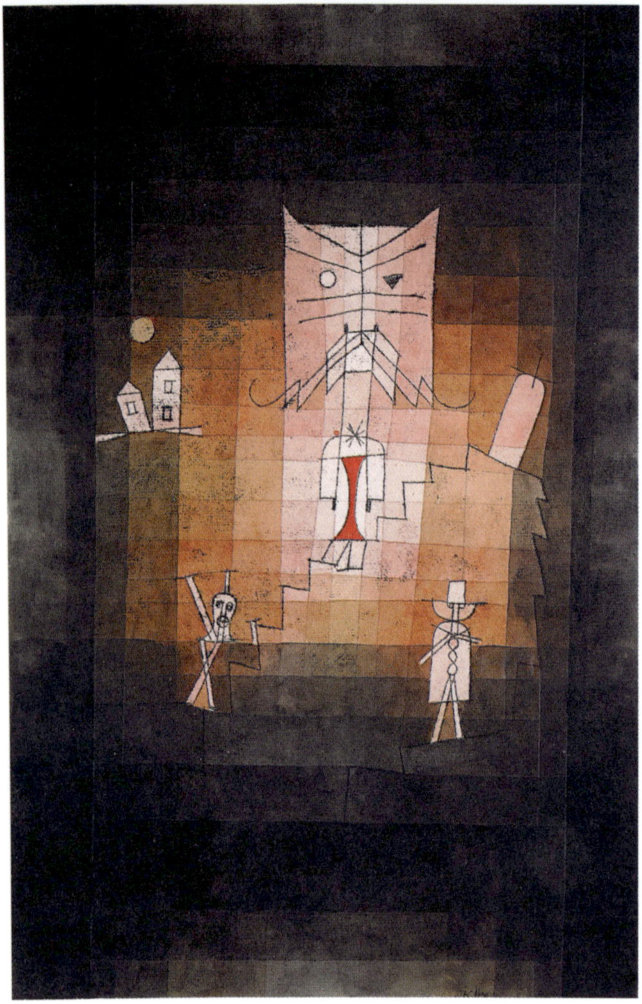

Paul Klee, *The Mountain of the Sacred Cat*, 1923

Cat (1923), the central feline figure – set against an orange-pink background of geometric shapes – dwarfs the tiny stick people beneath it. Here, as the title suggests, Klee elevates the cat to the level of a deity.

A cat features prominently in an early work by Marc Chagall, *Paris through the Window* (1913), painted three years after the artist moved to the French capital from Russia. Chagall famously resisted literal interpretations of his paintings, and this work deliberately blurs the boundaries between the worlds of dream and reality. Dominated by the unmistakable shape of the Eiffel Tower, the scene appears to show the Paris skyline through an open window. However, on closer inspection, the cat has a human face. Other dreamlike elements include a human figure with two faces, an upside-down train and a couple who seem to float horizontally.

Other surrealists who featured cats of one kind or another in their works include Toyen, Leo Dohmen, Leonora Carrington, Remedios Varo, Edward Burra, Francis Picabia and Victor Brauner.

Marc Chagall, *Paris through the Window*, 1913

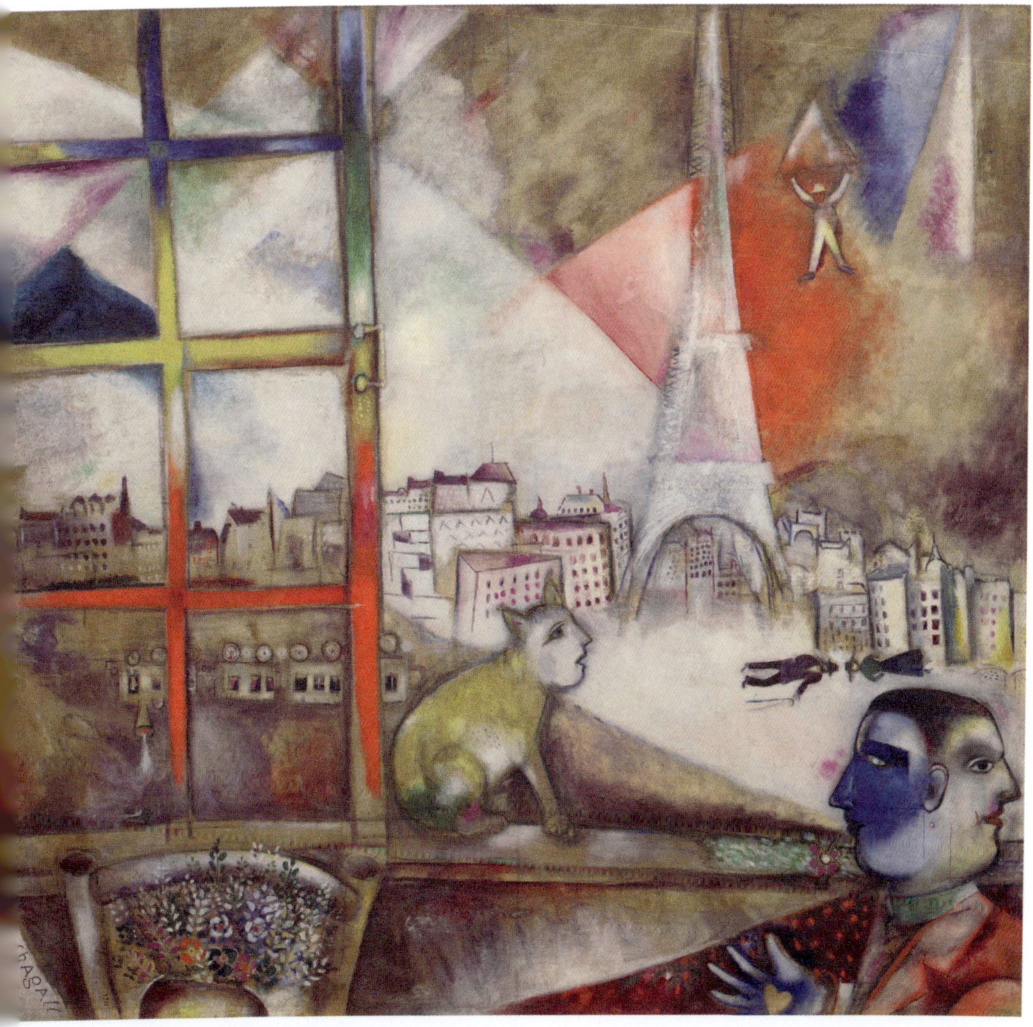

Lion

As one of the great predators at the top of the food chain, and with its distinctive male mane, the lion is, for surrealist artists, the most popular of the big cats. Tigers, jaguars, leopards and cheetahs also appear occasionally, but they are outnumbered by images of lions. There is a leonine presence in works by Salvador Dalí, Óscar Domínguez, Max Ernst, Toyen, Conroy Maddox and Clovis Trouille.

The best of Dalí's lions appears in *The Accommodations of Desire* (1929), which explores the artist's anxieties over his affair with his future wife Gala, who was married to the surrealist poet Paul Éluard at the time. The painting includes seven pebbles on which Dalí has envisioned what his future would hold. The head of a male lion is shown on four of the pebbles. These lion heads were not painted by the artist but cut out – presumably from a children's book – and stuck onto the work. On one pebble, we see only the mouth of the lion. On another, the red silhouette of the lion's head has been applied. On a third pebble, the face has been removed to leave only the mane, and on the fourth the lion appears in its complete form. With the arrogance of the artist, Dalí dismembers the great beast, playing fast and loose with its image.

In 1939, obsessed with Hollywood extremes, Dalí gave us the memorable chimera, part lion, part actress, that he called *Shirley Temple, the Youngest, Most Sacred Monster of the Cinema in her Time.* In this disturbingly sexualized portrayal of Temple, a blistering attack on the adult overtones imposed on child stars, the

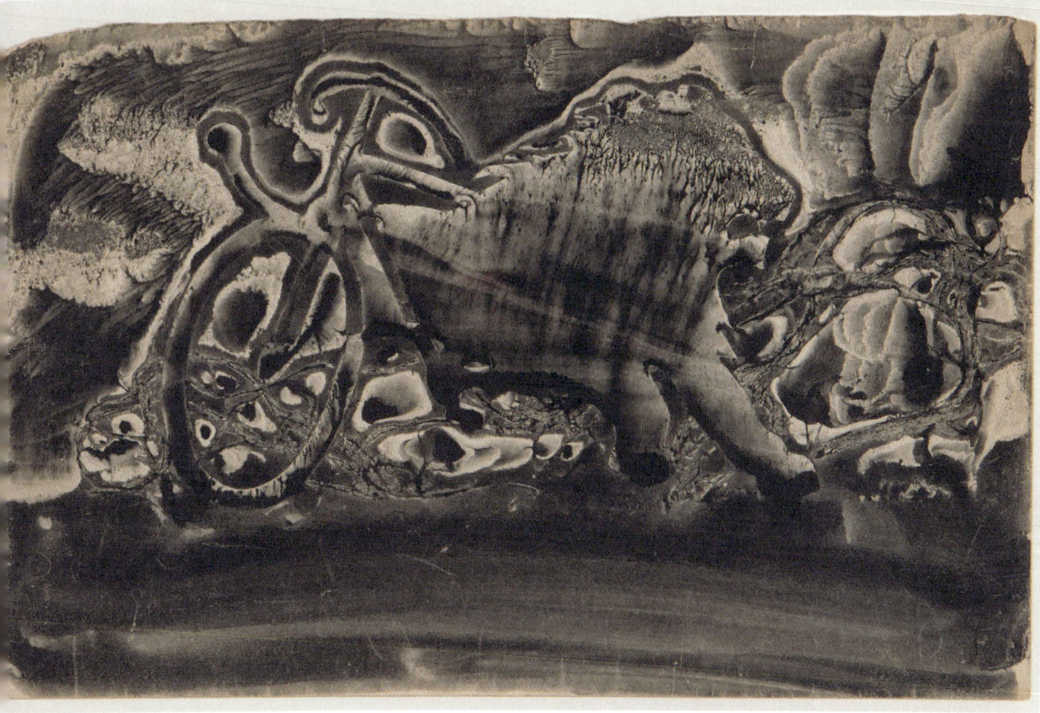

Óscar Domínguez, *Lion-Bicycle*, 1936

Salvador Dalí, *The Accommodations of Desire*, 1929

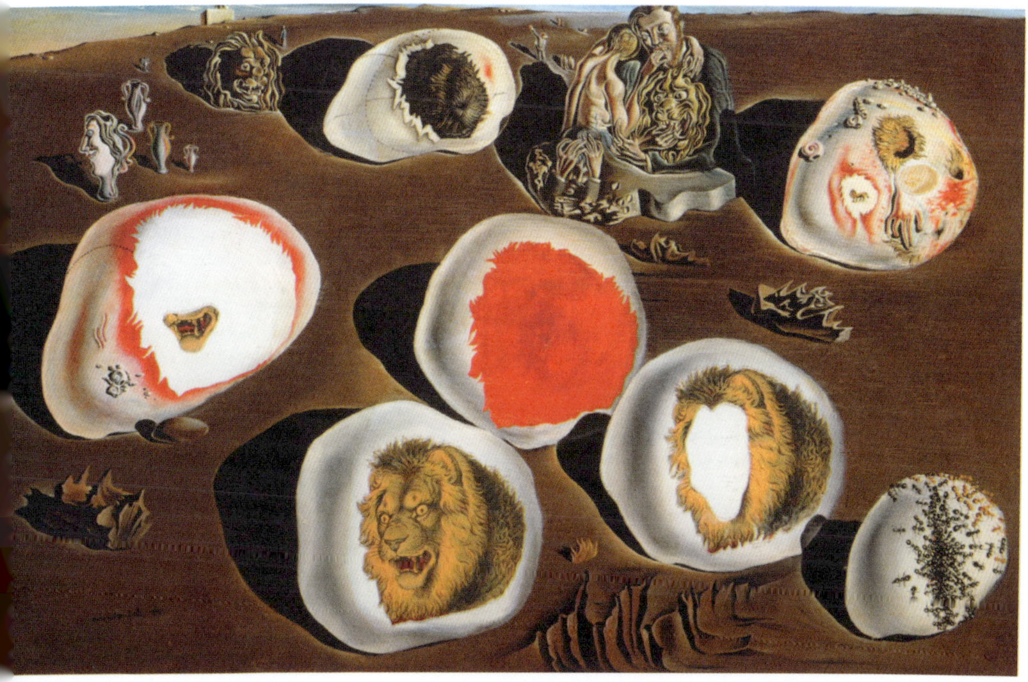

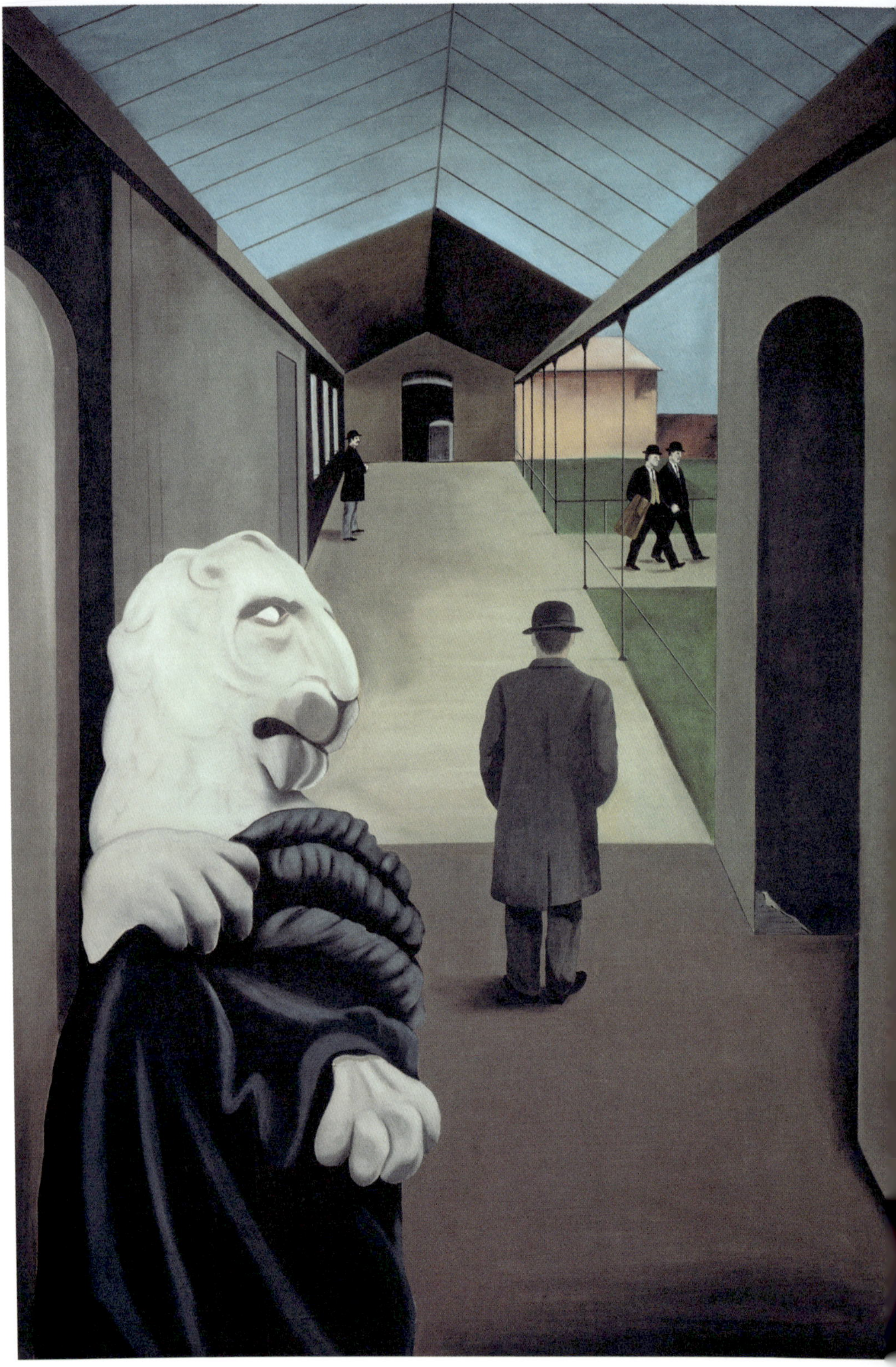

 Conroy Maddox, *Passage de l'Opéra*, 1940/1970–71

artist applies a cutout from a black-and-white newspaper image of Temple's face onto the body of a busty red lioness with long claws. We know it is a lioness, incidentally, because it has the leonine tufted tail-tip. For good measure, Dalí has added a vampire bat with spread wings on Temple's head, while the discarded bones from her latest kills are scattered over the ground.

Óscar Domínguez's unique chimera is part lion and (of all things) part bicycle. The lion's mane has been created by the clever use of decalcomania. This was a surrealist technique that Domínguez himself had created in 1936, the year he painted his *Lion-Bicycle*. Decalcomania consisted of pressing painted paper against a sheet of glass and then pulling it free to create complex patterns that could be modified to make unusual surrealist images.

In Conroy Maddox's *Passage de l'Opéra* (1940/1970–71), an upright stone lion in the foreground is given a human stance and is made all the more human by the addition of a robe. Like some stern Roman emperor, standing stiffly at one end of the passageway, the white lion in the black cloak surveys the scene and one can't help wondering if it is considering the possibility of making a meal of the man in a bowler hat (a reference, perhaps, to Magritte?). British-born Maddox travelled to Paris in the 1930s, and this depiction of the Passage de l'Opéra – an arcade that the surrealist poet Louis Aragon had written about at length, lamenting its demolition – was painted from memory.

Clovis Trouille's *Justine* (1937) portrays a realistic male lion that has been strapped to the floor. Trouille gives this helpless beast the most unusual task of using the tuft at the end of its tail as a fig-leaf for a naked redhead who has been tied to a giant phallic post, which is supported by a metal tripod. Bizarrely, this purple 'phallus' seems to have grown a pair of hands that are clasping the woman's body.

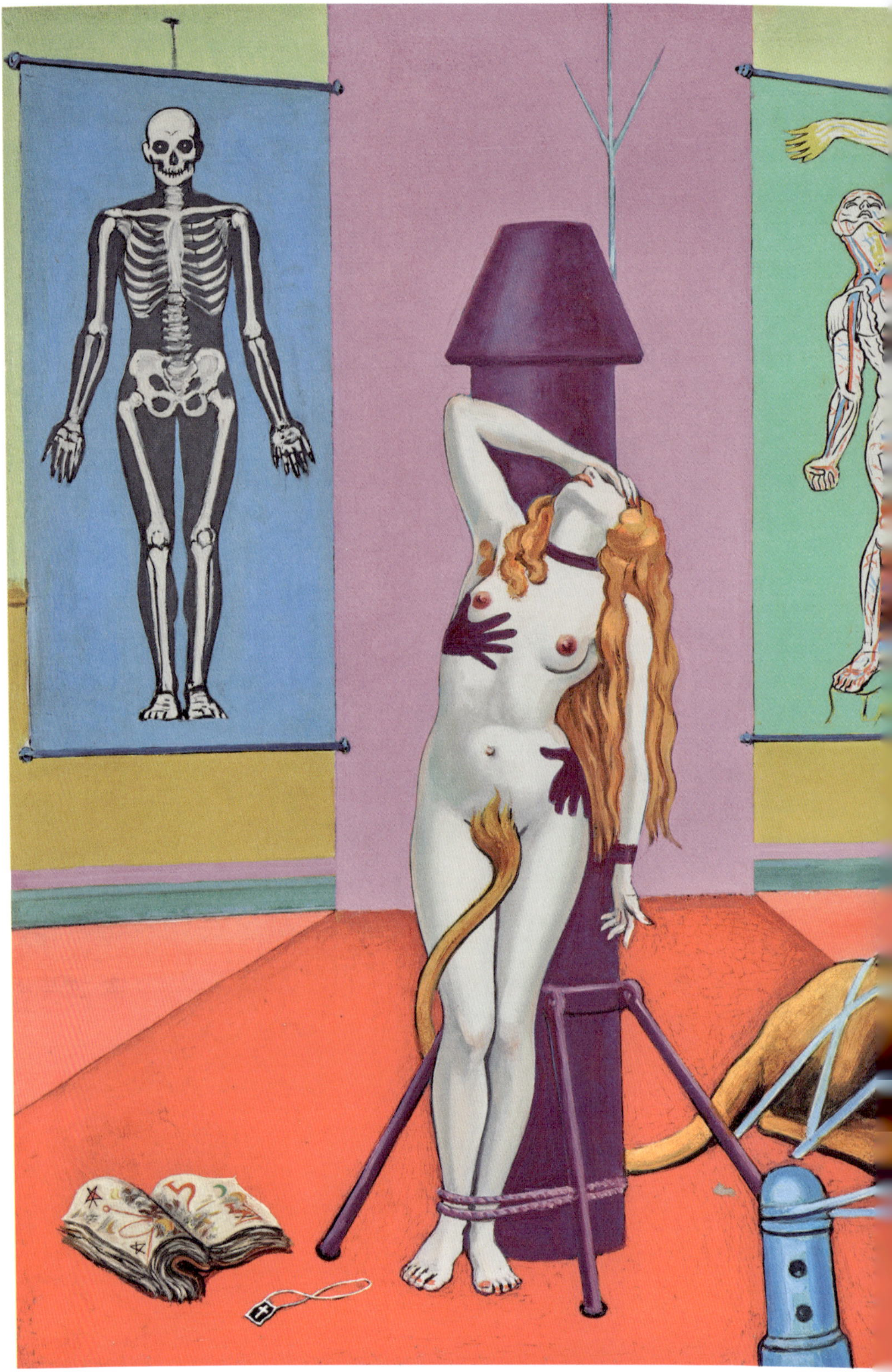

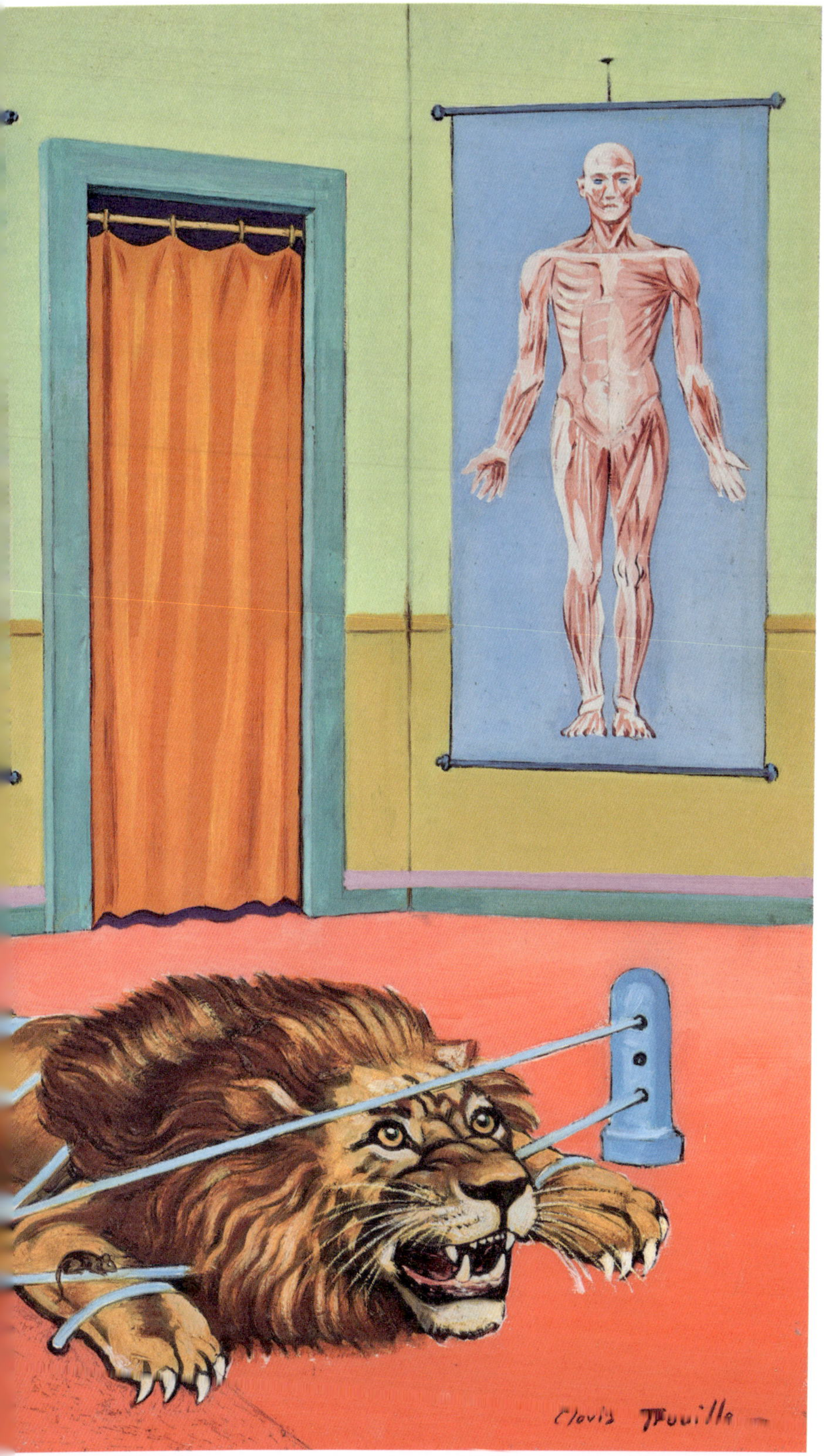

Clovis Trouille, *Justine*, 1937

Tiger

Like the lion, the tiger is a powerful presence in any work of art – the ultimate predator, fearless and immensely strong. It lacks the lion's great mane, but its striped coat allows the surrealist artist to play visual games. In Jane Graverol's *The Evil Star* (1956), the stripes of the huge cat become confused with the vertical bars of its zoo cage.

In Dalí's technical masterpiece of 1944, with the elaborate title *Dream Caused by the Flight of a Bee around a Pomegranate a Second before Waking*, two foreshortened tigers are shown leaping together into a savage attack. They are a pair, with the male on the left and the female on the right. The male has a larger, wider head, with a ruff or collar that is absent in the female. Bizarrely, Dalí's male tiger is emerging from the widely gaping mouth of a red fish, which itself appears to spring from an exploding pomegranate. The jaws of this tiger are wide open, exposing its massive canine teeth. Next to it, the tigress is also snarling and appears to be trying to grab hold of a floating bayonet that will wake the sleeping figure of Gala, Dalí's wife and muse, who floats above rocks in the lower half of the painting. The pomegranate and bee of the title float beside her – the buzzing of the bee appearing

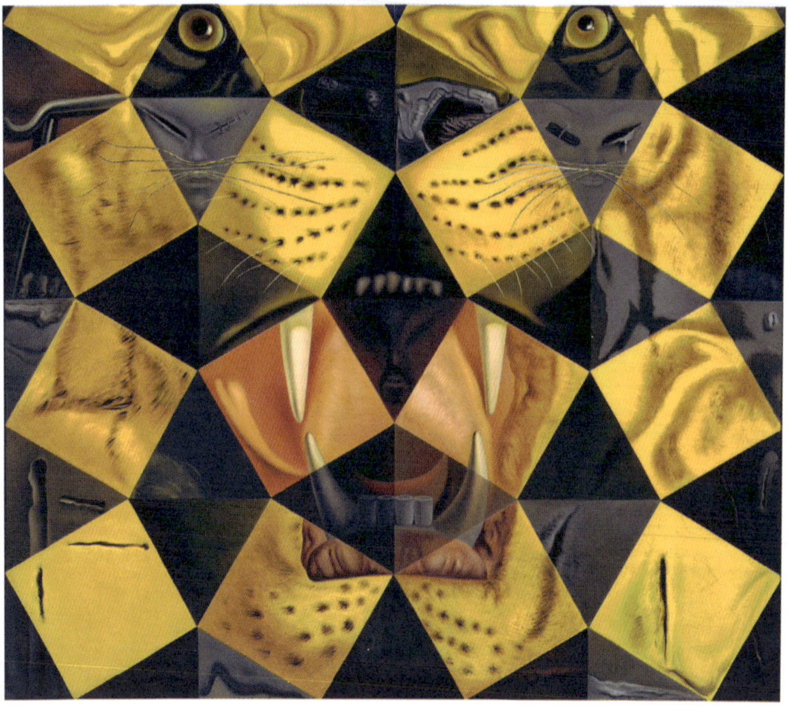

Salvador Dalí, *Lenin Tiger*, 1962

Jane Graverol, *The Evil Star*, 1956

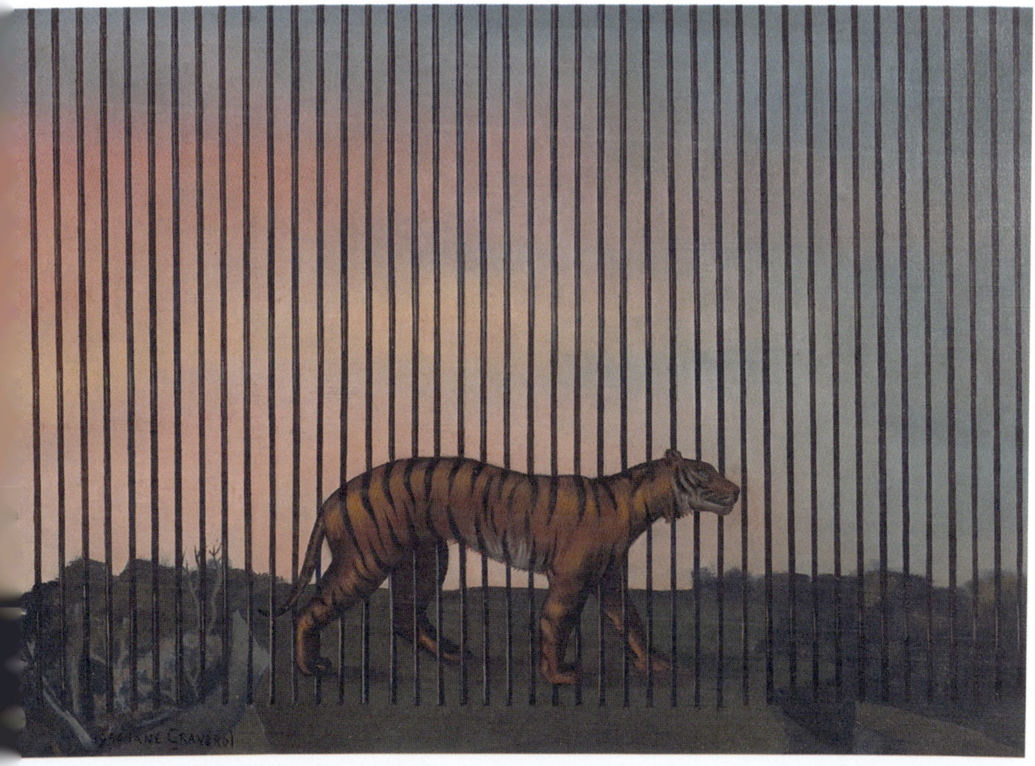

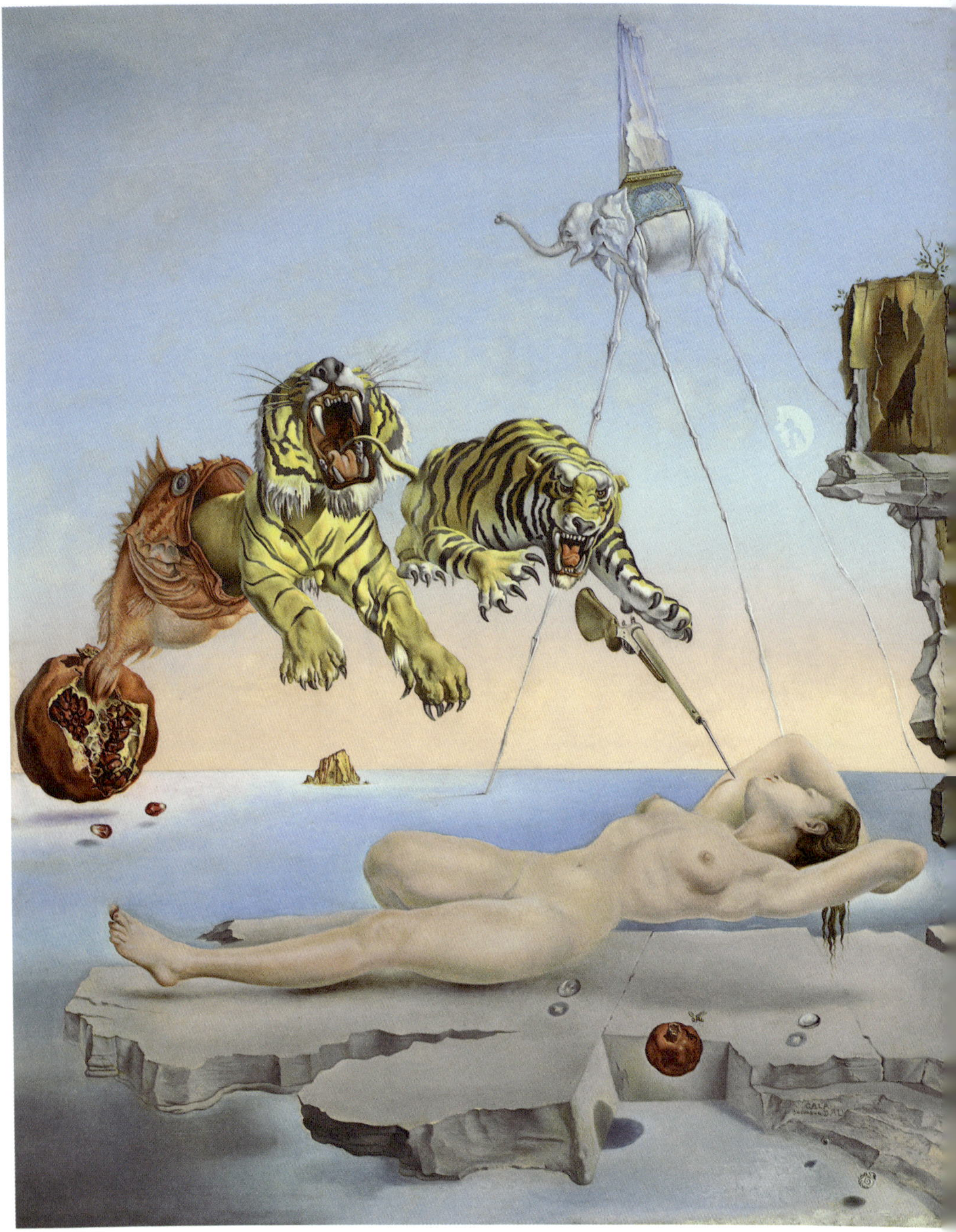

Salvador Dalí, *Dream Caused by the Flight of a Bee around a Pomegranate a Second before Waking*, 1944

to have stimulated the dream unfolding in the upper part of the painting. These elements are given an unusual backdrop: the sea, on which an elephant with impossibly long, spindly legs walks on water, teetering precariously.

In a later Dalí work, commonly known as *Lenin Tiger* (1962), the outline of the tiger's head is hard to make out. This abstract oil on canvas is one of Dalí's complex, layered compositions that plays with our perception, tricking the eye into seeing multiple different versions of the work depending on where the viewer is standing. As Dalí explains in the much longer, official title, this work consists of *Fifty Abstract Paintings that from Two Metres Change into Three Lenins Disguised as a Chinese and from Six Metres Form the Head of a Royal Tiger.*

Cheetah

The cheetah is synonymous with slender, elegant speed. It is the fastest mammal on earth, able to reach speeds of up to 68 mph (109 kmph) over short distances.

It features only rarely in the surrealist menagerie, but it does appear in several works by the Czech surrealist Toyen. In *The New World of Love* (1968), six cheetahs dissolve into a chequerboard background, their stern faces fixing us with a cold stare, as though we are about to become the next meal – if we cannot run fast enough. We can only hope that these are resting cheetahs and that we are safe, at least for the moment.

In a strange painting made a few years earlier, *The Dream* (1964), Toyen reduces the animal to just its forelegs – the athletic limbs on which it depends for survival. The cheetah's legs emerge, in parallel symmetry, from what appears to be the interior wall of a building. The rest of the cheetah's body is obscured and only visible as a black shadow, trapped behind the wall. Another shadow, of an unseen woman, also appears on the adjacent wall. The predator appears resting but is poised, ready for the chase.

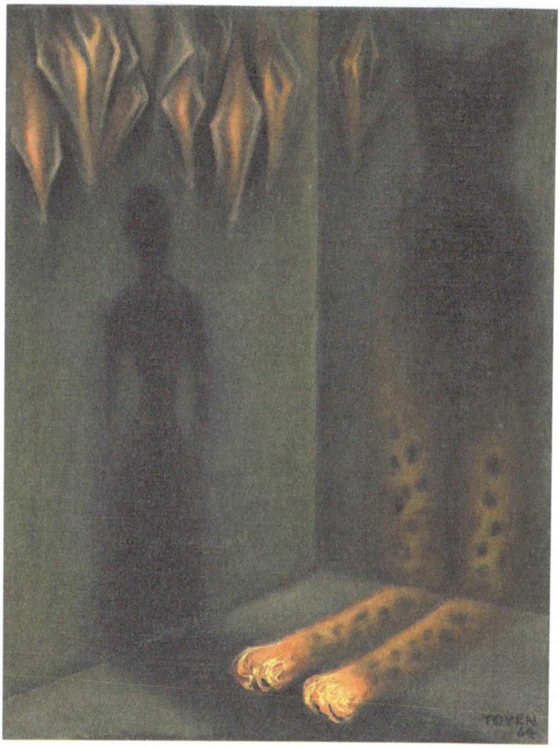

Toyen, *The Dream*, 1964

Toyen, *The New World of Love*, 1968

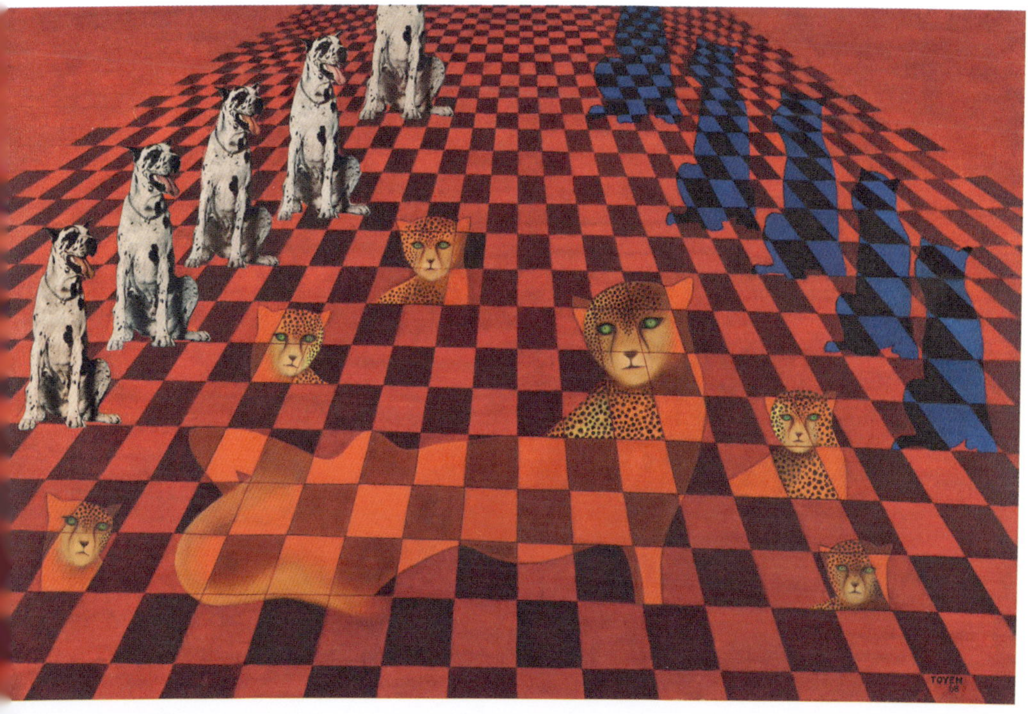

Sea Lion

The sea lion is rarely encountered in surrealist art, but there are two amusing examples, both of which take the old-fashioned, performing circus sea lion as their starting point.

The most iconic image of the circus sea lion shows the animal cleverly balancing a ball on the tip of its nose, and the obvious surrealist strategy is to ask what would be the most irrelevant, irrational object to introduce as a replacement for that familiar ball.

In *Le Ludion* (1956), the Belgian surrealist photographer Leo Dohmen decided to give his sea lion a traditional Christian crucifix to balance on its nose, thus reducing the sacred symbol of Christianity to the level of a circus joke. This deliberate insult fits in well with André Breton's well-known hatred of all things religious. Dohmen's title for this work refers to the dancers who came to ancient Rome and performed in circus games, where they improvised movements without the accompaniment of music.

New Zealander Michael Parekōwhai returns the insult by making his sea lion balance a surrealist icon on its nose. Instead of a crucifix we now find Marcel Duchamp's mounted bicycle wheel (1913), the first of his famous 'readymades', held perilously aloft. Parekōwhai, of a younger generation of surrealists, is of Māori and European descent, and his art commonly features familiar objects in unfamiliar situations, in the tradition so favoured by Magritte. Another of his sea lions balances a full-size grand piano on its nose. Parekōwhai's obscure titles would also have pleased Magritte. His Duchamp piece has the enigmatic title *My Sister, My Self*, while the version with the piano is called *The Horn of Africa* (both 2006).

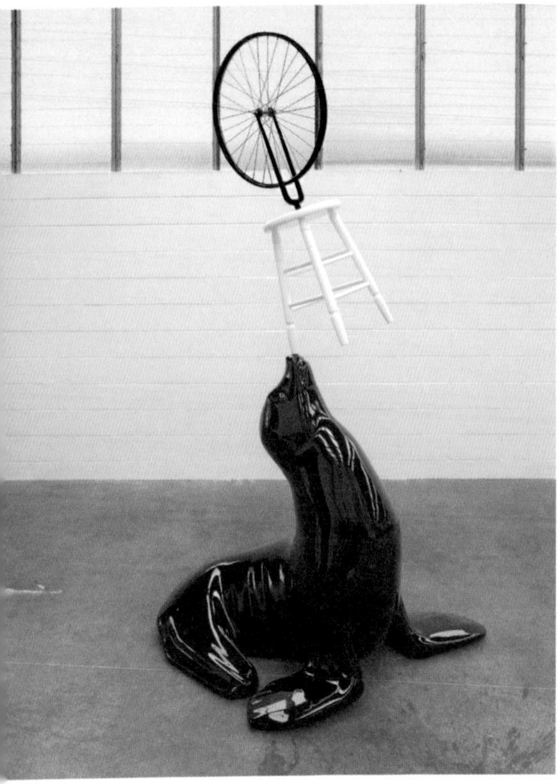

Michael Parekōwhai, *My Sister, My Self*, 2006

Leo Dohmen, *Le Ludion*, 1956

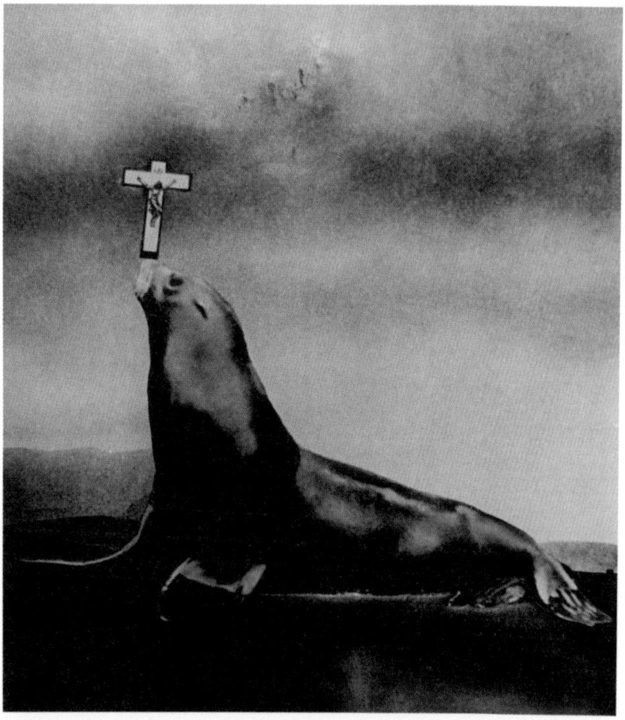

The Ele

phants

Elephant

The most famous of all surrealist elephants must surely be Max Ernst's *Celebes* (1921). For those who do not know the history of this iconic work, it may come as a surprise to learn that we owe its central image not to Ernst, but to a certain Major Hans Schomburgk. He was an early 20th-century explorer, and it was he who, in 1915, photographed a huge earthenware construction with a rounded, elephantine body shape, standing on short, stocky legs. This communal grain bin, made by the Konkomba people of Tschopowa in Togoland (which encompassed what is now the nation of Togo and parts of Ghana in West Africa), was filled from the top and was able to hold several tons of grain and protect it from rats, mice and fire. It is unique in shape and its resemblance to the rear end of an elephant must have amused Ernst, who used it as the basis for his painting, adding a pair of tusks and a variety of irrational details to create an unforgettable surrealist composition. Scholarly attempts to interpret these irrational additions are misguided: the essence of this painting is its dreamlike mystery.

The name *Celebes*, given to the painting by Ernst, is said to come from an obscene German schoolboy rhyme. 'The Elephant

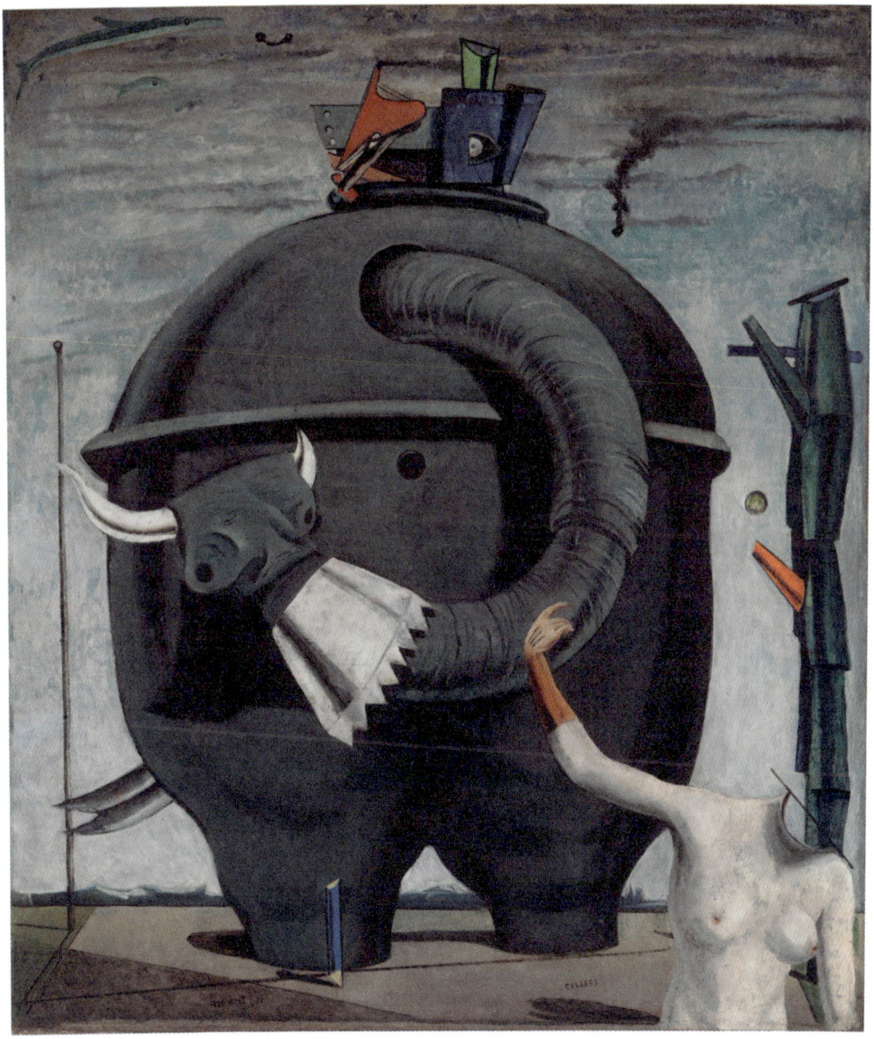

Max Ernst, *Celebes*, 1921

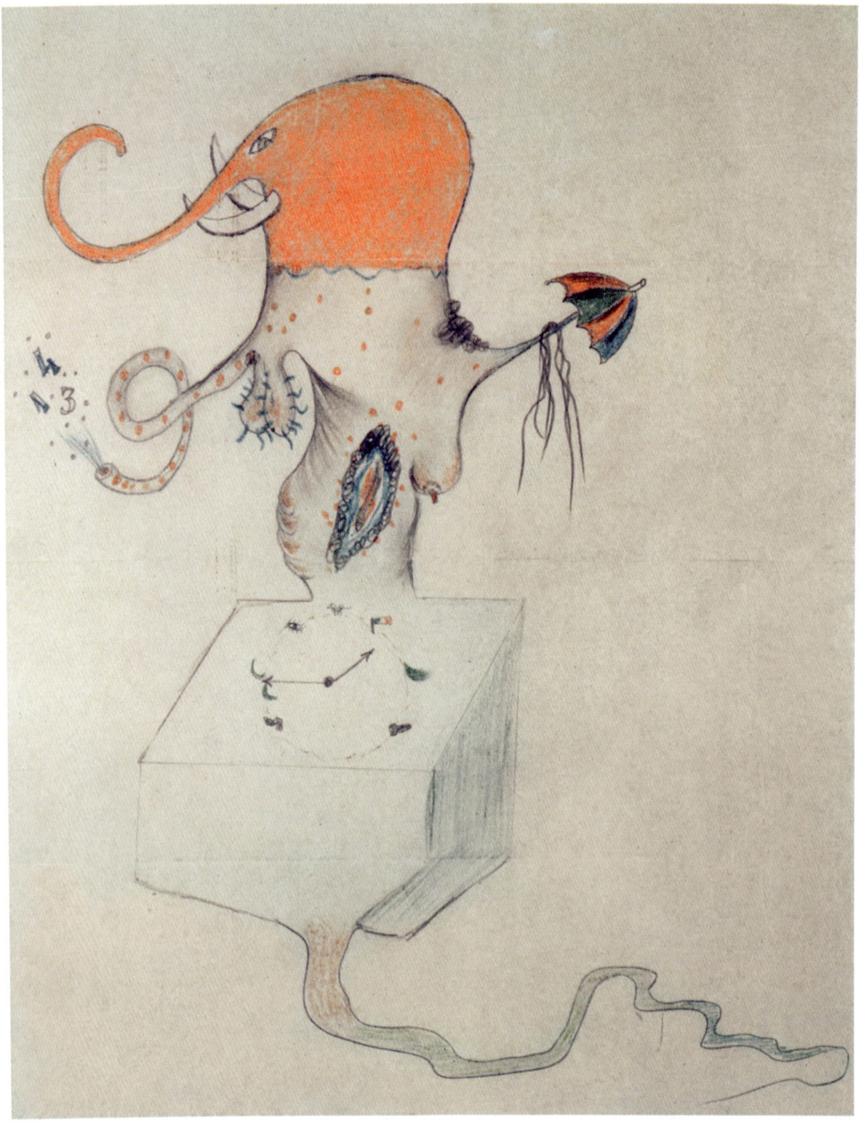

André Breton, *Head Section of an Exquisite Corpse*, 1926

of Celebes', as it appears in that rhyme, probably got its name from the fact that the Indonesian island of Celebes (now known as Sulawesi), when viewed on a map, has the rough outline of an elephant with a raised trunk.

A lesser-known surrealist elephant appears in 1926, in the head section of an exquisite corpse drawing. Exquisite corpse – a game in which participants take it in turns to add elements to a drawing on a folded piece of paper, without seeing the others' contributions – became popular in the 1920s when surrealist artists adopted it as a technique to create collaborative compositions. This example was made in crayon by André Breton. Among its strange features, the grotesque elephantine-human hybrid has acquired a pair of testicles and a second 'trunk' that doubles as a penis ejaculating numerals.

Salvador Dalí, *The Temptation of St Anthony*, 1946

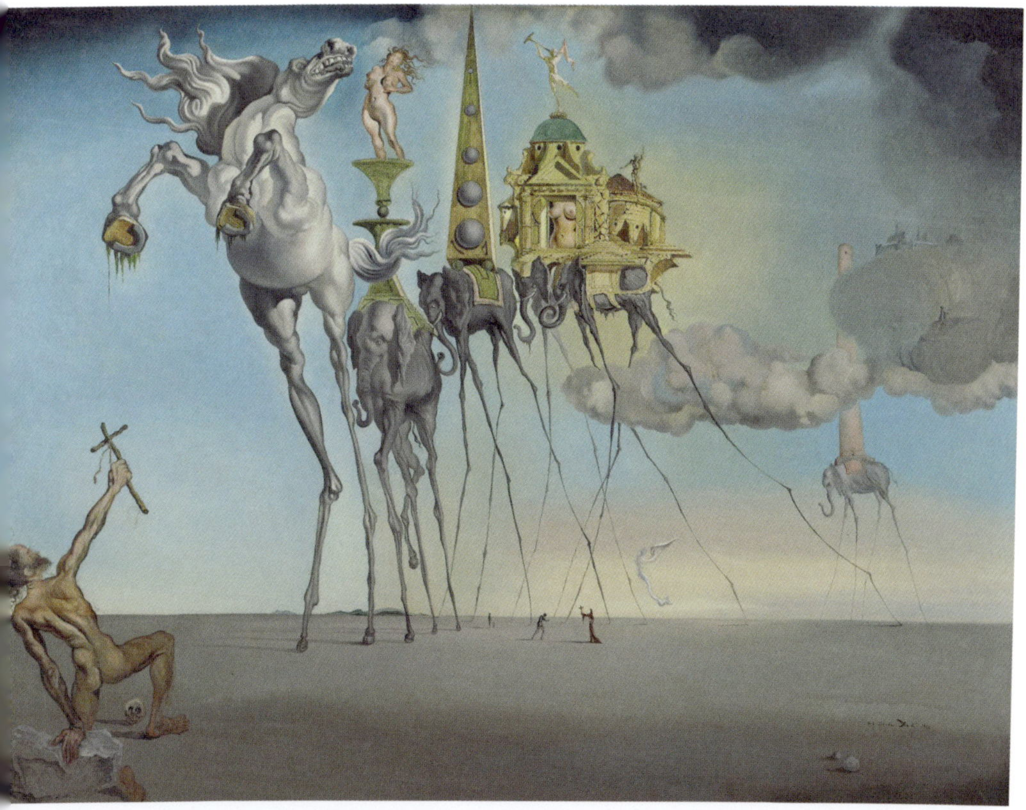

Much more celebrated elephants appear in Salvador Dalí's masterpiece *The Temptation of St Anthony* (1946). Four elephants are shown in a bizarre procession that is threatening a naked Saint Anthony, who is seen half-kneeling in the lower left-hand corner of the painting; a fifth elephant is visible in the distance. A horse leads the procession, rearing up as if to trample the saint. Each elephant carries on its back a towering structure that has no rational reason for being there. But the most iconic invention with Dalí's elephants is the replacement of the normal, thick elephantine legs with the long, spindly legs of a spider. Such legs could never support an elephant and are the most perversely unsuitable limbs imaginable for this heavyweight giant of an animal. Dalí repeated this feature in several paintings, and it also appears in the artist's later sculptures of elephants.

The British sculptor Henry Moore was obsessed with elephants and loved the rough texture of their skin. In particular, he was fascinated by the sculptural quality of the elephant's skull. When visiting his friend, the biologist Sir Julian Huxley, he spotted the skull of an African elephant that had been presented to Huxley during one of his safaris and which now stood proudly in his Hampstead garden. Moore startled his host by urgently requesting that he should be allowed to take the skull away with him and place it in his studio. By nature, Moore was a quietly polite man, and this request was strangely out of character. Huxley, who was very fond of his elephant skull, tried to think of some reason to refuse his friend's request. 'I am sorry,' he said, 'but there are birds nesting in the skull's eye-sockets and I cannot have them disturbed.' This was not a good move because Moore replied that he was happy to wait until the nestlings had fledged. When Huxley informed him that this had happened, within hours a truck arrived to remove the skull to Moore's studio, where, in the 1960s and 1970s, it inspired some powerful drawings and sculptures.

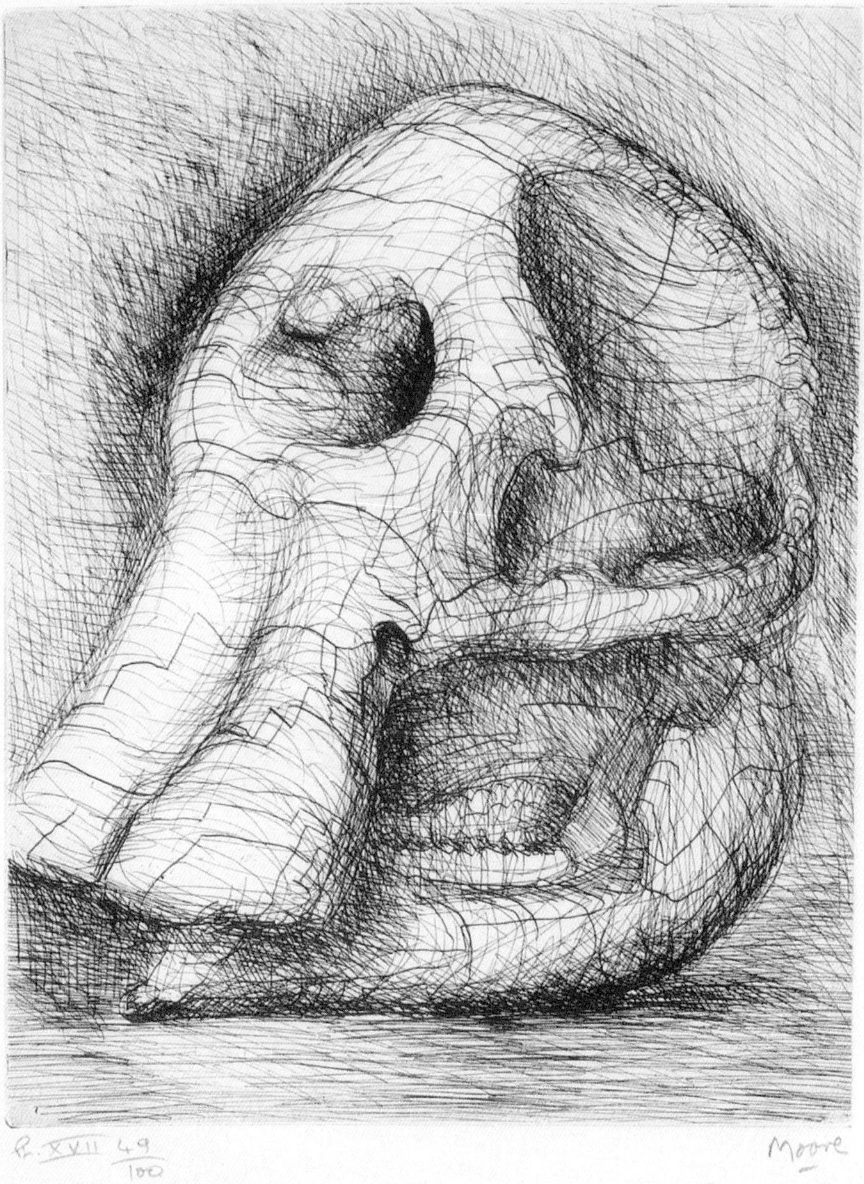

Henry Moore, *Elephant Skull*, 1970

In Óscar Domínguez's *Cementerio de Elefantes* (1938), the elephants are all trunks and little else, their undulating shapes forming a disquieting landscape. These trunks protrude horizontally from eyeless heads and join one another in a jumble of tubular connections. It is as if the trunk, being the most characteristic feature of the animal, has been allowed to dominate it to the exclusion of almost everything else. The title translates as 'Elephant Graveyard', the mythical place where elderly elephants go to die – the fleshy red detail, broken tusks and thorns, however, suggesting a violent end.

Roger Hilton's *Elephant* (1973) has the charm of a child's portrayal. It is simple in the extreme and, with a deliberate exclusion of any attempt at anatomical accuracy, his ruthless Art Brut approach follows Breton's demand, in his *Surrealist Manifesto*, that surrealism shall be 'exempt from any aesthetic or moral concern'.

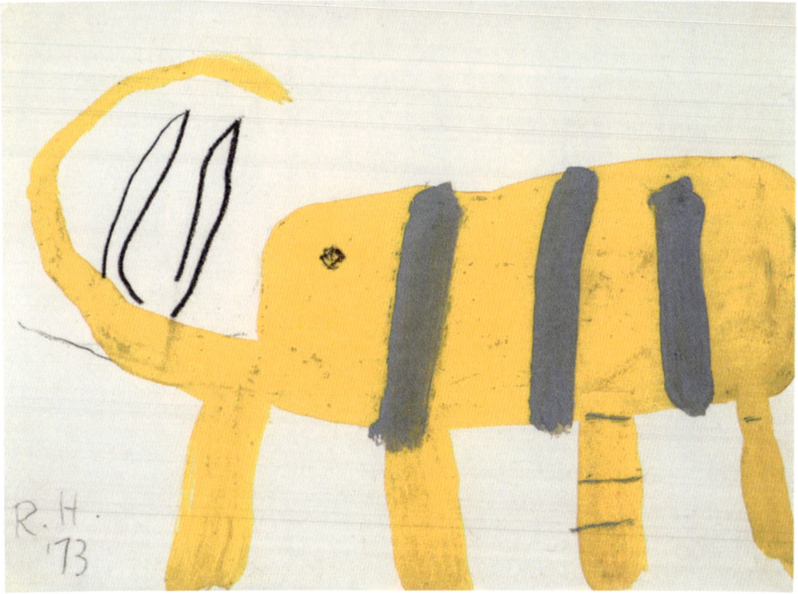

Roger Hilton, *Elephant*, 1973

Óscar Domínguez,
Cementerio de Elefantes, 1938

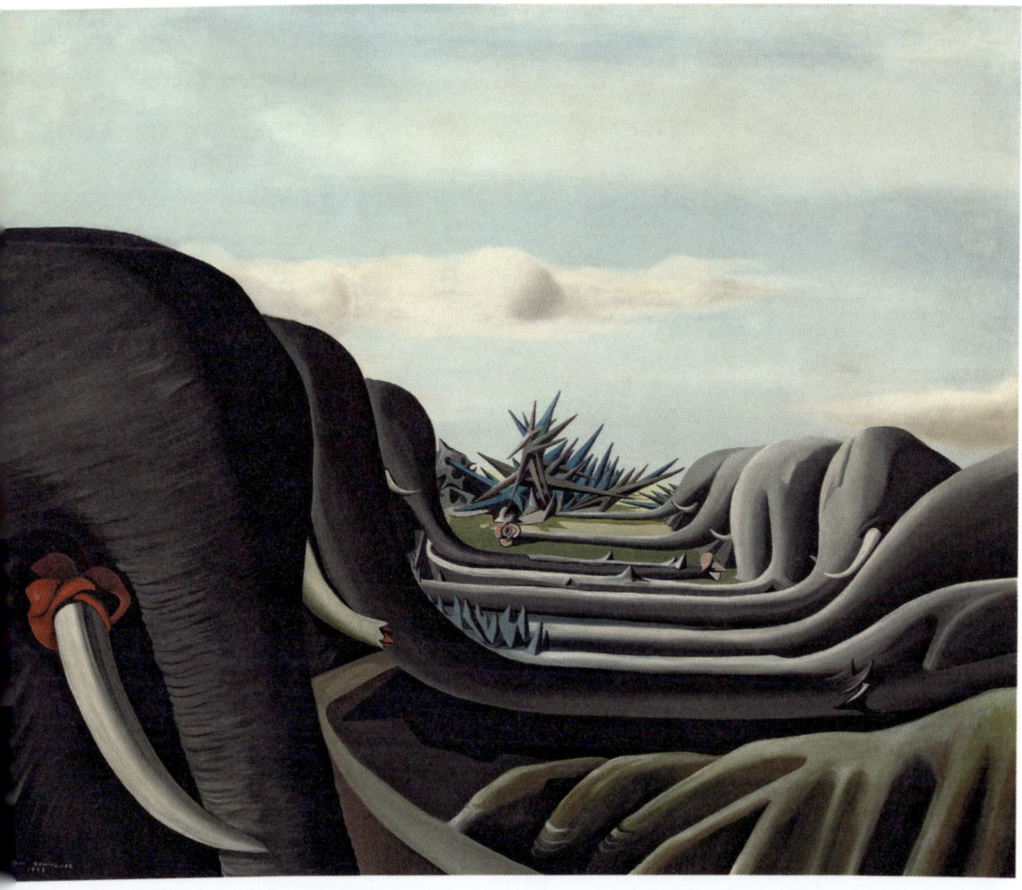

The Hoofe

Animals

Horse

For centuries, the horse was the almost constant companion of growing civilizations. Unlike the zebra, the horse's ancestor was an amenable beast that allowed itself to be ridden, harnessed and yoked. It took us to war, worked on our farms, gave us improved forms of transport and provided us with all kinds of sport. Even after it was overtaken in so many ways by the motor vehicle, it remained a major source of pleasure, as an animal to be ridden and raced.

Little wonder that the horse appears in countless surrealist compositions. Indeed, there are so many surrealist horses that a whole book could be written about them alone. A small sample are illustrated here.

Victor Brauner, who was unusually fond of amalgamating totally unrelated species, decided to combine the rear end of a horse with a young nude. The woman sits on the ground, with two pairs of forearms – one pair coming from the body of the horse, and the other from her own shoulders. In this seemingly unfinished sketch of 1941, Brauner's irrational creation stares blankly into space, like a celebrity posing for photographs on the red carpet. Many an accomplished rider has remarked that,

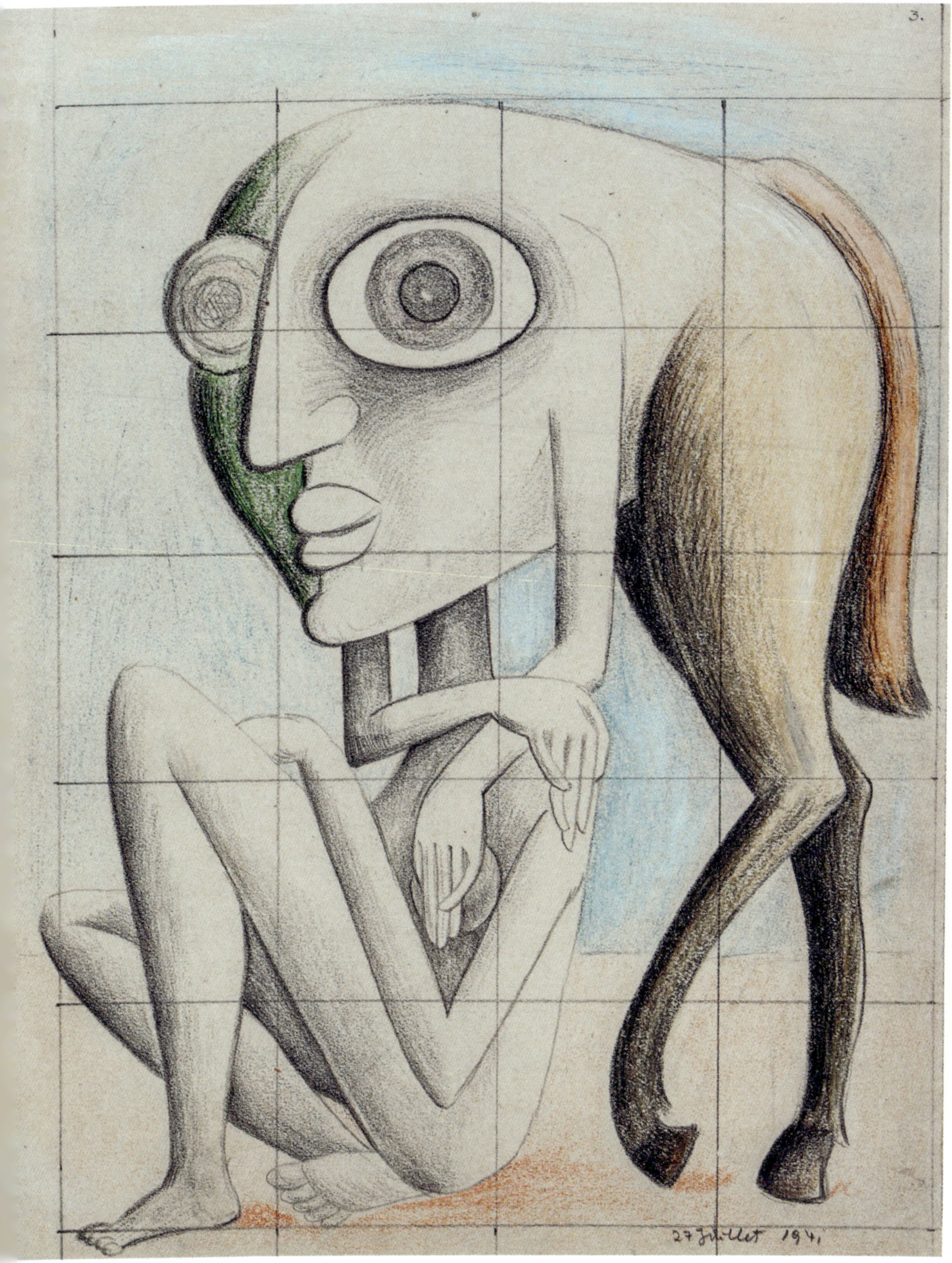

Victor Brauner, *Untitled*, 1941

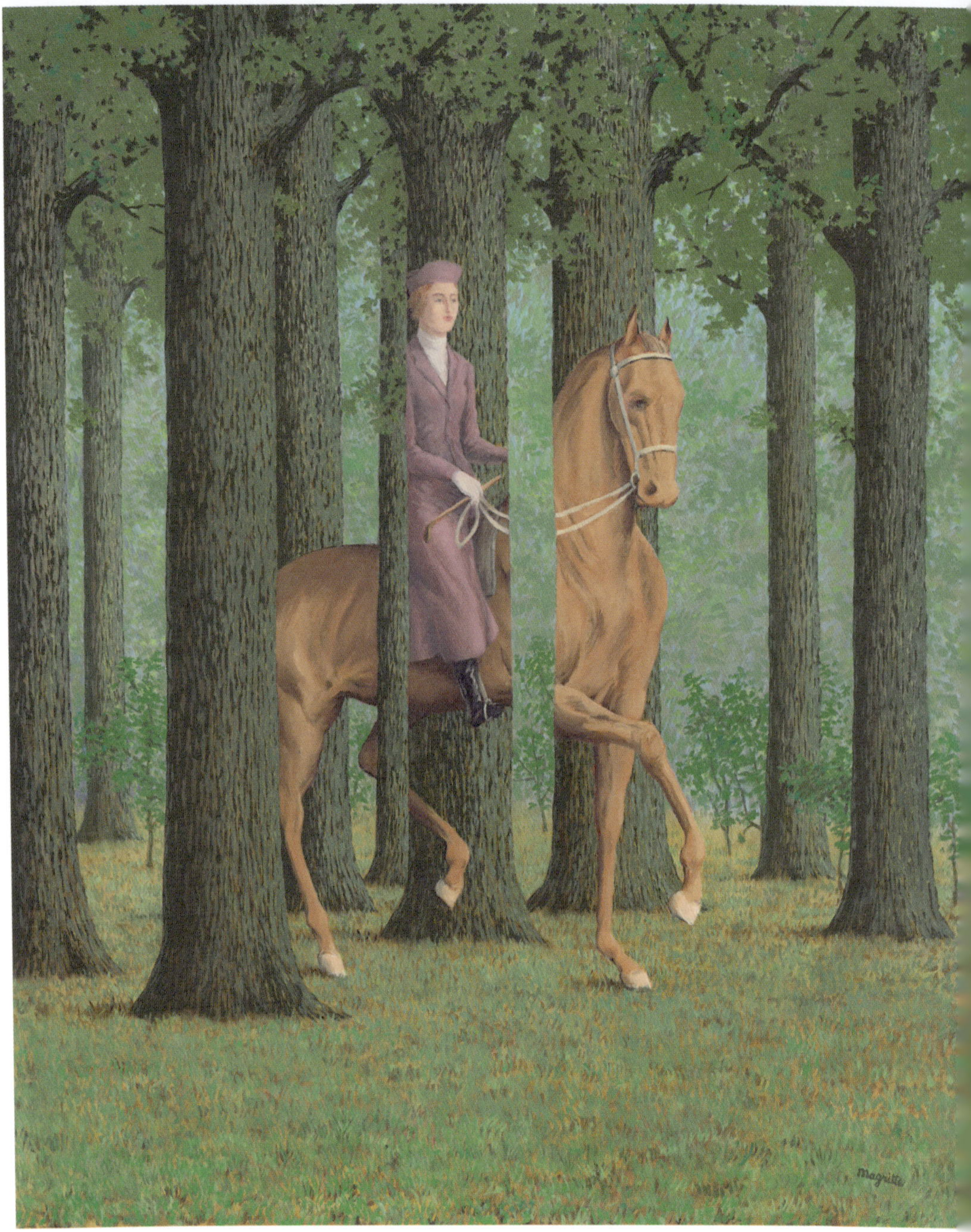

René Magritte, *The Blank Signature*, 1965

when they are in the saddle, they begin to feel like the horse's body is part of their own. Brauner's subject looks rather stunned to find that, for her, this has actually happened.

The Blank Signature (1965), by Magritte, also shows a young woman at one with her horse. Clad in a stylish riding costume, she trots through a forest where the trees and the horse/rider have become hopelessly confused with one another. Like an impossible riddle, the painting presents an optical illusion, a scene that could never exist in real life. Our eyes dart back and forth, scanning the tree trunks and strips of green, as we try to work out where exactly the various elements begin and end.

In *Song of Songs IV* (1958), part of Marc Chagall's series of illustrations of the Old Testament, the horse has magically grown a pair of wings. It flies through the sky with a bride and groom, still in their wedding clothes and tenderly embracing, on its back.

Marc Chagall, *Song of Songs IV*, 1958

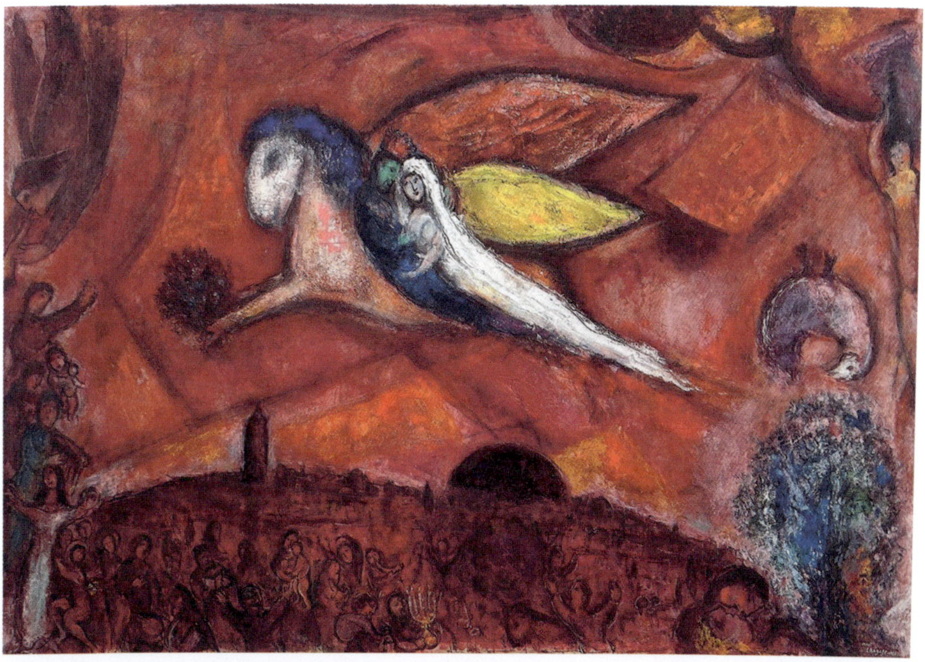

The horse holds a bunch of flowers between its legs, suggesting that it has caught the wedding bouquet. Most of Chagall's domestic animals are pictured floating in the air as they whirl around his imagination and he fondly recalls his childhood pleasures.

The rider in Cruzeiro Seixas's *Untitled* composition of 1972 is having trouble with his horse. The poor animal appears to have lost its hind legs. Or, at the very least, they have collapsed under him. Perhaps the rider has ridden the animal literally into the ground. The horse is certainly complaining and turns its head to confront him, as the rider attempts to hold his balance and retain his grip on his spear or lance.

Óscar Domínguez gives us two horses in *Sunday or Marine Rutting* (1935). This deliberately enigmatic painting appears to show two horses, each on a broad step, divided by a huge, fitted mirror. On the viewer's side of the mirror, we see the front end of one horse and the rear end of the other. The mismatched reflections appear to give one of the horses two heads and the other two tails. The two-headed horse, weighed down by anchors, seems to pull itself in opposite directions. Scholars have interpreted this strange painting as a symbol of duality or the contradiction that exists in the human condition.

When Dalí paints a horse, we are immediately reminded of his extraordinary technical skill. In *Equestrian Portrait of Carmen Martínez-Bordiú* (1972), his prancing horse becomes a window through which we see a distant landscape, while his rider sits placidly bareback on the horse, with her hands folded in her lap. The model's expression appears sombre, as if she was less than happy to be posing for the notorious artist but accepted it as her aristocratic duty. Martínez-Bordiú is the granddaughter of the Spanish dictator General Franco, and there are photos of Dalí presenting the canvas to Franco on 8 November 1972. Later, in 1982, he accepted a noble title from the Spanish king,

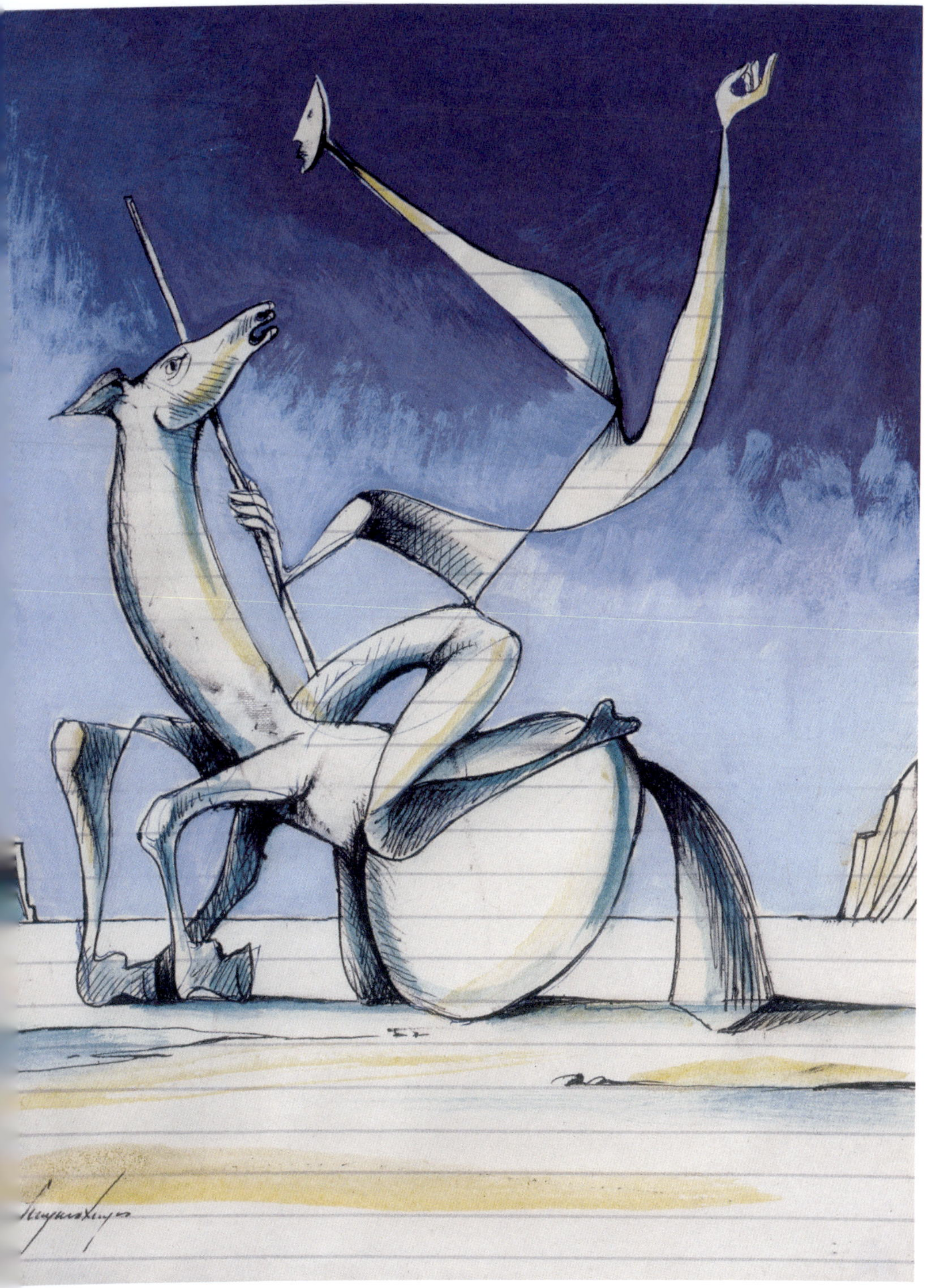

Cruzeiro Seixas, *Untitled*, 1972

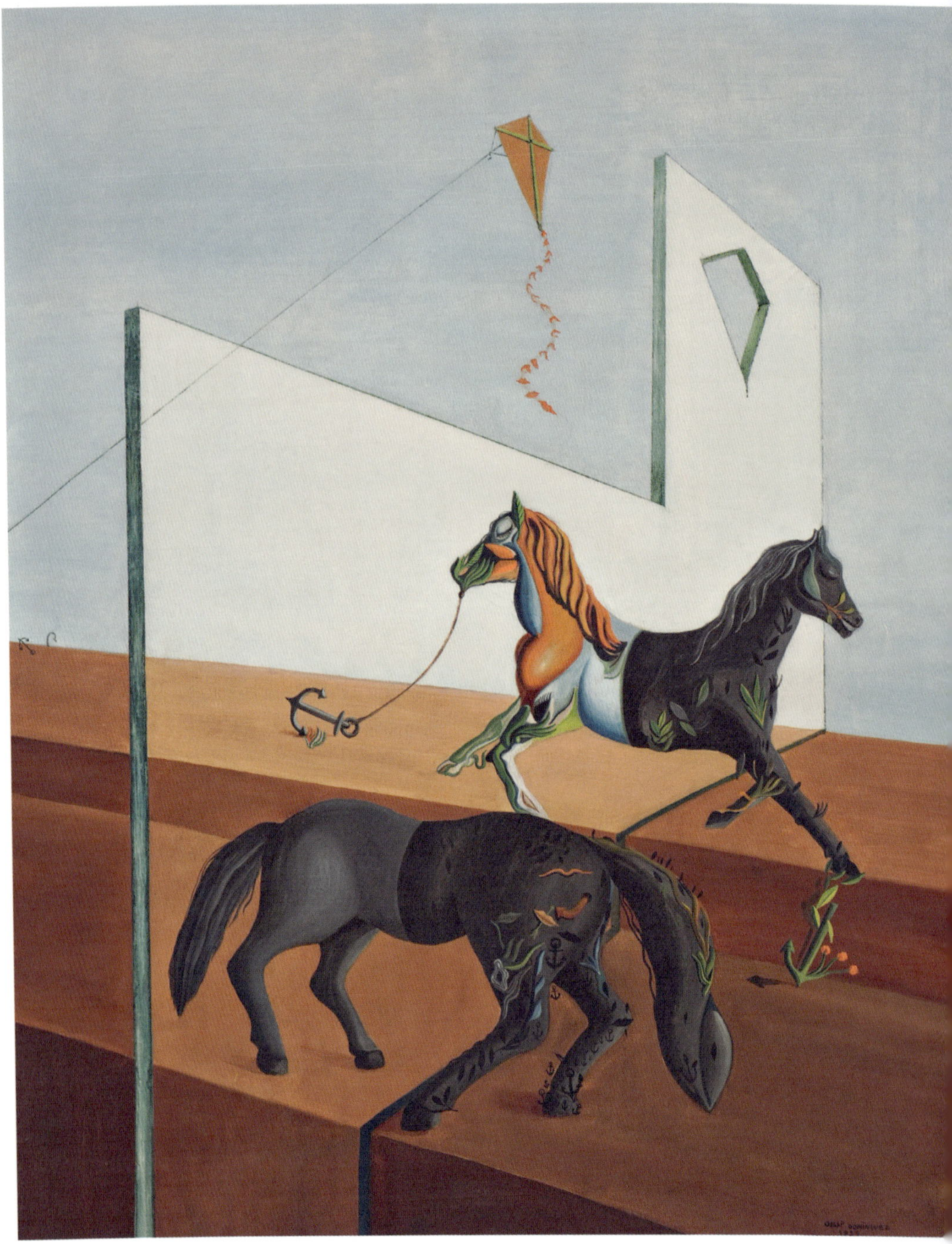

Óscar Domínguez, *Sunday or Marine Rutting*, 1935

Juan Carlos, and became the Marquis of Dalí de Púbol. These actions and the fact that he once said he thought Adolf Hitler was 'sexy', seem to have been done deliberately to enrage his surrealist colleagues, all of whom were intensely left-wing.

By nature, the other great Spanish surrealist, Joan Miró, was a quiet, private person, with a stable family life. Only when he entered his studio did his wild visual imagination take wing. His little blue circus horses of 1927 – he painted ten of them – are charmingly free of complex draughtsmanship and technical fireworks. He reduces his horses to the bare essentials.

Salvador Dalí, *Equestrian Portrait of Carmen Martínez-Bordiú*, 1972

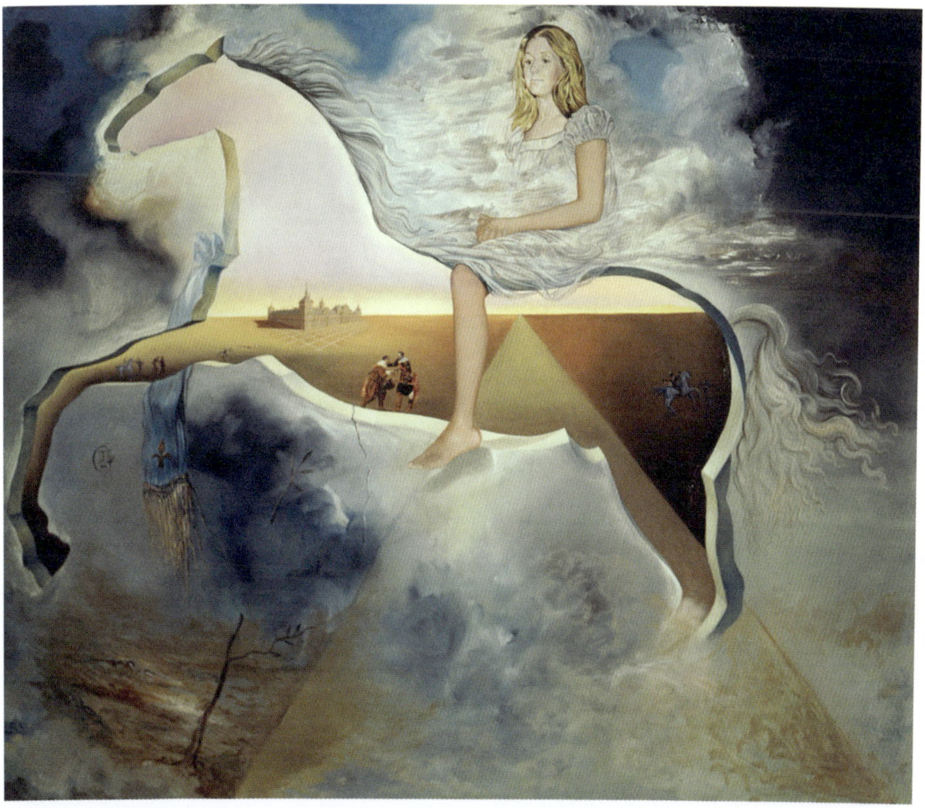

Donkey

The donkey has often been seen as the poor relation of the horse. While the horse is admired as a magnificent, fast steed, the donkey takes the role of a humble, long-suffering and sometimes stubborn beast of burden.

At various times, it has been said to represent stupidity, simplicity, gentleness, endurance, laziness, service, suffering, peace and the ability to endure hard labour. Considering how well it has been working in the service of humanity for thousands of years, it has been harshly treated and never given the respect offered to its close relative, the dazzlingly athletic horse.

Salvador Dalí was obsessed with donkeys and ensured their inclusion in the classic surrealist film that he made with Luis Buñuel in 1929, *Un Chien Andalou*. There is a rumour that this may have been partly due to the fact that both he and Buñuel had in the past been engaged in a fierce attack on a Spanish book called *Platero y yo*, about a man and his donkey.

In one scene in the film, a man drags two grand pianos across a room, each with a dead donkey on top of it – the large teeth of the carcasses echoing the pianos' white keys. Dalí reportedly poured glue over the dead donkeys to enhance their putrefaction, as well

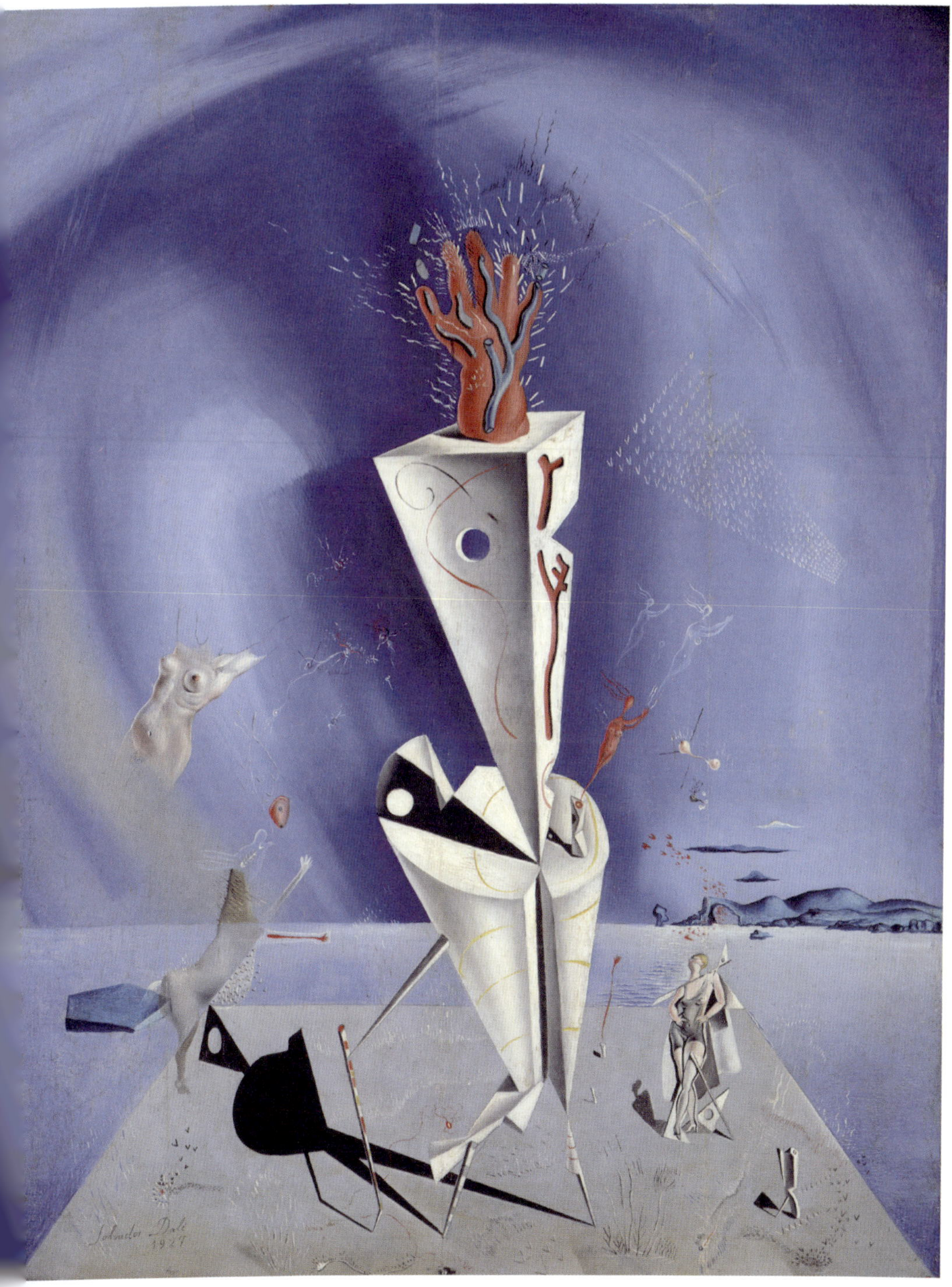

Salvador Dalí, *Apparatus and Hand*, 1927

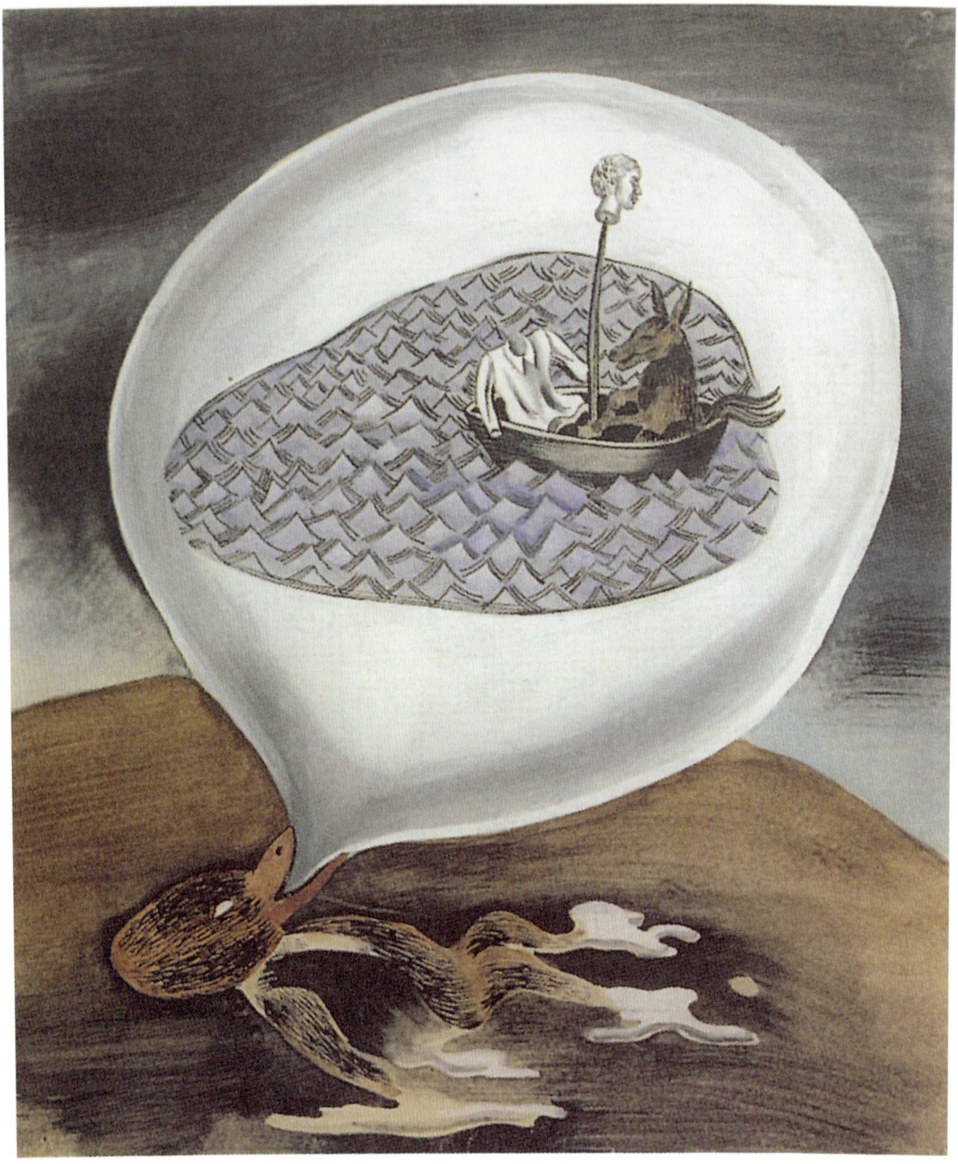

Remedios Varo, *The Journey*, 1935

as hacking at their eye sockets and mouths to show off their rows of white teeth.

Donkeys also appear in several Dalí paintings. In *Apparatus and Hand* (1927), a donkey with human hands is shown leaping up into the air, trying to catch hold of a strange object that appears to be falling from the sky. Bizarrely, the ghostly face of the animal has become the skeleton of a fish. Dalí also includes a swarm of flies that are covering the swollen belly of the donkey, suggesting that this is another of his decomposing, rotting donkeys, despite the fact that it is rearing up on its hind legs.

Remedios Varo is kinder to her donkey. In *The Journey* (1935), she provides it with a small boat in which it appears to float happily on the sea. Opposite the donkey, there is a smart white shirt that contains no body. However, a decapitated female head is impaled on top of the mast. Even more sinister is the fact that the sea is contained in the vomit of a dying bird.

Rhinoceros

The rhinoceros is a symbol of physical strength and aggression, charging fearlessly at its enemies. More specifically, thanks to its thick, central horn, it is a symbol of phallic arousal and sexual assault. Sadly, thanks to the immense power of its thrusting horn, in classical Chinese medical texts, it has long been claimed that, if swallowed, powdered rhino horn will transmit its strength to the sick and will cure many ailments, from fevers and rheumatism to carbuncles and vomiting, food poisoning, snakebite, hallucinations and even demonic possession. Recent research, however, has proved beyond doubt that it has no health benefits of any kind and that, in reality, it is composed almost entirely of keratin of the type found in human fingernails. Despite this, poachers in Africa are still killing many rhinoceroses every year. Their horns are severed, while the de-horned bodies of the animals are simply left to rot. At the beginning of the 20th century there were 500,000 rhinos in existence, but today that figure has fallen to only 27,000.

Conservationists are doing their best to stamp out this mindless slaughter and they would doubtless be horrified to see a shelf in the Spanish home of Salvador Dalí, on which he displayed his personal collection of severed rhino horns. By modern standards,

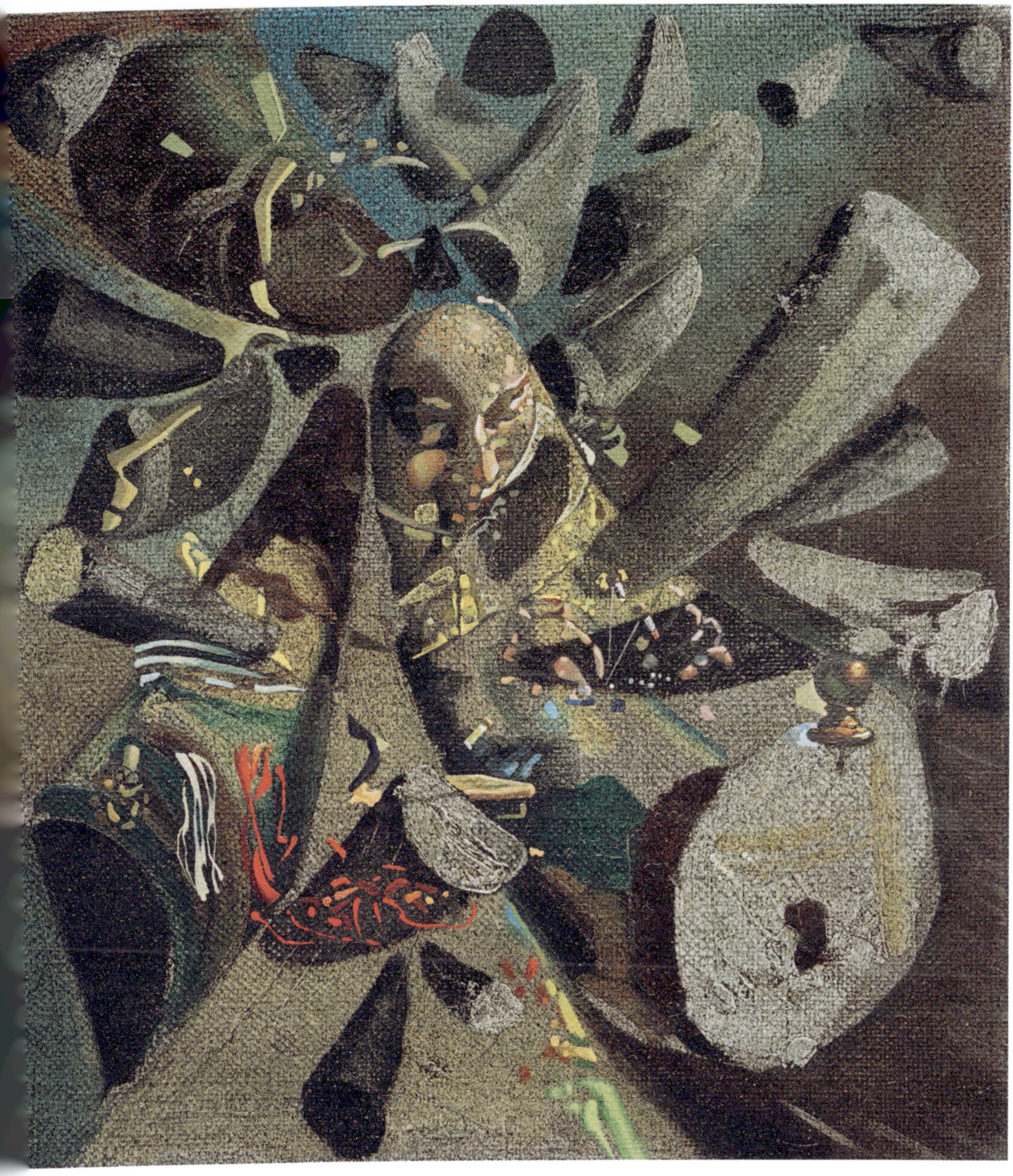

Salvador Dalí, *Paranoiac-Critical Study of Vermeer's Lacemaker*, 1955

Dalí's attitude towards wildlife was appalling. He famously disliked animals and once astonished American talk show host Dick Cavett and his guests by bringing a live anteater on stage during an interview. 'I don't like animals of any kind,' Dalí announced, before going on to say that the anteater and rhinoceroses were the only exception.

Dalí's obsession with the rhino horn had nothing to do with its supposedly medicinal properties. Instead, he was fascinated purely by its erotic, phallic shape. In 1954, he produced an aggressively sensual painting called *Young Virgin Auto-sodomized by Her Own Chastity*. It shows a nude woman leaning over a railing; two horns form her buttocks and two further horns float beneath them, nudging towards the buttock cleft. Three more severed rhino horns are floating in the sky above her. Controversially, the subject is Dalí's sister, Ana Maria, with whom he was estranged, although it comes as no surprise to discover that this painting was acquired by Hugh Hefner for his Playboy Mansion. The later *Goddess Leaning on Her Elbow – Virgin Formed by Five Rhinoceros Horns* (*c.* 1960) continues the theme of the *Young Virgin*, only now her body is reduced to little more than five huge rhino horns.

Also in 1954, Dalí staged a performance at the Louvre, where he sat in front of Vermeer's painting of *The Lacemaker* (1670–71) and promised his audience that he would produce a perfect copy of it in one hour. At the end of that time, the audience was startled to discover that the painting he was showing them portrayed four intersecting rhinoceros horns. The 'lacemaker' herself was nowhere to be seen. 'The lacemaker is morphologically the horn of a rhinoceros,' Dalí explained. (He did also do a faithful copy of Vermeer's masterpiece around the same time, now in the collection of the Met.)

In the following year, 1955, Dalí's *Paranoiac-Critical Study of Vermeer's Lacemaker* shows the lacemaker's face surrounded

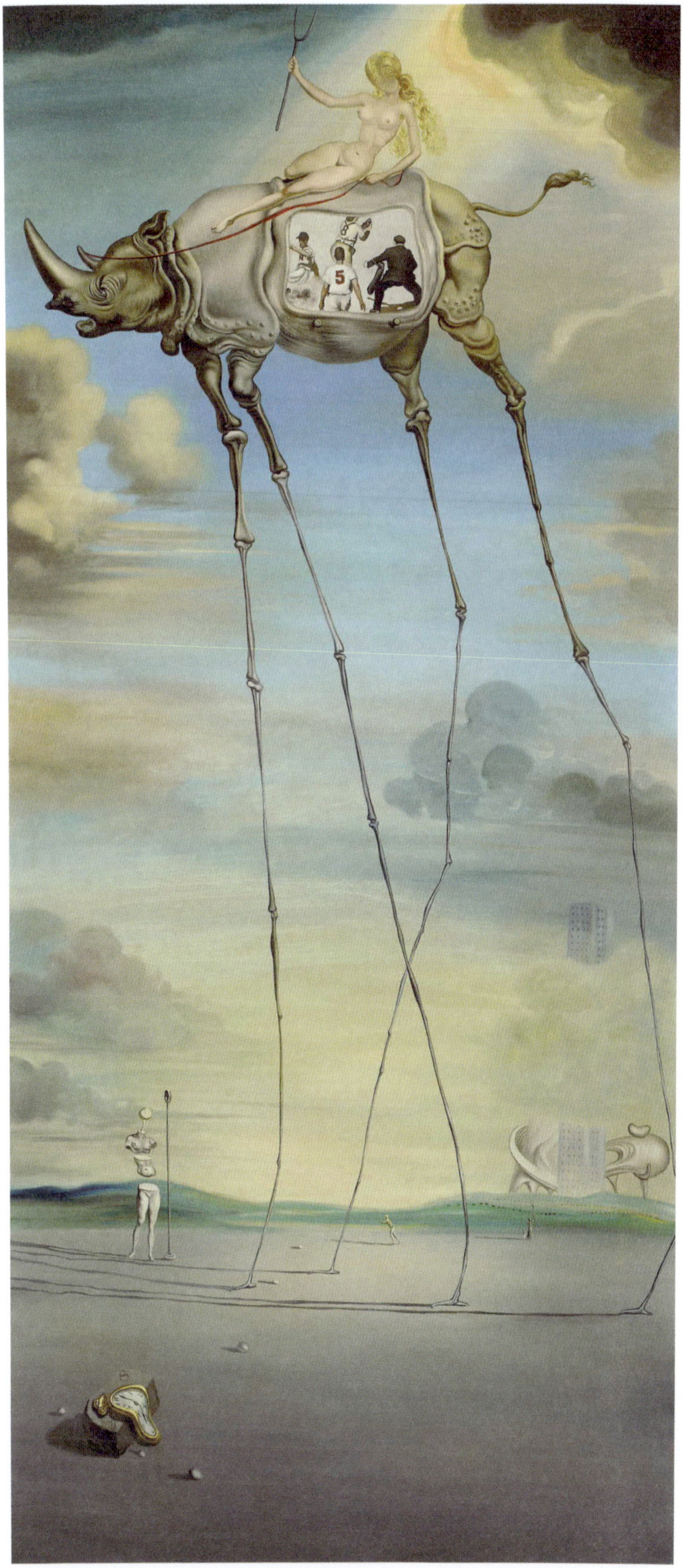

Salvador Dalí, *Celestial Ride*, 1957

by a shower of severed rhino horns and other detritus. He said of this work: 'I had to make the *Lacemaker* explode in the form of rhinoceros horns. These horns being the only ones in the animal kingdom constructed in accordance with a logarithmic spiral, as in this painting, it is the very logarithmic expression that guided Vermeer's hand in painting *The Lacemaker*.'

Dalí also made a film (sadly never finished) called *The Prodigious Story of the Lacemaker and the Rhinoceros*. For this film he created another painting called *Rhinocerotic Portrait of Vermeer's Lacemaker*. The making of the film was pure Dalí theatre. He had himself installed with his easel and paints inside the rhinoceros enclosure at Vincennes zoo. Protected by a barrier of stone blocks, and with one of his entourage holding the rounded end of a French baguette on top of his head, he started working on the piece, while at the same time encouraging the rhinoceros to charge at a large copy of the Vermeer painting, which was lowered in front of the animal. The bemused rhino refused to cooperate and Dalí was reduced to piercing *The Lacemaker* himself, using the long, spirally twisted tusk of a narwhal – which perhaps explains why the film was not completed.

In 1956 Dalí created a bronze sculpture called *Cosmic Rhinoceros*, giving the mighty animal long, spidery legs and balancing sea urchins on its back. In choosing the legs of a spider, he was seeking out the most inappropriate limbs for such a heavy body. He continued this theme with the painting *Celestial Ride* (1957), one of seven works originally commissioned for the Ziegfeld Theater in New York, under the series title *The Seven Lively Arts*. Depicting the arts of dance, opera, ballet, music, cinema, radio/television and theatre, these paintings were lost in a fire and later recreated and reworked by Dalí. Now, in addition to its spindly legs, the rhinoceros is being ridden by a nude female and its flank has become a television screen showing a sporting event.

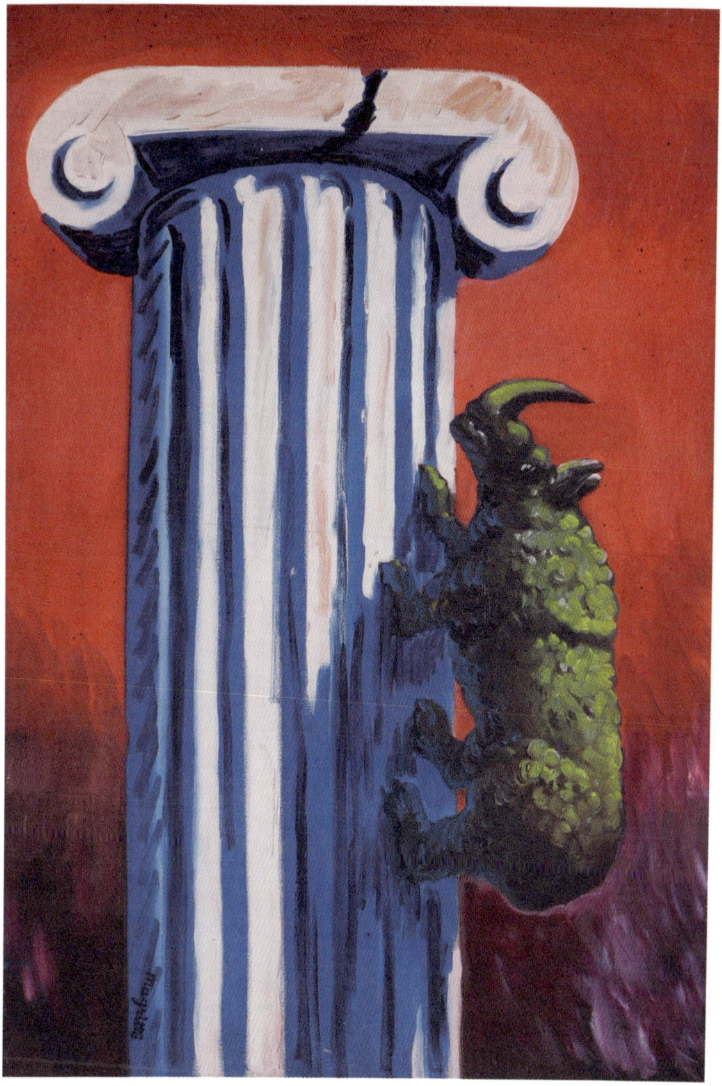

René Magritte, *The Mountain-Dweller*, 1948

Dalí's joy of the irrational knew no bounds, but being Dalí, he often felt the need to provide a spurious, pseudo-scientific explanation of what he was doing. René Magritte felt no such need. Instead, he enjoyed leaving his viewer with an irrational puzzle for which there was absolutely no explanation. What was the most unlikely activity he could impose on the majestic rhinoceros? His answer, in *The Mountain-Dweller* (1948), was to show it climbing vertically up a Greek Ionic column.

Pig

Symbolically, the pig is often associated with either prosperity or gluttony. It does not appear very often in the surrealist menagerie, perhaps because its body shape is too simple and rounded to be easily manipulated in a surrealist manner. Indeed, the few pigs that do appear, do so largely as themselves, with little distortion.

Leonora Carrington's *The Temptation of St Anthony* (1945) includes a beautifully formed pig whose only modification is its slightly pointed nose – a feature of many of her animal figures. It is portrayed sleeping peacefully, protected by the Saint's billowing cloak. When asked about the painting, Carrington replied, 'The picture seems pretty clear to me, being a more or less literal rendering of St Anthony complete with pig.' She included a pig because Anthony was the patron saint of pigs and pig-farmers. There is a legend that, one day, he healed a wild pig and befriended the animal, who remained with him in the desert.

Marc Chagall included so many farm animals in his village scenes that the pig was bound to be among them. In *The Watering Trough* (1923), his rather emaciated pig is bright green in colour and appears to be keeping a watchful eye on some unseen companion.

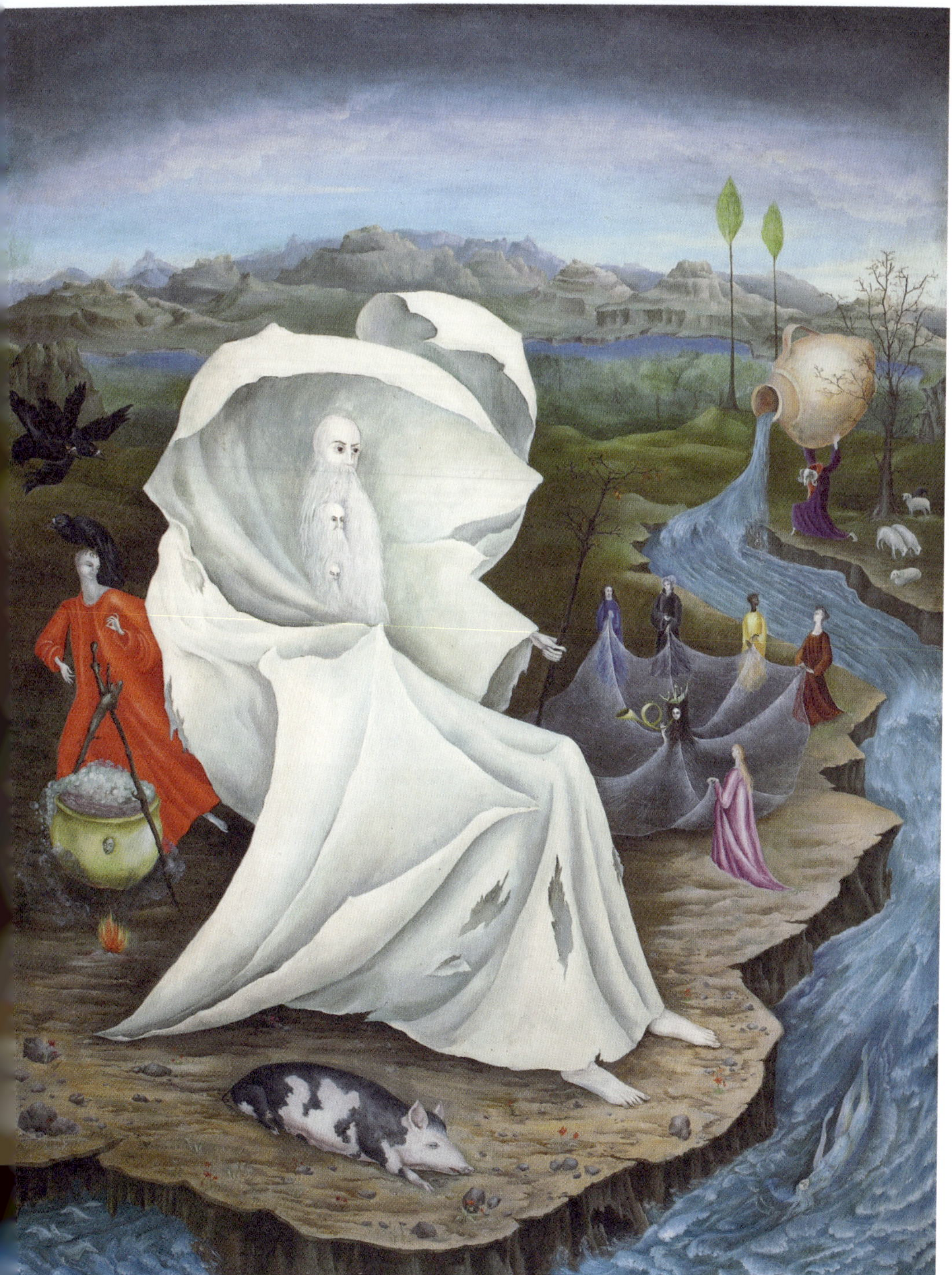

Leonora Carrington,
The Temptation of St Anthony, 1945

Camel

It is surprising that the camel has not been a popular subject for surrealist artists. Its fleshy humps cry out for surrealist manipulation. However, apart from a small, realistic camel that appears in the background of a Dalí painting (*Sun-table*, 1935), a couple of comical sculptures by Alexander Calder and an obscure portrait of a camel by Jane Graverol (who transforms its hump into a sharply pointed Egyptian pyramid and its head into the face of the Great Sphinx of Giza), only a handful of surrealist works feature this 'ship of the desert'.

In the mixed-media *Spanish Woman with Camel* (c. 1927), Francis Picabia employs one of his favourite 'overlay' devices. This is one of a series of works known as 'transparencies' in which Picabia superimposed translucent layers of imagery. Here, the outline of a two-headed camel lies on top of a Spanish señorita and her jealously attentive companion, thought to be a toreador. The image of the señorita first appeared in *Spanish Woman with Butterfly* in 1926, with Picabia revisiting (and renaming) the work on cardboard to include the male figure, and finally the camel, the following year. He borrowed the image of the camel from a fresco in the 11th-century Romanesque church at Sant Joan de Boí.

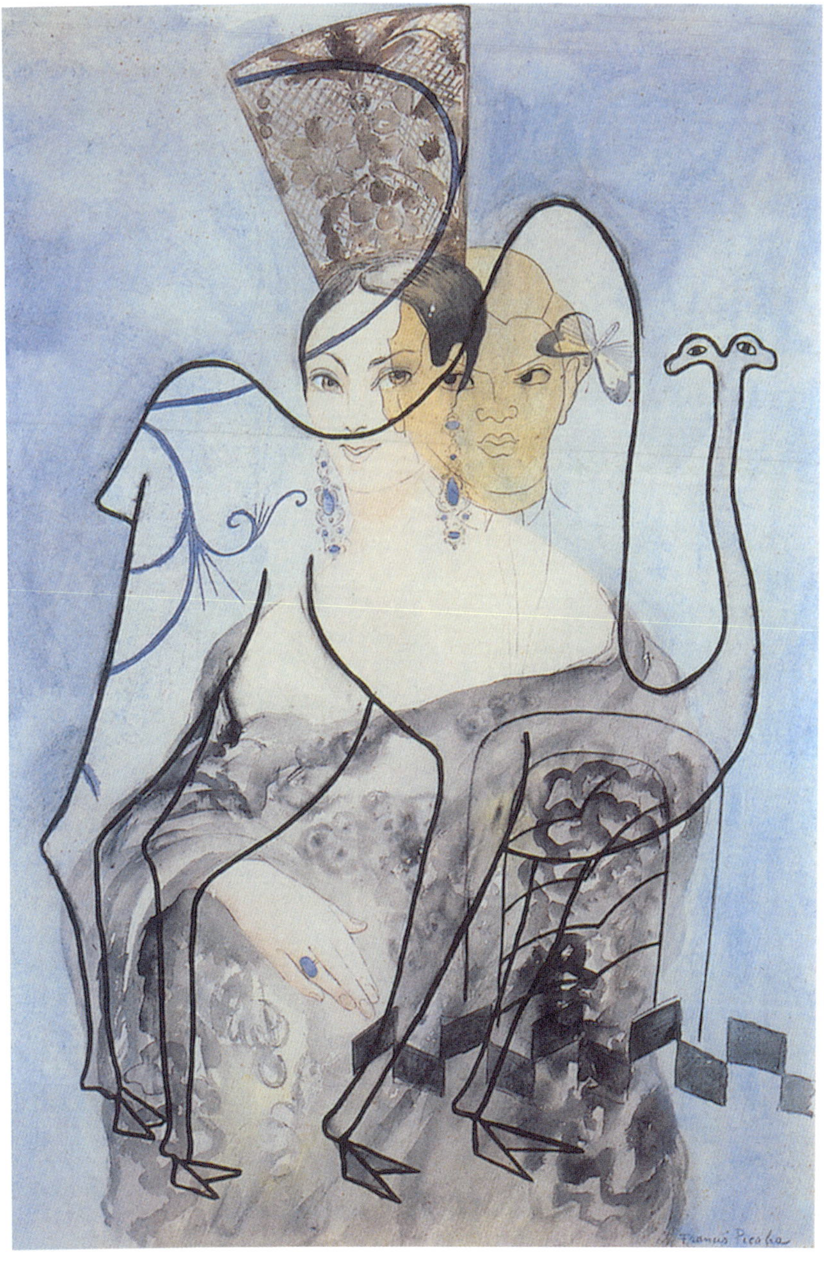

Francis Picabia,
Spanish Woman with Camel, c. 1927

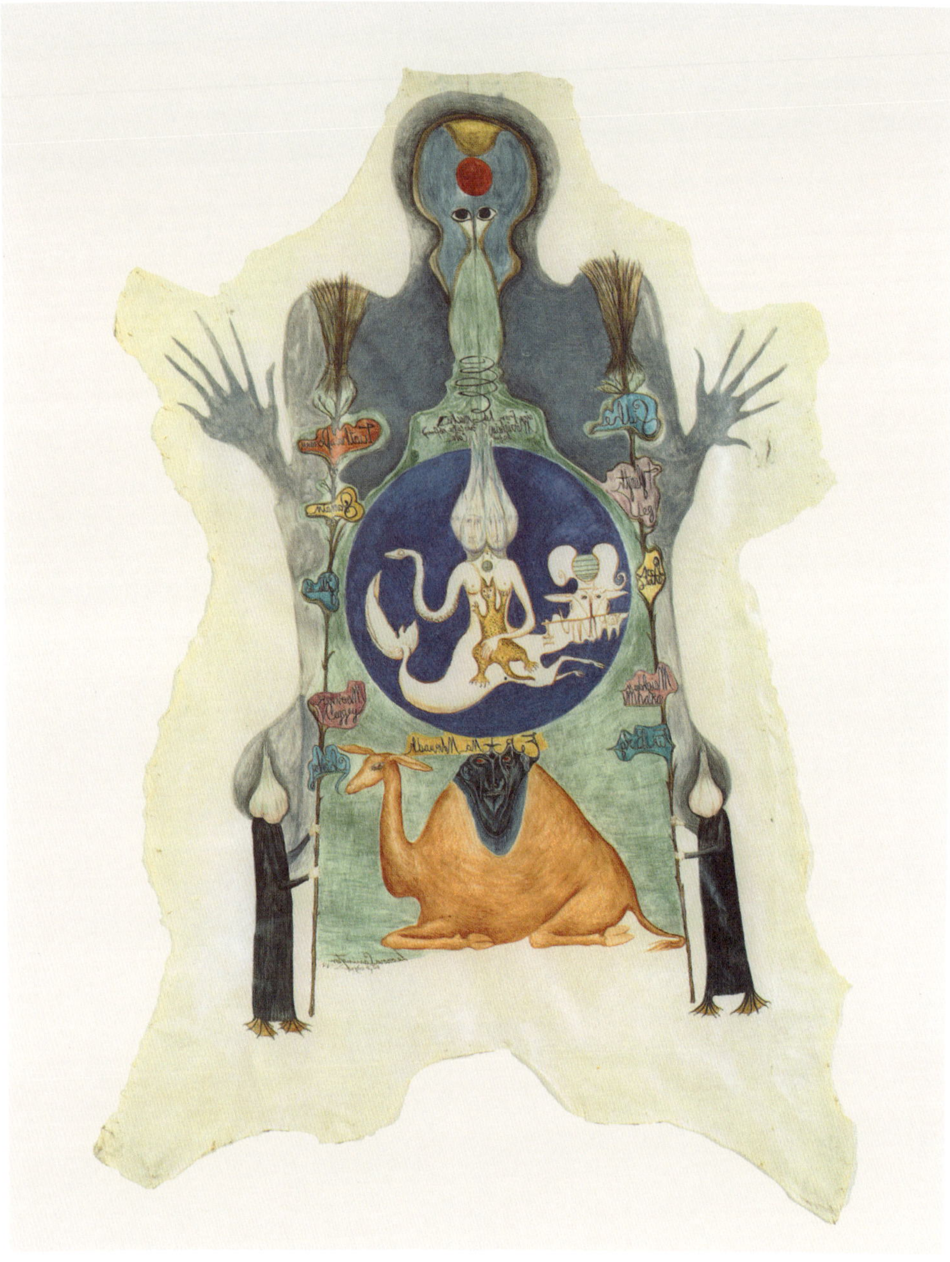

Leonora Carrington, *Samhain Skin*, 1975

Leonora Carrington's *Samhain Skin* (1975) shows a resting camel with a very slender head, draped in a black cloth on which there appears a sinister, bearded face. The title of this painting refers to the ancient Celtic festival of Samhain, which was held every year between the evening of 31 October and 1 November, to mark the end of summer and the start of winter. Halloween is thought to be a later development of this ancient festival. Carrington painted this work on vellum – actual animal skin – on which she reveals strange creatures, human hybrids, and reverse-handwritten Celtic words referring to Gaelic deities. The main centres for these ancient Celtic rituals were Ireland, Scotland and Wales, so the inspiration for Carrington's resting camel is something of a mystery.

Deer

There is one feature that confirms the identity of an animal as a deer – its branching antlers. No matter how distorted the image of its body becomes, the presence of antlers is sufficient to recognize it as a member of the *Cervidae*, the deer family. Among the surrealists, the deer has not been a particularly popular subject, but it does appear in works by Frida Kahlo, Edith Rimmington, Leonora Carrington, Georgia O'Keeffe and Óscar Domínguez.

Of these, by far the most impressive is Kahlo's *The Wounded Deer* (also known as *The Little Deer*, 1946). Her deer is shown running through a wooded landscape. It has Kahlo's face, with the distinctive monobrow, and is being attacked by hunters who have shot nine arrows into its body. The wounds from these arrows are all dripping blood and the animal is clearly not going to survive these injuries. Although the animal must be in great pain, Kahlo's face is expressionless. Symbolically, this portrayal relates to Kahlo's own physical agonies, resulting from a tragic accident when she was young. She painted this work shortly before she underwent a major operation in New York and gave it to two friends of hers as a wedding gift, accompanied by a poem that read: 'Sadness haunts my paintings, it's in them through and through, and so it is for me today, as calm has left me too.'

Edith Rimmington's deer, occupying the left-hand side of *Mythical Composition* (1950), are very different. Close inspection

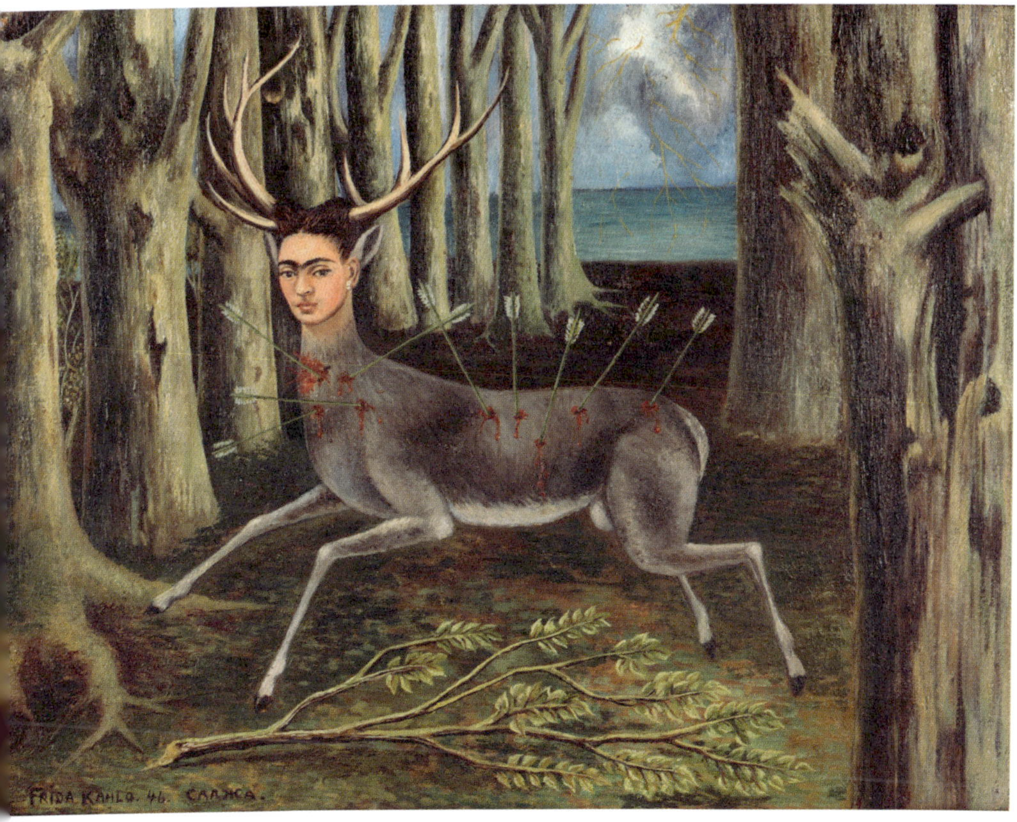

Frida Kahlo, *The Wounded Deer*, 1946

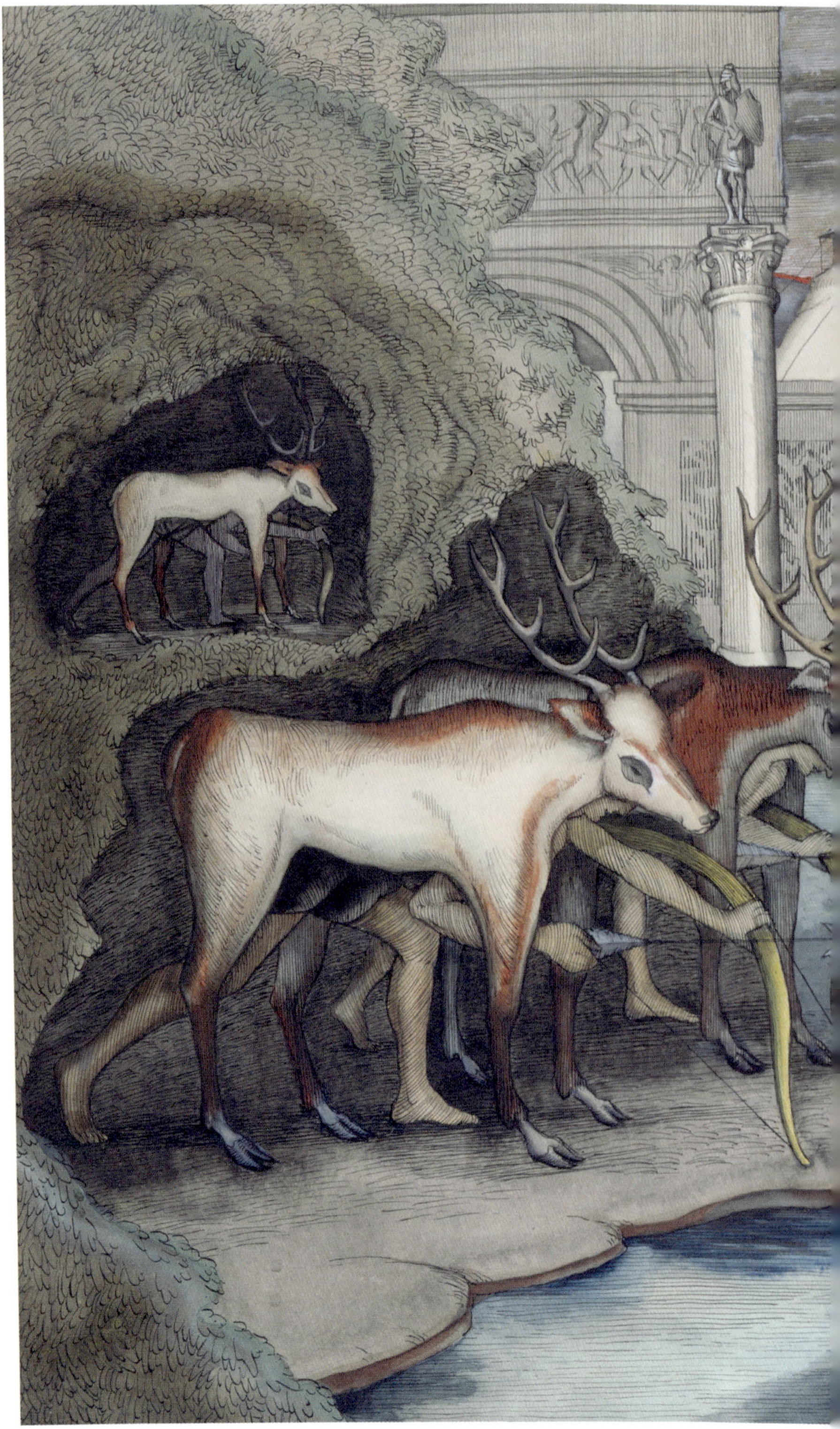

 Edith Rimmington, *Mythical Composition*, 1950

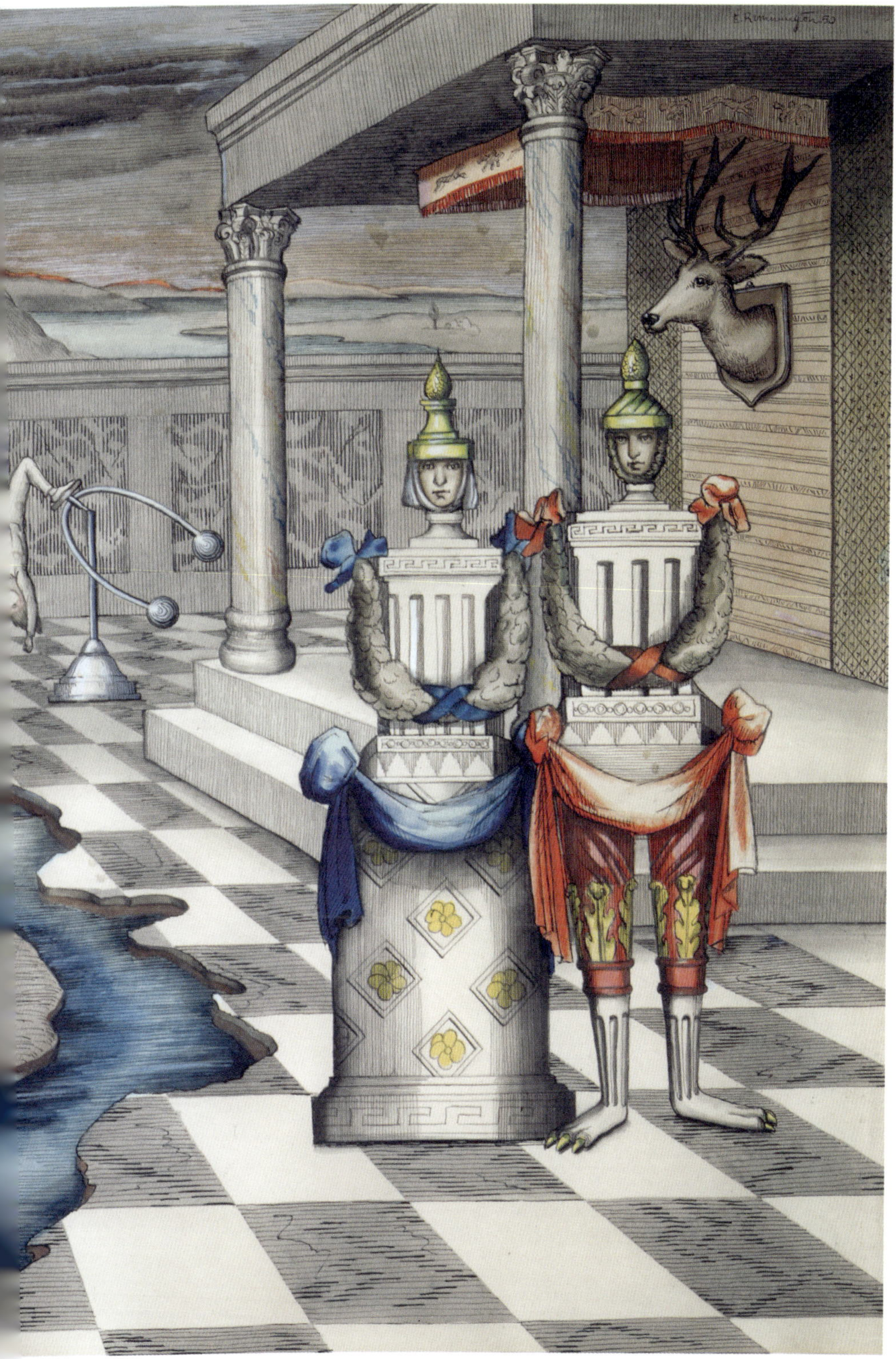

reveals that they are, in reality, archers disguised as deer. With the skins and heads of deer worn on their backs as camouflage, the archers crouching beneath them are poised to fire arrows from their bows. Here, the prey has become the predator. This otherworldly, dreamlike scene is divided into two halves by a river, with the target appearing to be two hybrid figures – a king and a queen – on the right of the composition.

Leonora Carrington's deer are different again. In *Green Tea* (1942), four stags sit in a strange pot reminiscent of an alchemical alembic, as if about to be cooked alive. The pot, however, is not what it seems because it has the legs and hooves of a deer. It stands in a verdant landscape that recalls England, where the artist grew up, alongside a strange human figure wrapped tightly in cowhide. At the bottom of the painting, below the lush surface, lurks a world of decay.

Óscar Domínguez's deer, in *The Levels of Desire* (1932–33), is also being transformed into something else – but in this case it is becoming a woman who is naked except for black stockings. The desire of the title is expressed through watching: the lecherous stares of a horse and a wolf, on the right of the painting, and a male head observing a female figure whose hands have become torches – literally burning with desire – in the background. This painting was one of fifteen works exhibited by the artist at the Circulo de Bellas Artes in Tenerife, in May 1933, Domínguez's first solo show.

In *Deer's Skull with Pedernal* (1936), Georgia O'Keeffe's deer has been reduced to no more than an antlered skull, hanging on a dead tree. O'Keeffe felt a strong connection with the landscape depicted in this work, which was painted near her home in New Mexico, and animal bones and the familiar presence of the flat-topped mountain, called the Pedernal, seen in the distance at the bottom of the canvas, are themes she returned to repeatedly.

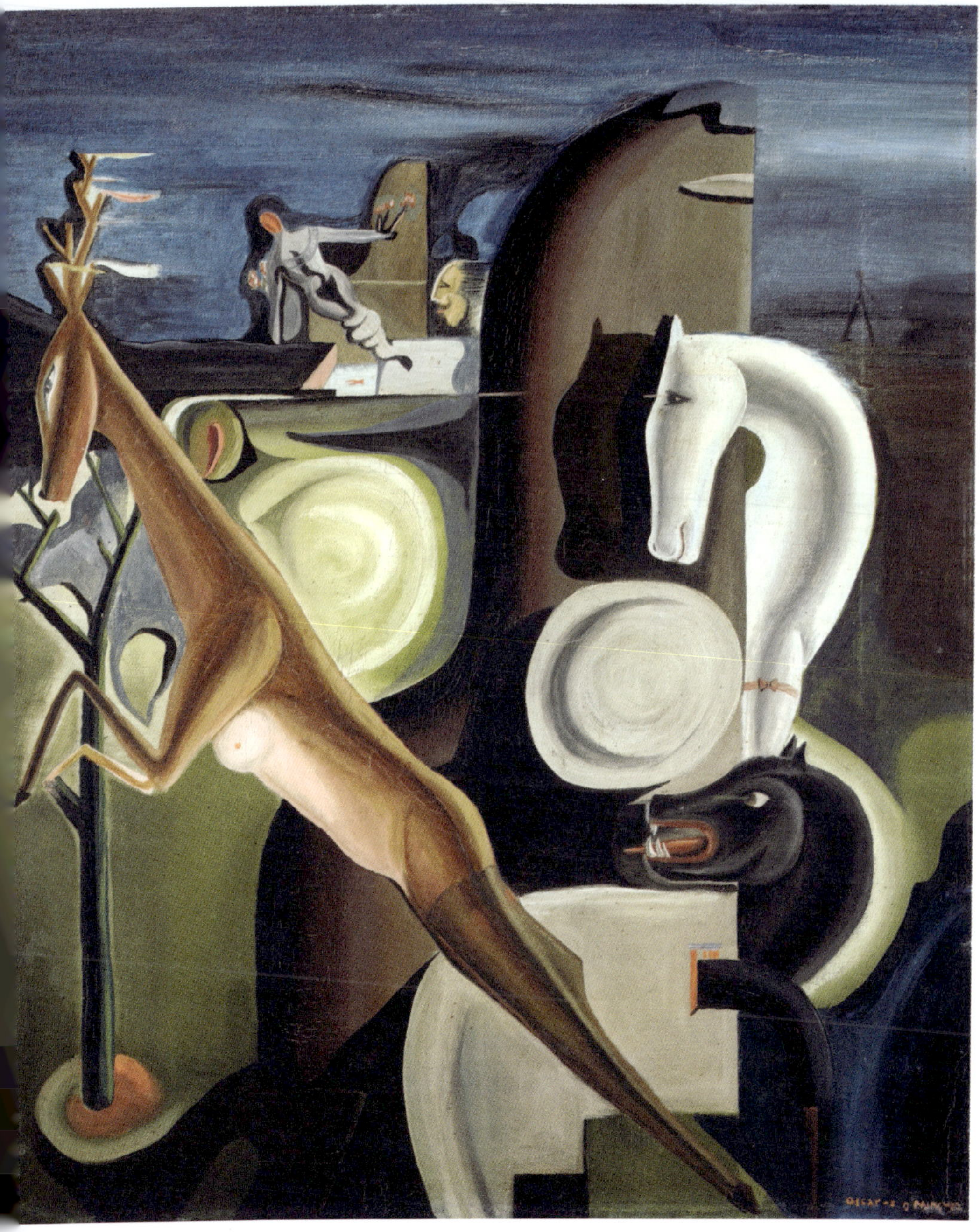

Óscar Domínguez,
The Levels of Desire, 1932–33

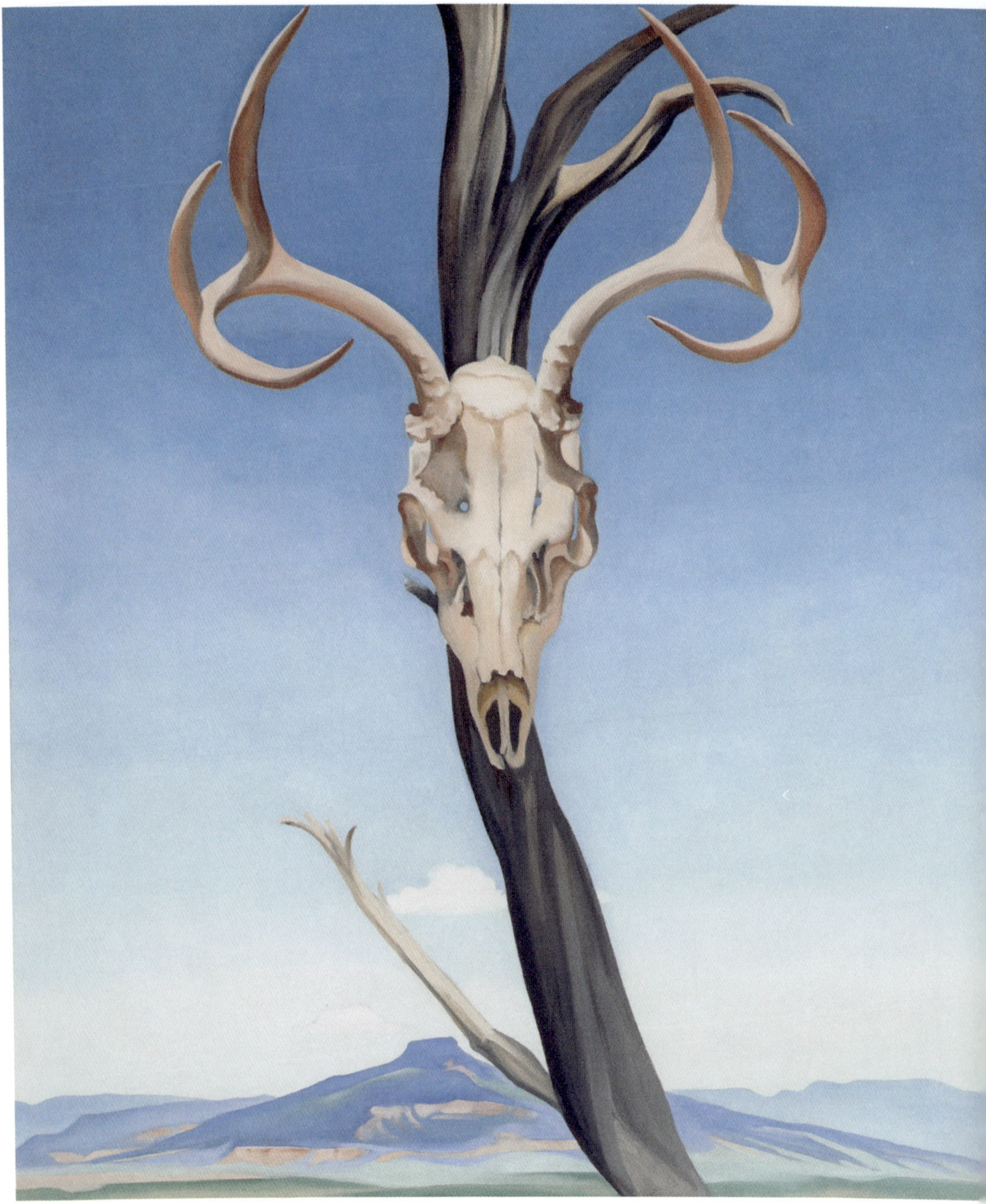

Georgia O'Keeffe, *Deer's Skull with Pedernal*, 1936

Leonora Carrington, *Green Tea*, 1942

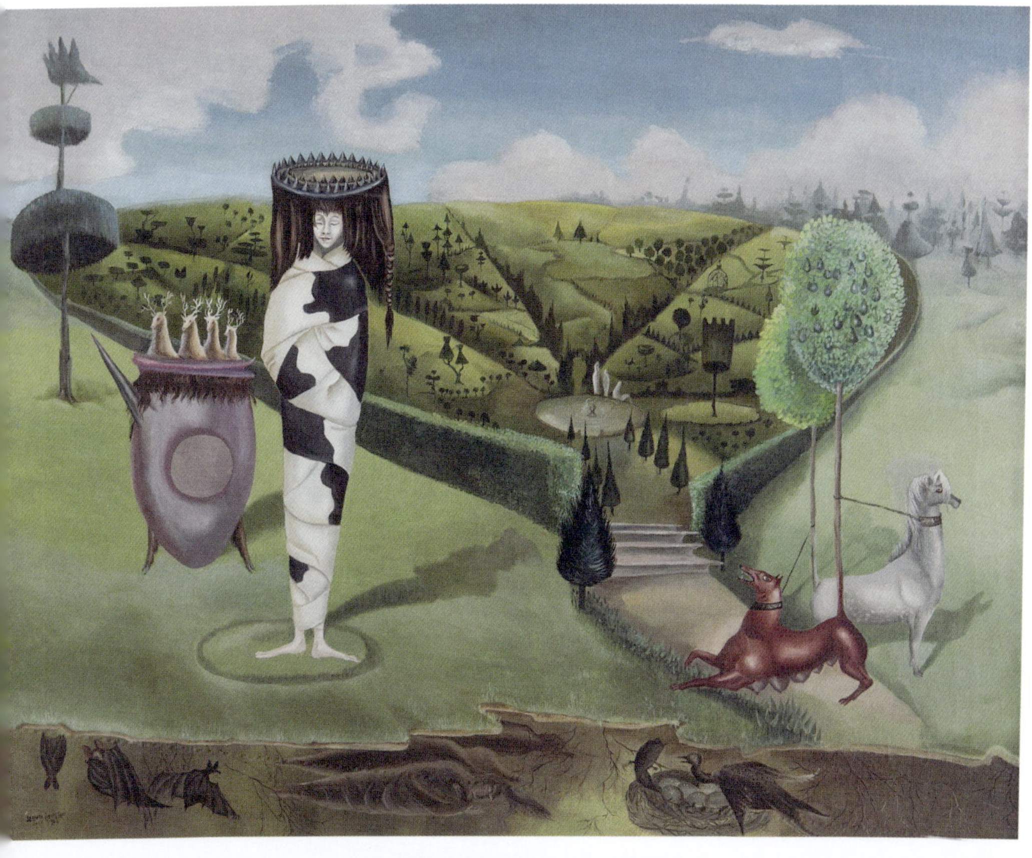

Giraffe

The Freudian significance of the giraffe is obvious, the father of psychoanalysis having drawn associations between its long neck and an erect penis. It therefore becomes a masculine symbol and one that was exploited in this role by Salvador Dalí.

Dalí portrayed the animal in a number of paintings, always showing it with its long mane bursting into flames. The first of these portrayals was *The Burning Giraffe* (1937), with Dalí describing the giraffe in this work as the 'masculine cosmic apocalyptic monster'. Despite being given prominence in the title, the giraffe appears in the background. The foreground is dominated by an elongated, human-like female that has drawers opening out of her chest and along her left leg – the 'secret drawers' of the unconscious described by Dalí, which can only be opened through psychoanalysis. A second such figure can be seen behind her and appears to be holding up a strip of meat. Created at the height of the Spanish Civil War, the 'giraffe in flames' is a foreboding of a worse conflict to come – the looming threat of the Second World War, which, in 1940, would drive Dalí himself to flee to the United States.

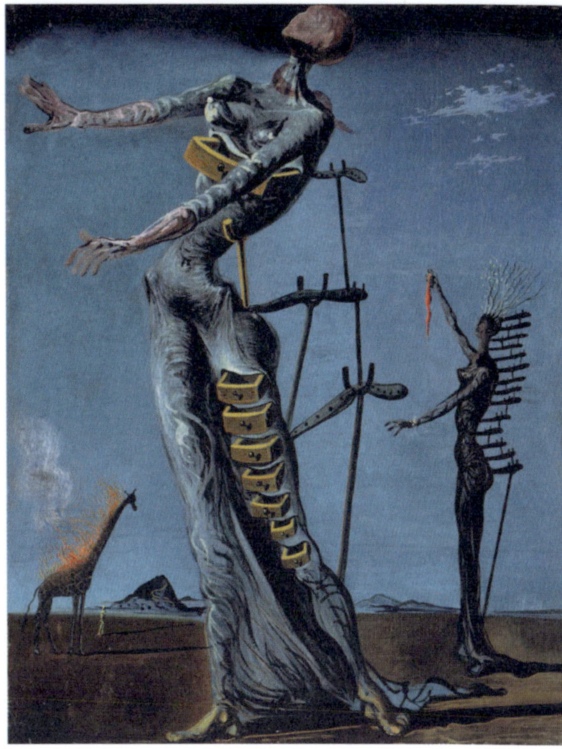

Salvador Dalí, *The Burning Giraffe*, 1937

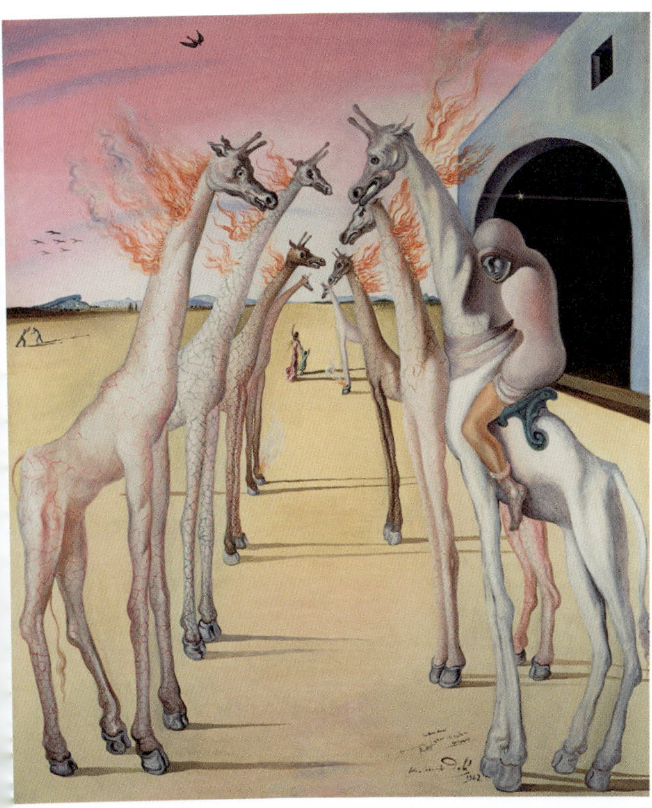

Salvador Dalí, *The Flames, They Call*, 1942

Of the later versions of his burning giraffe, the most impressive is *The Flames, They Call* (1942). Here, with most of Europe now literally in flames, his single *Burning Giraffe* of 1937 has become a whole colony of flaming animals. These giraffes, their bodies reduced to an almost skeletal condition, confront one another in two opposing rows. This is a rare example of Dalí making a comment on current affairs. His imagery is nearly always intensely personal, but the impact of the Second World War on his life would be so great that it seeped into his otherwise relentlessly eccentric and irrational visual world.

Bull

The bull has always been a symbol of brute force. It is presented as the savage beast, nature's monster, that must be subdued by the brave human warrior wielding a sword. So basic is this conflict that the ancient bullfight has managed to survive into the 21st century, despite being little more than a bloody slaughter.

The surrealist who has best captured the muscular might of the bull is André Masson. In *Tauromachie* (1937), he expresses the overpowering strength of the bull as it bears down on its human victims. The bull bares its teeth as it crushes one bullfighter, whose billowing red cape forms the backdrop to the bloody scene. A second bullfighter lies lifeless behind the bull, and a toppled horse, trapped under the cape, rears its head in terror.

Bulls are a recurring theme in Óscar Domínguez's work. They are often shown at the point of being defeated, but in *Head of a Bull* (1941) the subject takes a different turn: the bull is becoming blended with a human hand, whose fingers clasp its face.

In Joan Miró's *The Bull Race* (1945), there is no killing. His bull stares at us with a startled expression that suggests the animal knows that the famous running of the bulls in Pamplona is about to start, and he would rather be elsewhere.

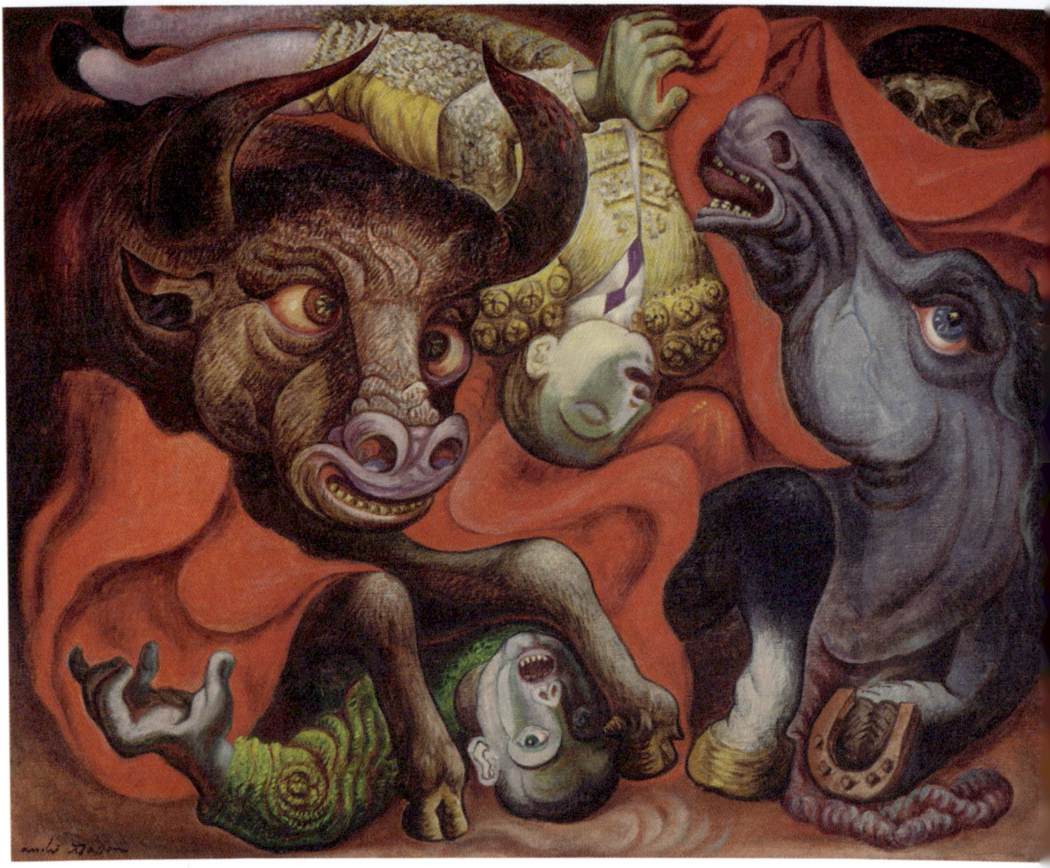

André Masson, *Tauromachie*, 1937

Dublin-born Francis Bacon was fascinated with bullfighting, and it was a subject he returned to repeatedly. In the most poignant of these works, *Study of a Bull* (1991), completed a year before his death in Madrid, the great beast is a shadow of its former self. Significantly, it was painted when Bacon knew he was dying: the bull emerges from the darkness of the bull pen into the light of the arena, where it stands reluctantly, almost invisibly, caught between life and death. For Bacon, this is a remarkably sympathetic, unmodified image of the animal, as if he wants to show the great bull his respect.

Finally, we come to a tame, placid, dehorned bull that is being held by its nose ring by a bridesmaid, as a bride in white watches on. In the background is a black-cloaked skeleton that reaches out an umbrella over the bull's head, as it appears to be raining. This is Oscar Mellor's *The Participants* (1990), and it presents us with the bull vanquished at last, but unharmed apart from its pierced nose.

Óscar Domínguez, *Head of a Bull*, 1941

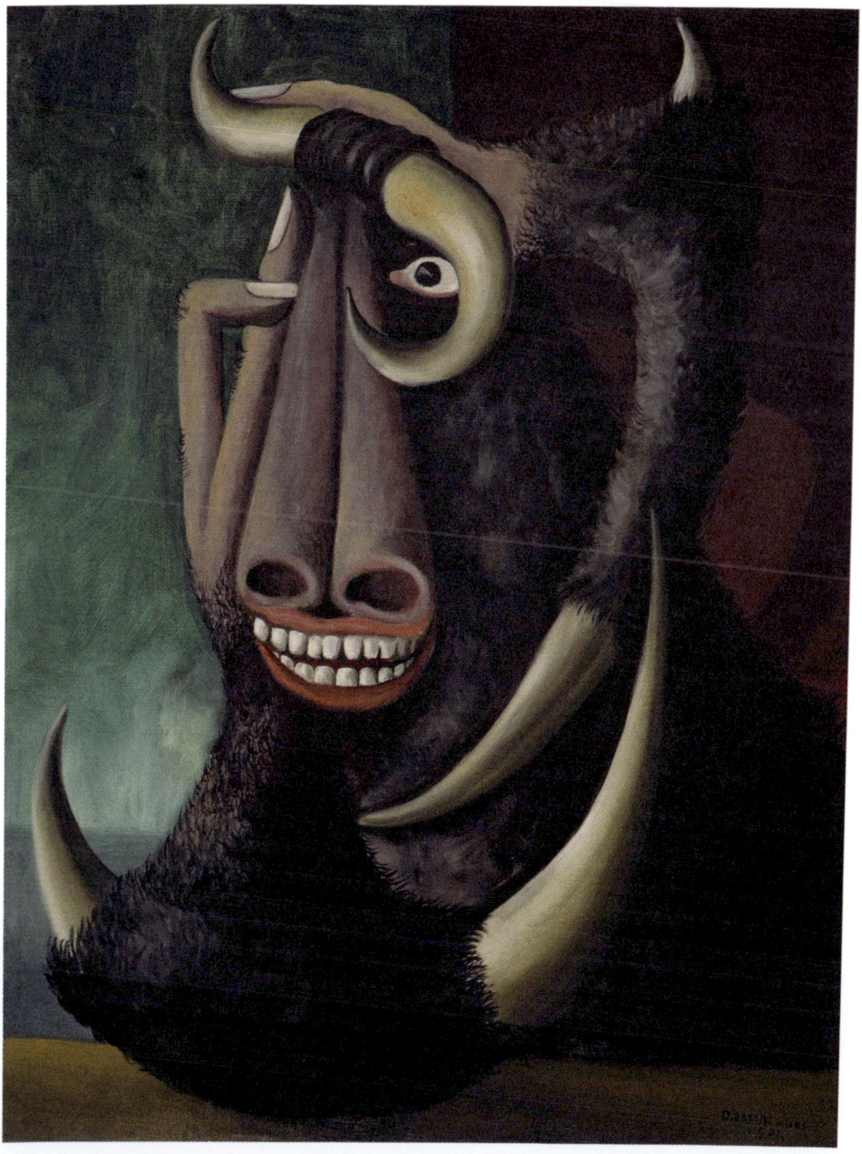

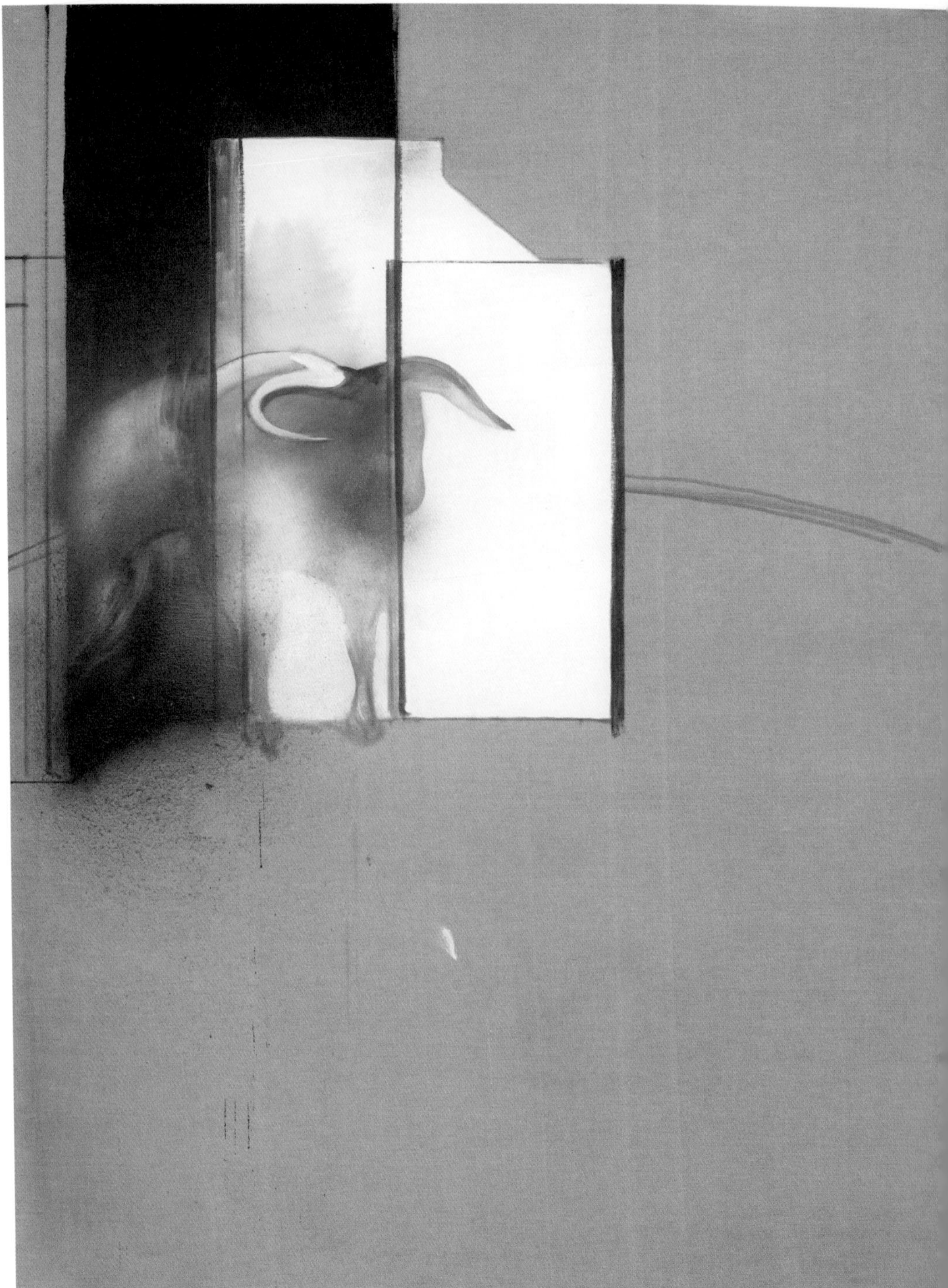

Francis Bacon, *Study of a Bull*, 1991

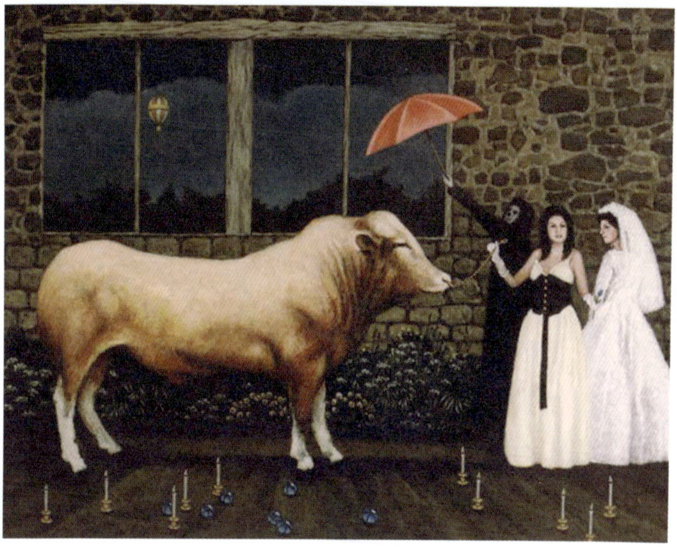

Oscar Mellor, *The Participants*, 1990

Joan Miró, *The Bull Race*, 1945

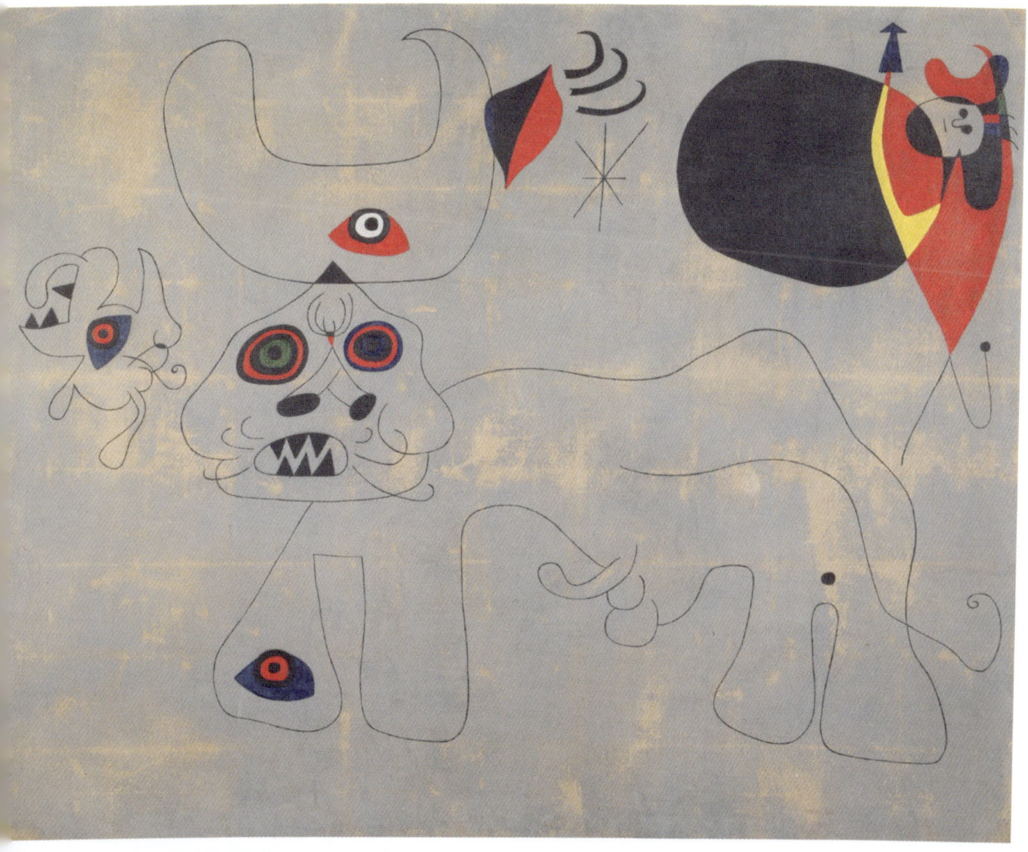

Cow

Unlike the bull, the cow rarely features in the surrealist menagerie, but there are a few exceptions.

In Félix Labisse's strangely haunting work, *The Isies* (1981), four cows' heads have become no more than draped headcoverings. In ancient Egypt, when Horus beheads his mother, the goddess Isis, because she has shown sympathy towards his enemy Seth, the god Thoth replaces her female head with the head of a cow. This explains the title of Labisse's work.

In a charming composition of 1928, called either *She Moos, We Play* or *She Bellows, We Play*, the Swiss master Paul Klee captures an anxious cow and her playful calves with a few deft lines.

In Marc Chagall's fanciful *Cow with a Parasol* (1946), a blue-headed cow, with a bunch of flowers on its back, holds a parasol in its front foot, to protect it from the glare of the sun. An inquisitive dog and a hen can be seen at the bottom of the painting. Chagall's lyrical treatment of farm animals is inspired by fond memories of his Jewish childhood in Vitebsk (then part of the Russian Empire, now in Belarus), where he was surrounded by domestic animals in the small wooden hut he shared with eight brothers and sisters.

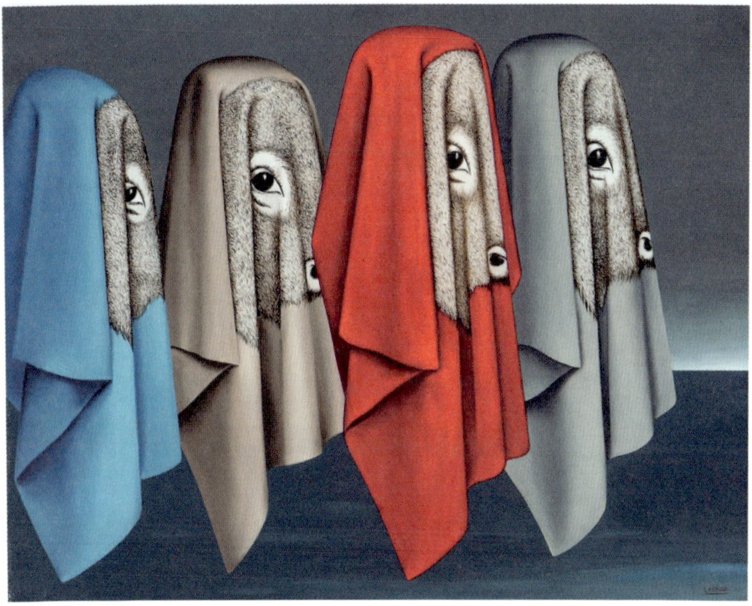

Félix Labisse, *The Isies*, 1981

Paul Klee, *She Moos, We Play*, 1928

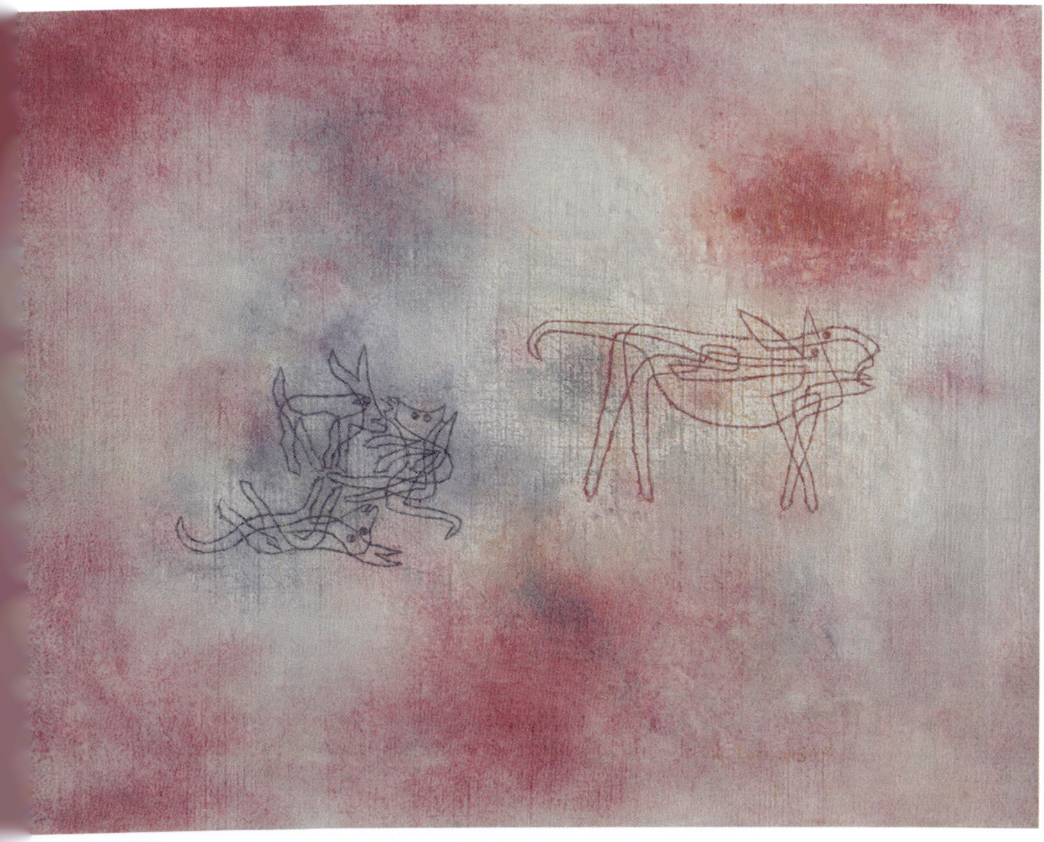

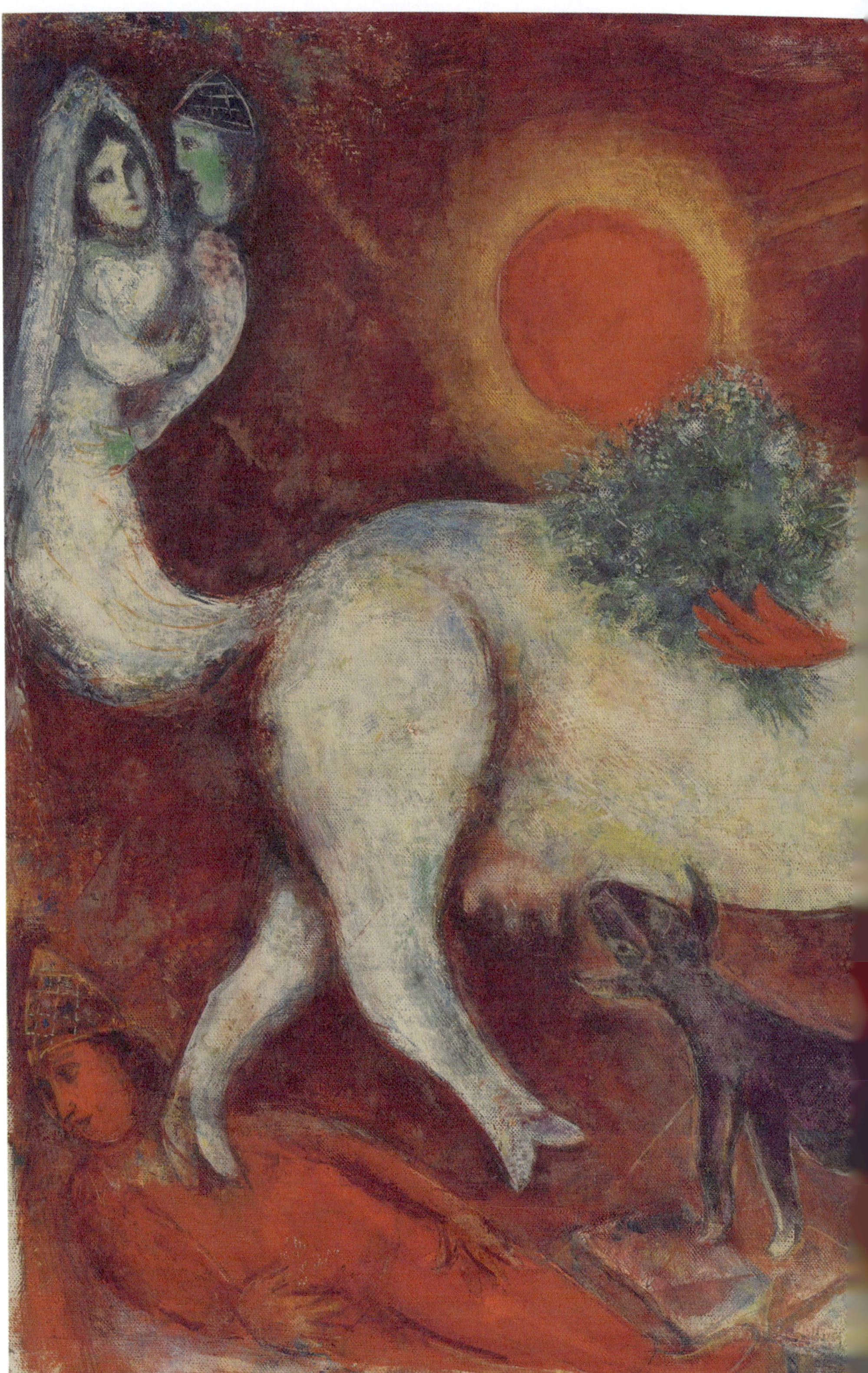

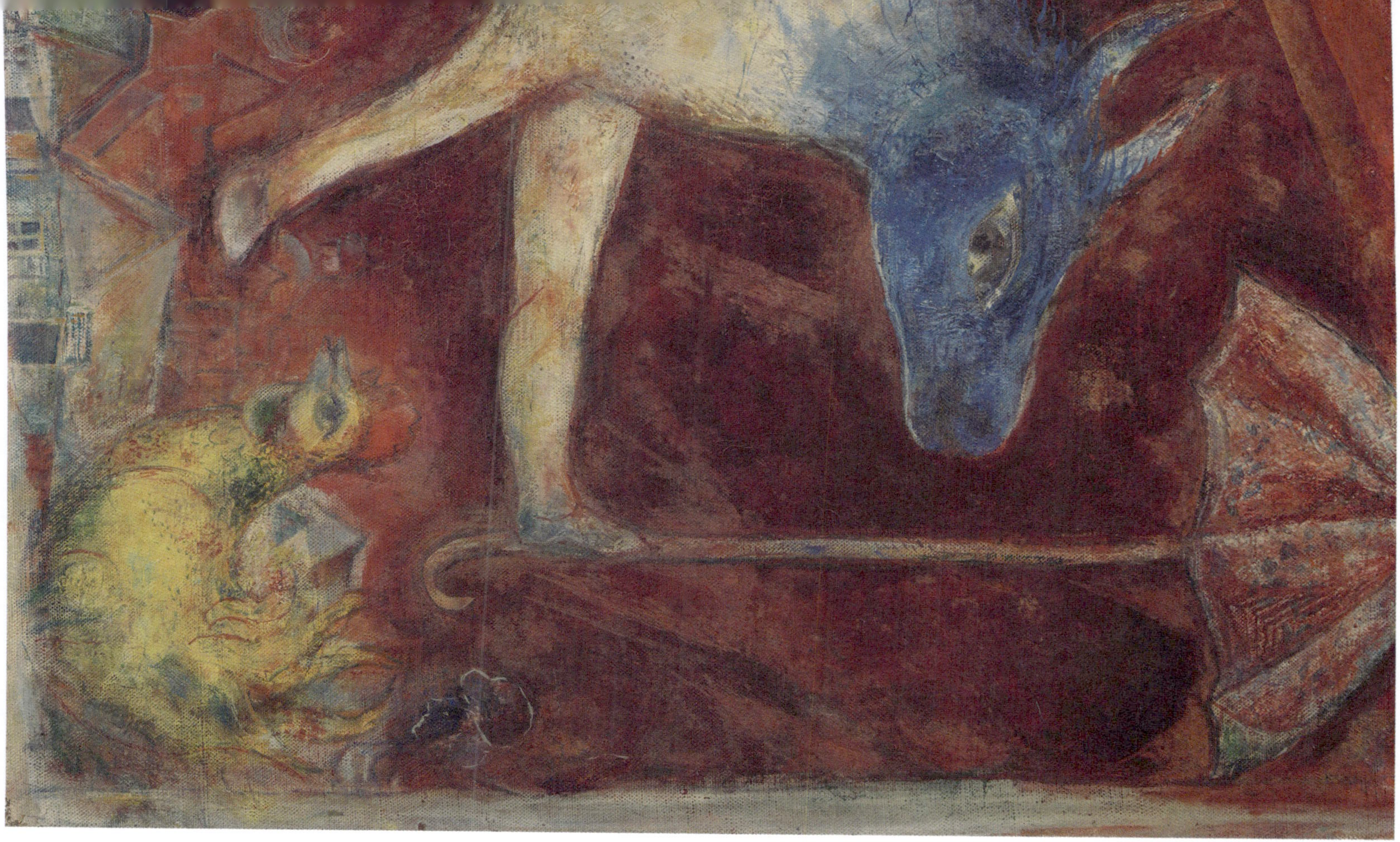

Marc Chagall, *Cow with a Parasol*, 1946

Gazelle

As a living animal, this graceful creature hardly features in the surrealist menagerie, but in the form of pieces of fur from a Chinese gazelle, it had a major role to play, and we know exactly how this came about.

Early in 1936, the Swiss surrealist Meret Oppenheim was sipping tea in a café in Paris. As she put the cup to her mouth, her raised arm revealed to her companion that she was wearing a strange metal bracelet lined with seal skin. The companion in question happened to be Pablo Picasso. The bracelet caught his attention, and she explained to him that she had designed it herself, playing with the idea of bringing together two radically different materials – hard metal and soft fur. Picasso then made the passing remark that would change her life, commenting that you could cover anything in fur. Oppenheim's reaction was to pick up her cup and saucer and joke, 'Even this!'

When she left the café, the bizarre idea of covering a cup and saucer with fur stuck in her mind. She found a Uniprix department store, where she selected a suitable cup, saucer and spoon, and then wrapped them in the fur of a Chinese gazelle. There was something so disturbing about the idea of drinking from a fur-lined cup that this object she had created on a whim became a famous surrealist icon and was widely exhibited. It came to overshadow all her other work, which led Oppenheim to lament, many years later: 'Ah, this eternal Fur-cup. You make an object, which gets placed on an altar, and everybody only speaks of it and nothing else.'

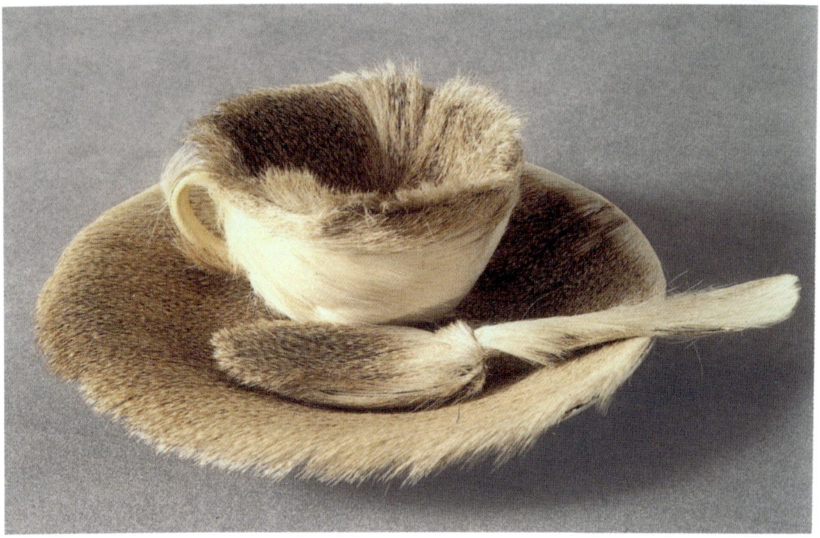

Meret Oppenheim, *Object*, 1936

The gazelle-cup, christened *Breakfast in Fur* by André Breton, but more commonly known simply as *Object*, was first exhibited in Paris in May 1936, in a show of surrealist objects organized by Breton. It caused such a sensation that, the following month, it was shipped across the Channel to appear in the momentous International Surrealist Exhibition in London. Soon afterwards, it was bought by the Museum of Modern Art in Manhattan, where it is still a major surrealist exhibit. Salvador Dalí appears to have taken inspiration from the work when he was asked, in 1939, to dress the windows of New York department store Bonwit Teller, whose short-lived displays included a bathtub lined with black sheepskin and filled with water; within hours the artist famously destroyed the displays, upending the bathtub and sending it crashing through the window.

In 1996, an exhibition called 'Meret Oppenheim: Beyond the Teacup' opened in New York – before travelling to other parts of the USA – to remind people of the artist's other work, which had been so badly overlooked.

Goat

Historically, the goat has long been a symbol of virility in many cultures, and it was associated with qualities such as curiosity and resilience. Due to its unruly nature, it has often been contrasted with the sheep, which follows obediently. With the rise of Christianity, it began to be associated with evil, with Satan being portrayed as having goat-like features, such as cloven hooves, hairy legs, horns, pointed ears and a beard. Perhaps because of this strong religious connection, the goat has not been favoured by the surrealists. The one exception is that great forerunner of the surrealists, Marc Chagall.

In his paintings, Chagall never forgot the childhood joys he experienced growing up in a village on the Russian border, surrounded by farm animals, music, dancing and family games. His first great masterpiece, *I and the Village* (1911), sums this up, and it is dominated by the head of a young goat. On the goat's cheek, the artist has added a vignette of a woman milking a cow, and colourful figures and buildings populate the background. Chagall painted this work a year after moving to Paris, and the fragmented geometrical forms in the dreamlike composition show the influence of Cubism, which he first experienced in the city.

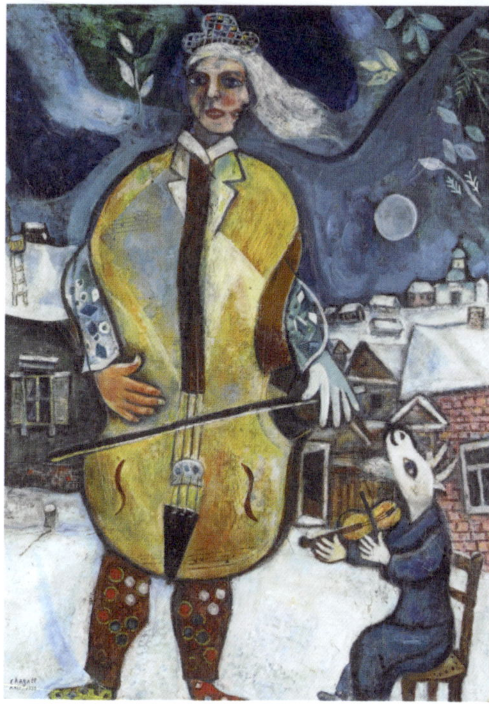

Marc Chagall, *The Cellist*, 1939

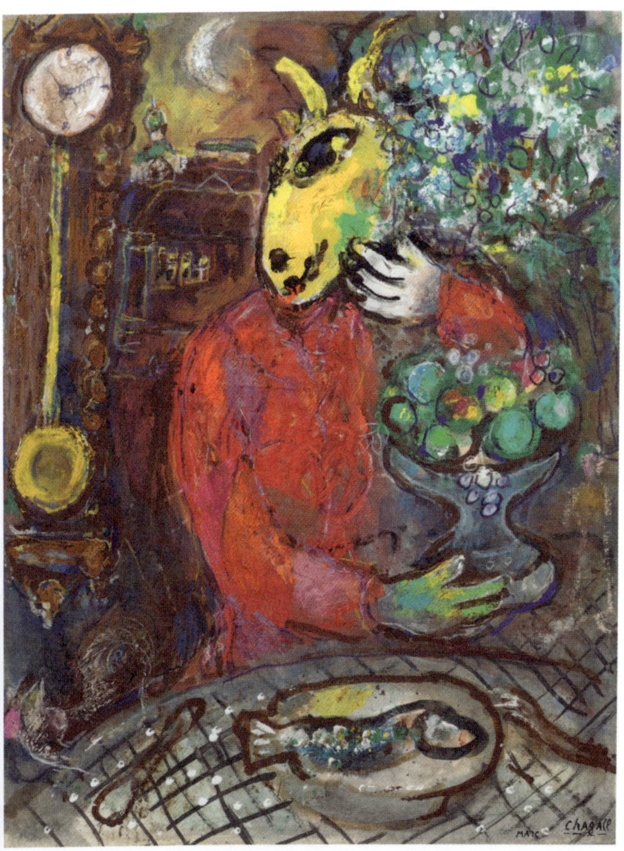

Marc Chagall, *The Red Jacket*, 1961

In later works, such as *The Cellist* (1939), his goat is often seen playing a stringed instrument. Here, the 'cellist' of the title refers to a central human figure whose body has morphed into the very instrument he is playing. The goat sits to one side with a violin, accompanying the cellist. *The Red Jacket* (1961), meanwhile, depicts a hybrid human figure with a goat's head. He is sat at a table and holds a bunch of flowers and a bowl of fruit. In the 1980s, Chagall depicted a painter in a red jacket, which is thought to be a self-portrait, suggesting that this human-hybrid figure may represent the artist himself. For Chagall, the goat has nothing to do with Satan. It is simply a fond reminder of the happy-go-lucky rural life that he enjoyed as a child.

Sheep

People who don't think for themselves, following blindly where others go, are sometimes compared to sheep, while gentle souls who pose no threat may be likened to lambs. Many of us associate sheep with warm clothing and comfort. None of these qualities makes them popular members of the darkly humorous surrealist menagerie. Perhaps, for this very reason, one particular surrealist, Salvador Dalí, took great care to portray them in detail in two of his works.

In *The Sheep* (1942), a flock of sheep has invaded a richly decorated room, where a woman – who, strangely, has a pigeon perched on her head – sits apparently undisturbed, sipping from a cup. Dressed in a long white robe, she has ill-defined, ghostly facial features – in contrast to the anatomically detailed sheep – and appears out of place, perhaps even from an earlier period in time than the room would suggest. A book has been placed on the back of one of the sheep, whose body – like others in the foreground – has been partially transformed into ornate furniture. As if enchanted, the living sheep are slowly becoming the fittings of this lavish abode.

In *Design for the Interior Decoration of a Stable-Library*, of the same year, an attractive woman is almost submerged by a family of sheep – two adults, with their thick, soft wool coats, and two lambs. One of the lambs has been given the full Dalí treatment, with a drawer having been pulled out of its flank and with a furry telephone resting on its back.

Salvador Dalí, *The Sheep*, 1942

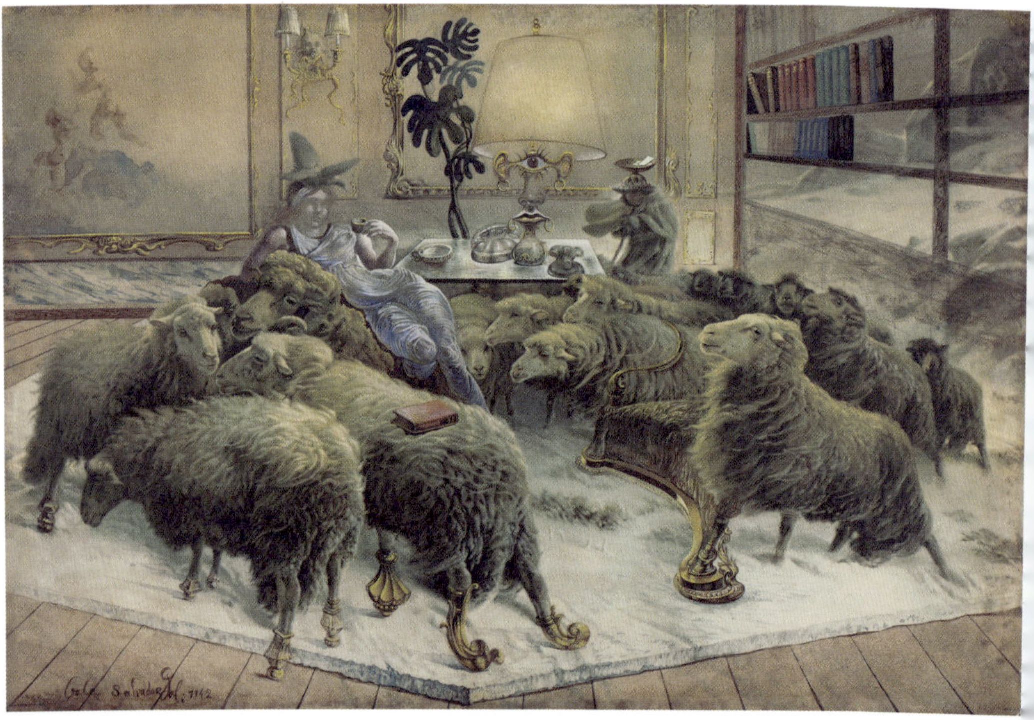

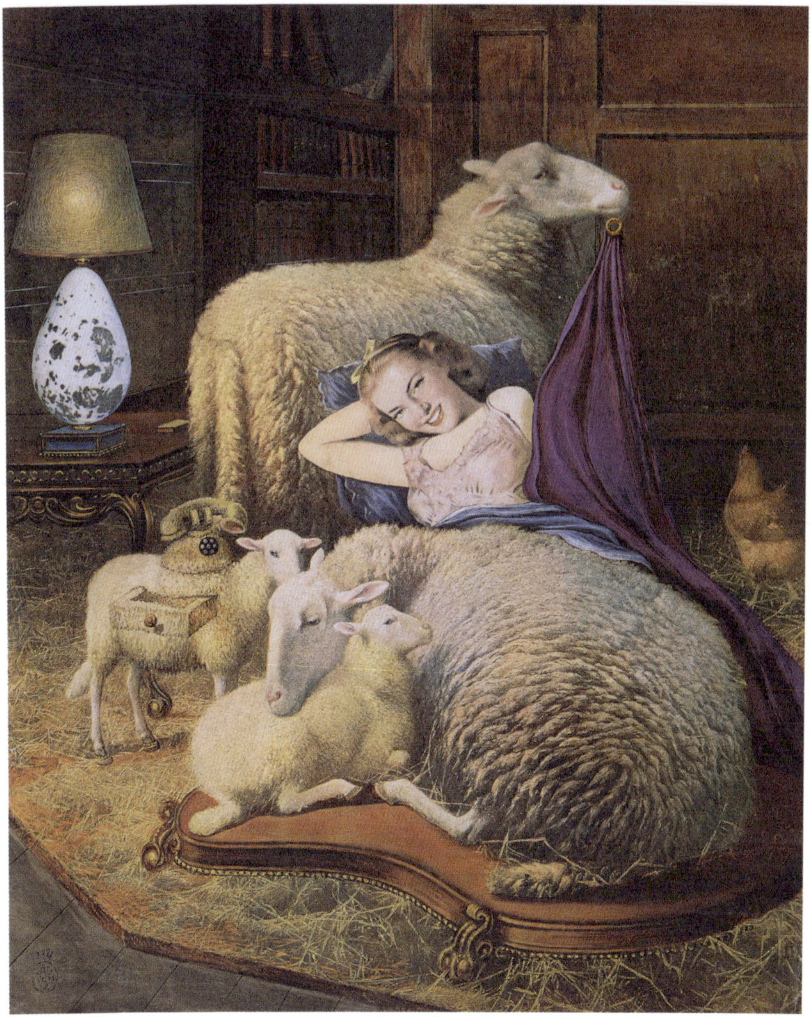

Salvador Dalí, *Design for the Interior Decoration of a Stable-Library*, 1942

The

Pr

nates

Monkey

The monkey played several distinct roles in surrealist art. It was seen as a foolish caricature of human existence, a colourful oddity, an irrational companion and an anatomical exaggeration.

The first notable example appeared on the eve of surrealism, in the notorious Dada poster *Still Lifes* created by Francis Picabia in 1920. The monkey in question was not a painted one, but a rather dilapidated toy wired to a canvas. Picabia had pulled the animal's tail between its legs so that it protruded obscenely as a long furry penis. In a savage attack on earlier art forms, he then wrote around the monkey – in capital letters – 'Portrait of Cézanne, Portrait of Renoir, Portrait of Rembrandt, Still Lifes'. Because it was written in French, the term 'Still Lifes' reads as 'Natures Mortes', which taken literally becomes 'Dead Nature' – a savage condemnation of the earlier artists as 'dead meat'. This particular monkey image can therefore be seen as the herald of the whole surrealist rebellion against the establishment that was about to explode.

Two years later, Max Ernst, another Dadaist who would become a pioneering surrealist, created a dramatic portrait of a monkey's face. *The Blue Monkey with Flower* (1922) is a bizarre self-portrait in which the artist sees himself in animal form. When he painted it, he had just given in to his animal impulses to start a passionate affair with the young woman who would later become Salvador Dalí's wife, Gala. He dedicated the painting to Cécile, her four-year-old daughter, and there is a photograph of him with the child, taken in the summer of 1922, that shows her

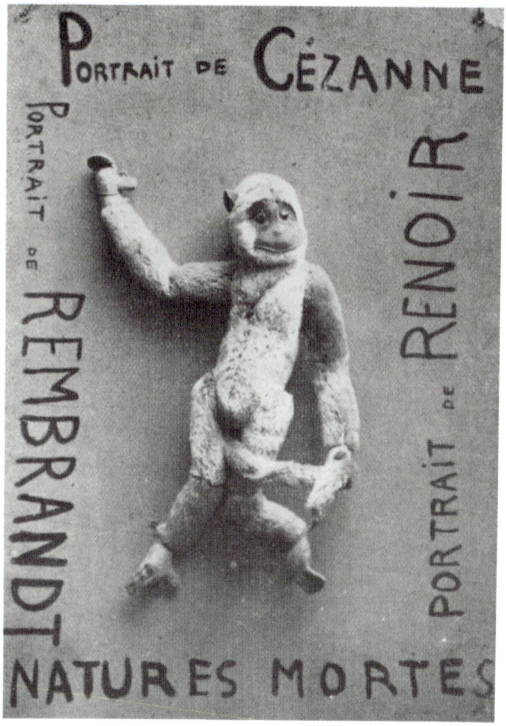

Francis Picabia, *Still Lifes*, 1920

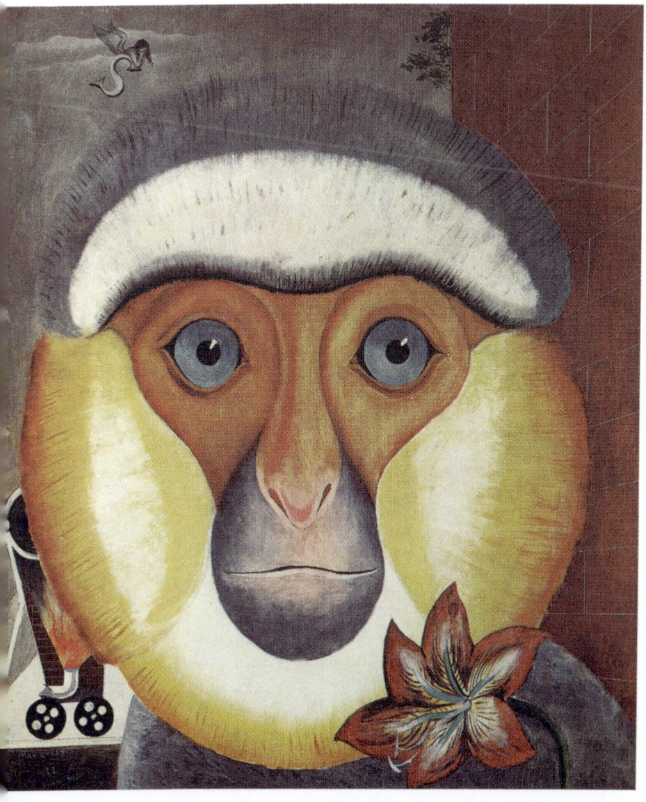

Max Ernst, *The Blue Monkey with Flower*, 1922

hugging a large toy monkey that may have been the inspiration for this painting.

There is a special reason why this picture can be seen as a self-portrait of the artist. Although Ernst refers to it as a blue monkey (*Cercopithecus mitis*), an African species, and it appears to be an accurate portrayal, it is not. The most significant alteration concerns the colour of the eyes. In nature, this monkey's eyes are pale orange in colour and are surrounded by blue-grey facial hair. Ernst has reversed these colours, making the eyes pale blue and the facial fur orange. Ernst's own eyes were a penetrating pale blue and so by this simple device he has placed himself inside the head of the monkey.

Although the face of the blue monkey occupies almost the whole canvas, there is a curious detail lurking in the bottom left-hand corner. It is partly obscured, but it is just possible to make

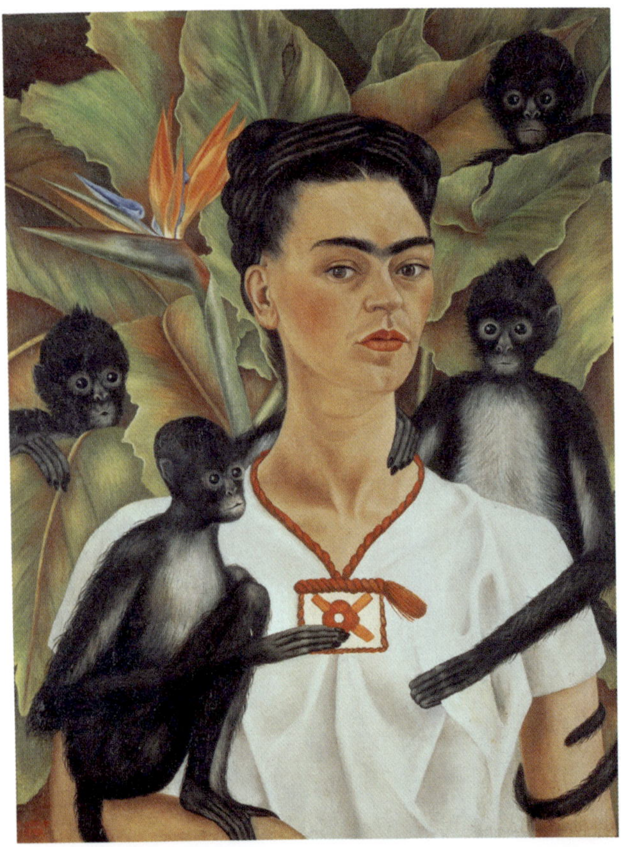

Frida Kahlo, *Self-Portrait with Monkeys*, 1943

out a burning furnace of the kind used by alchemists who sought to turn lead into gold. Alchemy is a subject that fascinated Ernst, who once described collage as the 'alchemy of the visual image' – the means by which to transform the lead of boring advertisements into the gold of surrealist compositions.

In the 1930s and early 1940s, the Mexican artist Frida Kahlo also painted a number of monkey-themed self-portraits. In the best of these works, *Self-Portrait with Monkeys* (1943), she depicts herself with four spider monkeys. One of the monkeys sits on her right forearm and clings to her neck, while another embraces her left shoulder and curls its prehensile tail around her left upper arm. The other two peer out of the dense vegetation behind her.

In the wild, the habitat of the spider monkey ranges from South America to Central America and even as far north as Mexico. Kahlo adored animals and kept several monkeys as pets – among them a Geoffroy's spider monkey (*Ateles geoffroyi*) called Fulang Chang, a gift from her husband Diego Rivera. The sadness she felt at not being able to have children of her own, following an accident in 1925, is a recurring theme in her self-portraits – the monkeys becoming symbols of the children she never had. Fulang Chang became a much-loved companion for Kahlo and appears with her in several self-portraits.

Around the time Kahlo painted *Self-Portrait with Monkeys*, her health was deteriorating and she became too ill to continue teaching at the National School of Painting, Sculpture and Printmaking ('La Esmeralda') in Mexico City. She started teaching a handful of her students, affectionately known as 'Los Fridos', from home and it has been suggested that the quartet of monkeys in this painting may symbolize the four students who remained with her during this period.

Toyen also lovingly portrays a monkey in a painting called simply *At the Blue Face* (1951). It is a curious work, showing a

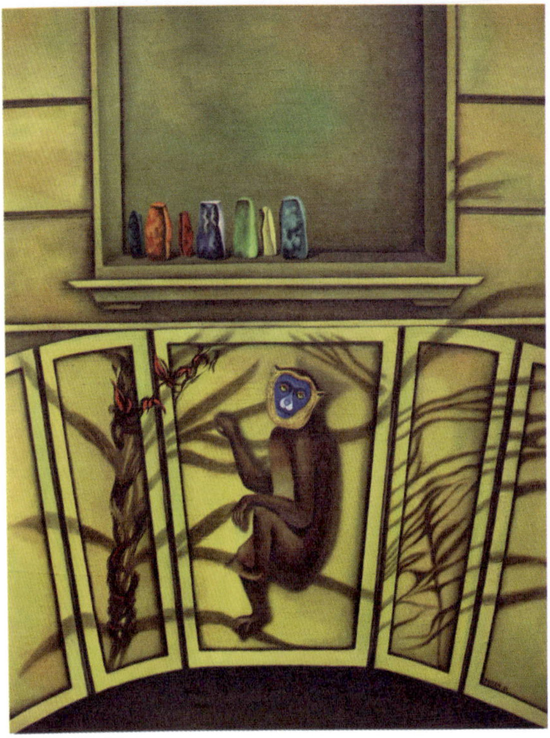

Toyen, *At the Blue Face*, 1951

five-panelled, folding screen propped against a wall. The large central panel is occupied by the blue-faced monkey, sitting on branches and apparently lacking its long tail. The species depicted is the West African moustached monkey (*Cercopithecus cephus*).

Finally, there is Francis Bacon's 'screaming' baboon of 1953. His animal is shown sitting in the fork of a dead tree in a large enclosure. The animal's head is tossed back and its jaws are wide open, in an expression that recalls his famous 'screaming popes'. The obvious conclusion is that the poor animal is tormented. This is unlikely, however, because when a baboon screams, it directs its action towards the source of its distress. When it gapes its mouth upwards, it is more likely to be yawning with boredom than screaming in agony. But this is a mere quibble because, either way, Bacon has managed to capture the very essence of a baboon with his brilliantly suggestive brushstrokes.

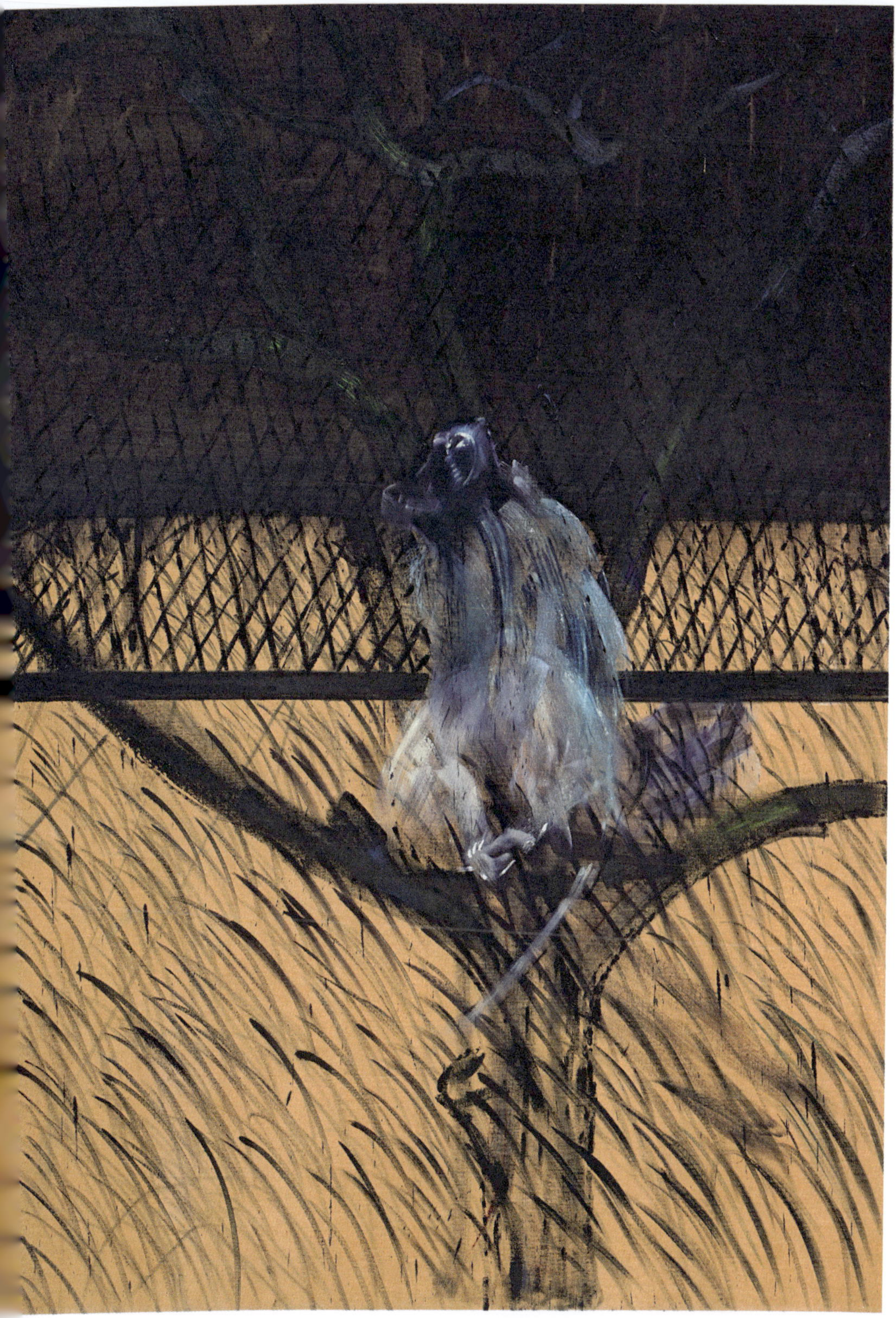

Francis Bacon, *Study of a Baboon*, 1953

Further Reading

All the books listed below were searched for examples of the animals featured in *The Surrealist Menagerie*.

Eileen Agar

Agar, Eileen, *A Look at My Life*, Methuen, London, 1988
Blazwick, Iwona, et al., *Eileen Agar: Angel of Anarchy*, Whitechapel Gallery, London, 2021
Byatt, A. S., *Eileen Agar 1899–1991: An Imaginative Playfulness*, Redfern Gallery, London, 2004
Lambirth, Andrew, *Eileen Agar: A Retrospective*, Birch & Conran, London, 1987
Remy, Michel, *Eileen Agar: Dreaming Oneself Awake*, Reaktion Books, London, 2017
Simpson, Ann, et al., *Eileen Agar 1899–1991*, National Galleries of Scotland, Edinburgh, 1999
Taylor, John Russell, 'Peek-a-boo with a Woman of Infinite Variety', *The Times* 'Arts' section, pp. 14–15, 15 December 2004

Francis Bacon

Ades, Dawn, and Andrew Forge, *Francis Bacon*, Tate Gallery, London, 1985
Alley, Ronald, and John Rothenstein (introduction), *Francis Bacon: Catalogue Raisonné*, Thames & Hudson, London, 1964
Archimbaud, Michel, *Francis Bacon: In Conversation with Michel Archimbaud*, Phaidon Press, London, 1993
Birch, James, *Bacon in Moscow*, Cheerio, London, 2022
Brighton, Andrew, *Francis Bacon*, Tate, London, 2001
Cappock, Margarita, *Francis Bacon's Studio*, Merrell, London, 2005
Davies, Hugh M., *Francis Bacon: The Papal Portraits of 1953*, Museum of Contemporary Art San Diego, 2001
Davies, Hugh M., and Sally Yard, *Francis Bacon*, Abbeville Press, New York, 1986
Edwards, John (foreword), and Perry Ogden (photographer), *7 Reece Mews: Francis Bacon's Studio*, Thames & Hudson, London, 2001
Farson, Daniel, *The Gilded Gutter Life of Francis Bacon*, Vintage, London, 1994
Ficacci, Luigi, *Bacon: 1909–1992*, Taschen, Cologne, 2003
Hammer, Martin, *Bacon and Sutherland*, Yale University Press for Paul Mellon Centre for Studies in British Art, New Haven, 2005
Hammer, Martin, *Francis Bacon and Nazi Propaganda*, Tate, London, 2012
Harrison, Martin, *In Camera: Francis Bacon*, Thames & Hudson, London, 2005
Harrison, Martin, *Francis Bacon: Catalogue Raisonné* (5 vols), The Estate of Francis Bacon, London, 2016
Leiris, Michel, *Francis Bacon: Full Face and in Profile*, Rizzoli, New York, 1983
Peppiatt, Michael, *Francis Bacon: Anatomy of an Enigma*, Weidenfeld and Nicolson, London, 1996
Peppiatt, Michael, et al., *Francis Bacon: Man and Beast*, Royal Academy of Arts, London, 2021
Sinclair, Andrew, *Francis Bacon: His Life and Violent Times*, Crown, New York, 1993
Stevens, Mark, and Annalyn Swan, *Francis Bacon: Revelations*, HarperCollins, London, 2021
Sylvester, David, *Interviews with Francis Bacon*, Thames & Hudson, London, 1975
Sylvester, David, *Looking Back at Francis Bacon*, Thames & Hudson, London, 2000

Victor Brauner

Anon., *Victor Brauner*, The Mayor Gallery, London, 1989
Alexandrian, Sarane, *Les Dessins Magiques de Victor Brauner*, Editions Denoel, Paris, 1965
Ballo, Guido, and Emilio Tadini, *Omaggio a Victor Brauner*, Galleria Schwarz, Milan, 1966
Bétard, Daphné, et al., *Victor Brauner: je suis le rêve, je suis l'inspiration*, Beaux Arts & Cie, Paris, 2020
Bozo, Dominique, *Les Dessins de Victor Brauner*, Musée National d'Art Moderne, Paris, 1972
Crispolti, Enrico, *Brauner*, Galleria Schwarz, Milan, 1962
Davidson, Susan, et al., *Victor Brauner: Surrealist Hieroglyphs*, Menil, Houston, 2001
Fréchuret, Maurice, *Cahiers Victor Brauner*, Musée d'Art Moderne Saint-Etienne, 1988
Jouffroy, Alain, *Brauner*, Le Musée de Poche, Paris, 1959
Semin, Didier, *Victor Brauner*, Filipacchi, Paris, 1990
Semin, Didier, *Victor Brauner*, Centre Pompidou, Paris, 1996
Semin, Didier, et al., *Dialogue des Mondes: Victor Brauner et les Arts Primitifs*, Galerie Schoffel-Valluet and Galerie Samy Kinge, Paris, 2010

André Breton

Breton, André, *Surrealism and Painting*, Museum of Fine Arts, Boston, 1965
Goutier, Jean-Michel, et al., *André Breton. 42 Rue Fontaine* (auction catalogue, vols 1–8), Calmels-Cohen, Paris, 2003
Gracq, Julien, et al., *André Breton. La Beauté Convulsive*, Editions du Centre Pompidou, Paris, 1991
Polizzotti, Mark, *Revolution of the Mind: The Life of André Breton*, Bloomsbury, London, 1995

Leonora Carrington

Aberth, Susan L., *Leonora Carrington: Surrealism, Alchemy and Art*, Lund Humphries, London, 2004
Carrington, Gabriel Weisz, *The Invisible Painting: My Memoir of Leonora Carrington*, Manchester University Press, 2021
Carrington, Leonora, *The Hearing Trumpet*, St Martin's Press/St James Press, New York/London, 1976
Chadwick, Whitney, *Leonora Carrington: La Realidad de la Imaginación*, Ediciones Era, Mexico City, 1994
Moorhead, Joanna, *The Surreal Life of Leonora Carrington*, Virago Press, London, 2017
Moorhead, Joanna, *Surreal Spaces: The Life and Art of Leonora Carrington*, Thames & Hudson, London, 2023

Marc Chagall

Compton, Susan, *Chagall*, Weidenfeld & Nicolson, London, 1985
Haftmann, Werner, *Chagall*, Abrams, New York, 1998
Meyer, Franz, *Marc Chagall. Leben und Werk*, DuMont Schauberg, Cologne, 1968
Sweeney, James Johnson, *Marc Chagall*, Museum of Modern Art, New York, 1946

Ithell Colquhoun

Colquhoun, Ithell, *The Crying of the Wind: Ireland*, Peter Owen, London, 2016
Hale, Amy, *The Supersensual Life of Ithell Colquhoun*, Francis Boutle, London, 2011
Levy, Silvano, 'The del Renzio Affair: A Leadership Struggle in Wartime Surrealism', *Papers of Surrealism*, Issue 3, Spring 2005
Ratcliffe, Eric, *Ithell Colquhoun, Pioneer Surrealist Artist, Occultist, Writer, and Poet*, Mandrake, Oxford, 2007
Shillitoe, Richard, *Ithell Colquhoun: Magician Born of Nature*, lulu.com, 2010

Joseph Cornell

Hartigan, Lynda Roscoe, et al., *Joseph Cornell. Shadowplay Eterniday*, Thames & Hudson, London, 2003
Lea, Sarah, and Lynda Roscoe Hartigan, *Joseph Cornell: Wanderlust*, Royal Academy of Arts, London, 2015

Solomon, Deborah, *Utopia Parkway: The Life and Work of Joseph Cornell*, Jonathan Cape, London, 1997

Salvador Dalí

Abadie, Daniel, et al., *Salvador Dalí. Retrospective 1920–1980*, Pompidou, Paris, 1979
Ades, Dawn, *Dalí's Optical Illusions*, Yale University Press, New Haven, 2000
Ades, Dawn, and Fiona Bradley, *Salvador Dalí: A Mythology*, Tate, London, 1998
Aguer i Teixidor, Montse, et al., *Dalí Multifaceted*, Chunichi Shimbun, Nagoya, Japan, 2007
Anguera, A. Oriol, *Mentira y Verdad de Salvador Dalí*, Ediciones Cobalto, Barcelona, 1948
Aguilera, Cesáreo Rodríguez, *Dalí*, Nauta, Barcelona, 1985
Caws, Mary Ann, *Salvador Dalí*, Reaktion Books, London, 2008
Cowles, Fleur, *Dalí: The Case of Salvador Dalí*, Heinemann, London, 1959
Dalí, Salvador, *Conquest of the Irrational*, Julien Levy, New York, 1935
Dalí, Salvador, *Metamorphosis of Narcissus*, Julien Levy, New York, 1937
Dalí, Salvador, *The Secret Life of Salvador Dalí*, Vision Press, London, 1948
Dalí, Salvador, *Dalí by Dalí*, Abrams, New York, 1970
Dalí, Salvador, *Hidden Faces*, Peter Owen, London, 1973
Dalí, Salvador, *The Wines of Gala*, Abrams, New York, 1978
Dalí, Salvador, *Diary of a Genius*, Creation Books, London, 1994
Dalí, Salvador, *Les Dîners de Gala*, Taschen, Cologne, 2021
De Burca, Jackie, *Salvador Dalí at Home*, White Lion Publishing, London, 2018
Descharnes, Robert, *The World of Salvador Dalí*, Macmillan, London, 1962
Descharnes, Robert, *Dalí: The Work, The Man*, Abrams, New York, 1984
Descharnes, Robert, and Gilles Néret, *Dalí: The Paintings* (2 vols), Taschen, Cologne, 1994
Duane, O.B., *Salvador Dalí*, Brockhampton Press, London, 1996
Etherington-Smith, Meredith, *Dalí: A Biography*, Sinclair-Stevenson, London, 1992
Eyraud, Clovis, et al., *La Divine Comédie...par Salvador Dalí*, Musée Galliera, Paris, 1960
Field, Albert, *The Official Catalog of the Graphic Works of Salvador Dalí*, Salvador Dalí Archives, New York, 1996
Friedewald, Boris, *Dalí's Moustaches: An Act of Homage*, Prestel, Munich, 2016
Gerard, Max, *Dalí*, Abrams, New York, 1968
Gibson, Ian, et al., *Salvador Dalí: The Early Years*, Thames & Hudson, London, 1994
Gibson, Ian, *The Shameful Life of Salvador Dalí*, Faber and Faber, London, 1997
Giménez-Frontín, J. L., *Teatre-Museu Dalí*, Electa, Madrid, 1995
King, Elliott H., et al., *Salvador Dalí: The Late Work*, Yale University Press, New Haven, 2011
Larkin, David (ed.), *Dalí*, Pan Books, London, 1976
Maddox, Conroy, *Dalí*, Hamlyn, London, 1981
Moorhouse, Paul, *Dalí*, Magna Books, Leicester, 1990
Mullins, Edwin, *Swimming with Dalí: And Other Encounters with Artists*, Unicorn, London, 2016
Néret, Gilles, *Salvador Dalí 1904–1989*, Taschen, Cologne, 2000
Parinaud, André, *The Unspeakable Confessions of Salvador Dalí*, Quartet Books, London, 1977
Pitxot, Antoni, and Josep Playa, *Casa-Museu Castell Gala Dalí Púbol*, Escudo de Oro, Barcelona, 2004
Radford, Robert, *Dalí*, Phaidon, London
Rogerson, Mark, *The Dalí Scandal*, Gollancz, London, 1997
Romero, Luis, *Dalí*, Chartwell Books, New Jersey, 1975
Secrest, Meryle, *Salvador Dalí: The Surrealist Jester*, Weidenfeld & Nicolson, London, 1986
Schaffner, Ingrid, *Salvador Dalí's Dream of Venus*, Princeton Architectural Press, New York, 2002
Serna, Ramón Gómez de la, *Dalí*, MacDonald, London, 1984
Shanes, Eric, *The Life and Masterworks of Salvador Dalí*, Parkstone Press International, New York, 2010
Soby, James Thrall, *Salvador Dalí*, Museum of Modern Art, New York, 1946
Volboudt, Pierre, et al., *Homage to Salvador Dalí*, Chartwell Books, New Jersey, 1980
Weinhardt, Carl J., et al., *Salvador Dalí 1910–1965*, Foundation for Modern Art, New York, 1965
Whitaker, Robert, *In the Company of Dalí*, Touchstone Books, Kent, 2006
Wilson, Simon, *Salvador Dalí*, Tate Gallery, London, 1980

Leo Dohmen

Canonne, Xavier, *Surrealism in Belgium 1924–2000*, Mercatorfonds, Brussels, 2007
Ceuleers, Jan, *Leo Dohmen 1929–1999: Look! Think! Win!*, Ronny Van de Velde, Antwerp, 2000
Moffett, Cleveland, et al., *Post-Columbian Art: Leo Dohmen*, Den Tijd, Antwerp, 1992
Moore, S. Derrickson, et al., *Leo Dohmen: Post-Columbian Art in Las Cruces*, Cutter Gallery, New Mexico, 1998

Óscar Domínguez

Guigon, Emmanuel, et al., *Eduardo Westerdahl – Óscar Domínguez. Colección Documental*, Guillermo de Osma Galería, Madrid, 1999
Molina, Antonio Fernández, *Óscar Domínguez 1906–1957*, Oriol Galería d'Art, Barcelona, 2000
Serrano, Véronique, et al., *Óscar Domínguez et le surrealisme 1906–1957*, Editions Hazan, Paris, 2005
Xuriguera, Gérard, *Óscar Domínguez*, Filipacchi, Paris, 1973

Max Ernst

Alexandrian, Sarane, and Patrick Waldberg, *Max Ernst*, Filipacchi, Paris, 1971
Anon., *Fragments of a Personal Universe: Max Ernst Collages and Microbes*, Nadada Editions, New York, 1998
Bischoff, Ulrich, *Max Ernst*, Taschen, Cologne, 1988
Bousquet, Joe, and Michel Tapié, *Max Ernst*, René Drouin, Paris, 1950
Camfield, William A., *Max Ernst: Dada and the Dawn of Surrealism*, Prestel, Munich, 1993
Damase, Jacques, *Max Ernst*, Jacques Damase Gallery, Paris, 1976
Derenthal, Ludger, and Jürgen Pech, *Max Ernst*, Nouvelles Editions Françaises, Paris, 1992
Diehl, Gaston, *Max Ernst*, Flammarion, Paris, 1973
Ernst, Max, *La Femme 100 Têtes*, Editions du Carrefour, Paris, 1929
Ernst, Max, et al., *Max Ernst: Beyond Painting*, Schultz, New York, 1948
Ernst, Max, *Max Ernst*, Arts Council, London, 1961
Ernst, Max, *Max Ernst. Ecritures*, Editions Gallimard, Paris, 1970
Ernst, Max, *Histoire Naturelle*, Thames & Hudson, London, 1972
Ernst, Max, *Max Ernst: Jenseits der Malerei – Das Grafische Oeuvre*, Kestner-Museum, Hanover, 1972
Ernst, Max, *Une Semaine de Bonté: A Surrealistic Novel in Collage by Max Ernst*, Dover, New York, 1976
Ernst, Max, *A Little Girl Dreams of Taking the Veil*, George Braziller, New York, 1982
Gatt, Giuseppe, *Max Ernst*, Hamlyn, London, 1970
Gee, Malcolm, *Ernst: Pietà or Revolution by Night*, Tate, London, 1986
Gehrts, Meg, *A Camera Actress in the Wilds of Togoland*, Lippincott, Philadelphia, 1915 (Source for 'Celebes')
Gimferrer, Pere, *Max Ernst*, Academy Editions, London, 1993

Goerg, Charles, *Max Ernst, Oeuvre Gravé*, Musée d'Art et d'Histoire, Geneva, 1970
Hentzen, Alfred, and Helmut R. Leppien, *Max Ernst. Das Graphische Werk*, Kunsthalle, Hamburg, 1967
Jouffroy, Alain, et al., *Max Ernst: The Sculpture*, Fruitmarket Gallery, Edinburgh, 1990
Marinotti, Paolo, et al., *Max Ernst: Oltre la Pittura*, Palazzo Grassi, Venice, 1966
Maurer, Evan M., et al., *Max Ernst*, Malingue, Paris, 2003
McNab, Robert, *Ghost Ships: A Surrealist Love Triangle*, Yale, New Haven, 2004
Motherwell, Robert, *Max Ernst: Beyond Painting*, Wittenborn & Schultz, New York, 1948
Pretzell, Lothar, et al., *Hommage à Max Ernst*, Kunstkreis Luzern, Stuttgart, 1971
Rainwater, Robert (ed.), *Max Ernst: Beyond Surrealism*, Oxford University Press, 1986
Quinn, Edward, *Max Ernst*, Ediciones Polígrafa, Barcelona, 1984
Russell, John, *Max Ernst: Life and Work*, Abrams, New York, 1967
Spies, Werner, *Max Ernst: Frottages*, Thames & Hudson, London, 1969
Spies, Werner, *The Return of La Belle Jardinière: Max Ernst 1950–1970*, Abrams, New York, 1971
Spies, Werner, *Max Ernst*, Pompidou, Paris, 1975
Spies, Werner, *Max Ernst. Oeuvre-Katalog* (6 vols), Menil Foundation, Houston, 1975–2004
Spies, Werner, *Max Ernst. Retrospektive 1979*, Prestel, Munich, 1979
Spies, Werner, *Max Ernst – Loplop*, George Braziller, New York, 1983
Spies, Werner (foreword), *Max Ernst, Graphik und Bücher*, Gerd Hatje, Stuttgart, 1991
Spies, Werner, *Max Ernst: A Retrospective*, Prestel, Munich, 1991
Spies, Werner, *Max Ernst. Sculptures – Maisons – Paysages*, Pompidou, Paris, 1998
Spies, Werner, *Max Ernst: Life and Work*, Thames & Hudson, London, 2006
Spies, Werner, *Max Ernst. Une Semaine de Bonté. Les Collages Originaux*, Gallimard, Paris, 2008
Turpin, Ian, *Max Ernst*, Phaidon Press, Oxford, 1979
Vowinckel, Andreas (ed.), *Max Ernst: Configurations*, Galerie Jan Krugier, Geneva, 1975
Waldberg, Patrick, *Max Ernst*, Jean-Jacques Pauvert, Paris, 1958
Waldberg, Patrick (foreword), *Max Ernst. Peintures pour Paul Eluard*, Denoël, Paris, 1969
Warlick, M. E., *Max Ernst and Alchemy: A Magician in Search of Myth*, University of Texas Press, Austin, 2001
Weiss, Gerlinder, *Max Ernst. Druckgraphische Werke*, Museum Ludwig, Cologne, 1991

Leonor Fini

Brion, Marcel, *Leonor Fini et son Oeuvre*, Jean-Jacques Pauvert, Paris, 1955
Fini, Leonor, *Leonor Fini: Peintures*, Editions Michele Trinckvel, Paris, 1994
Jelenski, Constantin, *Leonor Fini*, Editions Clairefontaine, Lausanne, 1968
Overstreet, Richard, and Neil Zukerman, *Leonor Fini. Catalogue Raisonné of the Oil Paintings* (2 vols), Weinstein, Scheidegger & Spiess, Zurich, 2021
Selsdon, Esther, *Leonor Fini*, Parkstone Press, New York, 1999
Villani, Tiziana, *Parcours dans l'Oeuvre de Leonor Fini*, Editions Michele Trinckvel, Paris, 1989
Webb, Peter, *Sphinx: The Life and Art of Leonor Fini*, Vendome Press, New York, 2009

Frida Kahlo

Herrera, Hayden, *Frida: The Biography of Frida Kahlo*, Bloomsbury, London, 2018
Lozano, Luis-Martín (ed.), *Frida Kahlo*, Taschen, Cologne, 2024
Milner, Frank, *Frida Kahlo*, Greenwich Editions, London, 2002

Paul Klee

Abboni, Fulvio, et al., *Paul Klee. Opere 1900–1940*, Electa, Florence, 1981
Alberghini, Marina, *Il Gatto Cosmico di Paul Klee*, Publigold, Milan, 1993
Anon., *Paul Klee. Handzeichnungen II. 1921–1930*, Müller & Kiepenheuer, Bergen, 1934
Anon., *Paul Klee*, Edizioni de' Foscherari, Bologna, 1971
Anon., *Paul Klee. The Great Masters: Illustrated Monograph*, Park Lane, London, 1993
Argan, G. C. (ed.), *Paul Klee, Diari. 1898–1918*, Il Saggiatore, Milan, 1984
Barr, Alfred H. Jr, et al., *Paul Klee*, Museum of Modern Art, New York, 1945
Comte, Philippe, *Paul Klee*, Tabard Press, New York, 1991
Cooper, Douglas, *Paul Klee*, Penguin, London, 1949
Giedion-Welcker, Carola, *Paul Klee*, Faber and Faber, London, 1952
Grohmann, Will, *Klee*, Thames & Hudson, London, 1987
Grohmann, Will, *Paul Klee*, Sansoni, Florence, 1954
Güse, Ernst-Gerhard (ed.), *Paul Klee: Dialogue with Nature*, Prestel, Munich, 1991
Jaffe, Hans L., *Klee*, Hamlyn, London, 1972
Jahrzehnt, Letzies, *Paul Klee. Ultimo decennio: 1930–1940*, Museo d'arte Mendrisio, 1990
Klee, Felix, *Paul Klee*, Eidos-Presse, Stuttgart, 1948
Klee, Paul, *Paul Klee on Modern Art*, Faber and Faber, London, 1948
Klee, Paul, *Pedagogical Sketchbook*, Faber and Faber, London, 1954
Klee, Felix, et al., *Paul Klee, His Life and Work*, Nottingham Castle Museum, Nottingham, 1983
Kuenzi, André, *Klee*, Fondation Pierre Gianadda, Martigny, Switzerland, 1985
Lanchner, Carolyn, *Paul Klee*, Museum of Modern Art, New York, 1987
Limbour, Georges, *Paul Klee*, Editions de la Connaissance, Brussels, 1948
Naubert-Riser, Constance, *Klee: The Masterworks*, Studio Editions, London, 1998
Naubert-Riser, Constance, *Klee*, Fernand Hazan, Paris, 1994
Novalis, *The Novices of Sais: Sixty Drawings by Paul Klee*, Curt Valentin, New York, 1949
Oliva, Achille Bonito, *Paul Klee: Disegni e Acquarelli*, Mazzotta, Milan, 1982
Partsch, Susanna, *Paul Klee*, Taschen, Cologne, 1990
Read, Herbert, *Klee (1879–1940)*, Faber and Faber, London, 1958
Rigo, Mario, et al., *Paul Klee*, Mazzotta, Milan, 1986
Rossi, Pierluigi, et al., *Paul Klee. Opere dal 1885 al 1933*, Museo d'Arte, Mendrisio, 1987
Rumelin, Christian (ed.), *Paul Klee: Catalogue Raisonné. Vols 1–9*, Thames & Hudson, London, 1998–2004
Sala, Aldo, et al., *Paul Klee*, Mazzotta, Milan, 1992
San Lazzaro, G. (Gualtieri) di, *Klee: A Study of his Life and Work*, Thames & Hudson, London, 1957
San Lazzaro, Gualtieri di, *Paul Klee*, Il Saggiatore, Milan, 1960

Félix Labisse

Anon., *Labisse. Les Mystères d'Isis*, Galerie Isy Brachot, Paris, 1981
Brachot, Christine and Isy, *Félix Labisse*, Galerie Isy Brachot, Paris, 1982
Cassou, Jean, *Labisse. Catalogue de l'Oeuvre Peint, 1927–1979*, Galerie Isy Brachot, Brussels, 1979
Dotremont, Christian, *Labisse*, Editions La Boétie, Brussels, 1946
Waldberg, Patrick, *Félix Labisse*, André de Rache, Brussels, 1970

Wifredo Lam

Anon., *Wifredo Lam: Early Works, 1942 to 1951*, Pierre Matisse Gallery New York, 1982
Benitez, Helena, *Wifredo and Helena: My Life with Wifredo Lam 1939–1950*, Acatos, Lausanne, 1999

Breton, André, et al., *Wifredo Lam, XXe Siècle*, Paris, 1979
Charpier, Jacques, *Lam*, Le Musée de Poche, 1960
Curzi, Lucien, *Wifredo Lam*, Edizioni Bora, Bologna, 1974
Fouchet, Max-Pol, *Wifredo Lam*, Ediciones Polígrafa, Barcelona, 1976
Laurin Lam, Lou, *Wifredo Lam: Catalogue Raisonné of the Painted Work. Vol. 1*, Acatos, Lausanne, 1996
Laurin Lam, Lou, and Eskil Lam, *Wifredo Lam: Catalogue Raisonné of the Painted Work. Vol. 2*, Acatos, Lausanne, 2002
Laurin-Lam, Lou, *Wifredo Lam: The Changing Image – Centennial Exhibition*, Yokohama Museum of Art, Yokohama, 2002
Sims, Lowery Stokes, *Wifredo Lam and the International Avant-Garde*, University of Texas Press, Austin, 2002
Tonneau-Ryckelynck, Dominique, and Pascaline Dron, *Wifredo Lam: Oeuvre Gravé et Lithographié; Catalogue Raisonné*, Musée de Gravelines, 1994
Xuriguera, Gérard, *Wifredo Lam*, Filipacchi, Paris, 1974

Jacqueline Lamba

Pace, Alba Romano, *Jacqueline Lamba: Peintre Rebelle, Muse de L'Amour Fou*, Gallimard, Paris, 2010

Conroy Maddox

Levy, Silvano (ed.), *Conroy Maddox: Surreal Enigmas*, Keele University Press, 1995
Levy, Silvano, *The Scandalous Eye: The Surrealism of Conroy Maddox*, Liverpool University Press, 2003
Rosemont, Penelope, and Paul Garon, *Conroy Maddox: Letters to Surrealists in the USA*, Black Swan Press, Chicago, 2019
Short, Robert, *Conroy Maddox: Surrealism Unlimited*, Camden Arts Centre, London, 1978

René Magritte

Benesch, Evelyn, et al., *René Magritte: The Key to Dreams*, Kunstforum, Vienna, and Fondation Beyeler, Basel, 2005
Calvocoressi, Richard, *Magritte*, Phaidon Press, London, 1984
Ceuleers, Jacques, *René Magritte, 135 Rue Esseghem, Jette-Brussels*, Pandora Press, Antwerp, 1999
Danchev, Alex, *Magritte: A Life*, Profile Books, London, 2020
Gablik, Suzi, *Magritte*, Thames & Hudson, London, 1970
Grunenberg, Christoph, et al., *Magritte A to Z*, Tate Publishing, London, 2011
Hammacher, A. M., *Magritte*, Abrams, New York, 1995
Kuller, George, et al., *René Magritte and the Contemporary Art*, Museum of Modern Art, Ostend, 1998
Levy, Silvano, *Decoding Magritte*, Samsom, Bristol, 2015
Meuris, Jacques, *Magritte*, Taschen, Cologne, 2004
Ollinger-Zinque, Gisèle, and Frederik Leen (eds), *René Magritte, 1898–1967*, Ludion, Ghent, 1998
Ottinger, Didier, et al., *Magritte*, Musée des Beaux-Arts de Montreal, 1996
Pritzker, Pamela, *Magritte*, Leon Amiel, New York, 1974
Robbe-Grillet, Alain, *René Magritte. La Belle Captive*, La Bibliothèque des Arts, Lausanne, 1975
Roegiers, Patrick, *Magritte and Photography*, Lund Humphries, London, 2005
Scutenaire, Louis, *Avec Magritte*, Lebeer Hossmann, Brussels, 1977
Scutenaire, Louis, et al., *Magritte*, Marlborough Fine Art, London, 1973
Sterckx, Pierre, *Un Hommage à Magritte*, Galerie Isy Brachot, Brussels, 1998
Sylvester, David, *Magritte*, Arts Council of Great Britain, London, 1969
Sylvester, David, *René Magritte. Catalogue Raisonné*, 5 vols, Philip Wilson, London, 1992–1997
Sylvester, David, *René Magritte. Peintures et Gouaches*, Ronny Van de Velde, Antwerp, 1994
Torczyner, Harry, *Magritte: The True Art of Painting*, Abrams, New York, 1985
Whitfield, Sarah (ed.), *René Magritte: Newly Discovered Works. Catalogue Raisonné VI*, Menil Foundation, Houston, 2012

Marcel Mariën

Canonne, Xavier, *Surrealism in Belgium, 1924–2000*, Mercatorfonds, Brussels, 2007
Canonne, Xavier, *Marcel Mariën: The Stowaway*, Pandora, Antwerp, 2014

André Masson

Ades, Dawn, *André Masson*, Mayor Gallery, London, 1995
Ballard, Jean (foreword), *André Masson*, Musée Cantini, Marseille, 1968
Lambert, Jean-Clarence, *André Masson*, Filipacchi, Paris, 1979
Leiris, M., and G. Limbour, *André Masson and his Universe*, Horizon, London, 1947
Masson, André, *Mythologies*, Editions de la Revue Fontaine, Paris, 1946
Poling, Clark V., *André Masson and the Surrealist Self*, Yale University Press, New Haven, 2008
Rubin, William, and Carolyn Lanchner, *André Masson*, Museum of Modern Art, New York, 1976
Sylvester, David, et al., *André Masson: Line Unleashed*, South Bank Centre, London, 1987

Oscar Mellor

Mellor, Phoebe, *The Paintings of Oscar Mellor*, Taurus Gallery, Oxford, 2008
Morris, Desmond, *Oscar Mellor: Private Surrealist*, Dark Windows Press, Rhos-on-Sea, Wales, 2023

Joan Miró

Baumann, Felix, *Joan Miró*, Kunsthaus Zurich, 1986
Beaumelle, Agnes de la (ed.), *Joan Miró. 1917–1934*, Pompidou, Paris, 2004
Corredor-Matheos, J., and Gloria Picazo, *Miró's Posters*, Chartwell Books, New Jersey, 1980
Dupin, Jacques, *Miró*, Abrams, New York, 1962
Dupin, Jacques, *Miró*, Flammarion, Paris, 1993
Dupin, Jacques, *Miró Engraver* (4 vols), Rizzoli, New York, 1989–2001
Dupin, Jacques, and Ariane Lelong-Mainaud, *Joan Miró. Catalogue Raisonné. Paintings* (6 vols), Daniel Lelong, Paris, 1999–2004
Dupin, Jacques, and Ariane Lelong-Mainaud, *Joan Miró. Catalogue Raisonné. Drawings* (6 vols), Daniel Lelong, Paris, 2008–2018
Gimferrer, Pere, *The Roots of Miró*, Ediciones Polígrafa, Barcelona, 1993
Hunter, Sam, *Joan Miró: His Graphic Work*, Abrams, New York, 1958
Lanchner, Carolyn, *Joan Miró*, Museum of Modern Art, New York, 1993
Leiris, Michel, and Patrick Cramer, *Joan Miró. Litografo* (6 vols), Ediciones Polígrafa, Barcelona, and Maeght, Paris, 1972–1992
Malet, Rosa Maria (preface), *Joan Miró: The Illustrated Books. Catalogue Raisonné*, Patrick Cramer, Geneva, 1989
Malet, Rosa Maria (introduction), et al., *Joan Miró. 1893–1993*, Little Brown, Boston, 1993
Miró, Emilio Fernández, and Pilar Ortega Chapel, *Joan Miró: Sculptures. Catalogue Raisonné. 1928–1982*, Daniel Lelong, Paris, 2006
Miró, Joan Punyet, and Joan Gardy Artigas, *Joan Miró. Josep Llorens Artigas. Ceramics, Catalogue Raisonné. 1941–1981*, Daniel Lelong, Paris, 2007
Rowell, Margit, *Joan Miró: Selected Writings and Interviews*, Thames & Hudson, London, 1987
Weelen, Guy, *Miró*, Abrams, New York, 1989

Henry Moore

Berthoud, Roger, *The Life of Henry Moore*, Faber and Faber, London, 1987

Bowness, Alan (ed.), *Henry Moore: Complete Sculpture* (6 vols), Lund Humphries, London, 1944–1988
Compton, Susan, *Henry Moore*, Weidenfeld & Nicolson, London, 1988
Garrould, Ann, *Henry Moore: Complete Drawings* (7 vols), Lund Humphries, London, 1996–2003
Grigson, Geoffrey, *Henry Moore*, Penguin, Harmondsworth, 1943
Moore, Henry, and John Hedgecoe, *Henry Moore: My Ideas, Inspiration and Life as an Artist*, Ebury Press, London, 1986
Sweeney, James Johnson, *Henry Moore*, Museum of Modern Art, New York, 1946
Strachan, W. J., *Henry Moore Animals*, Aurum Press, London, 1983
Sylvester, David (ed.), *Henry Moore: Sculpture and Drawings* (vols 1–6), Lund Humphries, London, 1957
Wilkinson, Alan (ed.), *Henry Moore: Writings and Conversations*, Lund Humphries, London, 2002

Georgia O'Keeffe
Benke, Britta, *O'Keeffe*, Taschen, Cologne, 2000
Castro, Jan Garden, *The Art & Life of Georgia O'Keeffe*, Virago Press, London, 1986
Hoffman, Katherine, *An Enduring Spirit: The Art of Georgia O'Keeffe*, Scarecrow Press, Metuchen, New Jersey, 1984
Lynes, Barbara Buhler, *Georgia O'Keeffe: Catalogue Raisonné* (2 vols), Yale University Press, New Haven, 1999
Lynes, Barbara Buhler, *Georgia O'Keeffe and the Calla Lily in American Art, 1860–1940*, Yale University Press, New Haven, 2002
Lynes, Barbara Buhler, and Russell Bowman, *O'Keeffe's O'Keeffes: The Artist's Collection*, Thames & Hudson, London, 2001
Rathbone, Belinda, et al., *Georgia O'Keeffe & Alfred Stieglitz: Two Lives – A Conversation in Paintings and Photographs*, HarperCollins, London, 1992
Robinson, Roxana, *Georgia O'Keeffe: A Life*, Bloomsbury, London, 1990
Turner, Elizabeth Hutton, *Georgia O'Keeffe: The Poetry of Things*, Yale University Press, New Haven, 1999

Meret Oppenheim
Burckhardt, Jacqueline, Bice Curiger et al., *Meret Oppenheim: Beyond the Teacup*, Independent Curators International, New York, 1996
Helfenstein, Josef, *Meret Oppenheim und der Surrealismus*, Gerd Hatje, Stuttgart, 1993
Meyer-Thoss, Christiane, *Meret Oppenheim. Buch der Ideen*, Gachnang & Springer, Bern, 1996. Published in English as *Meret Oppenheim: Book of Ideas*, Walther König, 1999.
Pagé, Suzanne, et al., *Meret Oppenheim*, Musée d'Art Moderne, Paris, 1984

Roland Penrose
Anon., *Roland Penrose and Lee Miller: The Surrealist and the Photographer*, Scottish National Gallery of Modern Art, Edinburgh, 2001
Baum, Timothy, *Two Old Pals: Man Ray and Roland Penrose*, Mayor Gallery, London, 1990
King, James, *Roland Penrose: The Life of a Surrealist*, Edinburgh University Press, 2016
Penrose, Antony, *The Home of the Surrealists: Lee Miller, Roland Penrose and Their Circle at Farley Farm*, Frances Lincoln, London, 2001
Penrose, Antony, *Roland Penrose: The Friendly Surrealist*, Prestel, London, 2001
Penrose, Roland, *The Road Is Wider than Long*, London Gallery, London, 1939
Penrose, Roland, *Scrap Book 1900–1981*, Thames & Hudson, London, 1981
Slusher, Katherine, *Lee Miller – Roland Penrose: The Green Memories of Desire*, Prestel, London, 2007

Francis Picabia
Borràs, María Lluïsa, *Picabia*, Thames & Hudson, 1985
Camfield, William A., et al., *Francis Picabia: Catalogue Raisonné* (4 vols), Yale University Press, New Haven, 2015–2022
Mundy, Jennifer, *Duchamp, Man Ray, Picabia*, Tate, London, 2008
Pagé, Suzanne (preface), et al., *Francis Picabia. Singulier Idéal*, Musée d'Art Moderne, Paris, 2002
Van de Velde, Ronny, *Francis Picabia*, Ronny Van de Velde, Antwerp, 1993

Pierre Roy
Ades, Dawn, *Pierre Roy, Nantes 1880 – Milan 1950*, Somogy Editions d'Art, Paris, 1994

Cruzeiro Seixas
Almeida, Bernardo Pinto de, Mário Cesariny et al., *Cruzeiro Seixas*, Centro de Estudos do Surrealismo, Fundação Cupertino de Miranda, Famalicão, Portugal, 2000

Jindřich Štyrský
Srp, Karel, *Jindřich Štyrský*, Argo, Prague, 2010

Dorothea Tanning
Carruthers, Victoria, *Dorothea Tanning: Transformations*, Lund Humphries, London, 2020
Lyford, Amy, *Exquisite Dreams: The Art and Life of Dorothea Tanning*, Reaktion Books, London, 2023
Mahon, Alyce, et al., *Dorothea Tanning*, Tate, London, 2018
Plazy, Gilles, *Dorothea Tanning*, Filipacchi, Paris, 1976
Waddell, Roberta, et al., *Dorothea Tanning: Hail, Delirium*, New York Public Library, 1992

Toyen
Le Brun, Annie, et al., *Toyen, 1902–1980*, Hirmer, Frankfurt, 2021
Ivsic, Radovan, *Toyen*, Filipacchi, Paris, 1974

John Tunnard
Martin, Simon, et al., *John Tunnard: Inner Space to Outer Space*, Pallant House Gallery, Chichester, 2010
Peat, Alan, and Brian Whitton, *John Tunnard: His Life and Work*, Scolar Press, Aldershot, 1997

Remedios Varo
Blanco, Alberto, et al., *Remedios Varo: Catalogue Raisonné*, Ediciones Era, Mexico, 1994
Haskell, Caitlin, and Tere Areq (eds), *Remedios Varo: Science Fictions*, Art Institute of Chicago, 2023
Kaplan, Janet A., *Unexpected Journeys: The Art and Life of Remedios Varo*, Virago Press, London, 1988
Nonaka, Masayo, *Remedios Varo: The Mexican Years*, Editorial RM, Mexico City, 2024

Edward Wadsworth
Black, Jonathan, *Edward Wadsworth: Form, Feeling and Calculation*, Philip Wilson, London, 2005
Glazebrook, Mark (introduction), *Edward Wadsworth: Paintings, Drawings and Prints*, Colnaghi, London, 1974
Glazebrook, Mark, *Edward Wadsworth: Paintings from the 1920s*, The Mayor Gallery, London, 1982
Lewison, Jeremy (ed.), *A Genius of Industrial England: Edward Wadsworth*, Arkwright Arts Trust, 1990

Scottie Wilson
Levy, Mervyn, 'Scottie Wilson's Kingdom in Kilburn', *The Studio*, vol. 163, no. 830, pp. 226–231, 1962
Levy, Mervyn, 'Scottie Wilson: The Visionary Experience', *The Studio*, vol. 172, no. 883, pp. 244–247, 1966
Melly, George, *It's all writ out for you: The Life and Work of Scottie Wilson*, Thames & Hudson, London, 1986
Mesens, E. L. T., 'Scottie Wilson', *Horizon*, vol. XIII, no. 78, pp. 400–2, 1946
Petullo, Anthony J., and Katherine M. Murrell, *Scottie Wilson: Peddler Turned Painter*, Petullo Publishing, Milwaukee, 2004

Picture Credits

Works are listed by page number.
a = above, b = below
Dimensions of works are given in centimetres and inches, height before width before depth.

2 Leonora Carrington, *Ferret Race* (detail), 1952. Oil on canvas, 100.3 × 55.2 ($39\frac{1}{2}$ × 22). Private Collection. © 2026 Estate of Leonora Carrington/ARS, NY and DACS, London

13a Pierre Roy, *Andromeda Prisoner*, *c.* 1930. Oil on canvas, 55 × 38 ($21\frac{3}{4}$ × 15). Private Collection. Photo Christie's Images/Bridgeman Images

13b Félix Labisse, *The Field of the Cloth of Gold*, 1943. Oil on canvas, 54 × 73 ($21\frac{3}{8}$ × $28\frac{3}{4}$). Private Collection. Courtesy Galerie Brachot, Belgium. © 2026 ADAGP, Paris and DACS, London

14 Joseph Cornell, *Object (Soap Bubble Set)*, 1941. Box construction (black eglomise border with black velvet), 46.3 × 31.4 × 9.5 ($18\frac{1}{4}$ × $12\frac{3}{8}$ × $3\frac{3}{4}$). Collection of Robert and Aimee Lehrman, Washington, DC, in honour of Charlotte Lehrman. National Gallery of Art, Washington, DC (2023.124.15). © 2026 The Joseph and Robert Cornell Memorial Foundation/VAGA at ARS, NY and DACS, London

17a Marcel Mariën, *The Star Dancer*, 1991. Starfish and plastic shoe on card, 36 × 26 × 4.7 ($14\frac{1}{4}$ × $10\frac{1}{4}$ × $1\frac{7}{8}$). Tate, London (T12051). Photo Tate. © 2026 DACS

17b Eileen Agar, *Fish Circus*, 1939. Collage, pen and ink and watercolour on paper, 25.5 × 30.5 ($10\frac{1}{8}$ × $12\frac{1}{8}$). Bequeathed by Gabrielle Keiller 1995. National Galleries of Scotland, Edinburgh (GMA 3938). © Estate of Eileen Agar. All rights reserved 2026/Bridgeman Images

18a Joseph Cornell, *Untitled (Sand Tray with Map and Starfish)*, 1952. Box construction, 2.8 × 36.5 × 18.4 ($1\frac{1}{8}$ × $14\frac{3}{8}$ × $7\frac{1}{4}$). Collection of Robert and Aimee Lehrman, Washington, DC, in honour of Isabelle Scott and Heidi Berry. National Gallery of Art, Washington, DC (2023.124.23). © 2026 The Joseph and Robert Cornell Memorial Foundation/VAGA at ARS, NY and DACS, London

18b Edward Wadsworth, *The Beached Margin*, 1937. Tempera on canvas on wood, 71.1 × 101.6 (28 × 40). Tate, London (N04935). Photo Alamy

21 Salvador Dalí, *Lobster Telephone*, 1938. Steel, plaster, rubber, resin and paper, 17.8 × 33 × 17.8 (7 × 13 × 7). Tate, London (T03257). Photo Steve Vidler/SuperStock. © 2026 Salvador Dalí, Fundació Gala-Salvador Dalí, DACS

22 Salvador Dalí, *Gala and the Angelus of Millet Immediately Preceding the Arrival of the Conic Anamorphoses*, 1933. Oil on wood, 24.2 × 19.2 ($9\frac{5}{8}$ × $7\frac{5}{8}$). Purchased 1975. National Gallery of Canada, Ottawa (18456). © 2026 Salvador Dalí, Fundació Gala-Salvador Dalí, DACS

25 Leonora Carrington, *Untitled*, 1969. Gouache on parchment. Private Collection. © 2026 Estate of Leonora Carrington/ARS, NY and DACS, London

27 André Masson, *Summer Divertissement*, 1934. Oil on canvas, 91.7 × 73.2 ($36\frac{1}{8}$ × $28\frac{7}{8}$). Centre Pompidou, Paris (AM 1981-593). © 2026 ADAGP, Paris and DACS, London

28 Roger Van de Wouwer, *Tartuffe's Hairshirt*, 1961. Oil on canvas, 56 × 41 ($22\frac{1}{8}$ × $16\frac{1}{4}$). Flemish Art Collection, Ghent (T2025MAG_066-9). © The Estate of Roger Van de Wouwer

30a Remedios Varo, *The Double Agent*, 1936. Oil on copper, 22 × 17 ($8\frac{3}{4}$ × $6\frac{3}{4}$). Private Collection. © 2026 Remedios Varo, DACS/VEGAP

30b Salvador Dalí, *Face of the Great Masturbator*, 1929. Oil on canvas, 110 × 150 ($43\frac{3}{8}$ × $59\frac{1}{8}$). Salvador Dalí Bequest, 1990. Museo Nacional Centro de Arte Reina Sofia, Madrid (AS11140). © 2026 Salvador Dalí, Fundació Gala-Salvador Dalí, DACS

31 John Tunnard, *Self-Portrait*, 1959. Oil on board, 60.7 × 76.5 ($23\frac{7}{8}$ × $30\frac{1}{8}$). © National Portrait Gallery, London

33 Félix Labisse, *Amorous Mantises*, 1946. Oil on canvas, 35 × 55.4 ($13\frac{7}{8}$ × $21\frac{7}{8}$). Private Collection. © 2026 ADAGP, Paris and DACS, London

34–35 Max Ernst, *The Joy of Life*, 1936. Oil on canvas, 73.5 × 93 (29 × $36\frac{5}{8}$). Purchased with the assistance of The National Lottery Heritage Fund and Art Fund, 1995. National Galleries of Scotland, Edinburgh (GMA 3886). Photo Album/Alamy. © 2026 ADAGP, Paris and DACS, London

37 Victor Brauner, *The Crime of the Butterfly King*, 1930. Oil on canvas, 64 × 49 ($25\frac{1}{4}$ × $19\frac{3}{8}$). Private Collection. Photo akg-images. © 2026 ADAGP, Paris and DACS, London

38a Roland Penrose, *Winged Domino: Portrait of Valentine*, 1937. Oil on canvas, 60 × 46 ($23\frac{5}{8}$ × $18\frac{1}{8}$). The Penrose Collection. © Lee Miller Archives, England 2026. All rights reserved. www.leemiller.co.uk

38b Salvador Dalí, frontispiece for *La Limite*, 1951. From Maurice Sandoz, *La Limite* (Paris: La Table Ronde, 1951). © 2026 Salvador Dalí, Fundació Gala-Salvador Dalí, DACS

40a Francis Picabia, *Woman with Butterfly*, 1927. Watercolour, gouache and pencil on paper, 32 × 24.5 ($12\frac{5}{8}$ × $9\frac{5}{8}$). Private Collection

40b Jindřich Štyrský, *Untitled*, 1940. Collage, 14 × 30.5 ($5\frac{1}{2}$ × 12). Private Collection. Courtesy Ubu Gallery, New York

41a Óscar Domínguez, *Le Plus clair du temps II*, 1943. Oil on canvas, 73 × 59.5 ($28\frac{3}{4}$ × $23\frac{1}{2}$). Private Collection. © 2026 ADAGP, Paris and DACS, London

41b Henry Moore, *Large Divided Oval: Butterfly*, 1982 (cast 1985–86). Unique bronze, 800 (315). Haus der Kulturen der Welt, Berlin. Photo Justus/Panther Media Global/Alamy

43a Jane Graverol, *Lolita*, 1960. Oil on unalit, 35.2 × 40 ($13\frac{7}{8}$ × $15\frac{3}{4}$). Royal Museums of Fine Arts of Belgium, Brussels (11870). Photo J. Geleyns. © 2026 DACS

43b Edith Rimmington, *The Decoy*, 1948. Oil on canvas, 35.5 × 30.5 (14 × $12\frac{1}{8}$). Purchased by the Patrons of the National Galleries of Scotland 2002. National Galleries of Scotland, Edinburgh (GMA 4654). © The Estate of Edith Rimmington

47 Georges Malkine, *Sirens*, 1926. Oil on canvas, 75 × 54 ($29\frac{5}{8}$ × $21\frac{3}{8}$). Collection Soizic Audouard. © 2026 ADAGP, Paris and DACS, London

48a Ithell Colquhoun, *Sardine and Eggs*, *c.* 1941. Watercolour on paper, 22.3 × 17.3 ($8\frac{3}{4}$ × $6\frac{3}{4}$). Tate, London (TGA 201913). © Tate

48b René Magritte, *Collective Invention*, 1935. Oil on canvas, 73.5 × 97.5 (29 × $38\frac{1}{2}$). Private Collection. © 2026 ADAGP, Paris and DACS, London

49 Marc Chagall, *Time Is a River without Banks*, 1930–39. Oil on canvas, 99.7 × 81.3 ($39\frac{1}{4}$ × 32). Private Collection. © 2026 ADAGP, Paris and DACS, London

50a Dorothea Tanning, *Poached Trout*, 1952. Oil on canvas, 40.6 × 55.9 (16 × 22). Private Collection. © 2026 ADAGP, Paris and DACS, London

50b Félix Labisse, *Charlotte Corday*, 1946. Oil on canvas, 115.3 × 180.7 (45 3/8 × 71 1/8). Private Collection. Photo Christie's Images/Bridgeman Images. © 2026 ADAGP, Paris and DACS, London

52a Toyen, *Between the Long Shadows*, 1943. Oil on canvas, 52 × 90 (20 1/2 × 35 1/2). Private Collection. © 2026 ADAGP, Paris and DACS, London

52b Paul Klee, *Around the Fish*, 1926. Oil and tempera on canvas mounted on cardboard, 46.7 × 63.8 (18 3/8 × 25 1/8). Abby Aldrich Rockefeller Fund. The Museum of Modern Art, New York (271.1939). Photo JJs/Alamy

53 Victor Brauner, *Fish on Wheels*, 1965. Oil on canvas and painted wood, 93 × 170 (36 5/8 × 67). Musée d'Art Moderne et Contemporain, Abbaye Sainte-Croix, Les Sables d'Olonne (983.26.6). Photo Dana Shishmanian. © 2026 ADAGP, Paris and DACS, London

55 Victor Brauner, *The Object that Dreams II*, 1938. Oil on canvas, 80.6 × 65.1 (31 3/4 × 25 5/8). Gift of Joseph and Jory Shapiro. Museum of Contemporary Art Chicago. © 2026 ADAGP, Paris and DACS, London

57 Victor Brauner, *The Lure of Death*, 1930. Oil on board, 52 × 44 (20 1/2 × 17 1/4). Private Collection. Courtesy Galerie Samy Kinge, Paris. © 2026 ADAGP, Paris and DACS, London

59 Pierre Roy, *Danger on the Stairs*, 1927–28. Oil on canvas, 91.4 × 60 (36 × 23 5/8). Gift of Abby Aldrich Rockefeller (142.1935). Photo The Museum of Modern Art, New York/Scala, Florence

60a Félix Labisse, *The Daughter of Tiresias*, 1973. Oil on canvas, 60 × 50 (23 5/8 × 19 3/4). Private Collection. © 2026 ADAGP, Paris and DACS, London

60b Leonora Carrington, *Forbidden Fruit*, 1969. Oil on canvas, 49 × 46 (19 3/8 × 18 1/8). Private Collection. © 2026 Estate of Leonora Carrington/ARS, NY and DACS, London

65 Max Ernst, *Loplop Introduces Loplop*, 1930. Oil and various materials on wood, 100 × 180 (39 3/8 × 70 7/8). Private Collection. © 2026 ADAGP, Paris and DACS, London

66a Jane Graverol, *The Holy Spirit*, 1965. Oil on canvas, 63 × 54 (24 3/4 × 21 1/4). Private Collection. © 2026 DACS

66b Jane Graverol, *Cruelty of Memory*, 1956. Oil on Masonite, 56 × 46.3 (22 1/8 × 18 1/4). Private Collection. © 2026 DACS

69 Victor Brauner, *The Lovers (Messengers of the Number)*, 1947. Oil on canvas, 92 × 73 (36 1/4 × 28 3/4). Centre Pompidou, Paris (AM 1987-1204). © 2026 ADAGP, Paris and DACS, London

70a Leonora Carrington, *Bird Bath II*, 1978. Acrylic on canvas board, 71 × 56 (28 × 22). Private Collection. © 2026 Estate of Leonora Carrington/ARS, NY and DACS, London

70b Leonora Carrington, *Crow Catcher*, 1990. Oil on canvas, 46 × 76 (18 1/8 × 30). Galleria Nazionale d'Arte Moderna e Contemporanea, Rome. © 2026 Estate of Leonora Carrington/ARS, NY and DACS, London

71 René Magritte, *Clairvoyance*, 1936. Oil on canvas, 54 × 65 (21 3/8 × 25 5/8). Private Collection. © 2026 ADAGP, Paris and DACS, London

73a Edith Rimmington, *The Oneiroscopist*, 1947. Oil on canvas, 51 × 41 (20 1/8 × 16 1/4). Israel Museum, Jerusalem (B98.0566). © The Estate of Edith Rimmington

73b Salvador Dalí, *Bird*, 1928. Oil, sand, pebbles and shingle on board, 49 × 60 (19 3/8 × 23 5/8). Purchased with the support of The National Lottery Heritage Fund and Art Fund, 1995. National Galleries of Scotland, Edinburgh (GMA 3883). Photo Alamy. © 2026 Salvador Dalí, Fundació Gala-Salvador Dalí, DACS

74a Oscar Mellor, *The Gathering*, 1962. Oil on canvas, 90.5 × 75.5 (35 3/4 × 29 3/4). Private Collection. © The Estate of Oscar Mellor

74b Leonor Fini, *The Guardian of the Phoenix*, 1952. Oil on canvas, 65 × 46 (25 5/8 × 18 1/8). Private Collection. © 2026 ADAGP, Paris and DACS, London

76a Man Ray, *The Misunderstood*, 1938. Oil on canvas, 61 × 46.5 (24 1/8 × 18 3/8). Private Collection. Photo Telimage, Paris. © 2026 Man Ray 2015 Trust/DACS, London

76b Paul Klee, *Landscape with Yellow Birds*, 1923. Watercolour on paper mounted on cardboard, 35.5 × 44 (14 × 17 3/8). Private Collection. Photo Hans Hinz/ARTOTHEK

77 Scottie Wilson, *Untitled (Tree of Birds)*, *c.* 1960. Ink and crayon on paper, 86.4 × 61 (34 1/8 × 24 1/8). Private Collection. © The Artist's Estate

78a Félix Labisse, *The Foreign Leda*, 1950. Oil on canvas, 55 × 46 (21 3/4 × 18 1/8). Private Collection. Courtesy Galerie Brachot, Belgium. © 2026 ADAGP, Paris and DACS, London

78b Joan Miró, *The Bird's Song on the Dew of the Moon*, 1955. Oil on cardboard, 27 × 37 (10 3/4 × 14 5/8). Fundació Joan Miró Barcelona. On loan from a private collection (D 1989). © 2026 Successió Miró/ADAGP, Paris and DACS London

79 Wifredo Lam, *Black Wings*, 1972. Oil on canvas, 81 × 65 (32 × 25 5/8). Private Collection. © 2026 Wifredo Lam Estate, ADAGP, Paris and DACS, London

81 Salvador Dalí, *Leda Atómica*, 1949. Oil on canvas, 61 × 46 (24 1/8 × 18 1/8). Dalí Theatre-Museum, Figueres. © 2026 Salvador Dalí, Fundació Gala-Salvador Dalí, DACS

82a Clovis Trouille, *Make Me into a Swan*, 1959. Oil on canvas, 47.5 × 61.2 (18 3/4 × 24 1/8). Private Collection. © 2026 ADAGP, Paris and DACS, London

82b Mimi Parent, *Leda and the Swan*, 1997. Mixed-media assemblage, box under glass. Private Collection. © The Estate of Mimi Parent

85a Salvador Dalí, *Swans Reflecting Elephants*, 1937. Oil on canvas, 51 × 77 (20 1/8 × 30 3/8). Private Collection. © 2026 Salvador Dalí, Fundació Gala-Salvador Dalí, DACS

85b Salvador Dalí, *Horace's Chimera*, 1972. Lithograph, 65 × 50 (25 5/8 × 19 3/4). Private Collection. © 2026 Salvador Dalí, Fundació Gala-Salvador Dalí, DACS

86 Joseph Cornell, *Untitled (Object with Swan)*, 1967. Metal mirror with fabric backing, plastic swan and paper tag, 2.5 × 22.8 × 8.8 (1 × 9 × 3 1/2). Private Collection. Photo Christie's Images/Bridgeman Images. © 2026 The Joseph and Robert Cornell Memorial Foundation/VAGA at ARS, NY and DACS, London

87 Leonora Carrington, *Lepidopteros*, 1969. Oil on canvas, 90 × 90 (35 1/2 × 35 1/2). Private Collection. © 2026 Estate of Leonora Carrington/ARS, NY and DACS, London

89 Leonora Carrington, *Grandmother Moorhead's Aromatic Kitchen*, 1975. Oil on canvas, 79 × 124.5 (31 × 49). Goddard Center for Visual & Performing Arts, Ardmore, OK. © 2026 Estate of Leonora Carrington/ARS, NY and DACS, London

90 Salvador Dalí, *Inaugural Gooseflesh*, 1928. Oil on cardboard, 76 × 63.2 (30 × 25). Fundació Gala-Salvador Dalí, Figueres. Photo Album/Alamy. © 2026 Salvador Dalí, Fundació Gala-Salvador Dalí, DACS

91 Salvador Dalí, *Allegory of Spring*, c. 1979. Oil on plywood panel, 122 × 244 (48 1/8 × 96 1/8). Fundació Gala-Salvador Dalí, Figueres. © 2026 Salvador Dalí, Fundació Gala-Salvador Dalí, DACS

93 Edith Rimmington, *Relative Strength*, 1950. Pen, ink and watercolour on paper, 53 × 37 (20 7/8 × 14 5/8). Private Collection. © The Estate of Edith Rimmington

95a Meret Oppenheim, *Vulture and Yellow-Red Object*, 1975. Watercolour, pastel and charcoal on paper, 26 × 34 (10 1/4 × 13 1/2). Private Collection. © 2026 DACS

95b Salvador Dalí, *Chair with the Wings of a Vulture*, 1960. Photograph Robert Descharnes. Collection of The Dalí Museum, St Petersburg, FL (1995.3.64). Photo © Descharnes & Descharnes sarl 2026. Artwork © 2026 Salvador Dalí, Fundació Gala-Salvador Dalí, DACS

97 René Magritte, *The Domain of Arnheim*, 1938. Oil on canvas, 73 × 100 (28 3/4 × 39 3/8). Private Collection. © 2026 ADAGP, Paris and DACS, London

99a Jane Graverol, *The New Melancholy*, 1956. Oil on board, 59 × 48 (23 1/4 × 19). Private Collection. © 2026 DACS

99b Toyen, *The Dangerous Hour*, 1942. Oil on canvas, 73 × 92 (28 3/4 × 36 1/4). Private Collection. © 2026 ADAGP, Paris and DACS, London

101 André Masson, *Ibdes in Aragon*, 1935. Oil on canvas, 60 × 92.4 (23 5/8 × 36 1/2). Tate, London (N05646). Photo Tate. © 2026 ADAGP, Paris and DACS, London

103a Marc Chagall, *Listening to the Cock*, 1944. Oil on canvas, 92.5 × 74.5 (36 1/2 × 29 3/8). Private Collection. © 2026 ADAGP, Paris and DACS, London

103b Toyen, *At the Green Table*, 1945. Oil on canvas, 110 × 160 (43 3/8 × 63). Private Collection. © 2026 ADAGP, Paris and DACS, London

104 Remedios Varo, *Vegetarian Vampires*, 1962. Oil on canvas, 85.7 × 60.3 (33 3/4 × 23 3/4). Private Collection. © 2026 Remedios Varo, DACS/VEGAP

105 Francis Picabia, *Chicken Coop*, 1912. Oil on canvas, 130.6 × 163 (51 1/2 × 64 1/4). Private Collection

107a Max Ernst, *The Return of the Beautiful Gardener*, 1967. Oil on canvas, 161.9 × 129.5 (63 3/4 × 51). The Menil Collection, Houston (CA 7018). © 2026 ADAGP, Paris and DACS, London

107b Max Ernst and Jean Arp, *Physiomythological Diluvial Picture (Fatagaga)*. Collage with photography, gouache, pencil, pen and ink on paper on cardboard, 11.2 × 10 (4 1/2 × 4). Sprengel Museum Hannover (FBS 14.C). Ernst © 2026 ADAGP, Paris and DACS, London. Arp © 2026 DACS

109 René Magritte, *The Therapist*, 1937. Oil on canvas, 92.1 × 64.9 (36 3/8 × 25 5/8). Private Collection. © 2026 ADAGP, Paris and DACS, London

111 Frida Kahlo, *Me and My Parrots*, 1941. Oil on canvas, 82 × 62.8 (32 1/4 × 24 3/4). Private Collection

112 Joseph Cornell, *A Parrot for Juan Gris*, 1953–54. Box construction, 45.1 × 31 × 11.7 (17 7/8 × 12 1/4 × 4 5/8). Private Collection. Photo Bridgeman Images. © 2026 The Joseph and Robert Cornell Memorial Foundation/VAGA at ARS, NY and DACS, London

115 Max Ernst, *Attirement of the Bride*, 1940. Oil on canvas, 129.6 × 96.3 (51 × 37 7/8). The Solomon R. Guggenheim Foundation Peggy Guggenheim Collection, Venice, 1976 (76.2553.78). © 2026 ADAGP, Paris and DACS, London

116a Max Ernst, *Marlene (Woman and Child)*, 1941. Oil on canvas, 23.8 × 19.7 (9 3/8 × 7 3/4). The Menil Collection (CA 5834). © 2026 ADAGP, Paris and DACS, London

116b Morris Graves, *Little-Known Bird of the Inner Eye*, 1941. Tempera on transparentized paper, 52.8 × 93.1 (20 3/4 × 36 5/8). Purchase. Photo The Museum of Modern Art, New York/Scala, Florence. Courtesy Woodside/Braseth Gallery, Seattle. © Morris Grave Foundation

119 René Magritte, *The Companions of Fear*, 1942. Oil on canvas, 70 × 92.5 (27 3/8 × 36 3/8). Private Collection. © 2026 ADAGP, Paris and DACS, London

120–21 Remedios Varo, *Creation of the Birds*, 1957. Oil on Masonite, 54 × 64 (21 3/8 × 25 1/4). Museo de Arte Moderno, Mexico City. © 2026 Remedios Varo, DACS/VEGAP

121 Wifredo Lam, *The Fear of a Bird*, 1955. Oil on canvas, 152.5 × 106 (60 × 41 3/4). Private Collection. © 2026 Wifredo Lam Estate, ADAGP, Paris and DACS, London

124 Conroy Maddox, *The Conquest*, 1977. Oil on canvas, 121 × 93 (47 3/4 × 36 5/8). Private Collection. Photo Lyon & Turnbull/Bridgeman Images. Kind permission given by the artist's daughter

127 Max Ernst, *Two Children Are Threatened by a Nightingale*, 1924. Oil with painted wood elements and cut-and-pasted printed paper on wood with wood frame, 69.8 × 57.1 × 11.4 (27 1/2 × 22 1/2 × 4 1/2). Purchase. Photo The Museum of Modern Art, New York/Scala, Florence. © 2026 ADAGP, Paris and DACS, London

130a Jacqueline Lamba, *For the Pocket*, 1935. Pins, colour threads, black silk square and glass bead mounted on cardboard, 33 × 33 × 4.5 (13 × 13 × 1 7/8). Private Collection. Rowland Weinstein, courtesy Weinstein Gallery. Photo Michael Snyder. © 2026 ADAGP, Paris and DACS, London

130b Clovis Trouille, *Dream of the Vampire*, 1960. Oil on canvas, 46.3 × 55 (18 1/4 × 21 5/8). Private Collection. © 2026 ADAGP, Paris and DACS, London

135 Victor Brauner, *Frica Fear*, 1950. Oil on board, 65 × 81 (25 5/8 × 32). Private Collection. Photo Bridgeman Images. © 2026 ADAGP, Paris and DACS, London

137a Joan Miró, *Dog Barking at the Moon*, 1926. Oil on canvas, 73 × 92.1 (28 3/4 × 36 1/4). A. E. Gallatin Collection, 1952. Philadelphia Museum of Art (1952-61-82). © 2026 Successió Miró/ADAGP, Paris and DACS London

137b Toyen, *Fox Hunt*, 1964. Oil on canvas, 89 × 146 (35 × 57 1/2). Private Collection. © 2026 ADAGP, Paris and DACS, London

138 Francis Picabia, *Animal Trainer*, 1923. Ripolin on canvas, 250 × 200 (98 1/2 × 78 3/4). Centre Pompidou, Paris (AM 1998-174)

140a Frida Kahlo, *Self-Portrait with Small Monkey*, 1945. Oil on Masonite, 55.9 × 41.3 (22 × 16 1/4). Museo Dolores Olmedo, Mexico City

140b Dorothea Tanning, *Living Picture*, 1954. Oil on canvas, 116.6 × 88.8 (46 × 85). Purchased with help from the Henry and Sula Walton Fund and Art Fund, 2019. National Galleries of Scotland, Edinburgh (GMA 5634). © 2026 ADAGP, Paris and DACS, London

141 Francis Bacon, *Dog*, 1952. Oil on canvas, 199 × 138 (78 1/4 × 54 1/4). Private Collection. © 2026 The Estate of Francis Bacon. All rights reserved. DACS

143 Toyen, *At the Château Lacoste*, 1943. Oil on canvas, 65.1 × 87 (25 5/8 × 34 1/4). Private Collection. © 2026 ADAGP, Paris and DACS, London

144a Victor Brauner, *Fascination*, 1939. Oil on canvas, 64.8 × 53.3 (25.5 × 21). Anonymous gift. San Francisco Museum of Modern Art (94.424). © 2026 ADAGP, Paris and DACS, London

144b Leonora Carrington, *Nine, Nine, Nine*, 1948. Oil on canvas, 68 × 88.5 (27 × 35). Private Collection. © 2026 Estate of Leonora Carrington/ARS, NY and DACS, London

147 Leonora Carrington, *Ferret Race*, 1952. Oil on canvas, 100.3 × 55.2 (39½ × 22). Private Collection. © 2026 Estate of Leonora Carrington/ARS, NY and DACS, London

149 Leonora Carrington, *Self-Portrait*, *c.* 1937–38. Oil on canvas, 65 × 81.3 (25½ × 32). The Pierre and Maria-Gaetana Matisse Collection, 2002. The Metropolitan Museum of Art, New York (2002.456.1) © 2026 Estate of Leonora Carrington/ARS, NY and DACS, London

150 Victor Brauner, *Person with a Dragon*, 1931. Oil on canvas, 64.8 × 54 (25½ × 21¼). © 2026 ADAGP, Paris and DACS, London

153 Joan Miró, *Head (The White Cat)*, 1927. Oil on canvas, 147.3 × 114.6 (58 × 45⅛). Private Collection. © 2026 Successió Miró/ADAGP, Paris and DACS London

154 Leonor Fini, *Sunday Afternoon*, 1980. Oil on canvas. Private Collection. © 2026 ADAGP, Paris and DACS, London

155 Paul Klee, *Cat and Bird*, 1928. Oil and ink on gessoed canvas, mounted on wood, 38.1 × 53.2 (15 × 21). Sidney and Harriet Janis Collection Fund and gift of Suzy Prudden and Joan H. Meijer memory of F. H. Hirschland. Photo The Museum of Modern Art, New York/Scala, Florence

156 Paul Klee, *The Mountain of the Sacred Cat*, 1923. Oil transfer drawing, pencil and watercolour on paper, 48.5 × 31.8 (19⅛ × 12⅝). Private Collection. Photo Bridgeman Images

157 Marc Chagall, *Paris through the Window*, 1913. Oil on canvas, 136 × 141.9 (53⅝ × 55⅞). Solomon R. Guggenheim Founding Collection, By gift. Solomon R. Guggenheim Museum, New York (37.438). © 2026 ADAGP, Paris and DACS, London

159a Óscar Domínguez, *Lion-Bicycle*, 1936. Decalcomania and gouache on paper, 20 × 31 (7⅞ × 12¼). Museo Nacional Centro de Arte Reina Sofia, Madrid (AD06748). © 2026 ADAGP, Paris and DACS, London

159b Salvador Dalí, *The Accommodations of Desire*, 1929. Oil and cut-and-pasted printed paper on wood, 22.2 × 34.9 (8¾ × 13¾). Jacques and Natasha Gelman Collection, 1998. The Metropolitan Museum of Art, New York (1999.363.16). © 2026 Salvador Dalí, Fundació Gala-Salvador Dalí, DACS

160 Conroy Maddox, *Passage de l'Opéra*, 1940/1970–71. Oil on canvas, 137.2 × 94.2 (54⅛ × 37⅛). Tate, London (T03052). Photo Bridgeman Images. Kind permission given by the artist's daughter

162–63 Clovis Trouille, *Justine*, 1937. Oil on canvas, 46.2 × 61.3 (18¼ × 24¼). Private Collection. © 2026 ADAGP, Paris and DACS, London

165a Salvador Dalí, *Lenin Tiger*, 1962. Oil on canvas, 200 × 229 (78¾ × 90¼). Fundació Gala-Salvador Dalí, Figueres. © 2026 Salvador Dalí, Fundació Gala-Salvador Dalí, DACS

165b Jane Graverol, *The Evil Star*, 1956. Oil on canvas, 49.5 × 68.5 (19½ × 27). Private Collection. © 2026 DACS

166 Salvador Dalí, *Dream Caused by the Flight of a Bee around a Pomegranate a Second before Waking*, 1944. Oil on panel, 51 × 41 (20⅛ × 16¼). Museo Nacional Thyssen-Bornemisza, Madrid (510 (1974.46)). © 2026 Salvador Dalí, Fundació Gala-Salvador Dalí, DACS

169a Toyen, *The Dream*, 1964. Oil on canvas, 35 × 27 (13⅞ × 10¾). Private Collection. © 2026 ADAGP, Paris and DACS, London

169b Toyen, *The New World of Love*, 1968. Oil on canvas and collage, 60 × 92 (23⅝ × 36¼). Private Collection. © 2026 ADAGP, Paris and DACS, London

171a Michael Parekōwhai, *My Sister, My Self*, 2006. Fibreglass, mild steel, wood, automotive paint, 270 × 150 × 100 (106⅜ × 59⅛ × 39⅜). Courtesy the artist and Michael Lett Gallery

171b Leo Dohmen, *Le Ludion*, 1956. Black-and-white photograph, 19 × 16.5 (7½ × 6½). Private Collection. Courtesy the artist's estate and Galerie Ronny Van de Velde

175 Max Ernst, *Celebes*, 1921. Oil on canvas, 125.4 × 107.9 (49⅜ × 42½). Tate, London (T01988). Photo Tate. © 2026 ADAGP, Paris and DACS, London

176 André Breton, *Head Section of an Exquisite Corpse*, 1926. Coloured pencil on paper, 27 × 21 (10¾ × 8⅜). Private Collection. Photo Bridgeman Images. © 2026 ADAGP, Paris and DACS, London

177 Salvador Dalí, *The Temptation of St Anthony*, 1946. Oil on canvas, 89.5 × 119.5 (35¼ × 47⅛). Royal Museums of Fine Arts of Belgium, Brussels (7223). © 2026 Salvador Dalí, Fundació Gala-Salvador Dalí, DACS

179 Henry Moore, *Elephant Skull*, 1970. Etching on wove paper, 25.4 × 20 (10 × 7⅞). Private Collection. © 2026 The Henry Moore Foundation. All Rights Reserved, DACS/www.henry-moore.org

181a Roger Hilton, *Elephant*, 1973. Gouache and charcoal on paper, 27.9 × 36.8 (11 × 14½). Private Collection. © 2026 Estate of Roger Hilton. All rights reserved, DACS

181b Óscar Domínguez, *Cementerio de Elefantes*, 1938. Oil on canvas, 58.5 × 71 (23 × 28). Private Collection. Photo Christie's Images/Bridgeman Images. © 2026 ADAGP, Paris and DACS, London

185 Victor Brauner, *Untitled*, 1941. Graphite, coloured pencil and white chalk on vellum paper, 22.5 × 17.2 (8⅞ × 6⅞). Photo Musée d'Art moderne de Paris, Dist. GrandPalaisRmn/image ville de Paris

186 René Magritte, *The Blank Signature*, 1965. Oil on canvas, 81.3 × 65.1 (32 × 25⅝). Collection of Mr and Mrs Paul Mellon. National Gallery of Art, Washington, DC (1985.64.24). © 2026 ADAGP, Paris and DACS, London

187 Marc Chagall, *Song of Songs IV*, 1958. Oil on paper mounted on canvas, 144.5 × 210.5 (57 × 82⅞). Musée national Marc Chagall, Nice (MBMC16). © 2026 ADAGP, Paris and DACS, London

189 Cruzeiro Seixas, *Untitled*, 1972. Ballpoint pen and gouache on paper, 21 × 15.4 (8⅜ × 6⅛). Donated by Cruzeiro Seixas. Fundação Cupertino de Miranda, Vila Nova de Famalicão. © 2026 DACS

190 Óscar Domínguez, *Sunday or Marine Rutting*, 1935. Oil on canvas, 93 × 73 (36⅝ × 28¾). TEA Tenerife Espacio de las Artes (TEA1995-003). © 2026 ADAGP, Paris and DACS, London

191 Salvador Dalí, *Equestrian Portrait of Carmen Martínez-Bordiú*, 1972. Oil on canvas, 160 × 190.5 (63 × 75). Private Collection. Photo Album Archivo/SuperStock. © 2026 Salvador Dalí, Fundació Gala-Salvador Dalí, DACS

193 Salvador Dalí, *Apparatus and Hand*, 1927. Oil on panel, 62.2 × 47.6 (24½ × 18¾). Gift of A. Reynolds & Eleanor Morse. The Dalí Museum, St Petersburg, FL. © 2026 Salvador Dalí, Fundació Gala-Salvador Dalí, DACS

194 Remedios Varo, *The Journey*, 1935. Collage and tempera on paper, 23.5 × 19.7 (9⅜ × 7⅞). Private Collection. © 2026 Remedios Varo, DACS/VEGAP

197 Salvador Dalí, *Paranoiac-Critical Study of Vermeer's Lacemaker*, 1955. Oil on canvas, 27 × 22 (10¾ × 8¾). Anonymous gift. Solomon R. Guggenheim Museum, New York. Photo akg-images. © 2026 Salvador Dalí, Fundació Gala-Salvador Dalí, DACS

199 Salvador Dalí, *Celestial Ride*, 1957. Oil on canvas, 188 × 83.9 (74 × 33). Private Collection. © 2026 Salvador Dalí, Fundació Gala-Salvador Dalí, DACS

201 René Magritte, *The Mountain-Dweller*, 1948. Oil on canvas, 74 × 50 (29¼ × 19¾). Private Collection. Photo Christie's Images Ltd/SuperStock. © 2026 ADAGP, Paris and DACS, London

203 Leonora Carrington, *The Temptation of St Anthony*, 1945. Oil on canvas, 122 × 91 (48 × 35¾). Private Collection. © 2026 Estate of Leonora Carrington/ARS, NY and DACS, London

205 Francis Picabia, *Spanish Woman with Camel*, c. 1927. Watercolour, gouache, and pencil on cardboard, 81 × 56 (32 × 22⅛). Private Collection

206 Leonora Carrington, *Samhain Skin*, 1975. Gouache on vellum, 121.3 × 82.2 (47¾ × 32⅜). Gift of Wallace and Wilhelmina Holladay. National Museum of Women in the Arts, Washington, DC. © 2026 Estate of Leonora Carrington/ARS, NY and DACS, London

209 Frida Kahlo, *The Wounded Deer*, 1946. Oil on Masonite, 22.9 × 30.5 (9 × 12). Private Collection

210–11 Edith Rimmington, *Mythical Composition*, 1950. Pen and ink and watercolour on paper, 53 × 74 (20⅞ × 29¼). Private Collection. Photo Whitford Fine Art, London/Bridgeman Images. © The Estate of Edith Rimmington

213 Óscar Domínguez, *The Levels of Desire*, 1932–33. Oil on canvas, 61 × 49.5 (24 × 19½). Private Collection. © 2026 ADAGP, Paris and DACS, London

214 Georgia O'Keeffe, *Deer's Skull with Pedernal*, 1936. Oil on canvas, 91.4 × 76.5 (36 × 30⅛). Gift of the William H. Lane Foundation. Museum of Fine Arts, Boston (1990.432). © 2026 Georgia O'Keeffe Museum/DACS

215 Leonora Carrington, *Green Tea*, 1942. Oil on canvas, 61 × 76.2 (24 × 30). Gift of the Drue Heinz Trust (by exchange). The Museum of Modern Art, New York (145.2019). Photo Franck Legros/Alamy. © 2026 Estate of Leonora Carrington/ARS, NY and DACS, London

217a Salvador Dalí, *The Burning Giraffe*, 1937. Oil on panel, 35 × 27 (13⅞ × 10¾). Emanuel Hoffmann Foundation, on permanent loan to the Kunstmuseum Basel. © 2026 Salvador Dalí, Fundació Gala-Salvador Dalí, DACS

217b Salvador Dalí, *The Flames, They Call*, 1942. Oil on canvas, 145 × 123 (57⅛ × 48½). Private Collection. © 2026 Salvador Dalí, Fundació Gala-Salvador Dalí, DACS

220 André Masson, *Tauromachie*, 1937. Oil on canvas, 81.3 × 100.3 (32 × 39½). The Cone Collection, formed by Dr Claribel Cone and Miss Etta Cone of Baltimore, Maryland. Baltimore Museum of Art (1950.349). © 2026 ADAGP, Paris and DACS, London

221 Óscar Domínguez, *Head of a Bull*, 1941. Oil on canvas, 50 × 65 (19¾ × 25⅝). TEA Tenerife Espacio de las Artes (TEA2019-001). © 2026 ADAGP, Paris and DACS, London

222 Francis Bacon, *Study of a Bull*, 1991. Oil, aerosol paint and dust on canvas, 198 × 147.5 (78 × 58). Private Collection. © 2026 The Estate of Francis Bacon. All rights reserved. DACS

223a Oscar Mellor, *The Participants*, 1990. Oil on board, 45.7 × 61 (18 × 24). Private Collection. © The Estate of Oscar Mellor

223b Joan Miró, *The Bull Race*, 1945. Oil on canvas, 114 × 144 (45 × 56¾). Centre Pompidou, Paris (AM 2763 P). © 2026 Successió Miró/ADAGP, Paris and DACS London

225a Félix Labisse, *The Isies*, 1981. Oil on canvas, 63.5 × 80 (25 × 31½). Private Collection. © 2026 ADAGP, Paris and DACS, London

225b Paul Klee, *She Moos, We Play*, 1928. Oil on canvas, 43.5 × 56.5 (17⅛ × 22¼). Zentrum Paul Klee, Bern

226–27 Marc Chagall, *Cow with a Parasol*, 1946. Oil on canvas, 81.3 × 108 (32 × 42½). Bequest of Richard S. Zeisler, 2007. The Metropolitan Museum of Art, New York (2007.247.3). © 2026 ADAGP, Paris and DACS, London

229 Meret Oppenheim, *Object*, 1936. Fur-covered cup, saucer, and spoon. Purchase. The Museum of Modern Art, New York. Photo RDB/ullstein via Getty Images. © 2026 DACS

231a Marc Chagall, *The Cellist*, 1939. Oil on canvas, 101 × 74 (39¾ × 29⅛). Private Collection. © 2026 ADAGP, Paris and DACS, London

231b Marc Chagall, *The Red Jacket*, 1961. Oil, gouache and ink on paper, 66 × 50.5 (26 × 20). Private Collection. © 2026 ADAGP, Paris and DACS, London

234 Salvador Dalí, *The Sheep*, 1942. Gouache on chromolithograph, 22.9 × 34.3 (9 × 13½). Gift of A. Reynolds & Eleanor Morse. The Dalí Museum, St Petersburg, FL (2007.100b). © 2026 Salvador Dalí, Fundació Gala-Salvador Dalí, DACS

235 Salvador Dalí, *Design for the Interior Decoration of a Stable-Library*, 1942. Collage over chromolithograph, overpainted with gouache and India ink, 51 × 45 (20⅛ × 17¾). Dalí Theatre-Museum, Figueres. © 2026 Salvador Dalí, Fundació Gala-Salvador Dalí, DACS

239a Francis Picabia, *Still Lifes*, 1920. Toy monkey and oil on cardboard. Reproduced in *Cannibale* no. 1, Paris, 25 April 1920

239b Max Ernst, *The Blue Monkey with Flower*, 1922. Oil on canvas, 60 × 50.2 (23⅝ × 19¾). Galerie Beyeler, Basel. © 2026 ADAGP, Paris and DACS, London

240 Frida Kahlo, *Self-Portrait with Monkeys*, 1943. Oil on canvas, 81.6 × 62.9 (32⅛ × 24¾). Jacques and Natasha Gelman Collection, Mexico City

242 Toyen, *At the Blue Face*, 1951. Oil on canvas, 107 × 82.5 (42⅛ × 32¼). Private Collection. Photo Azoor Collection/Alamy. © 2026 ADAGP, Paris and DACS, London

243 Francis Bacon, *Study of a Baboon*, 1953. Oil on canvas, 198.3 × 137.3 (78⅛ × 54⅛). James Thrall Soby Bequest. Photo The Museum of Modern Art, New York/Scala, Florence. © 2026 The Estate of Francis Bacon. All rights reserved. DACS

Index of Artists and Works

Page references in *italics* indicate illustrations.

Acknowledgments

I would like to thank all those at Thames & Hudson who have worked so hard to bring this book to life: editorial director Roger Thorp, sales manager Dawn Shield, editor Rebecca Pearson, editorial manager Mohara Gill, designer Karolina Prymaka, art director Matt Watson Young, picture researcher Lise Seguin, production controller Ginny Liggitt and pre-press manager Elisa Merino.

Frontispiece: Leonora Carrington, *Ferret Race* (detail), 1952

First published in the United Kingdom in 2026 by
Thames & Hudson Ltd, 6–24 Britannia Street,
London WC1X 9JD

First published in the United States of America in 2026 by
Thames & Hudson Inc., 500 Fifth Avenue, New York,
New York 10110

Picture credits can be found on p. 249.

EU Authorized Representative: Interart S.A.R.L.
19 rue Charles Auray, 93500 Pantin, Paris, France
productsafety@thameshudson.co.uk
interart.fr

A CIP catalogue record for this book is available
from the British Library

Library of Congress Control Number 2025936072

ISBN 978-0-500-03057-8
01

Printed and bound in China by
C&C Offset Printing Co. Ltd

MIX
Paper | Supporting responsible forestry
FSC® C008047
www.fsc.org